MORGAN STATE SERIES IN AFRO-AMERICAN STUDIES

Walter Fisher, General Editor
Benjamin Quarles, Consulting Editor

The Series has been assisted by a grant from the Ford Foundation. Technical editorial support was provided by the Metropolitan Applied Research Center.

ALSO BY PHILIP BUTCHER

The William Stanley Braithwaite Reader
George W. Cable
George W. Cable: The Northampton Years

THE MINORITY PRESENCE IN AMERICAN LITERATURE, 1600–1900

A Reader and Course Guide

Edited by PHILIP BUTCHER

Volume I

 HOWARD UNIVERSITY PRESS, WASHINGTON D.C. 1977

Printed in the United States of America

Library of Congress Cataloging in Publication Data
Main entry under title:

The Minority presence in American literature, 1600–1900.

   Includes bibliographical references and index.
   1. American literature. 2. Minorities—United
States—Literary collections. I. Butcher, Charles
Philip.
PS509.M5M53   810'.9'353   77–5687
ISBN 0-88258-101-5 (v. 1)
ISBN 0-88258-061-2 (v. 1) pbk.

Edith, Nellie, Jennie, and James: For Them and Theirs

Preface

The Minority Presence in American Literature is designed both for the general reader pursuing an interest in American life and literature or in the role and status of minorities in the development of the nation and for the college student engaged in formal study of these subjects. While black Americans and American Indians are emphasized, the readings and study materials deal also with other minority groups, with some references to writing after 1900, and they provide a basis for examining the literary representation of any minority in any period.

This book will be most useful to persons who have had some exposure to the formal study of literature, who are capable of objective appraisals of various kinds of writing, and who are acquainted with the broad outlines of the writing and history of the United States. The reader must take care to deal with the selections in the context of the time of publication, to understand the writers and their works rather than to judge them, and to appreciate the authors' accomplishments rather than to disparage their work for flaws more easily detected from our perspective than from theirs. I have not meant to exalt poor writers unduly merely because they had social vision or humanitarian motives or to condemn fine writers whose genius did not include a generous understanding of some particular minority; but I consider that an author's response to the minority presence of his time and place is part of his record as a person and an artist and should not be disregarded. Yet I have wished to avoid chauvinism in preparing this book, and I would not want readers to use what they find here for chauvinistic purposes.

Incorporating the introductory essay in both volumes of this work assures that all readers are provided with two essentials for an intelligent response to the selections: a synthesis of the experience of "the other American" over three hundred years of our history and a guide to the principles that operate in the representation of minorities in literature. The readings are presented in chronological order, generally, the determining factor being the date of publication of the first selection by each writer. Each author's work is followed by a study guide that consists, in most instances, of a list of additional treatments of minorities, some recommended references, and questions and projects. The work from which a selection is taken is not listed among "Suggested Readings," and the selection, often given a title of my own, may not exhaust the relevance of that work. The projects differ greatly in scope and difficulty; students and teachers must adjust them to suit their needs, taking into account the library and other resources that are at hand. Students should be careful about inferring answers to the questions they do not pursue and should not undertake any project without checking the index and employing appropriate references from the bibliography at the end of the book. Some of the books I cite have been issued in several editions, including paperback, but I refer to one edition only. I make no comment about study tools such as the *Dictionary of American Biography*, the bibliographies in *American Literature*, *PMLA*, and other scholarly journals, or the standard references students are expected to use in advanced work in American literature, since it is assumed, as a matter of course, that these will be consulted as needed.

In my graduate classes in the minority presence I have found it helpful to insist that required reports treat more than one period and literary form and deal with more than one minority group. A particular student might discuss in one presentation the Indian woman in selected poetry of the romantic period, in a second the Quaker abolitionist as a character in certain fugitive slave narratives, and in a third Thoreau and the Irish. The range of the reports should allow the student to develop a topic related to his or her interests and should involve the study of unfamiliar material examined from an objective point of view. The stress should be on literary rather than other considerations. Reports may concentrate on a single minority as represented in several works or by several authors, a problem affecting several minorities (e.g., segregated housing or mixed marriage), a period (the age of local color), or a setting (the urban ghetto).

If readers of this book are to avoid the very sins they condemn when their indignation is aroused by bigotry and racism, they must keep in mind the human inclination toward xenophobia—the fear and hatred of strangers and foreigners—and the dismaying fact that man's reluctance to accept his fellows as equals is not limited to any single time or place or race or culture. Walther von der Vogelweide, a thirteenth century Minnesinger, observed in "My Brother Man" that "Mankind arises from one origin; / We are alike both outward and within." Yet many Christians, Jews, and heathens who worship God lack the true love that should be their salvation:

> *"For many call Thee Father, who*
> *Will not own me as brother too."*

PHILIP BUTCHER

CONTENTS

°Some titles, like this one, have been supplied by the editor. Sources from which selections are taken are indicated in the headnotes.

THE MINORITY
PRESENCE IN
AMERICAN LITERATURE, 1600–1900

INTRODUCTION

I. The Minority Presence: Principles, Practices, and Prospects (1600–1800)

> Do we call this the land of the free? What is it to be free from King George and continue the slaves of King Prejudice?
>
> THOREAU.

In "Waiting at the Station," from *Sketches and Travels in London,* written more than a hundred years ago about class distinctions in England, William Makepeace Thackeray dramatized the conscience-salving rationalizations that the dominant group in a society uses in dismissing its subordinates as essentially alien and beyond the pale:

> We are amongst a number of people waiting for the Blackwell train at the Fenchurch Street Station. Some of us are going a little farther than Blackwell—as far as Gravesend: some of us are going even farther than Gravesend—to Port Phillip in Australia, leaving behind the *patriae fines* and the pleasant fields of Old England. . . .
>
> Some eight-and-thirty women are sitting in the large Hall of the station, with bundles, baskets, and light baggage, waiting for the steamer, and the orders to embark. . . .
>
> You and I, let us suppose again, are civilised persons. We have been decently educated: and live decently every day, and wear tolerable clothes, and practise cleanliness: and love the arts and graces of life. As we walk down this rank of eight-and-thirty female emigrants, let us fancy that we are at Melbourne, and not in London, and that we have come down from our sheep-walks, or clearings, having heard of the arrival of forty honest, well-recommended

3

young women, and having a natural longing to take a wife home to the bush—which of these would you like? If you were an Australian Sultan, to which of these would you throw the hankerchief? I am afraid not one of them. I fear, in our present mood of mind, we should mount horse and return to the country, preferring a solitude, and to be a bachelor, than to put up with one of these for a companion. There is no girl here to tempt you by her looks: (and, world-wiseacre as you are, it is by these you are principally moved)—there is no pretty, modest, red-cheeked rustic,—no neat, trim little grisette, such as what we call a gentleman might cast his eyes upon without too much derogating, and might find favour in the eyes of a man about town. No; it is a homely bevy of women with scarcely any beauty amongst them—their clothes were decent but not the least picturesque—their faces are pale and care-worn for the most part—how, indeed, should it be otherwise, seeing that they have known care and want all their days?—there they sit, upon bare benches, with dingy bundles, and great cotton umbrellas—and the truth is, you are not a hardy colonist, a feeder of sheep, feller of trees, a hunter of kangaroos—but a London man, and my lord the Sultan's cambric handkerchief is scented with Bond Street perfumery—you put it in your pocket, and couldn't give it to any one of these women.

They are not like you, indeed. They have not your tastes and feeling: your education and refinements. They would not understand a hundred things which seem perfectly simple to you. They would shock you a hundred times a day by as many deficiencies of politeness, or by outrages upon the Queen's English—by practices entirely harmless, and yet in your eyes actually worse than crimes—they have large hard hands and clumsy feet. The woman you love must have pretty soft fingers that you may hold in yours: must speak your language properly, and at least when you offer her your heart, must return hers with its *h* in the right place, as she whispers that it is yours, or you will have none of it. If she says, "Hedward, I ham so unappy to think I shall never behold you again,"—though her emotion on leaving you might be perfectly tender and genuine, you would be obliged to laugh. If she said, "Hedward, my art is yours for hever and hever" (and anybody heard her), she might as well stab you,—you couldn't accept the most faithful affection offered in such terms—you are a town-bred man, I say, and your handkerchief smells of Bond Street musk and millefleur. A sun-burnt settler out of the Bush won't feel any of these exquisite tortures: or understand this kind of laughter: or object to Molly because her hands are coarse and her ankles thick: but he will take her back to his farm, where she will nurse his children, bake his dough, milk his cows, and cook his kangaroo for him.

But between you, an educated Londoner, and that woman, is not the union absurd and impossible? Would it not be unbearable for either? Solitude would be incomparably pleasanter than such a companion. . . . Well! out with it at once: you don't think Molly is your equal—nor indeed is she in possession of many artificial acquirements. She can't make Latin verses, for example, as you used to do at school; she can't speak French and Italian, as your wife very likely can, etc.—and in so far she is your inferior, and your amiable lady's.

What Thackeray perceived as estranging England's lower classes from their betters—"They are not like you, indeed"—may be seen as basic to the predicament of subordinate groups in a society concerned about religion, nationality, and race as well as class. Americans subscribe to assorted religious faiths, trace their ancestry to nations on scattered continents, and bear skins that are black, brown, red, white, yellow, and all possible mixtures thereof. But only white Anglo-Saxon Protestant males, the dominant group in our culture, entirely escape the stigma of minority[1] designation. All other Americans have been regarded historically as inferior to them on the convenient notions that, on the one hand, minorities are "all alike" (that is, are all like one another in their group) and, on the other, are fundamentally "different" (that is, are lamentably unlike the established norm for human beings as determined and supposedly exemplified by the male WASP). To the extent that these concepts have been in force in our culture at a given time, they have found expression in our literature.

Yet it has been the very presence on these shores of various ethnic groups, classes, and cultures that has characterized the American experience and has made American literature something more than writings in English composed on the North American continent.

---

[1]The term is used in this book in accordance with the statement adopted by the Modern Language Association's Commission on Minority Groups: "A minority group is not construed here simply in terms of relative numbers in the population—a voting booth minority. Rather it is construed as a group of significant size in the society whose culture not only differs from the conventional culture but is systematically underrepresented in the preferred activity of the society and undervalued in its eyes." *MLA Newsletter*, 5, No. 3 (May, 1973), 3.

American literature deals with the encounter of Europeans and the native inhabitants of the New World, with the frontier, advancing ever westward, providing a unique setting. It deals also, since Africans arrived here before the Pilgrims and Puritans, with a massive black-white confrontation and accommodation, once concentrated on, but not limited to, the plantation, and now taking place in almost all aspects of our highly complex society. And it includes in its picture of the nation's development millions of assimilated people of "foreign" extraction and more millions still in some phase of the Americanization process. What makes the United States what it is—what has always distinguished it—is the presence here of people of all the diverse races and cultures of the globe and the evidences in our culture of their contribution to our heritage and their participation in our daily life.

That heritage is not exclusively English. It was an Italian, Columbus, who discovered in the western ocean the islands that were first thought to be part of Asia. Cabot, whose voyage in 1497 made possible England's territorial claims in the New World, was born in Genoa and became a citizen of Venice. Amerigo Vespucci, an Italian navigator, gave the western hemisphere the name "America" in his treatise on geography. In 1513, Ponce de Leon discovered Florida, and Balboa, another Spaniard, discovered the Pacific Ocean. French explorers reached the coast of Canada as early as 1534. De-Soto, also a Spaniard, landed in Florida in 1539 and marched to the Mississippi River, possibly getting as far north as what is now Kentucky before he died. Estevanico, a Christian Negro who had been with Cabeza de Vaca in the Texas area for several years, in 1539 guided a Spanish expedition into what is now New Mexico. A year later Coronado, another Spaniard, led an expedition that probably reached the area of Oklahoma and Kansas. In Florida, Spaniards founded St. Augustine, the oldest city in North America, twenty years before Sir Walter Raleigh's ill-fated English colonists landed on Roanoke Island off the coast of North Carolina in 1585.

The colony at Jamestown, the first permanent English settlement in America, included in its population settlers who do not conform to the aristocratic image of romantic tradition. Among the laborers there in 1608 were Poles and Germans. Only two English women were present, one of whom, a lady's maid named Anne Buras, mar-

ried that year another laborer, John Laydon, in the first wedding of
Europeans on Virginia soil. No courtly dame and cavalier were
they, Stephen Vincent Benét noted in *Western Star* (1943):

> And yet, while they lived (and they had not long to live),
> They were half of the first families in Virginia.

The sponsors of the colony came to understand the value of women
to the enterprise and sent ninety English maidens to become settlers'
wives in 1619, the same year in which a Dutch vessel landed the first
Africans there. That was the year, too, when the House of Burgesses
was convened. America's first representative assembly ruled that
only English men had the right to vote, but Poles exerted pressure
and were not long denied the franchise.

In 1620 the Pilgrims founded Plymouth, the first English colony
in New England. Most of the passengers on the *Mayflower*, and on
all the later Pilgrim ships, were not English Separatists seeking a
place to worship as they pleased but "Strangers," as the Pilgrims
called them, who came to better their economic lot. From the Pilgrim's friend Samoset, a man named John Brown bought 12,000
acres of Maine land for fifty beaver skins in 1625. A year later the
Dutch bought Manhattan Island in exchange for trinkets worth
twenty-four dollars. They encouraged in New Amsterdam a polyglot
population symbolic of New York's later character; there were
people of eighteen nationalities and several religions on hand when
the English took over the colony less than thirty years later. Of
course that population included blacks, for Africans were to be
found in each of the thirteen original English colonies from the earliest years of settlement. The Massachusetts Bay Colony was established in 1630, and by the time these Puritans adopted Nathaniel
Ward's *Body of Liberties* in 1641, making theirs the first English
colony to give legal sanction to Negro slavery, 20,000 Europeans
were in the New England area. Finns and Swedes established a permanent settlement in Delaware in 1636, two years after Catholics
landed in Maryland. And all the while the original Americans, the
Indians, were all over the land.

In any literature, aliens or minorities are likely to be depicted unfavorably when they are readily distinguishable by their appearance, language, costume, etc. If the benighted people are few in numbers, docile, useful, and no threat to vested interests, they may be shown as quaint or exotic. But if they are hostile or have potential power that threatens the status quo, they must expect to be demeaned, ridiculed, exploited, and persecuted in literature as well as in life. As the group moves toward accommodation with the dominant culture, or as the value judgments or the power structure of the society is transformed, the literary treatment the group receives will improve in range and quality, with a general decline in the use of denigrating stereotypes and an increase in the favorable portrayal of figures conforming most fully to majority values.

Two incidents in the early history and literature of the American people are relevant to the principles stated above and serve as starting points for the study of the literary expression of the minority presence. The first was reported somewhat belatedly by John Smith, notable for his achievement as leader of the colony at Jamestown. Captain Smith wrote of being captured by Indians who were about to beat his brains out when the chief's daughter Pocahontas, "got his head in her armes, and laid her owne upon his to save him from death." This famous story of an eponymous hero who is rescued from the enemy through the devotion of an attractive alien woman who prefers him to her own people fits the classic pattern of folk literature, fairy tales, and man's universal erotic dream. Later, when Pocahontas was visiting England, Smith wrote to recommend her to Queen Anne for risking her life to save his. For two or three years after that incident, he said, she had visited the Jamestown settlement and had been God's instrument "to preserve this Colonie from death, famine and utter confusion." He noted "her extraordinairie affection to our Nation" and praised her for marrying John Rolfe and "rejecting her barbarous condition." The Indian princess was, he said, "the first Christian ever of that Nation, the first Virginian ever spake English, or had a childe in marriage by an Englishman." It is not surprising that Londoners, admiring her hat and ruff and ladylike demeanor, approved of her or that generations of Virginians proudly acknowledged descent from the alliance of Rolfe and his Indian wife. A defector from her native culture, Pocahontas did more than adopt Christianity; she converted to white. A popular figure in

American literature, she has not been depicted in accordance with derogatory Indian stereotypes.

Another illuminating account is that in William Bradford's history of the Pilgrim settlement at Plymouth. After they landed late in 1620 the colonists suffered from severe weather, hunger, disease, and hostile natives. But to their astonishment, an Indian they met the following March spoke some English, was acquainted with European ways, and was disposed to be friendly. This man, Samoset, introduced them to Squanto, who had been to England and spoke even better English. Over the years the help of Samoset and Squanto did a great deal to make possible the survival of the colony. Expressing the conviction that Providence determined the colonists' fortunes, Bradford said that Squanto was a special instrument sent of God for their good. Calling his death a great loss, Bradford mourned for the colonists, not for Squanto.

The works of other colonial writers demonstrate that man is often motivated by self-interest and is prone to judge other humans by their relationship to himself, but there is evidence in this writing also of man's capacity for a more generous treatment of his fellows. Gradually there is an enlargement of the role of Indians and blacks and an increased understanding of minority experience. As cultural differences are blurred and intergroup associations assume more varied and intimate patterns the minority figures gain identity as persons. Once merely creatures notable for their divergence from established norms, they cease to be things and begin to acquire human rights that must be respected. Blacks and Indians are converted to Christianity. Miscegenation and intermarriage take place. The justice of slavery is challenged. And exceptional individuals prove by their achievement that people of all colors and creeds have creative intelligence as well as souls.

But a few individuals may deviate from a society's image of a subordinate group without greatly affecting that image. Many exceptions are needed to change the rule, to break the force of stereotypes rooted in bigotry and racism. The treatment of red men and black men in the literature of the English colonies relied on the assumption of their inferiority even as it advanced in range and gave some sympathetic representations of their character and their plight in a culture that exploited them. That culture became more complex and the society increasingly multi-ethnic. When cries of independence and freedom filled the air, writers were inspired to think of the rights of all—if only all white males. But the equalitarian ideals that were proclaimed when the thirteen colonies established their political independence from England and King George were not conceived as extending to Indians and blacks, either slave or free.

The literary emancipation of a minority comes about when its members are perceived as equals and as single and unique beings who are more notable for their basic human qualities than for the distinctions that set the group apart. When at last the minority is seen and depicted in terms of its own culture, which is accepted as having as much validity as any other, the literary artist—whatever his own ethnic identity—will have broken free from the shackles of King Prejudice.

II.
The Minority Presence Looms Larger
(1800–1865)

> Our fellow countrymen in chains!
> Slaves—in a land of light and law!
> Slaves—crouching on the very plains
> Where rolled the storm of Freedom's war!

WHITTIER.

Most early American writing dealt with the lives and concerns of Englishmen endeavoring to establish an outpost of European civilization in a new physical environment. What the writers of the nineteenth century found themselves obliged to record and interpret was the development of a new nation and a unique culture created by the interaction of American Indians, Africans, Asians, and assorted Europeans. Some of the diverse ingredients that went into the melting pot blended readily, while others made their contribution to the whole but kept distinct identities. The interaction was often a struggle and was frequently violent, with uprisings, raids, massacres, riots, and wars marking the course of the years from the opening of the century to its close. But there was an advance toward accommodation, with separate cultures fusing into new patterns and national and racial groups losing some of the sharp outlines of their alienation. It was a period of conflict and social change. And it was a time when the nation's literature became truly American in character.

As the century opened, Parson Weems published his *Life of Washington* and added the cherry tree fable to our tradition. At his death the year before, the victorious commander of the American forces, in what Whittier called "Freedom's war," had freed his slaves, having finally become "principalled against . . . traffic in the human species." In his late years he must also have seen the error of a youthful provincialism that led him to write in his journal at sixteen about some German immigrants he met on the frontier he was

11

surveying, "ignorante . . . they would never speak English but, when spoken too, they speak all Dutch." When he died, the nation Washington had done so much to create stretched from the Atlantic coast to the Mississippi River. Its territory doubled in 1803 with President Jefferson's Louisiana Purchase, reaching across the plains to the Rocky Mountains. In the next sixty years Americans would extend their control all the way to the Pacific Ocean and would establish the country's present continental borders.

This expansion meant making and breaking treaties with the Indians, driving them from their lands and steadily consolidating white victories and advances. Forty-eight million acres of Indian hunting grounds passed into white hands between 1795 and 1809. The Shawnee chief, Tecumseh, offered brilliant resistance to the conquest, and was perhaps the ablest leader the Americans faced in the War of 1812. General Andrew Jackson, whose military reputation was important to his rise to the presidency, first came to national attention when he defeated the Creeks at Horseshoe Bend in 1814. It took two wars to clear the Seminoles from Florida and Black Hawk's War of 1832 to dispossess the Indians of the Old Northwest. As trains of Conestoga wagons and prairie schooners carried the pioneers westward, the epic struggle shifted to the prairies and plains. The Manifest Destiny that justified the conquest of the Indians served to cover also the annexation of Texas and the thousands of acres that were the fruit of victory in the war the United States provoked with Mexico in 1848.

The "fellow countrymen" whose enslavement Whittier protested in his poem were in bondage in the South, since, by 1800, virtually all the North's Negroes had been freed. Once a tottering system given somewhat apologetic approval, slavery became of crucial importance to southern states following the perfection of the cotton gin that Eli Whitney produced in 1793; and soon a spirited defense was provided for the "peculiar institution" that let the cotton kingdom flourish. The black race, it was argued, was biologically inferior and slavery was the Negro's natural state. Southern leaders emphasized the Bible's endorsement of servitude and insisted that theirs were happy slaves contented with their lot. That claim lacks confirmation in the record of slave rebellions and the steady flow of blacks escaping to freedom in the North and Canada. There was the

Gabriel uprising in Virginia in 1800, the Denmark Vesey conspiracy in South Carolina in 1822, and, most important of all, Nat Turner's rebellion in Virginia in 1831. From that time to the Civil War, some 2,500 slaves made their escape to liberty each year by way of the underground railroad.

Opposition to slavery mounted as the plantation system strengthened its hold; internal traffic in human beings with Virginia and its neighbors kept the cotton fields of the deep South supplied with bondsmen; and the spread of slavery to new states threatened to alter the regional relationships of the nation's political structure. For thirty years before the war broke out between the states, slavery was the dominant issue in American public affairs. Garrison founded his *Liberator* in 1831, and the American Anti-Slavery Society was organized in 1833, the climactic year when Parliament abolished slavery in all lands under British control. As historian Benjamin Quarles has pointed out, "although practically all slaves were Negroes, not all Negroes were slaves." In 1830, when the black population was more than 2,300,000 and constituted 18.1 percent of the national total, the free proportion of the Negro population reached the all-time high of 13.7 percent. The census of 1860 reported 3,953,000 slaves and 488,000 free blacks. Free blacks were no inconsequential force in the antislavery struggle.

The literary war, engaging black writers and white, Northerners and Southerners, was waged with increasing vigor and reached its climax with the publication of Harriet Beecher Stowe's *Uncle Tom's Cabin* in 1852. Its dramatization added to sectional animosities. John Brown's insurrection in 1859 was followed in the next year by Lincoln's election to the presidency and South Carolina's secession from the Union. Whatever other conflicts of interest combined to bring on the Civil War of 1861–65, the issue of slavery was of crucial importance to both the Union and the Confederacy. If Lincoln's Emancipation Proclamation of 1863 was more rhetoric and military policy than an instrument to liberate the South's slaves, the victories of Northern troops did bring freedom to blacks throughout the land. They did not end the Negro's minority status.

Other minorities were in evidence now more than ever before, though Europeans of many nationalities had been arriving in the English colonies for decades and had played an important role in the war for independence. Colonists of non-English extraction were more than willing to sever the ties with King George III. Thousands of General Washington's troops were Germans, and sometimes his Irish soldiers amounted to about a third of his whole command. Blacks, of course, saw service in both the Continental army and navy, fighting side by side with whites. When independence was won, St. Jean de Crèvecoeur was not alone in seeing Americans as a new breed, "a mixture of English, Scotch, Irish, French, Dutch, Germans, and Swedes."

Though immigration lagged after the Revolution, it picked up early in the nineteenth century. More than 50,000 immigrants arrived from Ireland between 1820 and 1830, and more than 200,000 came in the following decade. The first federal census of the foreign-born reported in 1850 that nearly a million of them were of Irish descent. Another half million Irish, driven by the potato famine at home, joined them in the next ten years, when 90,000 new German immigrants also landed on American soil. Newcomers beset by poverty and language problems met with residential segregation, religious intolerance, and job exploitation. They were crowded into urban slums, restricted to manual labor, and victimized by riot mobs. "The Negro is black outside," agitators said, "the Irishman is black inside." When the Civil War came, more than 140,000 Irish and 175,000 Germans fought in Union ranks. So did more than 180,000 black volunteers. Shouldering heavy burdens in the crisis, the nation's largest minorities affirmed their commitment to its interests, their claims to American identity.

A clear sense of the national identity and a truly American literature were called for immediately after independence was achieved, but took time to develop. It was not until after the romantic period had begun that Americans could take pride in writers of really major stature. Irving and Cooper won both critical and popular approval at home and abroad for fiction that still has a hold on our imagination. Both wrote a good deal about the nation's minorities and had a part in conceiving the American image held by their countrymen and the world. In retrospect they seem deficient in appreciation for some of the minorities they depicted and guilty of contributing to the stereotypes that fastened themselves to our collective consciousness. Though they may be charged with racism, their guilt diminishes when it is remembered that contrived plots and patronizing humor suited the taste of their audience. Irving's minstrel blacks offend modern readers who fail to observe that he assigned similarly grotesque anatomy and stereotyped behavior to some white characters. Cooper is interesting for his use of interracial romances but annoying for his care in frustrating the lovers, whether the couples are Indian-white, white-black, or black-Indian. The tragedy of these alliances anticipates a multitude of arbitrarily blighted love affairs in fiction from Cooper's day to the present.

Poe wrote too little about the daily life of the real world to give much attention to the minority presence, and Hawthorne provides less material on blacks than might be expected of a man of public affairs and alert intelligence writing in the midst of the slavery controversy. But Melville balances Hawthorne's neglect with a wealth of provocative characters, incidents, and symbols, and an understanding of depths of human nature few writers have explored. Emerson and Thoreau, revered as speculative thinkers and proponents of transcendentalism, were more active participants in the struggles of the time and more important as social critics than literary textbooks generally indicate. But as sympathetic as they were to the plight of enslaved blacks, they shared indifference to the predicament of immigrants who were near at hand. Sometimes it is easier to love mankind than a neighbor, easier, too, to pity the slave, confront the aborigine, and open the door to the alien than to conceive of these diverse types as one's countrymen. But Whittier's compassion conceded that status to blacks, and Walt Whitman, professed champion of the common man, deliberately included all humanity in his catalogs of brotherhood. In the nation's literature, the minority presence, whether trite and wooden or infused with new humanity, was firmly established as the identifying ingredient.

III.
Old Blood and New: The Minority Presence from 1865 to 1900

> There is something in the contemplation of the mode in which America has been settled, that, in a noble breast, should forever extinguish the prejudices of national dislikes.
>
> Settled by the people of all nations, all nations may claim her for their own. You can not spill a drop of American blood without spilling the blood of the whole world.
>
> MELVILLE

From the surrender of the Confederacy at Appomatox to the end of the nineteenth century, black Americans found that they were not emancipated from the stigma of slavery and the burdens of subordination; they had not won full civil rights. Indians, the victims of continuing attrition, were the nation's enemies or its wards. And masses of European immigrants, marked by ethnic identities they could not efface for a generation or more, suffered the limitations of second-class citizenship in the promised land. People of minority status or alien origin discovered that being Americans did not make them white Anglo-Saxon Protestants.

The hopes of black citizens, both freedmen and freemen, were raised as the nation embarked on Reconstruction. Constitutional amendments affirmed their full citizenship, the Freedman's Bureau gave aid to the ailing and destitute, newly established systems of public education became available to them, and they achieved political representation in the South. But the benefits proved to be temporary or limited gains. Slavery was replaced by rigid segregation as the Jim Crow system built a wall that confined the Negro to "his place." The Ku Klux Klan, founded in 1866, became a powerful force for tyranny. Sharecropping doomed tenant farmers to poverty. Mob violence and lynchings assured white dominance. In 1866 mobs

16

burned schools and churches and killed or seriously wounded more than a hundred blacks in Memphis and New Orleans, and lynchings reached a peak of 235 victims for one year in 1892. The struggle for civil rights was lost in the courts and in the public forum as northern humanitarians fell silent or shifted their support from the ex-slave to other underprivileged groups. The twentieth century opened with white supremacists firmly in control of the solid South and enjoying the approval of most Americans everywhere, except for the 8,830,000 citizens (11.6 percent of the total population) whose African ancestry made them members of the country's largest racial minority.

A military campaign to "pacify" the Plains Indians was begun during the Civil War and continued for twenty-five years until they had been driven from the lands coveted for settlement, mining, or railroad development. The doctrine that "the only good Indian is a dead Indian" threatened their extermination. The final conquest of the West was marked by bloody and ignoble victories. Soldiers massacred hundreds of Cheyennes and Arapahos at Sand Creek in Colorado in 1864. General Custer's column was wiped out at the Battle of Little Big Horn in 1876, but the victory sealed the Indians' doom. Geronimo and his Apaches were finally defeated about the time the last buffalo herd was destroyed in 1884. The greatest victory for federal troops came in 1890 when some two hundred unarmed Sioux, women and children among them, were massacred at Wounded Knee in South Dakota. By 1900 the Indian population, ravaged by disease, assimilation, conquest, and oppression, was down to about 250,000, less than a third of what estimates say it was before Europeans arrived on their continent.

After the Civil War the same nationalities that had dominated the ranks of the nation's immigrants for decades continued to outnumber other new arrivals. Irish and Germans and Scandinavians flocked to America. Two million Germans landed here between 1870 and 1890, and 400,000 Swedes and many other Scandinavians came during the same period. But after 1880 immigration began to take on a different character. With people of northern European extraction well settled and advanced in the Americanization process, new peoples, more alien and less easily assimilated, began to constitute the bulk of the immigrants. They came largely from southern and eastern Europe: Italians, Greeks, Czechs, Slovaks, Russian Jews, Poles, Hungarians. These huddled masses seeking refuge bore unpronounceable names, spoke strange tongues, and might be identified by dark complexions and different profiles. On the west coast the tide of Chinese immigrants reached such a height that Congress passed the Chinese Exclusion Act in 1882, the first racist closing of America's golden door of opportunity.

The earliest immigrants had encountered some hostility, and many an ad for employment in the 1860s read "No Irish need apply," but now the new arrivals met with rising disfavor. They were herded into urban ghettos, and poorly paid for heavy labor. Still the immigrants came. By 1890 one third of the people of Boston were of alien birth. And in New York then there were twice as many Irish as in Dublin, half as many Italians as in Naples, as many Germans as in Hamburg, and two and a half times as many Jews as in Warsaw. Benjamin Franklin once argued that "white" should be reserved for Saxons and the English, Francis Parkman denied that the term included Mexicans, and later Americans often withheld that accolade from the Balkan and Mediterranean peoples. Persuaded that the Anglo-Saxon was superior to the Celt, the Chinese, and the southern Europeans, many American writers ignored the presence of these groups on the national scene, patronized them, or otherwise treated them in the stereotypical fashion reserved for minorities.

The status of any minority in the period can be determined by examining the representation of that group in jokes, cartoons, stage comedy, and other informal and often anonymous productions roughly classified as humor. The comic relief selections in American journals, even those in a magazine of the stature of *Scribner's Monthly*, can be as illuminating in regard to the image of a minority as is the serious treatment accorded that group elsewhere in the same periodicals.

Humor can be lighthearted or vicious. Human beings find it difficult, if not impossible, to resist the conclusion that persons who are different from themselves are laughable. Foreigners speak a funny language and wear preposterous clothes. We laugh *with* those whose condition or human frailty is of the sort to which we, too, are prone; we laugh *at* inferiors. We "poke fun" at those we would

demean. Ridicule of unalterable liabilities of appearance or condition is at best thoughtless, at worst malicious.

The most frequent butt of amateur and professional humorists in
America has been the black man, whose physical difference and cultural distance from the accepted norm made him exceedingly vul-
nerable. But other subordinate groups have also been subjected to
abuse and mockery in the guise of humor, among them the Irish and
the Chinese. Like other minorities, the Chinese were most ridiculed
when their difference from the dominant group was exaggerated, in
their case by pigeon-English and queue. Once it seemed that their
prospects for full acceptance in American society had no better than
"a Chinaman's chance," a popular expression meaning no chance at
all.

The selection that follows appeared anonymously in *Scribner's
Monthly* for January, 1871, but was revealed later as the work of
Mary Mapes Dodge, a writer of juvenile fiction best known for *Hans
Brinker: or, the Silver Skates.* Serious treatments of the "Chinese
Question" appeared in articles in the same journal in March, May,
and September of that year. An anonymous review in the May issue
praised William Dean Howells for *Suburban Sketches,* without
commenting on his allusion, in the selection from his book that is
included in this volume, to the alleged threat to the nation's well-
being from the Chinese immigrants in the West and the Irish immigrants in the East.

MISS MALONY ON THE CHINESE QUESTION

Och! don't be talkin'. Is it howld on, ye say? An' didn't I howld on
till the heart of me was clane broke entirely, and me wastin' that
thin you could clutch me wid yer two hands. To think o' me toilin'
like a nager for the six year I've been in Ameriky—bad luck to the
day I iver left the owld counthry! to be bate by the likes o' them!
(faix an' I'll sit down when I'm ready, so I will, Ann Ryan, an' ye'd
better be listnin' than drawin' your remarks) an' is it mysel, with five
good charac'ters from respectable places, would be herdin' wid the
haythens? The saints forgive me but I'd be buried alive sooner'n put
up wid it a day longer. Sure an' I was the granehorn not be lavin' at
onct when the missus kim into me kitchen wid her perlaver about
the new waiter man which was brought out from Californy. "He'll

be here the night," says she, "and Kitty, it's meself looks to you to
be kind and patient wid him, for he's a furriner," says she, a kind
o'lookin' off. "Sure an it's little I'll hinder nor interfare wid him nor
any other, mum," says I, a kind o' stiff, for I minded me how these
French waiters, wid their paper collars and brass rings on their fingers, isn't company for no gurril brought up dacint and honest. Och!
sorra a bit I knew what was comin' till the missus walked into me
kitchen smilin', and says kind o'shcared: "Here's Fing Wing, Kitty,
an' you'll have too much sinse to mind his bein' a little strange."
Wid that she shoots the doore, and I, misthrusting if I was tidied up
sufficient for me fine buy wid his paper collar, looks up and—Howly
fathers! may I niver brathe another breath, but there stud a rale
haythen Chineser a-grinnin' like he'd just come off a tay-box. If
you'll belave me, the crayture was that *yeller* it'ud sicken you to see
him; and sorra stitch was on him but a black night-gown over his
trowsers and the front of his head shaved claner nor a copper biler,
and a black tail a-hanging down from it behind, wid his two feet
stook into the heathenestest shoes you ever set eyes on. Och! but I
was up-stairs afore you could turn about, a givin' the missus warnin,' an' only stopt wid her by her raisin' me wages two dollars, and
playdin' wid me how it was a Christian's duty to bear wid haythens
and taitch'em all in our power—the saints save us! Well, the ways
and trials I had wid that Chineser, Ann Ryan, I couldn't be tellin'.
Not a blissed thing cud I do but he'd be lookin' on wid his eyes
cocked up'ard like two poomp-handles, an'he widdout a speck or
smitch o' whiskers on him, an' his finger nails full a yard long. But
it's dyin' you'd be to see the missus a'larnin him, and he grinnin' an'
waggin' his pig-tail (which was pieced out long wid some black
stoof, the haythen chate!) and gettin' into her ways wonderful quick,
I don't deny, imitatin' that sharp, you'd be shurprised, and ketchin'
an' copyin' things the best of us will be a-hurried wid work, yet
don't want comin' to the knowledge of the family—bad luck to him!

Is it ate wid him? Arrah, an' would I be sittin' wid a haythen an'
he a-atin' wid drum-sticks—yes, an' atin' dogs an' cats unknownst to
me, I warrant you, which it is the custom of them Chinesers, till the
thought made me that sick I could die. An' didn't the crayture prof-
fer to help me a wake ago come Toosday, an' me a foldin' down me
clane clothes for the ironin', and fill his haythin mouth wid water,
an' afore I could hinder squirrit it through his teeth stret over the
best linen table-cloth, and fold it up tight as innercent now as a
baby, the dirrity baste! But the worrest of all was the copyin' he'd be
doin' till ye'd be dishtracted. It's yersel' knows the tinder feet that's

on me since ever I've bin in this counthry. Well, owin' to that, I fell
into a way o' slippin' me shoes off when I'd be settin' down to pale
the praities or the likes o' that, and, do ye mind! that haythin would
do the same thing after me whinivir the missus set him to parin'
apples or tomaterses. The saints in heaven couldn't have made him
belave he cud kape the shoes on him when he'd be paylin' anything.

   Did I lave fur that? Faix an' I didn't. Didn't he get me into trouble wid my missus, the haythin? You're aware yersel' how the
boondles comin' in from the grocery often contains more'n 'll go
into anything dacently. So, for that matter I'd now and then take out
a sup o'sugar, or flour, or tay, an' wrap it in paper and put it in me
bit of a box tucked under the ironin' blankit the how it cuddent be
bodderin' any one. Well, what shud it be, but this blessed Sathurday
morn the missus was a spakin' pleasant and respec'ful wid me in me
kitchen when the grocer boy comes in an' stands fornenst her wid
his boondles, an' she motions like to Fing Wing (which I never
would call him by that name ner any other but just haythin), she motions to him, she does, for to take the boondles an' empty out the
sugar an' what not where they belongs. If you'll belave me, Ann
Ryan, what did that blatherin' Chineser do but take out a sup o'
sugar, an' a handful o' tay, an' a bit o' chaze right afore the missus,
wrap them into bits o' paper, an' I spacheless wid shurprize, an' he
the next minute up wid the ironin' blankit and pullin' out me box
wid a show o' bein' sly to put them in. Och, the Lord forgive me,
but I clutched it, and the missus sayin', "O Kitty!" in a way that 'ud
cruddle your blood. "He's a haythin nager," says I. "I've found you
out," says she. "I'll arrist him," says I. "It's you ought to be arris-
ted," says she. "You won't," says I. "I will," says she—and so it went
till she give me such sass as I cuddent take from no lady—an' I give
her warnin' and' I left that instant, an' she a-point-in' to the doore.

"Miss Malony on the Chinese Question" shows very clearly the influence of local color, the literary movement of the 1870s and 1880s
brought on by Bret Harte's popular verses and stories about life in
the mining camps of the Far West. The genre featured racial, regional, occupational, and other minorities which might be depicted
as quaint and humorous. Every group and every section had its
spokesman, as writers staked claims to literary materials like
prospectors asserting their rights to the earth's minerals. The movement enriched our literature by adding new subjects and attitudes,

for often the author's intent was to gain favorable attention for some little-known people or place. Though the writer did not belong to the group and was prone to misrepresent its values and patronize his characters, at least one professed purpose of the work was to present a novel subject with sympathetic understanding. Some of this writing, like the best fiction of George W. Cable and Kate Chopin, moved on toward regionalism and realism, producing a gallery of notable minority characters.

When realism became the prevailing literary style in the United States, William Dean Howells set the model for close observation and careful reporting on the commonplaces of middle-class life. His incidental treatment of immigrants gives us insights into the reaction of Americans to newcomers whose inferiority was not attested by gross physical deviations from the dominant standard. For such supposedly disappearing minorities a full accommodation to the majority values might seem to promise early release from the handicaps that attend cultural difference. Howells's references to Jews, Irish, and urban blacks have the virtue of quiet directness. More impassioned is the work of Mark Twain, whose misanthropy grew as he pondered the abuse and persecution visited upon minorities and the underprivileged in all human societies. Twain's spirited defenses of the rights of blacks and Chinese are sometimes misunderstood by readers unable to identify irony or appreciate sophisticated humor. Although not all his work is equally admirable for its rendering of minority experience, his *Adventures of Huckleberry Finn* is rightly called a "hymn to freedom."

Stereotyping of minorities—races, nationalities, etc.—comes about when writers and readers generalize and oversimplify. The attainable task for the artist is to depict with fidelity, depth, and compassion a woman or certain particular women, not *everywoman;* a Navaho bride or modern Mohawk steelworkers, not *the* Indian. Writers should write about what they know about, whatever that may be, which is not to say either that only Chicanos should write about Chicanos, or that a Nisei author should write only about Nisei. Minority identity does not automatically confer artistic skill and profound understanding of human nature and human society. Genius may produce a brilliant representation of some condition or identity the writer does not share in his or her own person. But for the fullest expression of the minority presence in America there must be artists who are part of the culture they depict and products of the tradition they describe.

Unfortunately, literary genius is not on call and does not appear in response to every need. Accomplishment in belles lettres takes time and opportunity. Oppressed people must put their energies into the daily battle for life and freedom; formal art is obliged to wait. Yet by the beginning of the twentieth century, Theodore Dreiser, a second-generation American, had made the first of his several major contributions to the mainstream of our literature, and Abraham Cahan, born in Russia, was producing authoritative studies of life in the ghettos where the new immigrants were herded. Charles W. Chesnutt and Paul Laurence Dunbar, whose ancestry traced to African slaves, had attained national recognition for their interpretations of black experience. They were heralds of a multitude of twentieth century writers of many ethnic identities whose works have added the indispensible inside view to the representation of these Americans in the nation's literature.

The theme of many of these writers is the predicament of people who are torn between the customs and values of the culture of their birth and those of the dominant society of which they are a part. Often they see the melting pot as merely a metaphor and feel that the majority culture induces them to abandon their heritage but withholds full participation and an equal status in American life. They write of the frustrations of the outsider who may possibly attain material success and public recognition but not admission to an inner circle. Joseph P. Kennedy, the first man of Irish descent to serve as American ambassador to England, once remarked before his son became President, "I was born in the United States and so was my father. Yet my children are still called Irish. What the hell do we have to do to become Americans?" They write also of the ambivalence of members of minority groups that leads them, as did Ambassador Kennedy at the Court of St. James, to take pride in their ethnic identity and to measure their advance by the distance they have come from their origin. "Tell them we are rising" was the message the struggling freedmen sent to their well-wishers; "We're movin' on up" is the theme song of modern blacks who have left Harlem for Manhattan's East Side. Upward mobility remains enough of a possibility in American life to make the national dream a compelling force.

And the flow of immigrants seeking refuge and opportunity continues. More than forty million people have migrated to the United States since the first European settlers arrived. By 1930 there were more people of Italian birth living in New York than in Rome. In the midst of the racial turmoil of the 1960s, about 33,000 black immigrants, ranging from laborers to professionals, came each year from the West Indies and Africa. Ethnic confusion goes on unabated: there are about 7,000 black Jews in the United States—among them some who have been Jews for generations—and one might find at an American university a black student majoring, as a matter of course, in Hebrew Studies. The newest immigrants—Puerto Ricans, Cubans, Mexicans, Hungarians, Koreans, Vietnamese—repeat the patterns experienced by their predecessors.

If each group advances in status as its members gain economic toeholds and make accommodations and contributions to the dominant culture, there are also penalties for whatever degree of alienation or identification persists. If some minorities have made dramatic progress up the ladder, it is yet true that there is a long way to go before all have a fair share of the rewards of American life. Discrimination and exploitation are meted out in heavy doses for some groups, while others experience them in lesser measure. In top corporations in Chicago in the early 1970s the number of black directors was only 0.4 percent, but those of Polish or Hispanic identity were even fewer. The number of people in Pittsburgh with incomes under $3,500 per year was twice as great for the foreign stock as for blacks. Indians, their numbers increased to almost 800,000 by the time of the 1970 census, constituted the most economically and educationally deprived minority in the nation, more than half of them living on reservations.

The cries of "Black Power" that dominated headlines of a decade ago have been followed by shouts of "Chicano Power" and "Women's Liberation," and virtually all the nation's minority groups have become vocal in protests and in formal literature. The study of their image becomes increasingly, but by no means exclusively, the study of works by ethnic writers. But these are, of course, also American writers, whose products are contributions to the growth and development of our national literature. The ever growing minority presence, a test and a challenge, remains central to the American experience.

THOMAS HARIOT
(1560–1621)

A mathematician and geographer who was tutor to Sir Walter Raleigh, Hariot accompanied an expedition to the British territory in the New World and, after spending over a year in the area, wrote *A Briefe and True Report of the New Found Land of Virginia* (1588). By painting its attractions for settlers and investors, this pamphlet supported Raleigh's ambitions to plant a colony in the region. Now very rare, it was translated into Latin and circulated on the Continent. When Richard Hakluyt included Hariot's work in the third volume of *The Principal Navigations, Voyages, Traffics, and Discoveries of the English Nation* (1600) it became readily accessible to English readers.

Their interest in the climate, terrain, and commodities of the New World was matched by concern about the character and condition of the inhabitants, whose numbers and friendly or hostile attitude would be important to the success of colonizing Europeans. Hariot's description of the natives was supplemented by the illustrations of one of his companions on the expedition, John White, whose classic renderings of the handsome physique of the Indians probably did much to encourage the Noble Savage concept. This selection from Hariot's work, the first English survey of what is now part of the United States, established the minority presence in the literature of America.

OF THE NATURE AND
MANNERS OF THE PEOPLE

It resteth I speake a word or two of the naturall inhabitants, their natures and maners, leauing large discourse thereof vntill time more conuenient hereafter: nowe onely so farre foorth, as that you may know, how that they in respect of troubling our inhabiting and planting, are not to be feared; but that they shall haue cause both to feare and loue vs, that shall inhabite with them.

They are a people clothed with loose mantles made of Deere skins, & aprons of the same rounde about their middles; all els naked; of such a difference of statures only as wee in England; hauing no edge tooles or weapons of yron or steele to offend vs withall, neither know they how to make any: those weapons ȳ[1] they haue, are onlie bowes made of Witch hazle, & arrowes of reeds; flat edged truncheons also of wood about a yard long, neither haue they any thing to defèd thèseluos but targets made of barks; and some armours made of stickes wickered together with thread.

Their townes are but small, & neere the sea coast but few, some containing but 10. or 12. houses: some 20. the greatest that we haue seene haue bene but of 30. houses: if they be walled it is only done with barks of trees made fast to stakes, or els with poles onely fixed vpright and close one by another.

Their houses are made of small poles made fast at the tops in rounde forme after the maner as is vsed in many arbories in our gardens of England, in most townes couered with barkes, and in some with artificiall mattes made of long rushes; from the tops of the houses downe to the ground. The length of them is commonly double to the breadth, in some places they are but 12. and 16. yardes long, and in other some wee haue seene of foure and twentie.

In some places of the countrey one onely towne belongeth to the gouernment of a *Wiróans* or chiefe Lorde; in other some two or three, in some sixe, eight, & more; the greatest *Wiróans* that yet we had dealing with had but eighteene townes in his gouernment, and able to make not aboue seuen or eight hundred fighting men at the

[1] ȳ, that.

27

most: The language of euery gouernment is different from any other, and the farther they are distant the greater is the difference.

Their maner of warres amongst themselues is either by sudden surprising one an other most comonly about the dawning of the day, or moone light; or els by ambushes, or some suttle deuises: Set battels are very rare, except it fall out where there are many trees, where eyther part may haue some hope of defence, after the deliuerie of euery arrow, in leaping behind some or other.

If there fall out any warres between vs & them, what their fight is likely to bee, we hauing aduantages against them so many maner of waies, as by our discipline, our strange weapons and deuises els; especially by ordinance great and small, it may be easily imagined; by the experience we haue had in some places, the turning vp of their heeles against vs in running away was their best defence.

In respect of vs they are a people poore, and for want of skill and iudgement in the knowledge and vse of our things, doe esteeme our trifles before thinges of greater value: Notwithstanding in their proper manner considering the want of such meanes as we haue, they seeme very ingenious; For although they haue no such tooles, nor any such craftes, sciences and artes as wee; yet in those thinges they doe, they shewe excellencie of wit. And by howe much they vpon due consideration shall finde our manner of knowledges and craftes to exceede theirs in perfection, and speed for doing or execution, by so much the more is it probable that they shoulde desire our friendships & loue, and haue the greater respect for pleasing and obeying vs. Whereby may bee hoped if meanes of good gouernment bee vsed, that they may in short time be brought to ciuilitie, and the imbracing of true religion.

Some religion they haue alreadie, which although it be farre from the truth, yet beyng as it is, there is hope it may bee the easier and sooner reformed. . . .

SELECTED REFERENCE

Rukeyser, Muriel. *Traces of Thomas Hariot* (1971).

PROJECTS AND PROBLEMS

Compare Hariot's work with some other "true report." Choose from the writings of John Smith, George Alsop, Francis Higginson, William Wood, Thomas Morton, John Hammond, Daniel Denton, William Penn, Thomas Ashe, and Gabriel Thomas. Focus on the description of Indian life and culture.

Did Hariot seem to anticipate dealing with the Indians on terms of equality?

The reports on the New World followed a pattern established centuries earlier. Giraldus Cambrensis (c. 1146–1223), a Norman-Welsh churchman and historian, wrote accounts of Ireland ("a country so remote from the rest of the world, and lying at its farthest extremity") that resemble Hariot's work. See "The Character and Customs of the Irish," an excerpt from his *Topography of Ireland*, in *The Portable Medieval Reader* (1949), ed. by James Bruce Ross and Mary Martin McLaughlin, and compare the description of the "barbarous" Irish with Hariot's picture of the aborigines of Virginia. Consider also George Alsop's description of Indian "Customs and Absurdities" in *A Character of the Province of Maryland*, first published in 1666.

JOHN SMITH
(1580–1631)

Traditionally the study of American literature begins
with the narratives of the English adventurer and
explorer whose leadership was a major factor in the
success of the first permanent English colony, the
settlement at Jamestown in Virginia. Smith's earliest
book on his experience in the New World appeared in
1608. This selection is from *The Generall Historie of
Virginia, New-England, and the Summer Isles* (1624).

SAVED BY POCAHONTAS

At last they brought him to Meronocomo, where was Powhatan their Emperor. Here more then two hundred of those grim Courtiers stood wondering at him, as he had beene a monster; till Powhatan and his trayne had put themselves in their greatest braveries. Before a fire upon a seat like a bedsted, he sat covered with a great robe, made of Rarowcun skinnes, and all the tayles hanging by. On either hand did sit a young wench of 16 or 18 yeares, and along on each side the house, two rowes of men, and behind them as many women, with all their heads and shoulders painted red; many of their heads bedecked with the white downe of Birds; but every one with something: and a great chayne of white beads about their necks. At his entrance before the King, all the people gave a great shout. The Queene of Appamatuck was appointed to bring him water to wash his hands, and another brought him a bunch of feathers, in stead of a Towell to dry them: having feasted him after their best barbarous manner they could, a long consultation was held, but the conclusion was, two great stones were brought before Powhatan: then as many as could layd hands on him, dragged him to them, and thereon laid his head, and being ready with their clubs, to beate out his braines, Pocahontas the Kings dearest daughter, when no intreaty could prevaile, got his head in her armes, and laid her owne upon his to save him from death: whereat the Emperour was contented he should live to make him hatchets, and her bells, beads, and copper; for they thought him aswell of all occupations as themselves. . . .

SELECTED REFERENCES

Emerson, Everett H. *Captain John Smith* (1971).
Nash, Gary B. "The Image of the Indian in the Southern Colonial Mind." *William and Mary Quarterly*, 29 (1972), 197–230.
Smith, Alan, ed. *Virginia, 1584–1607: The First English Settlement in North America* (1975).

Vaughan, Alden T. *American Genesis: Captain John Smith and the Founding of America* (1975).

PROJECTS AND PROBLEMS

Speculate on possible explanations for Smith's failure to publish the story of his rescue by Pocahontas in December of 1607 until seventeen years later, when she was not alive to confirm it.

Consider Smith's story about Pocahontas in connection with the comment in John Marston's *Eastward Hoe* (1605) that Virginia, longing for Englishmen to "share the rest of her maiden-head," had already "a whole country" of Englishmen who "have married with the Indians." These unions, he said, "bring forth as beautiful faces as any we have in England; and therefore the Indians are so in love with 'hem that the treasure they have they lay at their feete."

Compare the story of Smith's rescue by the Indian princess with one of the many other accounts in history and fiction of a beautiful woman who defects from her people to save or serve a man of alien or hostile identity. Is the woman in the narrative depicted as renegade or heroine? Is the man represented as villain or hero? What factors determine which interpretation the story offers?

Not long after she was captured by English colonists near Jamestown in 1613, Pocahontas adopted Christianity, put on European clothing, and changed her name to Rebecka. After her marriage to John Rolfe she never again saw her father or acknowledged her Indian culture. Might some modern young woman—a radical, idealist, or fanatic—perceive her as a model? Consider the kidnapping and ransom of Pocahontas that Smith reports in Book IV of his history.

Pocahontas was royally received when she and her husband visited London in 1616. Explain that reception. Explain why President Woodrow Wilson's second wife and other descendants of Rolfe and Pocahontas were not regarded in Virginia as half-breeds, mixed-bloods, or Indians. Instead, as J. Fenimore Cooper said in *Notions of the Americans* (1828), "it is a matter of boast among many of the most considerable persons of Virginia, that they are descended from the renowned Pocahontas."

Pocahontas has captured the imagination of many American writers. In "Our Mother Pocahontas" she is represented by Vachel Lindsay as a symbol of the American spirit. Is the poet's praise for her in his closing stanza a different kind of tribute than her Virginia contemporaries would have offered? For an illuminating comment on earlier treatments of Pocahontas see "Archetype into Stereotype" in *O Brave New World: American Literature from 1600 to 1840* (1968), ed. by Leslie A. Fiedler and Arthur Zeiger.

JOHN ROLFE
(1585–1622)

No literary man, John Rolfe nevertheless made his mark on American life and letters. He landed in the Virginia colony in 1610 and two years later introduced the regular cultivation of tobacco. A widower, he fell in love with Pocahontas, daughter of the Indian chief Powhatan, and married her in April, 1614. The first of the following selections is from his letter to Sir Thomas Dale, deputy governor of the colony. Written prior to his marriage, it was published in London the following year. The second selection is from his letter to Sir Edwin Sandys, treasurer of the Virginia Company of London, written after August of 1618. With it begins the record of the African in what is now the United States.

BETROTHED TO POCAHONTAS
Letter to Sir Thomas Dale

Honourable Sir, and most worthy Governor:

... to avoid tedious preambles, and to come neerer the matter: first suffer me with your patence, to sweepe and make cleane the way wherein I walke, from all suspicions and doubts, which may be covered therein, and faithfully to reveale unto you, what should move me hereunto.

Let therefore this my well advised protestation, which here I make betweene God and my own conscience, be a sufficient witnesse, at the dreadfull day of judgement (when the secret of all mens harts shall be opened) to condemne me herein, if my chiefest intent and purpose be not, to strive with all my power of body and minde, in the undertaking of so mightie a matter, no way led (so farre forth as mans weakenesse may permit) with the unbridled desire of carnall affection: but for the good of this plantation, for the honour of our countrie, for the glory of God, for my owne salvation, and for the converting to the true knowledge of God and Jesus Christ, an unbeleeving creature, namely Pokahuntas. To whom my hartie and best thoughts are, and have a long time bin so intangled, and inthralled in so intricate a laborinth, that I was even awearied to unwinde my selfe thereout. But almighty God, who never faileth his, that truely invocate his holy name hath opened the gate, and led me by the hand that I might plainely see and discerne the safe paths wherein to treade.

To you therefore (most noble Sir) the patron and Father of us in this countrey doe I utter the effects of this my setled and long continued affection (which hath made a mightie warre in my meditations) and here I doe truely relate, to what issue this dangerous combate is come unto, wherein I have not onely examined, but throughly tried and pared my thoughts even to the quicke, before I could finde any fit wholesome and apt applications to cure so daungerous an ulcer. I never failed to offer my daily and faithfull praiers to God, for his sacred and holy assistance. I forgot not to set before

mine eies the frailty of mankinde, his prones[1] to evill, his indul-
gencie of wicked thoughts, with many other imperfections wherein
man is daily insnared, and oftentimes overthrowne, and them compared to my present estate. Nor was I ignorant of the heavie displeasure which almightie God conceived against the sonnes of Levie
and Israel for marrying strange wives, nor of the inconveniences
which may thereby arise, with other the like good motions which
made me looke about warily and with good circumspection, into the
grounds and principall agitations, which thus should provoke me to
be in love with one whose education hath bin rude, her manners barbarous, her generation accursed, and so discrepant in all nurtriture
from my selfe, that oftentimes with feare and trembling, I have
ended my private controversie with this: surely these are wicked instigations, hatched by him who seeketh and delighteth in mans destruction; and so with fervent praiers to be ever preserved from such
diabolical assaults (as I tooke those to be) I have taken some rest.

Thus when I had thought I had obtained my peace and quietnesse,
beholde another, but more gracious tentation hath made breaches
into my holiest and strongest meditations; with which I have bin put
to a new triall, in a straighter manner than the former: for besides
the many passions and sufferings which I have daily, hourely, yea
and in my sleepe indured, even awaking mee to astonishment, taxing
mee with remisnesse, and carelesnesse, refusing and neglecting to
performe the duetie of a good Christian, pulling me by the eare, and
crying: why dost not thou indeavour to make her a Christian? And
these have happened to my greater wonder, even when she hath bin
furthest seperated from me, which in common reason (were it not an
undoubted worke of God) might breede forgetfulnesse of a farre
more worthie creature. Besides, I say the holy spirit of God hath
often demaunded of me, why I was created? If not for transitory
pleasures and worldly vanities, but to labour in the Lords vineyard,
there to sow and plant, to nourish and increase the fruites thereof,
daily adding with the good husband in the Gospell, somewhat to the
tallent, that in the end the fruites may be reaped, to the comfort of
the labourer in this life, and his salvation in the world to come? And
if this be, as undoubtedly this is, the service Jesus Christ requireth of
his best servant: wo unto him that hath these instruments of pietie

[1]proneness

put into his hands, and wilfully despiseth to worke with them. Like-wise, adding hereunto her great apparance of love to me, her desire to be taught and instructed in the knowledge of God, her capable-nesse of understanding, her aptnesse and willingnesse to receive anie good impression, and also the spirituall, besides her owne incite-ments stirring me up hereunto.

What should I doe? shall I be of so untoward a disposition, as to refuse to leade the blind into the right way? Shall I be so unnaturall, as not to give bread to the hungrie? or uncharitable, as not to cover the naked? Shall I despise to actuate these pious dueties of a Chris-tian? Shall the base feare of displeasing the world, overpower and with holde mee from revealing unto man these spirituall workes of the Lord, which in my meditations and praiers, I have daily made knowne unto him? God forbid. . . .

Now if the vulgar sort, who square all mens actions by the base rule of their own filthinesse, shall taxe or taunt me in this my godly labour: let them know, it is not any hungry appetite, to gorge my selfe with incontinency; sure (if I would, and were so sensually in-clined) I might satisfie such desire, though not without a seared con-science, yet with Christians more pleasing to the eie, and lesse feare-full in the offence unlawfully committed. Nor am I in so desperate an estate, that I regard not what becommeth of mee; nor am I out of hope but one day to see my Country, nor so void of friends, nor mean in birth, but there to obtain a mach[2] to my great content: nor have I ignorantly passed over my hopes there, or regardlesly seek to loose the love of my friends, by taking this course: I know them all, and have not rashly overslipped any.

But shal it please God thus to dispose of me (which I earnestly de-sire to fulfill my ends before sette down) I will heartely accept of it as a godly taxe appointed me, and I will never cease, (God assisting me) untill I have accomplished, and brought to perfection so holy a worke, in which I will daily pray God to blesse me, to mine, and her eternall happines. And thus desiring no longer to live, to enjoy the blessing of God, then[3] this my resolution doth tend to such godly ends, as are by me before declared: not doubting of your favourable acceptance, I take my leave, beseeching Almighty God to raine

[2]match
[3]than

downe upon you, such plenitude of his heavenly graces, as your heart can wish and desire, and so I rest, At your commaund most willing to be disposed off

JOHN ROLFE.

THE BLACK RECORD BEGINS

About the latter end of August, a Dutch man of Warr of the burden of a 160 tunes arrived at *Point Comfort,* the commanders name Capt. Jope, his pilott for the West Indyes, one Mr. Marmaduke an Englishman. They mett with the Trer[1] in the West Indyes, and determyned to hold consort shipp hetherward, but in their passage lost one the other. He brought not anything but 20 and odd Negroes, which the Governor and Cape Marchant bought for victualle (whereof he was in great need as he ptended) at the best and easiest rates they could. . . .

SELECTED REFERENCES

Nash, Gary B. *Red, White, and Black: The Peoples of Early America* (1974).

Tyler, Lyon Gardiner, ed. *Narratives of Early Virginia, 1606-1625* (1907).

PROJECTS AND PROBLEMS

See the full text of Rolfe's letter to Sir Thomas Dale in Tyler's book or in *The Indian and the White Man* (1964), ed. by Wilcomb E. Washburn and respond to Nash's assertion that "the marriage was political." Does Rolfe's letter offer any support to Washburn's statement that "the carnal bond . . . was immediately established between Europeans and Indians"?

Rolfe states that he is worried about his forthcoming marriage and acknowledges that Pocahontas may seem a strange mate for him. Does he refer to her race? Does he express concern because she is an Indian or because she is "an unbeleeving creature"?

Were the blacks who arrived in 1619 the vanguard of the enormous number of Africans who—unlike all the other immigrants to

[1]An English ship, the *Treasurer,* had sailed from Virginia in the summer of 1618, supposedly to get salt and goats for the colony but outfitted as a war vessel.

the New World—arrived in chains, disposed of to the Virginia colonists as slaves or indentured servants? Were the three women
granted a different status from the others? Compare their condition
with that of the white indentured servants who performed the bulk
of the labor in the English colonies during their first fifty years of
existence. See *The Negro in Virginia* (1940), compiled by the Virginia Writers' Project of the WPA.

WILLIAM BRADFORD
(1590–1657)

A passenger on the *Mayflower* when it arrived in
Massachusetts in 1620, Bradford became governor of the
Plymouth Colony the following April and was frequently
reelected to that position. *Of Plymouth Plantation*, the
history he began to write in 1630, was completed in
1651. This selection presents the Pilgrim leader's version
of an important early encounter of the English
Separatists and the first Americans.

PROFITABLE UNTO THEM

...All this while the Indians came skulking about them, and would sometimes show them selves aloofe of, but when any aproached near them, they would rune away. And once they stoale away their tools wher they had been at worke, and were gone to diner. But about the 16. of March[1] a certaine Indian came bouldly amongst them, and spoke to them in broken English, which they could well understand, but marvelled at it. At length they understood by discourse with him, that he was not of these parts, but belonged to the eastrene parts, wher some English-ships came to fhish, with whom he was aquainted, and could name sundrie of them by their names, amongst whom he had gott his language. He became proftable to them in aquainting them with many things concerning the state of the cuntry in the east-parts wher he lived, which was afterwards profitable unto them; as also of the people hear, of their names, number, and strength; of their situation and distance from this place, and who was cheefe amongst them. His name was Samaset; he tould them also of another Indian whos name was Squanto, a native of this place, who had been in England and could speake better English then him selfe. Being, after some time of entertainmente and gifts, dismist, a while after he came againe, and 5. more with him, and they brought againe all the tooles that were stolen away before, and made way for the coming of their great Sachem, called Massasoyt; who, about 4. or 5. days after, came with the cheefe of his freinds and other attendance, with the aforesaid Squanto. With whom, after frendly entertainment, and some gifts given him, they made a peace with him (which hath now continued this 24 years) in these terms.

1. That neither he nor any of his, should injurie or doe hurte to any of their peopl.

2. That if any of his did any hurte to any of theirs, he should send the offender, that they might punish him.

3. That if any thing were taken away from any of theirs, he should cause it to be restored; and they should doe the like to his.

[1]1621.

42

4. If any did unjustly warr against him, they would aide him; if any did warr against them, he should aide them.

5. He should send to his neighbours confederats, to certifie them of this, that they might not wrong them, but might be likewise comprised in the conditions of peace.

6. That when ther men came to them, they should leave their bows and arrows behind them.

After these things he returned to his place caled Sowams, some 40. mile from this place, but Squanto continued with them, and was their interpreter, and was a spetiall instrument sent of God for their good beyond their expectation. He directed them how to set their corne, wher to take fish, and to procure other comodities, and was also their pilott to bring them to unknowne places for their profitt, and never left them till he dyed. He was a native of this place, and scarce any left alive besids him selfe. He was caried away with diverce others by one Hunt,[2] a m^r of a ship, who thought to sell them for slaves in Spaine: but he got away for England, and was entertained by a marchante in London, and imployed to New-found-land and other parts, and lastly brought hither into these parts by one Mr. Dermer, a gentle-man imployed by Sr. Ferdinando Gorges and others, for discovery, and other designes in these parts. . . .

SELECTED REFERENCE

Miller, Perry, and Thomas H. Johnson. *The Puritans* (1938).

PROJECTS AND PROBLEMS

The friendly services of Samoset and Squanto were of the greatest value to the colonists. Does Bradford's history accord full acceptance to these allies?

Is Bradford's attitude toward the Indians traceable to the principles of Providential History or to other influences? Is it at all differ-

---

[2]Thomas Hunt, captain of one of the ships in John Smith's expedition to New England in 1614, captured twenty-seven Indians, carried them to Malaga, and sold them.

ent from that of John Smith? Explain possible reasons for any differences you detect.

Compare Bradford's account of the massacre of four hundred Indians and the burning of a Pequot village in 1637 with Benjamin Franklin's "A Narrative of the Late Massacres, in Lancaster County." What are some explanations for the differences?

See the journals and letters of John Winthrop, Bradford's contemporary and leader of the Puritan Massachusetts Bay Colony, and compare his attitude toward the Indian with that of Bradford and John Eliot.

JOHN ELIOT
(1604–1690)

A few years after he arrived in Boston, Eliot began to preach to the Indians around Roxbury in their native tongue, for he took seriously the announced intention of the settlers of the Massachusetts Bay Colony to convert the natives to Christianity. In 1651 he established the first of his villages of praying Indians. His translation of the Bible into the Algonquian language is his principal memorial. The following passage is from a tract, *The Day-Breaking, If Not the Sun-Rising of the Gospell with the Indians in New England,* printed in London in 1647.

CONVERTS OF "THE APOSTLE TO THE INDIANS"

Wee have cause to be very thankfull to God who hath moved the hearts of the generall court to purchase so much land for them to make their towne in which the *Indians* are much taken with,[1] and it is somewhat observable that while the Court were considering where to lay out their towne, the *Indians* (not knowing of any thing) were about that time consulting about Lawes for themselves, and there company who sit downe with *Waaubon;* there were ten of them, two of them are forgotten.

Their Lawes were these

1. That if any man be idle a weeke, at most a fortnight, hee shall pay five shillings.

2. If any unmarried man shall lie with a young woman unmarried, he shall pay twenty shillings.

3. If any man shall beat his wife, his hands shall bee tied behind him and carried to the place of justice to bee severely punished.

4. Every young man if not anothers servant, and if unmarried, hee shall be compelled to set up a *Wigwam* and plant for himselfe, and not live shifting up and downe to other *Wigwams.*

5. If any woman shall not have her haire tied up but hang loose or be cut as mens haire, she shall pay five shillings.

6. If any woman shall goe with naked breasts they shall pay two shillings sixpence.

7. All those men that weare long locks shall pay five shillings.

8. If any shall kill their lice betweene their teeth, they shall pay five shillings. This Law though ridiculous to English eares yet tends to preserve cleanliness among *Indians.*

Tis wonderfull in our eyes to understand by these two honest *Indians,* what Prayers *Waaubon* and the rest of them use to make, for

[1]The towne the Indians did desire to know what name it should have, and it was told them it should bee called Noonatomen, which signifies in English rejoycing, because they hearing the word, and seeking to know God, the English did rejoyce at it, and God did rejoyce at it, which pleased them much, & therefore that is to be the name of their town. [Eliot's note.]

hee that preacheth to them professeth hee never yet used any of
their words in his prayers, from whom otherwise it might bee
thought that they had learnt them by rote, one is this.

Amanaomen	*Jehovah*	*tahassen metagh.*
Take away	Lord	my Stony heart
	Another	
Cheehesom	*Jehovah*	*kekowhogkew,*
Wash	Lord	my soule.
	Another	

Lord lead me when I die to heaven.

These are but a taste, they have many more, and these more enlarged then thus expressed, yet what are these but the sprinklings of
the spirit and blood of Christ Jesus in their hearts? and 'tis no small
matter that such dry barren and long-accursed ground should yeeld
such kind of increase in so small a time, I would not readily com-
mend a faire day before night, nor promise much of such kind of
beginnings, in all persons, nor yet in all of these, for wee know the
profession of very many is but a meere paint, and their best graces
nothing but meere flashes and pangs, which are suddainly kindled
and as soon go out and are extinct againe, yet God doth not usually
send his Plough & Seedsman to a place but there is a least some little peece of good ground, although three to one bee naught: and
mee thinkes the Lord Jesus would never have made so fit a key for
their locks, unlesse hee had intended to open some of their doores,
and so to make way for his comming in. Hee that God hath raised up
and enabled to preach unto them, is a man (you know) of a most
sweet, humble, loving gratious and enlarged spirit, whom God hath
blest, and surely will still delight in & do good by. I did thinke never
to have opened my mouth to any, to desire those in England to further any good worke here, but now I see so many things inviting to
speake in this businesse, that it were well if you did lay before those
that are prudent and able these considerations.

1 That it is prettie heavy and chargeable to educate and traine up
those children which are already offered us, in schooling,
cloathing, diet, and attendance, which they must have.

2 That in all probabilities many *Indians* in other places, expe-
cially under our jurisdiction, will bee provoked by this example in

these, both to desire preaching, and also to send their children to us, when they see that some of their fellows fare so well among the English, and the civill authoritie here so much favouring and countenancing of these, and if many come in, it will bee more heavy to such as onely are fit to keepe them, and yet have their hands and knees infeebled so many wayes besides.

3 That if any shall doe any thing to encourage this worke, that it may be given to the Colledge for such an end and use, that so from the Colledge may arise the yeerly revenue for their yeerly maintenance. I would not have it placed in any particular mans hands for feare cousenage or misplacing or carelesse keeping and improving; but at the Colledge it's under many hands and eyes the chief and best of the country who have ben & will be exactly carefull of the right and comely disposing of such things; and therefore, if any thing bee given, let it be put in such hands as may immediately direct it to the President of the Colledge, who you know will soone acquaint the rest with it; and for this end if any in England have thus given any thing for this end, I would have them speake to those who have received it to send it this way, which if it bee withheld I thinke 'tis no lesse than sacrilege: but if God moves no hearts to such a work, I doubt not then but that more weake meanes shall have the honour of it in the day of Christ.

A FOURTH MEETING WITH THE INDIANS.

This day being *Decemb,* 9. the children being catechised, and that place of *Ezekiel* touching the dry bones being opened, and applyed to their condition; the *Indians* offered all their children to us to bee educated amongst us, and instructed by us, complaining to us that they were not able to give any thing to the English for their education: for this reason there are therefore preparations made towards the schooling of them, and setting up a Schoole among them or very neare unto them. Sundry questions also were propounded by them to us, and of us to them; one of them being askt what is sinne? hee answered a noughty heart. Another old man complained to us of his feares, *viz,* that hee was fully purposed to keepe the Sabbath, but still he was in feare whether he should go to hell or heaven; and thereupon the justification of a sinner by faith in Christ was opened unto him as the remedy against all feares of hell. Another complayned of other *Indians* that did revile them, and call them Rogues and such like speeches for cutting off their Locks, and for cutting their Haire in a modest manner as the New-English generally doe; for since the word hath begun to worke upon their hearts, they have discerned the vanitie and pride which they placed in their haire, and have therefore of their owne accord (none speaking to them that wee know of) cut it modestly; there were therefore encouraged by some there present of chiefe place and account with us, not to feare the reproaches of wicked *Indians,* nor their witchcraft and *Pawwaws* and poysonings, but let them know that if they did not dissemble but would seeke God unfaignedly, that they would stand by them, and that God also would be with them. They told us also of divers *Indians* who would come and stay with them three or foure dayes, and one Sabbath, and then they would goe from them, but as for themselves, they told us they were fully purposed to keepe the Sabbath, to which wee incouraged them, and night drawing on were forced to leave them, for this time.

SELECTED REFERENCES

Russell, Francis. "Apostle to the Indians." *American Heritage,* 9, No. 1 (1957), 5–9, 117–19.

Tyler, Moses Coit. *A History of American Literature, 1607–1765* (1949).

PROJECTS AND PROBLEMS

Daniel Gookin, superintendent of the praying Indians and John Eliot's main colleague, is one of the historic figures used as characters in Nathaniel Hawthorne's "Young Goodman Brown." Discuss King Philip's War and the work of Eliot and Gookin in relation to that story. Gookin's humanitarian attitude is expressed in his *Historical Account of the Doings and Sufferings of the Christian Indians of New England* (1836).

MARY ROWLANDSON
(c. 1635–c. 1678)

During King Philip's War, Mrs. Rowlandson, wife of the pastor of the church at Lancaster, Massachusetts, was abducted by the Narragansett Indians and held for eleven weeks and five days before she was ransomed. Her account, the first New England captivity narrative, was published in 1682 and many times thereafter. The qualities that made the genre popular for many decades are apparent in this selection from *The Sovereignty and Goodness of God, Together With the Faithfulness of His Promises Displayed; Being a Narrative of the Captivity and Restauration of Mrs. Mary Rowlandson.*

IN GRIEVOUS CAPTIVITY

On the tenth of February 1675, Came the Indians with great numbers upon Lancaster: Their first coming was about Sun-rising; hearing the noise of some Guns, we looked out; several Houses were burning, and the Smoke ascending to Heaven. There were five persons taken in one house, the Father, and the Mother and a sucking Child, they knockt on the head; the other two they took and carried away alive. Their were two others, who being out of their Garison upon some occasion were set upon; one was knockt on the head, the other escaped: Another their was who running along was shot and wounded, and fell down; he begged of them his life, promising them Money (as they told me) but they would not hearken to him but knockt him in head, and stript him naked, and split open his Bowels. Another seeing many of the Indians about his Barn, ventured and went out, but was quickly shot down. There were three others belonging to the same Garison who were killed; the Indians getting up upon the roof of the Barn, had advantage to shoot down upon them over their Fortification. Thus these murtherous wretches went on, burning, and destroying before them.

At length they came and beset our own house, and quickly it was the dolefullest day that ever mine eyes saw. The House stood upon the edg of a hill; some of the Indians got behind the hill, others into the Barn, and others behind any thing that could shelter them; from all which places they shot against the House, so that the Bullets seemed to fly like hail; and quickly they wounded one man among us, then another, and then a third, About two hours (according to my observation, in that amazing time) they had been about the house before they prevailed to fire it (which they did with Flax and Hemp, which they brought out of the Barn, and there being no defence about the House, only two Flankers at two opposite corners and one of them not finished) they fired it once and one ventured out and quenched it, but they quickly fired it again, and that took. Now is the dreadfull hour come, that I have often heard of (in time of War, as it was the case of others) but now mine eyes see it. Some in our house were fighting for their lives, others wallowing in their blood, the House on fire over our heads, and the bloody Heathen ready to knock us on the head, if we stirred out. Now might we hear Mothers and Children crying out for themselves, and one another, Lord, What shall we do? Then I took my Children (and one of my sisters, hers) to go forth and leave the house: but as soon as we came to the dore and appeared, the Indians shot so thick that the bulletts rattled against the House, as if one had taken an handfull of stones and threw them, so that we were fain to give back. We had six stout Dogs belonging to our Garrison, but none of them would stir, though another time, if any Indian had come to the door, they were ready to fly upon him and tear him down. The Lord hereby would make us the more to acknowledge his hand, and to see that our help is always in him. But out we must go, the fire increasing, and coming along behind us, roaring, and the Indians gaping before us with their Guns, Spears and Hatchets to devour us. No sooner were we out of the House but my Brother in Law (being before wounded, in defending the house, in or near the throat) fell down dead, wherat the Indians scornfully shouted, and hallowed, and were presently upon him, stripping off his cloaths, the bulletts flying thick, one went through my side, and the same (as would seem) through the bowels and hand of my dear Child in my arms. One of my elder Sisters Children, named William, had then his Leg broken, which the Indians perceiving, they knockt him on head. Thus were we butchered by those merciless Heathen, standing amazed, with the blood running down to our heels. My eldest Sister being yet in the House, and seeing those wofull sights, the Infidels haling Mothers one way, and Children another, and some wallowing in their blood: and her elder Son telling her that her Son William was dead, and my self was wounded, she said, And, Lord, let me dy with them; which was no sooner said, but she was struck with a Bullet, and fell down dead over the threshold. I hope she is reaping the fruit of her good labours, being faithfull to the service of God in her place. In her younger years she lay under much trouble upon spiritual accounts, till it pleased God to make that precious Scripture take hold of her heart, 2 Cor. 12. 9. *And he said unto me, my Grace is sufficient for thee.* More then twenty years after I have heard her tell how sweet and comfortable that place was to her. But to return: The Indians laid hold of us, pulling me one way, and the Children another, and said, Come go along with us; I told them they would kill me: they answered, If I were willing to go along with them, they would not hurt me.

Oh the dolefull sight that now was to behold at this House! *Come, behold the works of the Lord, what dissolations he has made in the Earth.* Of thirty seven persons who were in this one House, none escaped either present death, or a bitter captivity, save only one, who might say as he, Job 1. 15, *And I only am escaped alone to tell the News.* There were twelve killed, some shot, some stab'd with their Spears, some knock'd down with their Hatchets. When we are in prosperity, Oh the little that we think of such dreadfull sights, and to see our dear Friends, and Relations ly bleeding out their heart-blood upon the ground. There was one who was chopt into the head with a Hatchet, and stript naked, and yet was crawling up and down. It is a solemn sight to see so many Christians lying in their blood, some here, and some there, like a company of Sheep torn by Wolves, All of them stript naked by a company of hell-hounds, roaring, singing, ranting and insulting, as if they would have torn our very hearts out; yet the Lord by his Almighty power preserved a number of us from death, for there were twenty-four of us taken alive and carried Captive.

I had often before this said, that if the Indians should come, I should chuse rather to be killed by them then taken alive but when it came to the tryal my mind changed; their glittering weapons so daunted my spirit, that I chose rather to go along with those (as I may say) ravenous Beasts, then that moment to end my dayes; and that I may the better declare what happened to me during that grievous Captivity, I shall particularly speak of the severall Removes we had up and down the Wilderness.

THE FIRST REMOVE.

Now away we must go with those Barbarous Creatures, with our bodies wounded and bleeding, and our hearts no less than our bodies. About a mile we went that night, up upon a hill within sight of the Town, where they intended to lodge. There was hard by a vacant house (deserted by the English before, for fear of the Indians). I asked them whither I might not lodge in the house that night to which they answered, what will you love English men still? this was the dolefullest night that ever my eyes saw. Oh the roaring, and singing and danceing, and yelling of those black creatures in the night, which made the place a lively resemblance of hell. And as miserable was the wast that was there made, of Horses, Cattle, Sheep, Swine, Calves, Lambs, Roasting Pigs, and Fowl (which they had plundered in the Town) some roasting, some lying and burning, and some boyling to feed our merciless Enemies; who were joyful enough though we were disconsolate. To add to the dolefulness of the former day, and the dismalness of the present night: my thoughts ran upon my losses and sad bereaved condition. All was gone, my Husband gone (at least separated from me, he being in the Bay,[1] and to add to my grief, the Indians told me they would kill him as he came homeward) my Children gone, my Relations and Friends gone, our House and home and all our comforts within door, and without, all was gone, (except my life) and I knew not but the next moment that might go too. There remained nothing to me but one poor wounded Babe, and it seemed at present worse than death that it was in such a pitiful condition, bespeaking Compassion, and I had no refreshing for it, nor suitable things to revive it. Little do many think what is the savageness and bruitishness of this barbarous Enemy, I[2] even those that seem to profess more than others among them, when the English have fallen into their hands.

Those seven that were killed at Lancaster the summer before upon a Sabbath day, and the one that was afterward killed upon a week day, were slain and mangled in a barbarous manner, by one-ey'd John, and Marlborough's Praying Indians,[3] which Capt. Mosely brought to Boston, as the Indians told me. . . .

SELECTED REFERENCES

Leach, Douglas E. *Flintlock and Tomahawk: New England and King Philip's War* (1958).

Pearce, Roy Harvey. *The Savages of America: A Study of the Idea of Civilization* (1953).

[1]Massachusetts Bay, at or near Boston.
[2]Aye.
[3]Settlement of Christian Indians at Marlborough, Massachusetts.

PROJECTS AND PROBLEMS

Did the Indian captivity narrative serve as source material for the later romances of the frontier? Did it offer many of the literary and other values later provided in belles lettres, especially the novel?

Mrs. Rowlandson's charges against the Marlborough Indians are countered by the report of her contemporary, Daniel Gookin, who saw them as victims of persecution by some of the colonists. Compare the accounts of these partisans and study *Transactions of the American Antiquarian Society*, II, 451–61, to decide which is more nearly correct.

SAMUEL SEWALL
(1652–1730)

The Diary, from which the first selection is taken, reveals much about the character as well as the affairs of Samuel Sewall and his contemporaries in Boston at the twilight of the Puritan period. Judge Sewall's *The Selling of Joseph*, one of the earliest antislavery tracts, was published in 1700. Sewall favored humane treatment of the Indians, as is evident in his letter to Sir William Ashhurst.

SLAVES AND THE
SLAVE TRADE

Fourth–day, June, 19. 1700. . . . Having been long and much dissatisfied with the Trade of fetching Negros from Guinea; at last I had a strong Inclination to Write something about it; but it wore off. At last reading Baynes, Ephes.[1] about servants, who mentions Blackamoors; I began to be uneasy that I had so long neglected doing any thing. When I was thus thinking, in came Bro[r] Belknap to shew me a Petition he intended to present to the Gen[l] Court for the freeing a Negro and his wife, who were unjustly held in Bondage. And there is a Motion by a Boston Comittee to get a Law that all Importers of Negros shall pay 40[s] p̄ head, to discourage the bringing of them. And Mr. C. Mather resolves to publish a sheet to exhort Masters to labour their Conversion. Which makes me hope that I was call'd of God to Write this Apology for them; Let his Blessing accompany the same.[2]

○   ○   ○   ○   ○

Thorsday Sept[r] 26th 1700. Mr. John Wait and Eunice his wife, and Mrs. Debora Thair come to Speak to me about the Marriage of Sebastian, Negro serv[t] of said Wait, with Jane, Negro servant of said Thair. Mr. Wait desired they might be published in order to marriage Mrs. Thair insisted that Sebastian might have one day in six allow'd him for the suport of Jane, his intended wife and her children, if it should please God to give her any. Mr. Wait now wholly declin'd that, but freely offer'd to allow Bastian Five pounds, in Money p̄ añum towards the suport of his children p̄ said Jane (besides Sebastians cloathing and Diet). I persuaded Jane and Mrs. Thair to agree to it, and so it was concluded; and Mrs. Thair gave up the Note of Publication to Mr. Wait for him to carry it to W[m]

[1]Paul Baynes, "Commentary on the First Chapter of the Ephesians," 1618.
[2]*The Selling of Joseph,* was published June 24, 1700.

Griggs, the Town Clerk, and to Williams in order to have them published according to Law. . . .

o   o   o   o   o

Oct ^{r} 20. [1700] Mr. Cotton Mather came to Mr. Wilkins's shop, and there talked very sharply against me as if I had used his father worse than a Neger; spake so loud that people in the street might hear him. Then went and told Sam, That one pleaded much for Negros, and he had used his father worse than a Negro, and told him that was his Father. . . .

Octr 9. [1701] I sent Mr. Increase Mather a Hanch of very good Venison; I hope in that I did not treat him as a Negro.

THE SELLING OF JOSEPH

A MEMORIAL.

Forasmuch as Liberty *is in real value next unto* Life: *None ought to part with it themselves, or deprive others of it, but upon most mature Consideration.*

The Numerousness of Slaves at this day in the Province, and the Uneasiness of them under their Slavery, hath put many upon thinking whether the Foundation of it be firmly and well laid; so as to sustain the Vast Weight that is built upon it. It is most certain that all Men, as they are the Sons of *Adam*, are Coheirs; and have equal Right unto Liberty, and all other outward Comforts of Life. *GOD hath given the Earth* (with all its Commodities) *unto the Sons of* Adam, *Psal 115. 16. And hath made of One Blood, all Nations of Men, for to dwell on all the face of the Earth, and hath determined the Times before appointed, and the bounds of their habitation: That they should seek the Lord. Foreasmuch then as we are the Offspring of GOD &c. Act* 17.26, 27, 29. Now although the Title given by the last ADAM, doth infinitely better Mens Estates, respecting GOD and themselves; and grants them a most beneficial and inviolable Lease under the Broad Seal of Heaven, who were before only Tenants at Will: Yet through the Indulgence of GOD to our First Parents after the Fall, the outward Estate of all and every of their Children, remains the same, as to one another. So that Originally, and Naturally, there is no such thing as Slavery. *Joseph* was rightfully no more a Slave to his Brethren, than they were to him: and they had no more Authority to *Sell* him, than they had to *Slay* him. And if *they* had nothing to do to Sell him; the *Ishmaelites* bargaining with them, and paying down Twenty pieces of Silver, could not make a Title. Neither could *Potiphar* have any better Interest in him than the *Ishmaelites* had. *Gen.* 37.20, 27, 28. For he that shall in this case plead *Alteration of Property*, seems to have forfeited a great

59

part of his own claim to Humanity. There is no proportion between Twenty Pieces of Silver, and LIBERTY. The Commodity it self is the Claimer. If *Arabian* Gold be imported in any quantities, most are afraid to meddle with it, though they might have it at easy rates; lest if it should have been wrongfully taken from the Owners, it should kindle a fire to the Consumption of their whole Estate. 'Tis pity there should be more Caution used in buying a Horse, or a little lifeless dust; than there is in purchasing Men and Women: Whenas they are the Offspring of GOD, and their Liberty is,

.... '*Auro pretiosior Omni.*'[1]

And seeing GOD hath said, *He that Stealeth a Man and Selleth him, or if he be found in his hand, he shall surely be put to Death.* Exod. 21.16. This Law being of Everlasting Equity, wherein Man Stealing is ranked amongst the most atrocious of Capital Crimes: What louder Cry can there be made of that Celebrated Warning,

'Caveat Emptor!'[2]

And all things considered, it would conduce more to the Welfare of the Province, to have White Servants for a Term of Years, than to have Slaves for Life. Few can endure to hear of a Negro's being made free; and indeed they can seldom use their freedom well; yet their continual aspiring after their forbidden Liberty, renders them Unwilling Servants. And there is such a disparity in their Conditions, Colour & Hair, that they can never embody with us, and grow up into orderly Families, to the Peopling of the Land: but still remain in our Body Politick as a kind of extravasat Blood. As many Negro men as there are among us, so many empty places there are in our Train Bands, and the places taken up of Men that might make Husbands for our Daughters. And the Sons and Daughters of *New England* would become more like *Jacob,* and *Rachel,* if this Slavery were thrust quite out of doors. Moreover it is too well known what Temptations Masters are under, to connive at the Fornication of their Slaves; lest they should be obliged to find them Wives, or pay their Fines. It seems to be practically pleaded that they might be Lawless; 'tis thought much of, that the Law should have Satisfaction for their Thefts, and other Immoralities; by which means, *Holiness to the Lord,* is more rarely engraven upon this sort of Servitude. It is

[1]More precious than gold.
[2]Buyer beware.

likewise most lamentable to think, how in taking Negros out of *Africa*, and Selling of them here, That which GOD has joyned together men do boldly rend asunder; Men from their Country, Husbands from their Wives, Parents from their Children. How horrible is the Uncleanness, Mortality, if not Murder, that the Ships are guilty of that bring great Crouds of these miserable Men, and Women. Methinks, when we are bemoaning the barbarous Usage of our Friends and Kinsfolk in *Africa:* it might not be unseasonable to enquire whether we are not culpable in forcing the *Africans* to become Slaves amongst our selves. And it may be a question whether all the Benefit received by *Negro* Slaves, will balance the Accompt of Cash laid out upon them; and for the Redemption of our own enslaved Friends out of *Africa.* Besides all the Persons and Estates that have perished there.

Obj. 1. *These Blackamores are of the Posterity of* Cham, *and therefore are under the Curse of Slavery. Gen.* 9.25, 26, 27.

Answ. Of all Offices, one would not begg this; *viz.* Uncall'd for, to be an Executioner of the Vindictive Wrath of God; the extent and duration of which is to us uncertain. If this ever was a Commission; How do we know but that it is long since out of Date? Many have found it to their Cost, that a Prophetical Denunciation of Judgment against a Person or People, would not warrant them to inflict that evil. If it would, *Hazael* might justify himself in all he did against his Master, and the *Israelites,* from 2 *Kings* 8.10, 12.

But it is possible that by cursory reading, this Text may have been mistaken. For *Canaan* is the Person Cursed three times over, without the mentioning of *Cham.* Good Expositors suppose the Curse entaild on him, and that this Prophesie was accomplished in the Extirpation of the *Canaanites,* and in the Servitude of the *Gibeonites. Vide Pareum.* Whereas the Blackmores are not descended of *Canaan,* but of *Cush.* Psal. 68. 31. *Princes shall not come out of Egypt* [Mizraim], *Ethiopia* [Cush] *shall soon stretch out her hands unto God.* Under which Names, all *Africa* may be comprehended; and their Promised Conversion ought to be prayed for. *Jer.* 13.23. *Can the Ethiopian change his skin?* This shows that Black Men are the Posterity of *Cush:* Who time out of mind have been distinguished by their Colour. And for want of the true, *Ovid* assigns a fabulous cause of it.

'Sanguine tum credunt in corpora summa vocato
A Ethiopum populus nigrum traxisse colorem.
METAMORPH. LIB. 2.[3]

Obj. 2 *The* Nigers *are brought out of a Pagan Country, into places where the Gospel is Preached.*

Answ. Evil must not be done, that good may come of it. The extraordinary and comprehensive Benefit accruing to the Church of God, and to *Joseph* personally, did not rectify his brethrens Sale of him.

Obj. 3. *The* Africans *have Wars one with another: Our Ships bring lawful Captives taken in those Wars.*

Answ. For ought is known, their Wars are much such as were between *Jacob's* Sons and their Brother *Joseph.* If they be between Town and Town; Provincial, or National: Every War is upon one side Unjust. An Unlawful War can't make lawful Captives. And by Receiving, we are in danger to promote, and partake in their Barbarous Cruelties. I am sure, if some Gentlemen should go down to the *Brewsters* to take the Air, and Fish: And a stronger party from *Hull* should Surprise them, and Sell them for Slaves to a Ship outward bound: they would think themselves unjustly dealt with; both by Sellers and Buyers. And yet 'tis to be feared, we have no other kind of Title to our *Nigers. Therefore all things whatsoever ye would that men should do to you, do ye even so to them: for this is the Law and the Prophets. Matt.* 7. 12.

Obj. 4. Abraham *had Servants bought with his Money, and born in his House.*

Answ. Until the Circumstances of *Abraham's* purchase be recorded, no Argument can be drawn from it. In the mean time, Charity obliges us to conclude, that He knew it was lawful and good.

It is Observable that the *Israelites* were strictly forbidden the buying, or selling one another for Slaves. *Levit.* 25.39.46. *Jer.* 34 8....22. And GOD gaged His Blessing in lieu of any loss they might conceipt they suffered thereby. *Deut.* 15. 18. And since the partition Wall is broken down, inordinate Self love should likewise be demolished.

---

[3]Then it was [during Phaëthon's ride], as men think, that the peoples of Ethiopia became black-skinned, since the blood was drawn to the surface of their bodies by the heat. *Metamorphoses, II,* 325–36.

GOD expects that Christians should be of a more Ingenuous and benign frame of spirit. Christians should carry it to all the World, as the *Israelites* were to carry it one towards another. And for men obstinately to persist in holding their Neighbours and Brethren under the Rigor of perpetual Bondage, seems to be no proper way of gaining Assurance that God ha's given them Spiritual Freedom. Our Blessed Saviour has altered the Measures of the ancient Love-Song, and set it to a most Excellent New Tune, which all ought to be ambitious of Learning. *Matt.* 5. 43, 44. *John* 13. 34. These *Ethiopians,* as black as they are; seeing they are the Sons and Daughters of the First *Adam,* the Brethren and Sisters of the Last ADAM, and the Offspring of GOD; They ought to be treated with a Respect agreeable.

INDIAN BOUNDARIES
Letter to Sir William Ashhurst

May 3, 1700.

HONORABLE SIR,—The last Fall, I had notice of my being en-
trusted with a share in managing the Indian Affairs, And presently
upon it, the Commissoners were pleased to appoint me their Secretary. As I account it an honor to be thus employed; so according to
my mean ability, I shall endeavour faithfully to serve the Corpora-
tion and Commissioners, as I shall receive Instructions from them. I
have met with an Observation of some grave Divines, that ordinarily
when God intends Good to a Nation, He is pleasd to make use of
[some] . . . , to be instrumental in conveying of that Good unto them.
Now God has furnished several of the Indians with considerable
abilities for the Work of the Ministry, and Teaching School, And
therefore I am apt to believe, that if the Indians so qualified, were
more taken notice of in suitable Rewards, it would conduce very
much to the propagation of the Gospel among them. Besides the
Content they might have in a provision of necessary Food and Rai-
ment, the Respect and honor of it, would quicken their Industry, and
allure others to take pains in fitting themselves for a fruitfull discharge of those Offices. One thing more, I would crave leave to suggest, We have had a very long and grievous War with the Eastern
Indians, and it is of great Concernment to His Majesty's Interests
here that a peace be concluded with them upon firm and sure foundations. Which in my poor opinion cannot well be, while our Articles of Accord with them remain so very General as they doe. I
should think it requisite that convenient Tracts of Land should be
set out to them; and that by plain and natural Boundaries, as much
as may be; as Lakes, Rivers, Mountains, Rocks, Upon which for any
English man to encroach, should be accounted a Crime. Except this
be done, I fear their own Jealousies, and the French Friers will persuade them, that the English, as they encrease, and think they want
more room, will never leave till they have crouded them quite out
of all their Lands. And it will be a vain attempt for us to offer
Heaven to them, if they take up prejudices against us, as if we did
grudge them a Living upon their own Earth. The Savoy-Confession

of Faith, Engl. on one side and Indian on the other, has been lately printed here; as also several Sermons . . . have been Transcribed into Indian, and printed, Which I hope in God's Time will have a very good Effect. To see it and be employed in giving your Honor an Account of it would be a very desirable piece of Service to him who is

your Honors
most humble Servant
SAM. SEWALL.

SUGGESTED ADDITIONAL READING

"A Memorial Relating to the Kennebeck Indians"

SELECTED REFERENCES

Chamberlain, Nathan H. *Samuel Sewall and the World He Lived In* (1897).

Lawrence, Henry W. "Samuel Sewall: Revealer of Puritan New England." *South Atlantic Quarterly*, 33 (1934), 20–37.

Towner, Lawrence W. "The Sewall-Saffin Dialogue on Slavery." *William and Mary Quarterly*, 21 (1964), 40–52.

Winslow, Ola Elizabeth. *Samuel Sewall of Boston* (1964).

PROJECTS AND PROBLEMS

Both Sewall and Cotton Mather were involved in the Salem witchcraft trials. Compare their records. Was Sewall's behavior, in keeping with his authorship of *The Selling of Joseph*, humane and enlightened?

Compare Sewall's incidental references to blacks and Indians in his diary with the casual comments about minorities in *The Journals of Sarah Kemble Knight*, his contemporary. Consider as one example this entry in the judge's diary: "I essay'd June, 22, [1716] to prevent Indians and Negroes being Rated with Horses and Hogs; but could not prevail." And see *The Letters of Samuel Lee* and *Samuel Sewall Relating to New England and the Indians* in the Colonial Society of Massachusetts Collections, XIV, 1913.

Sewall and Cotton Mather mentioned in their works Indian raids and retribution by the colonists. Discuss the ways in which the accounts differ in their treatment of the warring parties.

Joseph Saffin's *A Brief and Candid Answer to a late Printed Sheet, entitled, The Selling of Joseph* (1701) was the first defense of slavery printed in Colonial America. Speculate on the extent to which the disagreement between Sewall and Saffin about the institution of slavery rested on different opinions (stated or implied) about the character and intellectual capacities of the slaves.

Compare *The Selling of Joseph* with the protest against slavery adopted by Germantown Quakers in 1688, reprinted in *Racial Thought in America* (1970), ed. by Louis Ruchames.

COTTON MATHER
(1663–1728)

A descendant of some of the most distinguished and influential Puritan divines, Cotton Mather wrote nearly five hundred books and pamphlets, mastered a dozen or so languages, and conducted a wide scholarly correspondence. Among his works are sermons, histories, biographies, and theological treatises. The first of the following selections is from *Magnalia Christi Americana* (1702); the second is from *The Negro Christianized* (1706).

HANNAH DUSTAN AND THE INDIANS

On *March* 15. 1697. The *Salvages* made a Descent upon the Skirts of *Haverhil*, murdering and Captiving about Thirty-nine Persons, and Burning about half a Dozen Houses. In this Broil, one *Hannah Dustan* having lain-in about a Week, attended with her Nurse, *Mary Neff*, a Widow, a Body of terrible *Indians* drew near unto the House where she lay, with Designs to carry on their Bloody Devastations. Her Husband hastened from his Employments abroad unto the relief of his Distressed Family; and first bidding *Seven* of his *Eight* Children (which were from *Two* to *Seventeen* Years of Age) to get away as fast as they could unto some Garrison in the Town, he went in to inform his Wife of the horrible Distress come upon them. E'er she could get up, the fierce *Indians* were got so near, that utterly despairing to do her any Service, he ran out after his Children; resolving that on the Horse which he had with him, he would Ride away with *That* which he should in this Extremity find his Affections to pitch most upon, and leave the rest unto the Care of the Divine Providence. He overtook his Children about Forty Rod from his Door; but then such was the *Agony* of his Parental Affections, that he found it impossible for him to distinguish any one of them from the rest; wherefore he took up a Courageous Resolution to Live and Die with them all. A Party of *Indians* came up with him; and now though they Fired at him, and he Fired at them, yet he Manfully kept at the Reer of his *Little Army* of Unarmed Children, while they Marched off with the Pace of a Child of Five Years Old; until, by the Singular Providence of God, he arrived safe with them all unto a Place of Safety about a Mile or two from his House. But his House must in the mean time have more dismal *Tragedies* acted at it. The *Nurse* trying to escape with the New-born Infant, fell into the Hands of the Formidable *Salvages;* and those furious Tawnies coming into the House, bid poor *Dustan* to rise immediately. Full of Astonishment she did go; and sitting down in the Chimney with an Heart full of most fearful *Expectation*, she saw the raging Dragons rifle all that they could carry away, and set the House on Fire. About Nineteen

or Twenty *Indians* now led these away, with about half a Score
other *English Captives;* but e'er they had gone many Steps, they
dash'd out the Brains of the *Infant* against a Tree; and several of the
other *Captives*, as they began to Tire in their sad *journey*, were soon
sent unto their *Long Home;* the *Salvages* would presently Bury their
Hatchets in their Brains, and leave their Carcases on the Ground for
Birds and Beasts to Feed upon. However, *Dustan* (with her Nurse)
notwithstanding her present Condition, Travelled that Night about
a Dozen Miles, and then kept up with their New Masters in a long
Travel of an Hundred and Fifty Miles, more or less, within a few
Days Ensuing, without any sensible Damage in their Health, from
the Hardships of their *Travel*, their *Lodging*, their *Diet*, and their
many other Difficulties. These Two poor Women were now in the
Hands of those whose *Tender Mercies are Cruelties;* but the good
God, who hath all *Hearts in his own Hands*, heard the Sighs of these
Prisoners, and gave them to find unexpected Favour from the *Mas-
ter* who laid claim unto them. That *Indian Family* consisted of
Twelve Persons; Two Stout Men, Three Women, and Seven Children; and for the Shame of many an *English Family* that has the
Character of *Prayerless* upon it, I must now Publish what these poor
Women assure me: 'Tis this, in Obedience to the Instruction which
the *French* have given them, they would have *Prayers* in their Family no less than Thrice every Day; in the *Morning*, at *Noon*, and in
the *Evening;* nor would they ordinarily let their Children *Eat* or
Sleep without first saying their *Prayers*. Indeed these *Idolaters* were
like the rest of their whiter Brethren *Persecutors*, and would not endure that these poor Women should retire to their *English Prayers*,
if they could hinder them. Nevertheless, the poor Women had nothing but Fervent Prayers to make their Lives Comfortable or Tolerable; and by being daily sent out upon Business, they had Opportunities together and asunder to do like another *Hannah*, in *Pouring out
their Souls before the Lord:* Nor did their praying Friends among
our selves forbear to *Pour out* Supplications for them. Now they
could not observe it without some Wonder, that their *Indian* Master
sometimes when he saw them dejected would say unto them, *What
need you Trouble your self? If your God will have you delivered,
you shall be so!* And it seems our God would have it so to be. This
Indian Family was now Travelling with these Two Captive

Women, (and an *English* Youth taken from *Worcester* a Year and half before,) unto a Rendezvous of *Salvages*, which they call a *Town* somewhere beyond *Penacook;* and they still told these poor Women, that when they came to this Town they must be Stript, and Scourg'd, and Run the *Gantlet* through the whole Army of *Indians*. They said this was the *Fashion* when the Captives first came to a Town; and they derided some of the Faint-hearted *English*, which they said, fainted and swoon'd away under the *Torments* of this Discipline. But on *April* 30. while they were yet, it may be, about an Hundred and Fifty Miles from the *Indian* Town, a little before break of Day, when the whole Crew was in a *Dead Sleep*, (Reader, see if it prove not so!) one of these Women took up a Resolution to intimate the Action of *Jael* upon *Sisera;* and being where she had not her own *Life* secured by any *Law* unto her, she thought she was not forbidden by any *Law* to take away the *Life* of the *Murderers*, by whom her *Child* had been Butchered. She heartened the *Nurse* and the *Youth* to assist her in this Enterprize; and all furnishing themselves with *Hatchets* for the purpose, they struck such home Blows upon the Heads of their *Sleeping Oppressors*, that e'er they could any of them struggle into any effectual resistance, *at the Feet* of those poor Prisoners, *they bow'd, they fell, they lay down; at their Feet they bowed, they fell; where they bowed, there they fell down Dead.* Only one *Squaw* escaped sorely Wounded from them in the Dark; and one *Boy*, whom they reserved asleep, intending to bring him away with them, suddenly wak'd and Scuttled away from this Desolation. But cutting off the *Scalps* of the *Ten Wretches*, they came off, and received *Fifty Pounds* from the General Assembly of the Province, as a Recompence of their Action; besides which, they received many *Presents of Congratulation* from their more private Friends; but none gave 'em a greater Taste of Bounty than Colonel *Nicholson*, the Governour of *Maryland*, who hearing of their Action, sent 'em a very generous Token of his Favour.

ON THE CONVERSION OF NEGROES

It is a *Golden Sentence* that has been sometimes quoted from *Chrysostom;*[1] That *for a man to know the Art of Alms, is more than for a man to be crowned with the Diadem of Kings. But to convert one Soul unto God, is more than to pour out Ten Thousand Talents into the Baskets of the Poor.* Truly, to Raise a *Soul* from a dark state of Ignorance and Wickedness, to the Knowledge of GOD and the Belief of CHRIST, and the practice of our Holy and Lovely Religion, 'Tis the noblest Work that ever was undertaken among the Children of men. An opportunity to endeavor the Conversion of a Soul, from a life of sin, which is indeed a woeful death, to fear God, and love Christ, and by a religious life to escape the Paths of the Destroyer, it cannot but be acceptable to all that have themselves had in themselves experience of such a conversion. And such an opportunity there is in your Hands, O all you that have any NEGROES in your Houses; an Opportunity to try Whether you may not be the Happy *Instruments* of Converting the Blackest Instances of Blindness and Baseness into admirable *Candidates* for Eternal Blessedness. Let not this Opportunity be Lost; if you have any concern for *Souls,* your Own or Others; but make a Trial, Whether by your Means, the most BRUITISH of Creatures upon Earth may not come to be disposed, in some Degree, like the *Angels* of Heaven, and the *Vassals* of Satan become the *Children* of God. Suppose these Wretched *Negroes* to be the Offspring of *Cham*[2] (which yet is not so very certain) yet let us make a Trial Whether the CHRIST who *dwelt in the Tents of Shem* have not some of His Chosen among them. Let us make a Trial Whether they that have been Scorched and Blacken'd by the Sun of Africa may not come to have their Minds Healed by the more Benign *Beams* of the *Sun of Righteousness.*

It is come to pass by the *Providence* of God, without which there comes nothing to pass, that Poor NEGROES are cast under your Government and Protection. You take them into your *Families;* you look

---

[1] Saint John Chrysostom (c. 347–407).
[2] Ham, second-born son of Noah.

on them as part of your *Possessions;* and you Expect from their Service a Support, and perhaps an Increase, of your other *Possessions.* How agreeable would it be, if a Religious Master or Mistress thus attended, would now think with themselves! *Who can tell but that this Poor Creature may belong to the Election of God! Who can tell but that God may have sent this Poor Creature into my Hands, that so One of the Elect may by my means be Called, & by my Instruction be made Wise unto Salvation! The glorious God will put an unspeakable Glory upon me if it may be so!* The Considerations that would move you To Teach your *Negroes* the *Truths* of the Glorious Gospel, as far as you can, and bring them, if it may be, to Live according to those *Truths,* a *Sober,* and a *Righteous,* and a *Godly* Life; They are innumerable; And, if you would after a *Reasonable* manner consider the Pleas which we have to make on the behalf of *God,* and of the *Souls* which He has made, one would wonder that they should not be *Irresistible. Show yourselves Men,* and let *Rational Arguments* have their Force upon you, to make you treat, not as *Bruits* but as *Men* those *Rational Creatures* whom God has made your *Servants....*

Be assured, Syrs, Your *Servants* will be the *Better Servants* for being made *Christian Servants.* To *Christianize* them aright will be to *fill them with all Goodness. Christianity* is nothing but a very Mass of Universal *Goodness.* Were your *Servants* well tinged with the spirit of *Christianity,* it would render them exceeding *Dutiful* unto their *Masters,* exceeding *Patient* under their *Masters,* exceeding faithful in their Business, and afraid of speaking or doing anything that may justly displease you. It has been observed that those *Masters* who have used their *Negroes* with most of *Humanity,* in allowing them all the Comforts of Life that are necessary and *Convenient* for them (Who have remember that by the Law of God, even an Ass was to be relieved when *Sinking under his Burden,* and an Ox might not be *Muzzled* when *Treading out the Corn;* and that if a *Just man will regard the Life of the Beast,* he will much more allow the comforts of life to and not [hide?] himself *from his own flesh)* have been better *Served,* had more work done for them, and better done, than those *Inhumane Masters* who have used their *Negroes* worse than their *Horses.* And those *Masters,* doubtless, who use their *Negroes* with most of *Christianity,* and use most pains to inform them in, and conform them to, *Christianity,* will find themselves no losers by it. . . . But many *Masters* whose *Negroes* have greatly vexed them, with miscarriages, may do well to examine Whether Heaven be not chastising of them for their failing in their Duty about their *Negroes.* Had they done more to make their *Negroes* the knowing and willing *Servants* of God, it may be God would have made their *Negroes* better *Servants* to them. Sirs, you may read your *Sin* in the *Punishment.*

And now, what *Objection* can any man living have, to refund the force of these *Considerations?* Produce *thy cause,* O Impiety, *Bring forth thy strong reasons,* and let all men see what Idle and silly cavils are thy best *Reasons* against this Work of God.

It has been cavilled by some that it is questionable Whether the *Negroes* have *Rational Souls* or no. But let that *Bruitish* insinuation be never Whispered any more. Certainly, their Discourse will abundantly prove that they have *Reason. Reason* shows itself in the *Design* which they daily act upon. The vast improvement that *Education* has made upon *some* of them argues there is a *Reasonable Soul* in *all* of them. . . . They are *Men,* and not *Beasts,* that you have bought, and they must be used accordingly. 'Tis true, they are Barbarous. But so were our own *Ancestors.* The *Britons* were in many things as Barbarous, but a little before our Saviour's nativity, as the Negroes are at this day, if there be any Credit in *Caesars Commentaries.* Their *Complexion* sometimes is made an Argument why nothing should be done for them. A *Gay* sort of argument! As if the great God went by the *Complexion* of Men in His Favours to them! As if none but *Whites* might hope to be Favoured and Accepted with God! Whereas it is well known That the Whites are the least part of Mankind. The biggest part of Mankind, perhaps, are *Copper-Coloured,* a sort of *Tawnies.* And our *English* that inhabit some Climates do seem growing apace to be not much unlike unto them. As if, because a people, from the long force of the African *Sun & Soil* upon them (improved, perhaps, to further Degrees by maternal imagination, and other accidents) are come at length to have the small *Fibers* of their *Veins,* and the Blood in them, a little more Interspersed through their Skin, than other People, this must render them less valuable to Heaven than the rest of Mankind? Away with such Trifles! The God who *looks on the Heart* is not moved by the color of the *Skin,* is not more propitious to one *Colour* than another.

Say rather, with the Apostle *Acts* 10.34, 35. *Of a truth I perceive, that God is no respecter of persons, but in every Nation he that feareth Him and worketh Righteousness is accepted with Him.* Indeed their *Stupidity* is a *Discouragement.* It may seem unto as little purpose to *Teach* as to *wash an Ethiopian.* But the greater their *Stupidity,* the greater must be our *Application.* If we can't learn them so much as we *Would,* let us learn them as much as we *Can.* A little divine *Light* and *Grace* infused into them will be of great account. And the more *Difficult* it is to fetch such *forlorn things* up out of the perdition whereinto they are fallen, the more *Laudable* is the undertaking. There will be the more of a *Triumph* if we prosper in the undertaking. Let us encourage ourselves from that word; *Mat.* 3.9. *God is able of these Stones to raise up Children unto Abraham.*

Well; But if the *Negroes* are *Christianized* they will be *Baptised;* and their *Baptism* will presently entitle them to their *Freedom;* so our *Money is thrown away.*

Man, if this were true, that a *Slave* bought with the *Money* were by thy means brought unto the *Things that accompany Salvation,* and thou shouldest from this time have no more Service from him, yet the *Money* were not thrown away. That Mans *Money will perish with him* who had rather the *Souls* in his family should *Perish* than that he should lose a little *Money.* And suppose it were so, that *Baptism* gave a legal Title to *Freedom.* Is there no guarding against this Inconvenience? You may by sufficient *Indentures* keep off the things which you reckon so Inconvenient. But it is all a Mistake. There is no such thing. What *Law* is it that sets the *Baptized Slave* at Liberty? Not the *Law of Christianity,* that allows of *Slavery.* Only it wonderfully Dulcifies and Mollifies and Moderates the Circumstances of it. *Christianity* directs a *Slave,* upon his embracing the *Law of the Redeemer,* to satisfy himself *That he is the Lord's Freeman,* tho he continues a *Slave.* It supposes (*Col.* 3.11.) that there are *Bond* as well as *Free* among those that have been *Renewed in the Knowledge and Image of Jesus Christ.* Will the *Canon-Law* do it? No, the *Canons* of numberless *Councils* mention the *Slaves* of *Christians* without any contradiction. Will the *Civil Law* do it? No: Tell, if you can, any part of *Christendom* wherein *Slaves* are not frequently to be met withal. But is not *Freedom* to be claim'd for a *Baptised Slave,* by the *English* Constitution? The English *Laws*

about *Villians* or *Slaves* will not say so; for by those *Laws*, they may
be granted *for Life*, like a *Lease*, and passed over with a *Manner*,
like other *Goods* or *Chattels*. And by those *Laws*, the Lords may
sieze the Bodies of their *Slaves* even while a *Writt . . .* is depending.
These English *Laws* were made when the *Lords* & the *Slaves* were
both of them *Christians*, and they stand still unrepealed. If there are
not now such *Slaves* in *England* as formerly, it is from the *Lords*
more than from the *Laws*. The *Baptised* then are not thereby entitled unto the *Liberty*. Howbeit, if they have arrived unto such a
measure of *Christianity* that *none can forbid Water for the Baptising
of them*, it is fit that they should enjoy those *comfortable circumstances* with us, which are due to them, not only as the *Children* of
Adam, but also as our *Brethren*, on the same level with us in the expectations of a blessed Immortality through the *Second Adam*.
Whatever Slaughter the Assertion may make among the pretensions
which are made unto *Christianity*, yet while the *sixteenth* chapter of
Matthew is in the Bible, it must be asserted: the *Christian* who cannot so far *Deny himself*, can be no *Disciple* of the Lord JESUS CHRIST.
But, O Christian, thy *Slave* will not serve thee one jot the worse for
that *Self-denial*.

SUGGESTED ADDITIONAL READINGS

Cotton Mather: Selections, ed. by Kenneth B. Murdock (1926).
Decennium Luctuosum
The Short History of New England

SELECTED REFERENCES

Cantor, Milton. "The Image of the Negro in Colonial Literature." *New England Quarterly*, 36 (1963), 452–77.
Friedman, Lee M. "Cotton Mather and the Jews." *Publications
of the American Jewish Historical Society*, No. 26 (1918),
201–10.
Haynes, Henry W. "Cotton Mather and His Slaves." *Proceed-
ings of the American Antiquarian Society*, n. s. 6 (1889–90),
191–95.

Read, Allen Walker. "The Speech of Negroes in Colonial America." *Journal of Negro History*, 24 (1939), 247–58.

Towner, Lawrence W. " 'A Fondness for Freedom': Servant Protest in Puritan Society." *William and Mary Quarterly*, 19 (1962), 201–19.

Twombly, Robert D., and Robert H. Moore. "Black Puritan: The Negro in Seventeenth-Century Massachusetts." *William and Mary Quarterly*, 26 (1967), 224–42.

PROJECTS AND PROBLEMS

In "Philip of Pokanoket" in this volume, Washington Irving charges an unnamed "worthy Clergyman" with bias in reporting the warfare between the Indians and the early settlers of Massachusetts. Was Cotton Mather or Increase Mather the guilty party?

Compare Cotton Mather's report on Hannah Dustan's experience with Nathaniel Hawthorne's "The Duston Family," in this volume, or with other stories of Indian captivity from Mather's *Decennium Luctuosum*, reprinted in *Narratives of the Indian Wars, 1675–1699* (1952), ed. by Charles H. Lincoln.

Review Mather's reaction to the Salem witchcraft trials and judge whether his attitudes were affected by racism as well as by superstition and religious training.

SARAH KEMBLE KNIGHT
(1666–1727)

A sprightly widow who proved herself to be a capable business woman, Mrs. Knight once kept a school that Benjamin Franklin is said to have attended. She left Boston in October of 1704 on a trip through Rhode Island and Connecticut to New York, no small undertaking at the time, arriving back home in March. Like many a traveler in a strange land, Mrs. Knight recorded her reaction to the people and manners she observed, measuring them against the standards that prevailed in Boston. Her journal, published in 1825 and frequently reprinted, is an entertaining source of information and reveals an author with a rare sense of humor.

INDULGENT CONNECTICUT

... About two o'clock afternoon we arrived in New Haven, where I was received with all Posible Respects and civility. Here I discharged Mr. Wheeler with a reward to his satisfaction, and took some time to rest after so long and toilsome a Journey; And Inform'd myselfe of the manners and customs of the place, and at the same time employed myselfe in the afair I went there upon.

They are Govern'd by the same Laws as wee in Boston, (or little differing,) thr'out this whole Colony of Connecticot, And much the same way of Church Government, and many of them good, Sociable people, and I hope Religious too: but a little too much Independent in their principalls, and, as I have been told, were formerly in their Zeal very Riggid in their Administrations towards such as their Lawes made Offenders, even to a harmless Kiss or Innocent merriment among Young people. Whipping being a frequent and counted an easy Punishment, about wch as other Crimes, the Judges were absolute in their Sentances. They told mee a pleasant story about a pair of Justices in those parts, wch I may not omit the relation of.

A Negro Slave belonging to a man in ye Town, stole a hogs head from his master, and gave it or sold it to an Indian, native of the place. The Indian sold it in the neighbourhood, and so the theft was found out. Thereupon the Heathen was Seized, and carried to the Justices House to be Examined. But his worship (it seems) was gone into the field, with a Brother in office, to gather in his Pompions.[1] Whither the malefactor is hurried, And Complaint made, and satisfaction in the name of Justice demanded. Their Worships cann't proceed in form without a Bench: whereupon they Order one to be Imediately erected, which, for want of fitter materials, they made with pompions—which being finished, down setts their Worships, and the Malefactor call'd, and by the Senior Justice Interrogated after the following manner. You Indian why did You steal from this man? You sho'dn't do so—it's a Grandy wicked wicked thing to steal. Hol't Hol't cryes Justice Junr. Brother, You speak Negro to him. I'le

[1]Pumpkins.

78

ask him. You sirrah, why did You steal this man's Hoggshead?
Hoggshead? (replys the Indian,) me no stomany. No? says his Worship; and pulling off his hatt, Patted his own head with his hand,
sais, Tatapa—You,Tatapa—you: all one this. Hah! Says Netop, now
me stomany that. Whereupon the Company fell into a great fitt of
Laughter, even to Roreing. Silence is comanded, but to no effect:
for they continued perfectly Shouting. Nay, said his worship, in an
angry tone, if it be so *take mee off the Bench.*

Their Diversions in this part of the Country are on Lecture days
and Training days mostly: on the former there is Riding from town
to town.

And on training dayes The Youth divert themselves by Shooting at
the Target, as they call it, (but it very much resembles a pillory,)
where hee that hitts neerest the white has some yards of Red Ribbin
presented him wch being tied to his hattband, the two ends streem-
ing down his back, he is Led away in Triumph, wth great applause,
as the winners of the Olympiack Games. They generally marry very
young: the males oftener as I am told under twentie than above;
they generally make public weddings, and have a way something singular (as they say) in some of them, *viz.* Just before Joyning hands
the Bridegroom quitts the place, who is soon followed by the Brides-
men, and as it were, [is] dragged back to duty—being the reverse to
ye former practice among us, to steal his Bride.

There are great plenty of Oysters all along by the sea side, as farr
as I Rode in the Collony, and those very good. And they Generally
lived very well and comfortably in their famelies. But too Indulgent
(especially ye farmers) to their slaves: sufering too great familiarity
from them, permitting them to sit at Table and eat with them, (as
they say to save time,) and into the dish goes the black hoof as freely
as the white hand. They told me there was a farmer lived nere the
Town where I lodgd who had some differences wth his slave, concerning something the master had promised him and did not punc-
tualy. perform; wch caused some hard words between them; But at
length they put the matter of Arbitration and Bound themselves to
stand to the award of such as they named—wch done, the Arbitrators
Having heard the Allegations of both parties, Order the master to
pay 40^s to black face, and acknowledge his fault. And so the matter
ended: the poor master very honestly standing to the award.

There are every where in the Towns as I passed, a Number of Indians the Natives of the Country, and are the most salvage of all the
salvages of that kind that I had ever Seen: little or no care taken (as I
heard upon enquiry) to make them otherwise. They have in some
places Landes of their owne, and Govern'd by Law's of their own
making;—they marry many wives and at pleasure put them away,
and on the least dislike or fickle humour, on either side, saying *stand
away* to one another is a sufficient Divorce. And indeed those uncomely *Stand aways* are too much in Vougue among the English in
this (Indulgent Colony) as their Records plentifully prove, and that
on very trivial matters, of which some have been told me, but are
not proper to be Related by a Female pen, tho some of that foolish
sex have had too large a share in the story.

If the natives committ any crime on their own precincts among
themselves, ye English takes no Cognezens of. But if on the English
ground, they are punishable by our Laws. They mourn for their
Dead by blackening their faces, and cutting their hair, after an Awk-
erd and frightfull manner; But can't bear You should mention the
names of their dead Relations to them: they trade most for Rum, for
wch theyd hazard their very lives; and the English fit them Generally as well, by seasoning it plentifully with water . . . .

SELECTED REFERENCES

Gunn, Sidney. "Sarah Kemble Knight." *Dictionary of American
Biography*, X, 468–69.

PROJECTS AND PROBLEMS

Compare Mrs. Knight's lively journal with the diary of her Boston
contemporary, Samuel Sewall.

Is Mrs. Knight's treatment of country bumpkins comparable to
her attitude toward Indians and blacks? Is her sense of superiority
based entirely on racial grounds?

Mrs. Knight had much to say about colonial inns. Compare the
patrons she describes with the traditional image of the puritanical
New England colonist. Did she find that only Indians overindulged
in rum?

WILLIAM BYRD
(1674–1744)

An urbane Virginia gentleman, Byrd owned many slaves,
an estate stretching over thousands of acres, and a
mansion on the James River. His *History of the Dividing
Line* (1841), was written when he was commissioned as
surveyor of the boundary between North Carolina and
Virginia. The following selection is from that work,
which circulated in manuscript during Byrd's lifetime.
His stature has increased with the publication of a more
personal account, *The Secret History of the Line* (1929)
and his secret diaries (1941, 1942, 1958).

A VISIT TO VIRGINIA'S INDIANS

April 7. [1728] The next day being Sunday, we ordered notice to be sent to all the neighborhood that there would be a sermon at this place, and an opportunity of christening their children. But the likelihood of rain got the better of their devotion, and what perhaps, might still be a stronger motive of their curiosity. In the morning we dispatched a runner to the Nottoway Town, to let the Indians know we intend them a visit that evening, and our honest landlord was so kind as to be our pilot thither, being about 4 miles from his house.

Accordingly in the afternoon we marched in good order to the town, where the female scouts, stationed on an eminence for that purpose, had no sooner spied us, but they gave notice of our approach to their fellow-citizens by continual whoops and cries, which could not possibly have been more dismal at the sight of their most implacable enemies.

This signal assembled all their great men, who received us in a body, and conducted us into the fort. This fort was a square piece of ground, inclosed with substantial puncheons, or strong palisades, about ten feet high, and leaning a little outwards, to make a scalade more difficult.

Each side of the square might be about 100 yards long, with loopholes at proper distances, through which they may fire upon the enemy.

Within this inclosure we found bark cabins sufficient to lodge all their people, in case they should be obliged to retire thither. These cabins are no other but close arbors made of saplings, arched at the top, and covered so well with bark as to be proof against all weather. The fire is made in the middle, according to the Hibernian fashion, the smoke whereof finds no other vent but at the door, and so keeps the whole family warm, at the expense both of their eyes and complexion.

The Indians have no standing furniture in their cabins but hurdles to repose their persons upon, which they cover with mats or deerskins. We were conducted to the best apartments in the fort, which just before had been made ready for our reception, and adorned with new mats that were sweet and clean.

The young men had painted themselves in a hideous manner, not so much for ornament as terror. In that frightful equipage they entertained us with sundry war-dances, wherein they endeavored to look as formidable as possible. The instrument they danced to was an Indian-drum, that is, a large gourd with skin braced taut over the mouth of it. The dancers all sang to this music, keeping exact time with their feet, while their heads and arms were screwed into a thousand menacing postures.

Upon this occasion the ladies had arrayed themselves in all their finery. They were wrapt in their red and blue match-coats, thrown so negligently about them that their mahogany skins appeared in several parts, like the Lacedaemonian damsels of old. Their hair was braided with white and blue peak, and hung gracefully in a large roll upon their shoulders.

This peak consists of small cylinders cut out of a conque-shell, drilled through and strung like beads. It serves them both for money and jewels, the blue being of much greater value than the white, for the same reason that Ethiopian mistresses in France are dearer than French, because they are more scarce. The women wear necklaces and bracelets of these precious materials, when they have a mind to appear lovely. Though their complexions be a little sad-colored, yet their shapes are very straight and well proportioned. Their faces are seldom handsome, yet they have an air of innocence and bashfulness, that with a little less dirt would not fail to make them desirable. Such charms might have had their full effect upon men who had been so long deprived of female conversation, but that the whole winter's soil was so crusted on the skins of those dark angels, that it required a very strong appetite to approach them. The bear's oil, with which they anoint their persons all over, makes their skins soft, and at the same time protects them from every species of vermin that use to be troublesome to other uncleanly people.

We were unluckily so many that they could not well make us the complement of bed-fellows, according to the Indian rules of hospitality, though a grave matron whispered one of the Commissioners very civily in the ear, that if her daughter had been but one year older, she should have been at this devotion.

It is by no means a loss of reputation among the Indians, for damsels that are single to have intrigues with the men; on the contrary,
they count it an argument of superior merit to be liked by a great
number of gallants. However, like the ladies that game they are a
little mercenary in their amours, and seldom bestow their favors out
of stark love and kindness. But after these women have once appropriated their charms by marriage, they are from thenceforth
faithful to their vows, and will hardly ever be tempted by an agreeable gallant, or be provoked by a brutal or even by a fumbling husband to go astray.

The little work that is done among the Indians is done by the poor
women, while the men are quite idle, or at most employed only in
the gentlemanly diversions of hunting and fishing.

In this, as well as in their wars, they now use nothing but fire-
arms, which they purchase of the English for skins. Bows and arrows
are grown into disuse, except only amongst their boys. Nor is it ill
policy, but on the contrary very prudent, thus to furnish the Indians
with fire-arms, because it makes them depend entirely upon the
English, not only for their trade, but even for their subsistence. Besides, they were really able to do more mischief while they made use
of arrows, of which they would let silently fly several in a minute
with wonderful dexterity, whereas now they hardly ever discharge
their fire-locks more than once, which they insidiously do from behind a tree, and then retire as nimbly as the Dutch Horse used to do
now and then formerly in Flanders.

We put the Indians to no expense, but only of a little corn for our
horses, for which in gratitude we cheered their hearts with what
rum we had left, which they love better than they do their wives and
children.

Though these Indians dwell among the English, and see in what
plenty a little industry enables them to live, yet they choose to continue in their stupid idleness, and to suffer all the inconveniences of
dirt, cold, and want, rather than to disturb their heads with care, or
defile their hands with labor.

The whole number of people belonging to the Nottoway Town, if
you include women and children, amount to about 200. These are
the only Indians of any consequence now remaining within the
limits of Virginia. The rest are either removed, or dwindled to a

very inconsiderable number, either by destroying one another, or else by the small-pox and other diseases. Though nothing has been so fatal to them as their ungovernable passion for rum, with which, I am sorry to say it, they have been but too liberally supplied by the English that live near them.

And here I must lament the bad success Mr. Boyle's charity has hitherto had towards converting any of these poor heathens to Christianity.[1] Many children of our neighboring Indians have been brought up in the College of William and Mary. They have been taught to read and write, and have been carefully instructed in the principles of the Christian religion, till they came to be men. Yet after they returned home, instead of civilizing and converting the rest, they have immediately relapsed into infidelity and barbarism themselves.

And some of them too have made the worst use of the knowledge they acquired among the English, by employing it against their benefactors. Besides, as they unhappily forget all the good they learn, and remember the ill, they are apt to be more vicious and disorderly than the rest of their countrymen.

I ought not to quit this subject without doing justice to the great prudence of Col. Spotswood in this affair. That gentleman was lieut. governor of Virginia when Carolina was engaged in a bloody war with the Indians. At that critical time it was thought expedient to keep a watchful eye upon our tributary savages, who we knew had nothing to keep them to their duty but their fears.

Then it was that he demanded of each Nation a competent number of their great men's children to be sent to the College, where they served as so many hostages for the good behavior of the rest, and at the same time were themselves principled in the Christian religion. He also placed a school-master among the Saponi Indians, at the salary of fifty pounds per annum, to instruct their children. The person that undertook that charitable work was Mr. Charles Griffin, a man of good family, who by the innocence of his life, and the sweetness of his temper, was perfectly well qualified for the pious undertaking. Besides, he had so much the secret of mixing pleasure

[1]Robert Boyle, an English physicist, left a bequest to educate Indians and convert them to Christianity.

with instruction, that he had not a scholar who did not love him affectionately.

Such talents must needs have been blest with a proportionable success, had he not been unluckily removed to the College, by which he left the good work he had begun unfinished. In short, all the pains he had undertaken among the infidels had no other effect but to make them something cleanlier than other Indians are.

The care Col. Spotswood took to tincture the Indian children with Christianity produced the following epigram, which was not published during his administration, for fear it might then have looked like flattery.

> Long has the furious priest assay'd in vain,
> With sword and faggot, infidels to gain.
> But now the milder soldier wisely tries
> By gentler methods to unveil their eyes.
> Wonders apart, he knew 'twere vain t'engage
> The fix'd preventions of misguided age.
> With fairer hopes he forms the Indian youth
> To early manners, probity and truth.
> The lion's whelp thus on the Lybian shore
> Is tam'd and gentled by the artful Moor,
> Not the grim sire, inured to blood before.

I am sorry I can't give a better account of the state of the poor Indians with respect to Christianity, although a great deal of pains has been and still continues to be taken with them. For my part, I must be of opinion, as I hinted before, that there is but one way of converting these poor infidels, and reclaiming them from barbarity, and that is, charitably to intermarry with them, according to the modern policy of the most Christian King in Canada and Louisiana.

Had the English done this at the first settlement of the Colony, the infidelity of the Indians had been worn out at this day, with their dark complexions, and the country had swarmed with people more than it does with insects.

It was certainly an unreasonable nicety, that prevented their entering into so good-natured an alliance. All nations of men have the same natural dignity, and we all know that very bright talents may be lodged under a very dark skin. The principal difference between one people and another proceeds only from the different opportunities of improvement.

The Indians by no means want understanding, and are in their figure tall and well-proportioned. Even their copper-colored complexion would admit of blanching, if not in the first, at the farthest in the second generation.

I may safely venture to say, the Indian women would have made altogether as honest wives for the first planters, as the damsels they used to purchase from aboard the ships. It is strange, therefore, that any good Christian should have refused a wholesome, straight bedfellow, when he might have had so fair a portion with her, as the merit of saving her soul.

8. We rested on our clean mats very comfortably, though alone, and the next morning went to the toilet of some of the Indian ladies, where, what with the charms of their persons and the smoke of their apartments, we were almost blinded. They offered to give us silkgrass baskets of their own making, which we modestly refused, knowing that an Indian present, like that of a nun, is a liberalıty put out to interest, and a bribe placed to the greatest advantage.

Our Chaplain observed with concern that the ruffles of some of our fellow travellers were a little discolored with pochoon,[2] wherewith the good man had been told those Ladies used to improve their invisible charms.

About 10 o'clock we marched out of town in good order, and the war captains saluted us with a volley of small-arms. From thence we proceeded over Black-water Bridge to Col. Henry Harrison's, where we congratulated each other upon our return into Christendom.

SUGGESTED ADDITIONAL READINGS

The Secret Diary of William Byrd of Westover, 1709-1712 (1941), ed. by Louis B. Wright and Marion Tinling.

The Writings of "Colonel William Byrd, of Westover in Virginia, Esqr" (1901), ed. by John S. Bassett.

[2]Bloodroot, which makes a red or yellow stain.

SELECTED REFERENCES

Arner, Robert D. "Westover and the Wilderness: William Byrd's Images of Virginia." *Southern Literary Journal*, 7, No. 2 (1975), 105–23.

Marambaud, Pierre. *William Byrd of Westover, 1674–1744* (1971).

PROJECTS AND PROBLEMS

Trace Byrd's image as a slaveholder by reviewing his diary accounts of the way he and his wife managed their human property. Did he assign a single character to all slaves or did he identify them as individuals? Did he dispense real justice or were his punishments and rewards personal and capricious?

Compare Byrd's generalizations about Indians, blacks, and poor whites. Which opinions are stereotypical? Which are defensible on the grounds of careful observation and objective reasoning? Consider his objection to the marriage of the daughter of a widow who was his friend to an Irish overseer: " . . . to stoop to a dirty Plebian, without any kind of merit, is the lowest Prostitution."

Does Byrd or Samuel Sewall deserve greater praise for the literary quality of his record of daily life? Does either really merit comparison with Samuel Pepys for accomplishment as a diarist?

See the letter Byrd wrote to "Lord Egremont" on July 12, 1736, and decide whether his objections to the "unchristian Traffic, of making Merchandise of our Fellow Creatures" are essentially moral and humanitarian or merely practical. Originally published in the *Virginia Magazine of History and Biography*, July, 1928, it is reprinted in *Racial Thought in America* (1970), ed. by Louis Ruchames.

Compare Byrd's comments about Indian women with the praise given them in *New England's Rarities* (1672), by John Josselyn, an English nobleman who paid long visits to America.

BENJAMIN FRANKLIN
(1706–1790)

The American dream of success is embodied in
Franklin's writings and made manifest in his rise from
poverty to wealth and power. His many works employ a
wide range of forms, including parody and satire, and
there are varied assaults on what he saw as the erroneous
opinions and injustices of his time. The third selection
that follows, which this editor has entitled "If It Be Right
to Kill Men," is from *A Narrative of the Late Massacres,
in Lancaster County* (1764). The last selection is taken
from *Concerning the Savages of North America* (1784).

OBSERVATIONS CONCERNING THE INCREASE OF MANKIND, PEOPLING OF COUNTRIES, ETC.

Written in Pensilvania, 1751

1. TABLES of the Proportion of Marriages to Births, of Deaths to Births, of Marriages to the Numbers of Inhabitants, &c., form'd on Observations made upon the Bills of Mortality, Christnings, &c., of populous Cities, will not suit Countries; nor will Tables form'd on Observations made on full-settled old Countries, as *Europe,* suit new Countries, as *America.* . . .

12. 'Tis an ill-grounded Opinion that by the Labour of slaves, *America* may possibly vie in Cheapness of Manufactures with *Britain.* The Labour of Slaves can never be so cheap here as the Labour of Working Men is in *Britain.* Any one may compute it. Interest of Money is in the Colonies from 6 to 10 per Cent. Slaves one with another cost 30£ Sterling per Head. Reckon then the Interest of the first Purchase of a Slave, the Insurance or Risque on his Life, his Cloathing and Diet, Expences in his Sickness and Loss of Time, Loss by his Neglect of Business (Neglect is natural to the Man who is not to be benefited by his own Care or Diligence), Expence of a Driver to keep him at Work, and his Pilfering from Time to Time, almost every Slave being by *Nature* a Thief, and compare the whole Amount with the Wages of a Manufacturer of Iron or Wool in *England,* you will see that Labour is much cheaper there than it ever can be by Negroes here. Why then will *Americans* purchase Slaves? Because Slaves may be kept as long as a *Man* pleases, or has Occasion for their Labour; while hired Men are continually leaving their masters (often in the midst of his Business,) and setting up for themselves.—Sec. 8.

13. As the Increase of People depends on the Encouragement of Marriages, the following Things must diminish a Nation, viz . . . 6. *The Introduction of Slaves.* The Negroes brought into the *English*

90

Sugar Islands have greatly diminish'd the Whites there; the Poor are by this Means deprived of Employment, while a few Families acquire vast Estates; which they spend on Foreign Luxuries, and educating their Children in the Habit of those Luxuries; the same Income is needed for the Support of one that might have maintain'd 100. The Whites who have Slaves, not labouring, are enfeebled, and therefore not so generally prolific; the Slaves being work'd too hard, and ill fed, their Constitutions are broken, and the Deaths among them are more than the Births; so that a continual Supply is needed from *Africa*. The Northern Colonies, having few Slaves, increase in Whites. Slaves also pejorate the Families that use them; the white Children become proud, disgusted with Labour, and being educated in Idleness, are rendered unfit to get a Living by Industry. . . .

21. The Importation of Foreigners into a Country, that has as many Inhabitants as the present Employments and Provisions for Subsistence will bear, will be in the End no Increase of People; unless the New Comers have more Industry and Frugality than the Natives, and then they will provide more Subsistence, and increase in the Country; but they will gradually eat the Natives out. Nor is it necessary to bring in Foreigners to fill up any occasional Vacancy in a Country; for such Vacancy (if the Laws are good, sec. 14, 16,) will soon be filled by natural Generation. Who can now find the Vacancy made in *Sweden, France,* or other Warlike Nations, by the Plague of Heroism, 40 years ago; in *France,* by the Expulsion of the Protestants; in *England,* by the Settlement of her Colonies; or in *Guinea,* by 100 Years Exportation of Slaves, that has blacken'd half *America?* The thinness of Inhabitants in *Spain* is owing to National Pride and Idleness, and other Causes, rather than to the Expulsion of the Moors, or to the making of new Settlements.

22. There is, in short, no Bound to the prolific Nature of Plants or Animals, but what is made by their crowding and interfering with each other's means of Subsistence. Was the Face of the Earth vacant of other Plants, it might be gradually sowed and overspread with one Kind only; as, for Instance, with Fennel; and were it empty of other Inhabitants, it might in a few Ages be replenish'd from one Nation only; as, for Instance, with *Englishmen.* Thus there are suppos'd to be now upwards of One Million *English* Souls in *North—America,* tho' 'tis thought scarce 80,000 have been brought over

Sea,) and yet perhaps there is not one the fewer in *Britain*, but rather many more, on Account of the Employment the Colonies afford to Manufacturers at Home. This Million doubling, suppose but once in 25 Years, will, in another Century, be more than the People of *England*, and the greatest Number of *Englishmen* will be on this Side the Water. What an Accession of Power to the *British* Empire by Sea as well as Land! What Increase of Trade and Navigation! What Numbers of Ships and Seamen! We have been here but little more than 100 years, and yet the Force of our Privateers in the late War, united, was greater, both in Men and Guns, than that of the whole *British* Navy in Queen *Elizabeth's* Time. How important an Affair then to *Britain* is the present Treaty for settling the Bounds between her Colonies and the *French*, and how careful should she be to secure Room enough, since on the Room depends so much the Increase of her People.

23. In fine, a Nation well regulated is like a Polypus; take away a Limb, its Place is soon supply'd; cut it in two, and each deficient Part shall speedily grow out of the Part remaining. Thus if you have Room and Subsistence enough, as you may by dividing, make ten Polypes out of one, you may of one make ten Nations, equally populous and powerful; or rather increase a Nation ten fold in Numbers and Strength.

And since Detachments of *English* from *Britain*, sent to *America*, will have their Places at Home so soon supply'd and increase so largely here; why should the *Palatine Boors* be suffered to swarm into our Settlements and, by herding together, establish their Language and Manners, to the Exclusion of ours? Why should *Pennsylvania*, founded by the *English*, become a Colony of *Aliens*, who will shortly be so numerous as to Germanize us instead of our Anglifying them, and will never adopt our Language or Customs any more than they can acquire our Complexion?

24. Which leads me to add one Remark, that the Number of purely white People in the World is proportionably very small. All *Africa* is black or tawny; *Asia* chiefly tawny; *America* (exclusive of the new Comers) wholly so. And in *Europe*, the *Spaniards*, *Italians*, *French*, *Russians*, and *Swedes*, are generally of what we call a swarthy Complexion; as are the *Germans* also, the *Saxons* only excepted, who, with the *English*, make the principal Body of White

People on the Face of the Earth. I could wish their Numbers were increased. And while we are, as I may call it, *Scouring* our Planet, by *clearing America* of Woods, and so making this Side of our Globe reflect a brighter Light to the Eyes of Inhabitants in *Mars* or *Venus*, why should we, in the Sight of Superior Beings, darken its People? Why increase the Sons of *Africa*, by planting them in *America*, where we have so fair an Opportunity, by excluding all Blacks and Tawneys, of increasing the lovely White and Red? But perhaps I am partial to the Complexion of my Country, for such Kind of Partiality is natural to Mankind.

INDIANS AND GERMANS
IN PENNSYLVANIA
Letter to James Parker

Dear Mr. Parker,   *Philadelphia, March 20, 1750/1*

I have, as you desire, read the Manuscript you sent me; and am of Opinion, with the publick-spirited Author, that securing the Friendship of the Indians is of the greatest Consequence to these Colonies; and that the surest Means of doing it, are to regulate the Indian Trade, so as to convince them, by Experience, that they may have the best and cheapest Goods, and the fairest Dealing from the English; and to unite the several Governments, so as to form a Strength that the Indians may depend on for Protection, in Case of a Rupture with the French; or apprehend great Danger from, if they should break with us . . .

The Observation concerning the Importation of Germans in too great Numbers into Pennsylvania, is, I believe, a very just one. This will in a few Years become a German Colony: Instead of their Learning our Language, we must learn their's, or live as in a foreign Country. Already the English begin to quit particular Neighbourhoods surrounded by Dutch, being made uneasy by the Disagreeableness of disonant Manners; and in Time, Numbers will probably quit the Province for the same Reason. Besides, the Dutch underlive, and are thereby enabled to under-work and under-sell the English; who are thereby extreamly incommoded, and consequently disgusted, so that there can be no cordial Affection or Unity between the two Nations. How good Subjects they may make, and how faithful to the British Interest, is a Question worth considering. And in my Opinion, equal Numbers might have been spared from the British Islands without being miss'd there, and on proper Encouragement would have come over: I say without being miss'd, perhaps I might say without lessening the Number of People at Home. I question indeed, whether there be a Man the less in Britain for the Establishment of the Colonies. An Island can support but a certain Number of People: When all Employments are full, Multitudes refrain Marriage, 'till they can see how to maintain a Family. The Number of Englishmen in England, cannot by their present common Increase be doubled in a Thousand Years; but if half of them were taken away and planted in America, where there is Room for them to encrease, and sufficient Employment and Subsistance; the Number of Englishmen would be doubled in 100 *Years:* For those left at home, would multiply in that Time so as to fill up the Vacancy, and those here would at least keep Pace with them.

Every one must approve the Proposal of encouraging a Number of sober discreet Smiths[1] to reside among the Indians. They would doubtless be of great Service. The whole Subsistance of Indians, depends on keeping their Guns in order; and if they are obliged to make a Journey of two or three hundred Miles to an English Settlement to get a Lock mended; it may, besides the Trouble, occasion the Loss of their Hunting Season. They are People that think much of their temporal, but little of their spiritual Interests; and therefore, as he would be a most useful and necessary Man to them, a Smith is more likely to influence them than a Jesuit; provided he has a good common Understanding, and is from time to time well instructed. . . .

[1]Gunsmiths.

IF IT BE RIGHT
TO KILL MEN

These Indians were the remains of a tribe of the Six Nations, settled at Conestogo, and thence called Conestogo Indians. On the first arrival of the English in Pennsylvania, messengers from this tribe came to welcome them, with presents of venison, corn, and skins; and the whole tribe entered into a treaty of friendship with the first proprietor, William Penn, which was to last "as long as the sun should shine, or the waters run in the rivers."

This treaty has been since frequently renewed, and the chain brightened, as they express it, from time to time. It has never been violated, on their part or ours, till now. As their lands by degrees were mostly purchased, and the settlements of the white people began to surround them, the proprietor assigned them lands on the manor of Conestogo, which they might not part with; there they have lived many years in friendship with their white neighbours, who loved them for their peaceable inoffensive behaviour.

It has always been observed, that Indians settled in the neighbourhood of white people do not increase, but diminish continually. This tribe accordingly went on diminishing, till there remained in their town on the manor but twenty persons, viz. seven men, five women, and eight children, boys and girls. . . .

Notwithstanding this proclamation [of John Penn], those cruel men again assembled themselves, and, hearing that the remaining fourteen Indians were in the workhouse at Lancaster, they suddenly appeared in that town, on the 27th of December. Fifty of them, armed as before, dismounting, went directly to the workhouse, and by violence broke open the door, and entered with the utmost fury in their countenances. When the poor wretches saw they had no protection nigh, nor could possibly escape, and being without the least weapon for defence, they divided into their little families, the children clinging to the parents; they fell on their knees, protested their innocence, declared their love to the English, and that, in their whole lives they had never done them injury; and in this posture they all received the hatchet! Men, women, and little children were every one inhumanly murdered in cold blood!

The barbarous men who committed the atrocious fact, in defiance of government, of all laws human and divine, and to the eternal disgrace of their country and color, then mounted their horses, huzzaed in triumph, as if they had gained a victory, and rode off *unmolested!*

The bodies of the murdered were then brought out and exposed in the street, till a hole could be made in the earth to receive and cover them.

But the wickedness cannot be covered; the guilt will lie on the whole land, till justice is done on the murderers. The blood of the innocent will cry to Heaven for vengeance. . . .

There are some, (I am ashamed to hear it,) who would extenuate the enormous wickedness of these actions, by saying, "The Inhabitants of the frontiers are exasperated with the murder of their relations, by the enemy Indians, in the present war." It is possible; but, though this might justify their going out into the woods, to seek for those enemies, and avenge upon them those murders, it can never justify their turning into the heart of the country, to murder their friends.

If an Indian injures me, does it follow, that I may revenge that injury on all Indians? It is well known, that Indians are of different tribes, nations, and languages, as well as the white people. In Europe, if the French, who are white people, should injure the Dutch, are they to revenge it on the English, because they too are white people? The only crime of these poor wretches seems to have been, that they had a reddish-brown skin and black hair; and some people of that sort, it seems, had murdered some of our relations. If it be right to kill men for such a reason, then, should any man, with a freckled face and red hair, kill a wife or child of mine, it would be right for me to revenge it, by killing all the freckled, red-haired men, women, and children, I could afterwards anywhere meet with.

But it seems these people think they have a better justification; nothing less than the Word of God. With the Scriptures in their hands and mouths, they can set at nought that express command, *Thou shalt do no murder;* and justify their wickedness by the command given Joshua to destroy the heathen. Horrid perversion of Scripture and of religion! To father the worst of crimes on the God of peace and love! Even the Jews, to whom that particular commission was directed, spared the Gibeonites, on account of their faith once given. The faith of this government has been frequently given to those Indians; but that did not avail them with people who despise government.

We pretend to be Christians, and, from the superior light we enjoy, ought to exceed heathens, Turks, Saracens, Moors, Negroes, and Indians, in the knowledge and practice of what is right. I will endeavour to show, by a few examples from books and history, the sense those people have had of such actions. . . .

Will it be permitted me to adduce, on this occasion, an instance of the like honor in a poor unenlightened African Negro. I find it in Captain Seagrave's account of his Voyage of Guinea. He relates, that a New England sloop, trading there in 1752, left their second mate, William Murray, sick on shore, and sailed without him. Murray was at the house of a black, named Cudjoe, with whom he had contracted an acquaintance during their trade. He recovered, and the sloop being gone, he continued with his black friend till some other opportunity should offer of his getting home. In the mean while, a Dutch ship came into the road, and some of the blacks going on board her were treacherously seized, and carried off as slaves. Their relations and friends, transported with sudden rage, ran to the house of Cudjoe to take revenge by killing Murray. Cudjoe stopped them at the door, and demanded what they wanted. "The white men," said they, "have carried away our brothers and sons, and we will kill all white men; give us the white man that you keep in your house, for we will kill him." "Nay," said Cudjoe, "the white men that carried away your brothers are bad men, kill them when you can catch them; but this white man is a good man, and you must not kill him." "But he is a white man," they cried; "the white men are all bad, and we will kill them all." "Nay," says he, "you must not kill a man, that has done no harm, only for being white. This man is my friend, my house is his fort, and I am his soldier. I must fight for him. You must kill me, before you can kill him. What good man will ever come again under my roof, if I let my floor be stained with a good man's blood!" The Negroes, seeing his resolution, and being convinced by his discourse that they were wrong, went away ashamed. In a few days, Murray ventured abroad again with Cudjoe, when several of them took him by the hand, and told him they were glad they had not killed him; for, as he was a good (meaning an innocent) man, their God would have been angry, and would have spoiled their fishing. "I relate this," says Captain Seagrave, "to show that some among these dark people have a strong sense of justice and honor, and that even the most brutal among them are capable of feeling the force of reason, and of being influenced by a fear of God, (if the knowledge of the true God could be introduced among them,) since even the fear of a false god, when their rage subsided, was not without its good effect."

Now I am about to mention something of Indians, I beg that I may not be understood as framing apologies for *all* Indians. I am far from desiring to lessen the laudable spirit of resentment in my countrymen against those now at war with us, so far as it is justified by their perfidy and inhumanity. I would only observe, that the Six Nations, as a body, have kept faith with the English ever since we knew them, now near a hundred years; and that the governing part of those people have had notions of honor, whatever may be the case with the rum-debauched, trader-corrupted vagabonds and thieves on the Susquehanna and Ohio, at present in arms against us. As a proof of that honor, I shall only mention one well-known recent fact. When six Catawba deputies, under the care of Colonel Bull, of Charlestown, went by permission into the Mohawks' country, to sue for and treat of peace, for their nation, they soon found the Six Nations highly exasperated, and the peace at that time impracticable. They were therefore in fear of their own persons, and apprehended that they should be killed in their way back to New York; which being made known to the Mohawk chiefs by Colonel Bull, one of them, by order of the council, made this speech to the Catawbas;

"Strangers and Enemies,

"While you are in this country, blow away all fear out of your breasts; change the black streak of paint on your cheek for a red one, and let your faces shine with bear's grease. You are safer here than if you were at home. The Six Nations will not defile their own land with the blood of men that come unarmed to ask for peace. We shall send a guard with you, to see you safe out of our territories. So far you shall have peace, but no farther. Get home to your own country, and there take care of yourselves, for there we intend to come and kill you."

The Catawbas came away unhurt accordingly. . . .

SAVAGES WE CALL THEM

Savages we call them, because their manners differ from ours, which we think the perfection of civility; they think the same of theirs.

Perhaps, if we could examine the manners of different nations with impartiality, we should find no people so rude as to be without rules of politeness; nor any so polite as not to have some remains of rudeness.

The Indian men, when young, are hunters and warriors; when old, counsellors, for all their government is by counsel of the sages; there is no force, there are no prisons, no officers to compel obedience or inflict punishment. Hence they generally study oratory, the best speaker having the most influence. The Indian women till the ground, dress the food, nurse and bring up the children, and preserve and hand down to posterity the memory of public transactions. These employments of men and women are accounted natural and honorable. Having few artificial wants, they have abundance of leisure for improvement by conversation. Our laborious manner of life, compared with theirs, they esteem slavish and base; and the learning, on which we value ourselves, they regard as frivolous and useless. An instance of this occurred at the treaty of Lancaster, in Pennsylvania, *anno* 1744, between the government of Virginia and the Six Nations. After the principal business was settled, the commissioners from Virginia acquainted the Indians by a speech that there was at Williamsburg a college, with a fund for educating Indian youth; and that, if the Six Nations would send down half a dozen of their young lads to that college, the government would take care that they should be well provided for, and instructed in all the learning of the white people. It is one of the Indian rules of politeness not to answer a public proposition the same day that it is made; they think it would be treating it as a light matter, and that they show it respect by taking time to consider it, as of a matter important. They therefore deferred their answer till the day following; when their speaker began, by expressing their deep sense of the kindness of the Virginia government, in making them that offer; "for we know," says he, "that you highly esteem the kind of learning taught in those colleges, and that the maintenance of our young men, while with you, would be very expensive to you. We are convinced, therefore, that you mean to do us good by your proposal, and we thank you heartily. But you, who are wise, must know that different nations have different conceptions of things; and you will therefore not take it amiss, if our ideas of this kind of education happen not to be the same with yours. We have had some experience of it; several of our young people were formerly brought up at the colleges of the northern provinces; they were instructed in all your sciences; but when they came back to us they were bad runners, ignorant of every means of living in the woods, unable to bear cold or hunger, knew neither how to build a cabin, take a deer, nor kill an enemy, spoke our language imperfectly, were therefore neither fit for hunters, warriors, nor counsellors; they were totally good for nothing. We are however not the less obliged by your kind offer, though we decline accepting it; and, to show our grateful sense of it, if the gentlemen of Virginia will send us a dozen of their sons, we will take great care of their education, instruct them in all we know, and make *men* of them."

Having frequent occasions to hold public councils, they have acquired great order and decency in conducting them. The old men sit in the foremost ranks, the warriors in the next, and the women and children in the hindmost. The business of the women is to take exact notice of what passes, imprint it in their memories (for they have no writing), and communicate it to their children. They are the records of the council, and they preserve the tradition of the stipulations in treaties a hundred years back; which, when we compare with our writings, we always find exact. He that would speak, rises. The rest observe a profound silence. When he has finished and sits down, they leave him five or six minutes to recollect that, if he has omitted any thing he intended to say, or has any thing to add, he may rise again and deliver it. To interrupt another, even in common conversation, is reckoned highly indecent. How different this is from the conduct of a polite British House of Commons, where scarce a day passes without some confusion, that makes the Speaker hoarse in calling *to order;* and how different from the mode of conversation in many polite companies in Europe, where, if you do not deliver your sentence with great rapidity, you are cut off in the middle of it by the impatient loquacity of those you converse with, and never suffered to finish it!

The politeness of these savages in conversation is indeed carried to excess, since it does not permit them to contradict or deny the truth of what is asserted in their presence. By this means they indeed avoid disputes; but then it becomes difficult to know their minds, or what impression you made upon them. The missionaries who have attempted to convert them to Christianity, all complain of this as one of the great difficulties of their mission. The Indians hear with patience the truths of the Gospel explained to them, and give their usual tokens of assent and approbation; you would think they were convinced. No such matter. It is mere civility.

A Swedish minister, having assembled the chiefs of the Susquehanna Indians, made a sermon to them, acquainting them with the principal historical facts on which our religion is founded; such as the fall of our first parents by eating an apple, the coming of Christ to repair the mischief, his miracles and sufferings, etc. When he had finished, an Indian orator stood up to thank him. "What you have told us," says he, "is all very good. It is indeed bad to eat apples. It is better to make them all into cider. We are much obliged by your kindness in coming so far, to tell us those things which you have heard from your mothers. In return, I will tell you some of those we have heard from ours: In the beginning, our fathers had only the flesh of animals to subsist on; and if their hunting was unsuccessful, they were starving. Two of our young hunters, having killed a deer, made a fire in the woods to broil some parts of it. When they were about to satisfy their hunger, they beheld a beautiful young woman descend from the clouds, and seat herself on that hill which you see yonder among the Blue Mountains. They said to each other, it is a spirit that perhaps has smelt our broiling venison and wishes to eat of it; let us offer some to her. They presented her with the tongue; she was pleased with the taste of it, and said: 'Your kindness shall be rewarded; come to this place after thirteen moons, and you shall find something that will be of great benefit in nourishing you and your children to the latest generations.' They did so, and, to their surprise, found plants they had never seen before; but which, from that ancient time, have been constantly cultivated among us, to our great advantage. Where her right hand had touched the ground, they found maize; where her left hand had touched it, they found kidney-beans, and where her backside had sat on it, they found tabacco." The good missionary, disgusted with this idle tale, said: "What I delivered to you were sacred truths; but what you tell me is mere fable, fiction, and falsehood." The Indian, offended, replied: "My brother, it seems your friends have not done you justice in your education; they have not well instructed you in the rules of common civility. You saw that we, who understand and practise those rules, believed all your stories; why do you refuse to believe ours?"

When any of them come into our towns, our people are apt to crowd round them, gaze upon them, and incommode them, where they desire to be private; this they esteem great rudeness, and the effect of want of instruction in the rules of civility and good manners. "We have," say they, "as much curiosity as you, and when you come into our towns, we wish for opportunities of looking at you; but for this purpose we hide ourselves behind bushes, where you are to pass, and never intrude ourselves into your company."

Their manner of entering one another's village has likewise its rules. It is reckoned uncivil in travelling strangers to enter a village abruptly, without giving notice of their approach. Therefore, as soon as they arrive within hearing, they stop and halloo, remaining there till invited to enter. Two old men usually come out to them, and lead them in. There is in every village a vacant dwelling, called *the strangers' house*. Here they are placed, while the old men go round from hut to hut, acquainting the inhabitants that strangers are arrived who are probably hungry and weary; and every one sends them what he can spare of victuals, and skins to repose on. When the strangers are refreshed, pipes and tobacco are brought, and then, but not before, conversation begins, with inquiries who they are, whither bound, what news, etc.; and it usually ends with offers of service, if the strangers have occasion for guides, or any necessaries for continuing their journey; and nothing is exacted for the entertainment.

The same hospitality, esteemed among them as a principal virtue, is practised by private persons; of which Conrad Weiser, our interpreter, gave me the following instance. He had been naturalized among the Six Nations, and spoke well the Mohock language. In going through the Indian country, to carry a message from our

governor to the council at Onondaga, he called at the habitation of
Canassetego, an old acquaintance, who embraced him, spread furs
for him to sit on, and placed before him some boiled beans and venison, and mixed some rum and water for his drink. When he was well
refreshed, and had lit his pipe, Canassetego began to converse with
him; asked how he had fared the many years since they had seen
each other, whence he then came, what occasioned the journey, etc.
Conrad answered all his questions; and when the discourse began to
flag, the Indian, to continue it, said: "Conrad, you have lived long
among the white people, and know something of their customs; I
have been sometimes at Albany, and have observed that once in
seven days they shut up their shops and assemble all in the great
house; tell me what it is for. What do they do there?" "They meet
there," says Conrad, "to hear and learn *good things.*" "I do not
doubt," says the Indian, "that they tell you so; they have told me the
same; but I doubt the truth of what they say, and I will tell you my
reasons. I went lately to Albany to sell my skins and buy blankets,
knives, powder, rum, etc. You know I used generally to deal with
Hans Hanson; but I was a little inclined this time to try some other
merchants. However, I called first upon Hans, and asked what he
would give for beaver. He said he could not give any more than four
shillings a pound; 'but,' says he, 'I cannot talk on business now; this
is the day when we meet together to learn *good things,* and I am
going to meeting.' So I thought to myself: 'Since I cannot do any
business to-day, I may as well go to the meeting too,' and I went
with him. There stood up a man in black, and began to talk to the
people very angrily. I did not understand what he said; but, perceiving that he looked much at me and at Hanson, I imagined he was
angry at seeing me there; so I went out, sat down near the house,
struck fire, and lit my pipe, waiting till the meeting should break up.
I thought, too, that the man had mentioned something of beaver,
and I suspected it might be the subject of their meeting. So when
they came out I accosted my merchant. 'Well, Hans,' says I, 'I hope
you have agreed to give more than four shillings a pound.' 'No,' says
he, 'I cannot give so much; I cannot give more than three shillings
and sixpence.' I then spoke to several other dealers, but they all sung
the same song,—three and sixpence—three and sixpence. This made
it clear to me that my suspicion was right; and that whatever they

pretended of meeting to learn *good things*, the real purpose was to consult how to cheat Indians in the price of beaver. Consider but a little, Conrad, and you must be of my opinion. If they met so often to learn *good things*, they would certainly have learned some before this time. But they are still ignorant. You know our practice. If a white man, in travelling through our country, encounters one of our cabins, we all treat him as I treat you; we dry him if he is wet, we warm him if he is cold, we give him meat and drink that he may allay his thirst and hunger, and spread soft furs for him to rest and sleep on; we demand nothing in return.[1] But if I go into a white man's house at Albany, and ask for victuals and drink, they say, 'Where is your money?' and if I have none, they say, 'Get out, you Indian dog!' You see they have not yet learned those little *good things*, that we need no meetings to be instructed in, because our mothers taught them to us when we were children; and therefore it is impossible their meetings should be, as they say, for any such purpose, or have any such effect; they are only to contrive *the cheating of Indians in the price of beaver.*"

SUGGESTED ADDITIONAL READINGS

"Information to Those Who Would Remove to America"
"To the Editor of the 'Federal Gazette' "
"Plan for Improving the Condition of the Free Blacks"

---

[1]It is remarkable that in all ages and countries hospitality has been allowed as the virtue of those whom the civilized were pleased to call barbarians.

The Greeks celebrated the Scythians for it. The Saracens possessed it eminently, and it is to this day the reigning virtue of the wandering Arabs.

St. Paul, too, in the relation of his voyage and shipwreck on the Island of Melita, says: *The barbarous people showed us no little kindness; for they kindled a fire and received every one because of the present rain and because of the cold.*—Acts, ch. xxvii. F. [Franklin's note]

SELECTED REFERENCES

Cohen, Bernard I. *Benjamin Franklin: His Contribution to the American Tradition* (1953).

Crane, Verner W. "Benjamin Franklin on Slavery and American Liberties." *Pennsylvania Magazine of History and Biography*, 62 (1938), 1–11.

Miller, Ross. "Autobiography as Fact and Fiction: Franklin, Adams, Malcolm X." *Centennial Review*, 16 (1972), 221–32.

Ohmann, Carol. *"The Autobiography of Malcolm X:* A Revolutionary Use of the Franklin Traditon." *American Quarterly*, 22 (1970), 131–49.

Pitt, A. Stuart. "Franklin and the Quaker Movement Against Slavery." *Bulletin of the Friends Historical Association*, 32 (1943), 13–31.

PROJECTS AND PROBLEMS

Did Franklin's feelings about minorities become more, or less, enlightened as he grew older? Use as one reference *Early American Views on Negro Slavery* (1969), ed. by Matthew T. Mellon.

Franklin has been called "the representative American" because of his pragmatism, inventiveness, and idealism. In his attitude toward slavery and toward treaties with the Indians, was he a spokesman for the majority of his fellows or was he ahead of his time?

Do Franklin's observations about the Dutch and the effect of their presence on residential areas anticipate the comments of later writers about how neighborhood property values respond to the arrival of minority residents?

Compare Franklin's ironic assault on the slave trade in his letter of March 23, 1790, to the editor of the *Federal Gazette* with the mock defense of slavery by John Trumbull, one of the Connecticut Wits, in "The Correspondent, No. 8," that first appeared in the *Connecticut Journal and New Haven Post-Boy*, July 6, 1770. Franklin's letter may be found in various editions of his works. Trumbull's piece is reprinted in Lorenzo Dow Turner's *Anti-Slavery Sentiment in American Literature Prior to 1865* (1966).

JOHN WOOLMAN
(1720-1772)

The humanitarian instincts of this Quaker preacher and leader led to a pioneer antislavery pamphlet in two parts, *Some Considerations on the Keeping of Negroes* (1754, 1762), and pleas for fairer treatment of the Indians and the poor. The following selection is from Woolman's *Journal*, a classic record of modest service and devotion to the inner life that is notable both for its content and its pure style.

I BELIEVE LIBERTY IS THEIR RIGHT

The seventh Day of the fifth Month, in the Year 1757, I lodged at a Friend's House; and the next Day, being the first of the Week, was at *Potapsco* Meeting; then crossed *Patuxent* River, and lodged at a Public-house. On the ninth breakfasted at a Friend's House; who, afterward, putting us a little on our Way, I had Conversation with him, in the Fear of the Lord, concerning his Slaves; in which my Heart was tender, and I used much Plainness of Speech with him, which he appeared to take kindly. We pursued our Journey without appointing Meetings, being pressed in Mind to be at the Yearly-meeting in *Virginia;* and, in my travelling on the Road, I often felt a Cry rise from the Center of my Mind, thus: O Lord, I am a Stranger on the Earth, hide not thy Face from me.

On the eleventh Day of the fifth Month, we crossed the Rivers *Patowmack* and *Rapahannock,* and lodged at *Port-Royal;* and on the Way we happening in Company with a Colonel of the Militia, who appeared to be a thoughtful Man, I took Occasion to remark on the Difference in general betwixt a People used to labour moderately for their Living, training up their Children in Frugality and Business, and those who live on the Labour of Slaves; the former, in my View, being the most happy Life: With which he concurred, and mentioned the Trouble arising from the untoward, slothful, Disposition of the Negroes; adding, that one of our Labourers would do as much in a Day as two of their Slaves. I replied, that free Men, whose Minds were properly on their Business, found a Satisfaction in improving, cultivating, and providing for their Families; but Negroes, labouring to support others who claim them as their Property, and expecting nothing but Slavery during Life, had not the like Inducement to be industrious.

After some farther Conversation, I said, that Men having Power too often misapplied it; that though we made Slaves of the Negroes, and the *Turks* made Slaves of the *Christians,* I believed that Liberty was the natural Right of all Men equally: Which he did not deny; but said, the Lives of the Negroes were so wretched in their own

Country, that many of them lived better here than there: I only said, there are great odds, in regard to us, on what Principle we act; and so the Conversation on that Subject ended: And I may here add, that another Person, some Time afterward, mentioned the Wretchedness of the Negroes, occasioned by their intestine Wars, as an Argument in Favour of our fetching them away for Slaves: To which I then replied, if Compassion on the *Africans,* in Regard to their domestic Troubles, were the real Motive of our purchasing them, that Spirit of Tenderness, being attended to, would incite us to use them kindly; that, as Strangers brought out of Affliction, their Lives might be happy among us; and as they are human Creatures, whose Souls are as precious as ours, and who may receive the same Help and Comfort from the holy Scriptures as we do, we could not omit suitable Endeavors to instruct them therein: But while we manifest, by our Conduct, that our Views in purchasing them are to advance ourselves; and while our buying Captives taken in War animates those Parties to push on that War, and increase Desolation amongst them, to say they live unhappy in *Africa,* is far from being an Argument in our Favour: And I farther said, the present Circumstances of these Provinces to me appear difficult; that the Slaves look like a burthensome Stone to such who burthen themselves with them; and that if the white People retain a Resolution to prefer their outward Prospects of Gain to all other Considerations, and do not act conscientiously toward them as fellow Creatures, I believe that Burthen will grow heavier and heavier, till Times change in a Way disagreeable to us: At which the Person appeared very serious, and owned, that, in considering their Condition, and the Manner of their Treatment in these Provinces, he had sometimes thought it might be just in the Almighty so to order it.

Having thus travelled through *Maryland,* we came amongst Friends at *Cedar-Creek* in *Virginia,* on the 12th Day of the fifth Month; and the next Day rode, in Company with several Friends, a Day's Journey to *Camp-Creek.* As I was riding along in the Morning, my Mind was deeply affected in a Sense I had of the Want of divine Aid to support me in the various Difficulties which attended me; and, in an uncommon Distress of Mind, I cried in secret to the Most High, O Lord, be merciful, I beseech thee, to thy poor afflicted Creature. After some Time, I felt inward Relief; and, soon after, a

Friend in Company began to talk in Support of the Slave-Trade, and said, the Negroes were understood to be the Offspring of *Cain,* their Blackness being the Mark God set upon him after he murdered *Abel* his Brother; that it was the Design of Providence they should be Slaves, as a Condition proper to the Race of so wicked a Man as *Cain* was: Then another spake in Support of what had been said. To all which, I replied in Substance as follows: That *Noah* and his Family were all who survived the Flood, according to Scripture; and, as *Noah* was of *Seth's* Race, the Family of *Cain* was wholly destroyed. One of them said, that after the Flood *Ham* went to the Land of *Nod,* and took a Wife; that *Nod* was a Land far distant, inhabited by *Cain's* Race, and that the Flood did not reach it; and as *Ham* was sentenced to be a Servant of Servants to his Brethren, these two Families, being thus joined, were undoubtedly fit only for Slaves. I replied, the Flood was a Judgment upon the World for its Abominations; and it was granted, that *Cain's* Stock was the most wicked, and therefore unreasonable to suppose they were spared: As to *Ham's* going to the Land of *Nod* for a Wife, no Time being fixed, *Nod* might be inhabited by some of *Noah's* Family, before *Ham* married a second Time; moreover the Text saith, "That all Flesh died that moved upon the Earth." *Gen.* vii.21. I farther reminded them, how the Prophets repeatedly declare, "That the Son shall not suffer for the Iniquity of the Father; but every one be answerable for his own Sins." I was troubled to perceive the Darkness of their Imaginations; and in some Pressure of Spirit said, the Love of Ease and Gain is the Motive in general for keeping Slaves, and Men are wont to take hold of weak Arguments to support a Cause which is unreasonable; and added, I have no Interest on either Side, save only the Interest which I desire to have in the Truth: And as I believe Liberty is their Right, and see they are not only deprived of it, but treated in other Respects with Inhumanity in many Places, I believe he, who is a Refuge for the Oppressed, will, in his own Time, plead their Cause; and happy will it be for such as walk in Uprightness before him: And thus our Conversation ended.

SUGGESTED ADDITIONAL READINGS

Some Considerations on the Keeping of Negroes
Remarks on Sundry Subjects

SELECTED REFERENCE

Rosenblatt, Paul. *John Woolman* (1969).

PROJECTS AND PROBLEMS

One of Woolman's admirers was John Greenleaf Whittier, who wrote appreciatively of the life of the "Quaker Saint" and his pioneer efforts in opposing slavery. Was Woolman, like Whittier, an abolitionist?

Consider Woolman's doctrines in relation to the career of Prudence Crandall, the Quaker schoolmistress whose school for black girls led to the enactment of Connecticut's "Black Law" in 1833. See Edmund Fuller's *Prudence Crandall: An Incident of Racism in Nineteenth-Century Connecticut* (1971).

A chapter in Woolman's *Journal* is devoted to his stay with Indians along the Susquehanna River in 1763. Compare his attitude toward "the Natives of this Land, who dwell far back in the wilderness" with that of his Quaker predecessor, William Penn.

Woolman opposed the slave trade, endorsed manumission, and urged his fellow Quakers not to own slaves. Compare his antislavery views with those of Samuel Sewall.

For a review of Quaker reactions to slavery in one Maryland locale over a two-hundred-year period, see Chapter IX of Kenneth Carroll's *Quakerism on the Eastern Shore* (1970). What was the effect of Woolman's visit to the area when he made his "walking journey" through Delaware and Maryland in 1766?

PHILLIS WHEATLEY
(c.1753–1784)

Brought from Africa to America as a slave in 1761 and reared in the home of a prosperous Boston tailor, Phillis Wheatley received an education there and wrote her first poems at twelve or thirteen. The extraordinary young woman's *Poems on Various Subjects, Religious and Moral,* from which these poems are taken, was published in London in 1773. Her verse is rooted in the religious instruction she received and expresses in conventional form the sentiments of her time.

TO THE UNIVERSITY OF CAMBRIDGE, IN NEW ENGLAND

While an intrinsic ardor prompts to write,
The muses promise to assist my pen;
'Twas not long since I left my native shore
The land of errors, and *Egyptian* gloom:
Father of mercy, 'twas thy gracious hand
Brought me in safety from those dark abodes.

Students, to you 'tis giv'n to scan the heights
Above, to traverse the ethereal space,
And mark the systems of revolving worlds.
Still more, ye sons of science ye receive
The blissful news by messengers from heav'n,
How *Jesus'* blood for your redemption flows.
See him with hands out-stretcht upon the cross;
Immense compassion in his bosom glows;
He hears revilers, nor resents their scorn:
What matchless mercy in the Son of God!
When the whole human race by sin had fall'n,
He deign'd to die that they might rise again,
And share with him in the sublimest skies,
Life without death, and glory without end.

Improve your privileges while they stay,
Ye pupils, and each hour redeem, that bears
Or good or bad report of you to heav'n.
Let sin, that baneful evil to the soul,
By you be shunn'd, nor once remit your guard;
Suppress the deadly serpent in its egg.
Ye blooming plants of human race devine,
An *Ethiop* tells you 'tis your greatest foe;
Its transient sweetness turns to endless pain,
And in immense perdition sinks the soul.

ON BEING BROUGHT FROM AFRICA TO AMERICA

'Twas mercy brought me from my *Pagan* land,
Taught my benighted soul to understand
That there's a God, that there's a *Saviour* too:
Once I redemption neither sought nor knew.
Some view our sable race with scornful eye,
"Their colour is a diabolic die."
Remember, *Christians*, *Negroes*, black as *Cain*,
May be refin'd, and join th' angelic train.

SUGGESTED ADDITIONAL READINGS

"On the Death of the Rev. Mr. George Whitefield, 1770"
"To the Right Honourable William, Earl of Dartmouth, . . ."
"To S.M. A Young African Painter on Seeing His Works"

SELECTED REFERENCES

Davis, Arthur. "Personal Elements in the Poetry of Phillis Wheatley." *Phylon*, 8 (1953), 192–98.

Kuncio, Robert C. "Some Unpublished Poems of Phillis Wheatley." *New England Quarterly*, 43 (1970), 287–97.

Robinson, William H. "Phillis Wheatley: Colonial Quandary." *CLA Journal*, 9 (1965), 25–38.

PROJECTS AND PROBLEMS

Relate the views on slavery expressed by Wheatley and Jupiter Hammon, another early black poet, to Cotton Mather's remarks on slavery in *The Negro Christianized*. Take into account Hammon's "An Address to Miss Phillis Wheatley."

Thomas Jefferson said of Phillis Wheatley in *Notes on Virginia*, "The compositions published under her name are below the dignity of criticism." Was this a just appraisal? How did the publisher of her book of poems attempt to prove the verses were really her work?

Compare Wheatley's "On Being Brought From Africa to America" with Francis E. W. Harper's "Bury Me in a Free Land." Account for the different attitudes of the two black women poets.

While she was in England, Phillis Wheatley wrote a letter to Samson Occum, an Indian schoolmaster and minister who was graduated from Dartmouth College. See the entry on Occum in the *Dictionary of American Biography*. Trace the parallels in the careers of Wheatley and Occum.

In "The Little Black Boy" (1789), the English poet William Blake reiterates the idea that Phillis Wheatley offers in "On Being Brought from Africa to America": that is, a black skin, though seen by some as external evidence of sin or degradation, is really no proof that its bearer may not be virtuous and destined for heaven. Study Mark Van Doren's critique of Blake's poem in his *Introduction to Poetry* (1951) and apply his comments on color symbolism to Wheatley's poem. Consider also the closing lines of the selection in this volume from Royall Tyler's *The Algerine Captive*.

What was George Washington's response to Phillis Wheatley's poem, "His Excellency Gen. Washington"? Might the poem have had an effect on his attitudes toward blacks and slavery? See Matthew T. Mellon, *Early American Views on Negro Slavery* (1969), and Edgar A. Toppin, "Blacks in the American Revolution," *Crisis*, 82 (1975), pp. 249–55.

ST. JEAN DE CRÈVECOEUR
(1735–1813)

Letters from an American Farmer, from which the following selection is taken, appeared in 1782. Born in France, Crèvecoeur emigrated to Canada and then settled in New York State with his American wife. A Loyalist, he fled to France during the Revolution. When he returned he found his wife dead, his home burned, and his children scattered as a result of an Indian raid. His portrait of America is both sentimental and perceptive.

ARE NOT THESE BLACKS
THY CHILDREN?

While all is joy, festivity, and happiness in Charles-Town, would you imagine that scenes of misery overspread in the country? Their ears by habit are become deaf, their hearts are hardened; they neither see, hear, nor feel for the woes of their poor slaves, from whose painful labours all their wealth proceeds. Here the horrors of slavery, the hardship of incessant toils, are unseen; and no one thinks with compassion of those showers of sweat and of tears which from the bodies of Africans, daily drop, and moisten the ground they till. The cracks of the whip urging these miserable beings to excessive labour, are far too distant from the gay Capital to be heard. The chosen race eat, drink, and live happy, while the unfortunate one grubs up the ground, raises indigo, or husks the rice; exposed to a sun full as scorching as their native one; without the support of good food, without the cordials of any chearing liquor. This great contrast has often afforded me subjects of the most afflicting meditation. On the one side, behold a people enjoying all that life affords most bewitching and pleasurable, without labour, without fatigue, hardly subjected to the trouble of wishing. With gold, dug from Peruvian mountains, they order vessels to the coasts of Guinea; by virtue of that gold, wars, murders, and devastations are committed in some harmless, peaceable African neighbourhood, where dwelt innocent people, who even knew not but that all men were black. The daughter torn from her weeping mother, the child from the wretched parents, the wife from the loving husband; whole families swept away and brought through storms and tempests to this rich metropolis! There, arranged like horses at a fair, they are branded like cattle, and then driven to toil, to starve, and to languish for a few years on the different plantations of these citizens. And for whom must they work? For persons they know not, and who have no other power over them than that of violence; no other right than what this accursed metal has given them! Strange order of things! Oh, Nature, where art thou?—Are not these blacks thy children as well as we? On the other side, nothing is to be seen but the most dif-

117

fusive misery and wretchedness, unrelieved even in thought or wish! Day after day they drudge on without any prospect of ever reaping for themselves; they are obliged to devote their lives, their limbs, their will, and every vital exertion to swell the wealth of masters; who look not upon them with half the kindness and affection with which they consider their dogs and horses. Kindness and affection are not the portion of those who till the earth, who carry the burdens, who convert the logs into useful boards. This reward, simple and natural as one would conceive it, would border on humanity; and planters must have none of it!

If negroes are permitted to become fathers, this fatal indulgence only tends to increase their misery: the poor companions of their scanty pleasures are likewise the companions of their labours; and when at some critical seasons they could wish to see them relieved, with tears in their eyes they behold them perhaps doubly oppressed, obliged to bear the burden of nature—a fatal present—as well as that of unabated tasks. How many have I seen cursing the irresistible propensity, and regretting, that by having tasted of those harmless joys, they had become the authors of double misery to their wives. Like their masters, they are not permitted to partake of those ineffable sensations with which nature inspires the hearts of fathers and mothers; they must repel them all, and become callous and passive. This unnatural state often occasions the most acute, the most pungent of their afflictions; they have no time, like us, tenderly to rear their helpless offspring, to nurse them on their knees, to enjoy the delight of being parents. Their paternal fondness is embittered by considering, that if their children live, they must live to be slaves like themselves; no time is allowed them to exercise their pious office, the mothers must fasten them on their backs, and, with this double load, follow their husbands in the fields, where they too often hear no other sound than that of the voice or whip of the taskmaster, and the cries of their infants, broiling in the sun. These unfortunate creatures cry and weep like their parents, without a possibility of relief; the very instinct of the brute, so laudable, so irresistible, runs counter here to their master's interest; and to that god, all the laws of nature must give way. Thus planters get rich; so raw, so unexperienced am I in this mode of life, that were I to be possessed of a plantation, and my slaves treated as in general they are here, never could I rest in peace; my sleep would be perpetually disturbed by a retrospect of the frauds committed in Africa, in order to entrap them; frauds surpassing in enormity every thing which a common mind can possibly conceive. I should be thinking of the barbarous treatment they meet with on ship-board; of their anguish, of the despair necessarily inspired by their situation, when torn from their friends and relations; when delivered into the hands of a people differently coloured, whom they cannot understand; carried in a strange machine over an ever agitated element, which they had never seen before; and finally delivered over to the severities of the whippers, and the excessive labours of the field. Can it be possible that the force of custom should ever make me deaf to all these reflections, and as insensible to the injustice of that trade, and to their miseries, as the rich inhabitants of this town seem to be? What then is man; this being who boasts so much of the excellence and dignity of his nature, among that variety of unscrutable mysteries, of unsolvable problems, with which he is surrounded? The reason why man has been thus created, is not the least astonishing! It is said, I know that they are much happier here than in the West-Indies; because land being cheaper upon this continent than in those islands, the fields allowed them to raise their subsistence from, are in general more extensive. The only possible chance of any alleviation depends on the humour of the planters, who, bred in the midst of slaves, learn from the example of their parents to despise them; and seldom conceive either from religion or philosophy, any ideas that tend to make their fate less calamitous; except some strong native tenderness of heart, some rays of philanthropy, overcome the obduracy contracted by habit.

I have not resided here long enough to become insensible of pain for the objects which I every day behold. In the choice of my friends and acquaintance, I always endeavour to find out those whose dispositions are somewhat congenial with my own. We have slaves likewise in our northern provinces; I hope the time draws near when they will be all emancipated: but how different their lot, how different their situation, in every possible respect! They enjoy as much liberty as their masters, they are as well clad, and as well fed; in health and sickness they are tenderly taken care of; they live under the same roof, and are, truly speaking, a part of our families. Many of them are taught to read and write, and are well instructed in the principles of religion; they are the companions of our labours, and treated as such; they enjoy many perquisites, many established holidays, and are not obliged to work more than white people. They marry where inclination leads them; visit their wives every week; are as decently clad as the common people; they are indulged in educating, cherishing, and chastising their children, who are taught subordination to them as to their lawful parents: in short, they participate in many of the benefits of our society, without being obliged to bear any of its burthens. They are fat, healthy, and hearty, and far from repining at their fate; they think themselves happier than many of the lower class whites: they share with their masters the wheat and meat provision they help to raise; many of those whom the good Quakers have emancipated, have received that great benefit with tears of regret, and have never quitted, though free, their former masters and benefactors.

But is it really true, as I have heard it asserted here; that those blacks are incapable of feeling the spurs of emulation, and the chearful sound of encouragement? By no means; there are a thousand proofs existing of their gratitude and fidelity: those hearts in which such noble dispositions can grow, are then like ours, they are susceptible of every generous sentiment, of every useful motive of action; they are capable of receiving lights, of imbibing ideas that would greatly alleviate the weight of their miseries. But what methods have in general been made use of to obtain so desirable an end? None; the day in which they arrive and are sold, is the first of their labours; labours, which from that hour admit of no respite; for though indulged by law with relaxation on Sundays, they are obliged to employ that time which is intended for rest, to till their little plantations. What can be expected from wretches in such circumstances? Forced from their native country, cruelly treated when on board, and not less so on the plantations to which they are driven; is there any thing in this treatment but what must kindle all the passions, sow the seeds of inveterate resentment, and nourish a wish of perpetual revenge? They are left to the irresistible effects of those strong and natural propensities; the blows they receive are they conducive to extinguish them, or to win their affections? They are neither soothed by the hopes that their slavery will ever terminate but with their lives; or yet encouraged by the goodness of their food, or the mildness of their treatment. The very hopes held out to mankind by religion, that consolatory system, so useful to the miserable, are never presented to them; neither moral nor physical means are made use of to soften their chains; they are left in their original and untutored state; that very state where in the natural propensities of revenge and warm passions, are so soon kindled. Cheered by no one single motive that can impel the will, or excite their efforts; nothing but terrors and punishments are presented to them; death is denounced if they run away; horrid delaceration if they speak with their native freedom; perpetually awed by the terrible cracks of whips, or by the fear of capital punishments, while even those punishments often fail of their purpose.

SUGGESTED ADDITIONAL READING

Crèvecoeur's Eighteenth-Century Travels in Pennsylvania and New York (1961), ed. and trans. by Percy G. Adams.

SELECTED REFERENCE

Philbrick, Thomas. St. John de Crèvecoeur (1970).

PROJECTS AND PROBLEMS

These lines from "What Is an American ?" are probably the best known passage in Letters from an American Farmer: "The next wish of this traveller will be to know whence came all these people? they are a mixture of English, Scotch, Irish, French, Dutch, Germans, and Swedes. From this promiscuous breed, that race now called Americans have arisen." Are the author's portraits of the Germans, Irish, etc., stereotypical? Are his comments in this essay free from class and regional prejudices?

Compare Crèvecoeur's position on slavery with that of his friends Thomas Jefferson and Benjamin Franklin.

Are Crèvecoeur's opinions about backwoodsmen similar to those of Virginia's William Byrd? May their views be explained by their intimate acquaintance with European culture? Which reporter seems more objective? Which is more humane?

Examine Crèvecoeur's account of travel on the frontier for evidence of uncommon sympathy for the Indian.

JOHN FILSON
(c.1747–1788)

A Kentucky pioneer, Filson wrote the first history of the area. *Discovery, Settlement and Present State of Kentucke* was published in 1784. It contained in an appendix "The Adventures of Col. Daniel Boon," from which the first selection is taken. The popular narrative, probably based on Boone's dictation and reputed to be his autobiography, was a major factor in the celebrated frontiersman's rise from historical figure to national legend. The second selection, originally entitled "Genius," was included in another appendix item, "An Account of the Indian Nations inhabiting within the Limits of the Thirteen United States."

DANIEL BOONE'S LAST ADVENTURES

... My wife, who despaired of ever seeing me again, expecting the Indians had put a period to my life, oppressed with the distresses of the country, and bereaved of me, her only happiness, had, before I returned, transported my family and goods, on horses, through the wilderness, amidst a multitude of dangers, to her father's house, in North-Carolina.

Shortly after the troubles at Boonsborough, I went to them, and lived peaceably there until this time. The history of my going home, and returning with my family, forms a series of difficulties, an account of which would swell a volume, and being foreign to my purpose, I shall purposely omit them.

I settled my family in Boonsborough once more; and shortly after, on the sixth day of October, 1780, I went in company with my brother to the Blue Licks; and, on our return home, we were fired upon by a party of Indians. They shot him, and pursued me, by the scent of their dog, three miles; but I killed the dog, and escaped. The Winter soon came on, and was very severe, which confined the Indians to their wigwams.

The severity of this Winter caused great difficulties in Kentucke. The enemy had destroyed most of the corn, the Summer before. This necessary article was scarce, and dear; and the inhabitants lived chiefly on the flesh of buffaloes. The circumstances of many were very lamentable: However, being a hardy race of people, and accustomed to difficulties and necessities, they were wonderfully supported through all their sufferings, until the ensuing Fall, when we received abundance from the fertile soil.

Towards Spring, we were frequently harassed by Indians; and, in May, 1782, a party assaulted Ashton's station, killed one man, and took a Negro prisoner. Capt. Ashton, with twenty-five men, pursued, and overtook the savages, and a smart fight ensued, which lasted two hours; but they being superior in number, obliged Captain Ashton's party to retreat, with the loss of eight killed, and four

124

mortally wounded; their brave commander himself being numbered among the dead.

The Indians continued their hostilities; and, about the tenth of August following, two boys were taken from Major Hoy's station. This party was pursued by Capt. Holder and seventeen men, who were also defeated, with the loss of four men killed, and one wounded. Our affairs became more and more alarming. Several stations which had lately been erected in the country were continually infested with savages, stealing their horses and killing the men at every opportunity. In a field, near Lexington, an Indian shot a man, and running to scalp him, was himself shot from the fort, and fell dead upon his enemy.

Every day we experienced recent mischiefs. The barbarous savage nations of Shawanese, Cherokees, Wyandots, Tawas, Delawares, and several others near Detroit, united in a war against us and assembled their choicest warriors at old Chelicothe, to go on the expedition, in order to destroy us, and entirely depopulate the country. Their savage minds were inflamed to mischief by two abandoned men, Captains McKee and Girty. These led them to execute every diabolical scheme; and, on the fifteenth day of August, commanded a party of Indians and Canadians, of about five hundred in number, against Briant's station, five miles from Lexington. Without demanding a surrender, they furiously assaulted the garrison, which was happily prepared to oppose them; and, after they had expended much ammunition in vain, and killed the cattle round the fort, not being likely to make themselves masters of this place, they raised the siege, and departed in the morning of the third day after they came, with the loss of about thirty killed, and the number of wounded uncertain. —Of the garrison four were killed, and three wounded.

On the eighteenth day Col. Todd, Col. Trigg, Major Harland, and myself, speedily collected one hundred and seventy-six men, well armed, and pursued the savages. They had marched beyond the Blue Licks to a remarkable bend of the main fork of Licking River, about forty-three miles from Lexington, as it is particularly represented in the map, where we overtook them on the nineteenth day. The savages observing us, gave way; and we, being ignorant of their numbers, passed the river. When the enemy saw our preceedings, having greatly the advantage of us in [our] situation, they formed the line of battle, as represented in the map, from one bend of Licking to the other, about a mile from the Blue Licks. An exceeding fierce battle immediately began, for about fifteen minutes, when we, being over-powered by numbers, were obliged to retreat, with the loss of sixty seven men; seven of whom were taken prisoners. The brave and much lamented Colonels Todd and Trigg, Major Harland and my second son, were among the dead. We were informed that the Indi-ans, numbering their dead, found they had four killed more than we; and therefore, four of the prisoners they had taken, were, by general consent, ordered to be killed, in a most barbarous manner, by the young warriors, in order to train them up to cruelty; and then they proceeded to their towns.

On our retreat we were met by Col. Logan, hastening to join us, with a number of well armed men. This powerful assistance we un-fortunately wanted in the battle; for, notwithstanding the enemy's superiority of numbers, they acknowledged that, if they had received one more fire from us, they should undoubtedly have given way. So valiantly did our small party fight, that, to the memory of those who unfortunately fell in the battle, enough of honour cannot be said. Had Col. Logan and his party been with us, it is highly probable we should have given the savages a total defeat.

I cannot reflect upon this dreadful scene, but sorrow fills my heart. A zeal for the defence of their country led these heroes to the scene of action, though with a few men to attack a powerful army of experienced warriors. When we gave way, they pursued us with the utmost eagerness, and in every quarter spread destruction. The river was difficult to cross, and many were killed in the flight, some just entering the river, some in the water, others after crossing in ascend-ing the cliffs. Some escaped on horse-back, a few on foot; and, being dispersed every where, in a few hours, brought the melancholy news of this unfortunate battle to Lexington. Many widows were now made. The reader may guess what sorrow filled the hearts of the in-habitants, exceeding any thing that I am able to describe. Being rein-forced, we returned to bury the dead, and found their bodies strewed every where, cut and mangled in a dreadful manner. This mournful scene exhibited a horror almost unparalleled: Some torn and eaten by wild beasts; those in the river eaten by fishes; all in such a putri-fied condition, that no one could be distinguished from another.

As soon as General Clark, then at the Falls of the Ohio, who was ever our ready friend, and merits the love and gratitude of all his country-men, understood the circumstances of this unfortunate action, he ordered an expedition, with all possible haste, to pursue the savages, which was so expeditiously effected, that we overtook them within two miles of their towns, and probably might have obtained a great victory, had not two of their number met us about two hundred poles before we come up. These returned quick as lightening to their camp with the alarming news of a mighty army in view. The savages fled in the utmost disorder, evacuated their towns, and reluctantly left their territory to our mercy. We immediately took possession of Old Chelicothe without opposition, being deserted by its inhabitants. We continued our pursuit through five towns on the Miami rivers, Old Chelicothe, Pecaway, New Chelicothe, Will's Towns, and Chelicothe, burnt them all to ashes, entirely destroyed their corn, and other fruits, and every where spread a scene of desolation in the country. In this expedition we took seven prisoners and five scalps, with the loss of only four men, two of whom were accidentally killed by our own army.

This campaign in some measure damped the spirits of the Indians, and made them sensible of our superiority. Their connections were dissolved, their armies scattered, and a future invasion put entirely out of their power; yet they continued to practice mischief secretly upon the inhabitants, in the exposed parts of the country.

In October following, a party made an excursion into that district called the Crab Orchard, and one of them, being advanced some distance before the others, boldly entered the house of a poor defenceless family, in which was only a Negro man, a woman and her children, terrified with the apprehensions of immediate death. The savage, perceiving their defenceless situation, without offering violence to the family attempted to captivate the Negro, who, happily proved an over-match for him, threw him on the ground, and, in the struggle, the mother of the children drew an ax from a corner of the cottage, and cut his head off, while her little daughter shut the door. The savages instantly appeared, and applied their tomahawks to the door. An old rusty gun-barrel, without a lock, lay in a corner, which the mother put through a small crevice, and the savages, perceiving it, fled. In the mean time, the alarm spread through the neighbour-

hood; the armed men collected immediately, and pursued the sav-
agers into the wilderness. Thus Providence, by the means of this
Negro, saved the whole of the poor family from destruction. From
that time, until the happy return of peace between the United States
and Great-Britain, the Indians did us no mischief. Finding the great
king beyond the water disappointed in his expectations, and conscious of the importance of the Long Knife, and their own wretchedness, some of the nations immediately desired peace; to which, at
present, they seem universally disposed, and are sending ambassa-
dors to General Clark, at the Falls of the Ohio, with the minutes of
their Councils; a specimen of which, in the minutes of the Pian-
kashaw Council, is subjoined.

To conclude, I can now say that I have verified the saying of an
old Indian who signed Col. Henderson's deed. Taking me by the
hand, at the delivery thereof, Brother, says he, we have given you a
fine land, but I believe you will have much trouble in settling it.—
My footsteps have often been marked with blood, and therefore I
can truly subscribe to its original name. Two darling sons, and a
brother, have I lost by savage hands, which have also taken from me
forty valuable horses, and abundance of cattle. Many dark and sleepless nights have I been a companion for owls, separated from the
chearful society of men, scorched by the Summer's sun, and pinched
by the Winter's cold, an instrument ordained to settle the wilderness. . . .

INDIAN GENIUS

The Indians are not so ignorant as some suppose them, but are a very understanding people, quick of apprehension, sudden in execution, subtle in business, exquisite in invention, and industrious in action. They are of a very gentle and amiable disposition to those they think their friends, but as implacable in their enmity; their revenge being only compleated, in the entire destruction of their enemies. They are very hardy, bearing heat, cold, hunger and thirst, in a surprising manner, and yet no people are more addicted to excess in eating and drinking, when it is conveniently in their power. The follies, nay mischief, they commit when inebriated, are entirely laid to the liquor; and no one will revenge any injury (murder excepted) received from one who is no more himself. Among the Indians, all men are equal, personal qualities being most esteemed. No distinction of birth, no rank, renders any man capable of doing prejudice to the rights of private persons; and there is no pre-eminence from merit, which begets pride, and which makes others too sensible of their own inferiority. Though there is perhaps less delicacy of sentiment in the Indians than amongst us; there is, however, abundantly more probity, with infinitely less ceremony, or equivocal compliments. Their public conferences shew them to be men of genius; and they have, in a high degree, the talent of natural eloquence.

They live dispersed in small villages, either in the woods, or on the banks of rivers, where they have little plantations of Indian-corn, and roots, not enough to supply their families half the year, and subsisting the remainder of it by hunting, fishing and fowling, and the fruits of the earth, which grow spontaneously in great plenty.

Their huts are generally built of small logs, and covered with bark, each one having a chimney, and a door, on which they place a padlock.

Old Chelicothe is built in form of a Kentucke station, that is, a parallelogram, or long square; and some of their houses are shingled. A long Council-house extends the whole length of the town, where the King and Chiefs of the nation frequently meet, and consult on all matters of importance, whether of a civil or military nature.

Some huts are built by setting up a frame on forks, and placing bark against it; others of reeds, and surrounded with clay. The fire is in the middle of the wigwam, and the smoke passes through a little hole. They join reeds together by cords run through them, which serve them for tables and beds. They mostly lie upon skins of wild beasts, and sit on the ground. They have brass kettles and pots to boil their food; gourds or calabashes, cut asunder, serve them for pails, cups and dishes.

SELECTED REFERENCES

Bakeless, John. *Daniel Boone* (1939).
Walton, John. *John Filson of Kentucke* (1956).

PROJECTS AND PROBLEMS

Other writers joined Filson in lauding Daniel Boone, among them Lord Byron (in *Don Juan*) and John James Audubon (in *Ornithological Biography*), but the most important tribute to him is James Fenimore Cooper's use of certain episodes in Filson's book as models for action in *The Last of the Mohicans*. Make a careful comparison of Boone and Hawkeye.

JOHN MARRANT
(1755– ?)

A Narrative of the Lord's Wonderful Dealings with John
Marrant, a Black, Taken Down from His Own Relation
first appeared in London in 1785. There were numerous
later editions, including the one in 1788 from which this
selection is taken. The book was one of the first by a
black American and enjoyed wide popularity for its vivid
account of Indian captivity. Marrant was an educated
free man who spent two years with the Cherokees and
was later an ordained minister among the Indians in
Nova Scotia.

A BLACK MINISTER HELD CAPTIVE BY THE CHEROKEES

By constant conversation with the hunter, I acquired a fuller knowledge of the Indian tongue: This, together with the sweet communion I enjoyed with God, I have considered as a preparation for the great trial I was soon after to pass through.

The hunting season being now at an end, we left the woods, and directed our course towards a large Indian town, belonging to the Cherokee nation; and having reached it, I said to the hunter, they will not suffer me to enter in. He replied, as I was with him, nobody would interrupt me.

There was an Indian fortification all round the town, and a guard placed at each entrance. The hunter passed one of these without molestation, but I was stopped by the guard and examined. They asked me where I came from, and what was my business there? My companion of the woods attempted to speak for me, but was not permitted; he was taken away, and I saw him no more. I was now surrounded by about 50 men, and carried to one of their chiefs to be examined by him. When I came before him, he asked me what was my business there? I told him I came there with a hunter, whom I met with in the woods. He replied, "Did I not know that whoever came there without giving a better account of themselves than I did, was to be put to death?" I said I did not know it. Observing that I answered him so readily in his own language, he asked me where I learnt it? To this I returned no answer, but burst out into a flood of tears, and calling upon my Lord Jesus. At this he stood astonished, and expressed a concern for me, and said I was young. He asked me who my Lord Jesus was?—To this I gave him no answer, but continued praying and weeping. Addressing himself to the officer who stood by him, he said he was sorry; but it was the law, and it must not be broken. I was then ordered to be taken away, and put into a place of confinement. They led me from their court into a low dark place, and thrust me into it, very dreary and dismal; they made fast the door, and set a watch. The judge sent for the executioner, and

132

gave him his warrant for my execution in the afternoon of the next day. The executioner came, and gave me notice of it, which made me very happy, as the near prospect of death made me hope for a speedy deliverance from the body: And truly this dungeon became my chapel, for the Lord Jesus did not leave me in this great trouble, but was very present, so that I continued blessing him, and singing his praises all night without ceasing: The watch hearing the noise, informed the executioner that somebody had been in the dungeon with me all night; upon which he came in to see and examine, with a great torch lighted in his hand, who it was I had with me; but finding nobody, he turned round, and asked me who it was? I told him it was the Lord Jesus Christ; but he made no answer, turned away, went out, and locked the door. At the hour appointed for my execution I was taken out, and led to the destined spot, amidst a vast number of people. I praised the Lord all the way we went, and when we arrived at the place I understood the kind of death I was to suffer, yet, blessed be God, none of those things moved me. The executioner shewed me a basket of turpentine-wood, stuck full of small pieces, like skewers; he told me I was to be stripped naked, and laid down in the basket, and these sharp pegs were to be stuck into me, and then set on fire, and when they had burnt to my body, I was to be turned on the other side, and served in the same manner, and then to be taken by four men and thrown into the flame, which was to finish the execution. I burst into tears, and asked what I had done to deserve so cruel a death! To this he gave me no answer. I cried out, Lord, if it be thy will that it should be so, thy will be done: I then asked the executioner to let me go to prayer; he asked me to whom? I answered, to the Lord my God; he seemed surprized, and asked me where he was? I told him he was present; upon which he gave me leave. I desired them all to do as I did, so I fell down upon my knees, and mentioned to the Lord his delivering of the three children in the fiery furnace, and of Daniel in the lion's den, and had close communion with God. I prayed in English a considerable time, and about the middle of my prayer, the Lord impressed a strong desire upon my mind to turn into their language, and pray in their tongue. I did so, and with remarkable liberty, which wonderfully affected the people. One circumstance was very singular, and strikingly displays the power and grace of God. I believe the executioner was savingly converted to God. He rose from his knees, and embraced me round the middle, and was unable to speak for about five minutes; the first words he expressed, when he had utterance, were, "No man shall hurt thee till thou hast been to the king."

I was taken away immediately, and as we passed along, and I was reflecting upon the deliverance which the Lord had wrought out for me, and hearing the praises which the executioner was singing to the Lord, I must own I was utterly at a loss to find words to praise him. I broke out in these words, what can't the Lord Jesus do! and what power is like unto his! I will thank thee for what is passed, and trust thee for what is to come. I will sing thy praise with my feeble tongue whilst life and breath shall last, and when I fail to sound thy praises here, I hope to sing them round thy throne above: And thus, with unspeakable joy, I sung two verses of Dr. Watts's hymns:

> "My God, the spring of all my joys,
> The life of my delights;
> The glory of my brightest days,
> And comfort of my nights.
> In darkest shades, if thou appear,
> My dawning is begun;
> Thou art my soul's bright morning star,
> And thou my rising sun."

Passing by the judge's door, he stopped us, and asked the executioner why he brought me back? The man fell upon his knees, and begged he would permit me to be carried before the king, which being granted, I went on, guarded by two hundred soldiers with bows and arrows. After many windings I entered the king's outward chamber, and after waiting some time he came to the door, and his first question was, how came I there? I answered, I came with a hunter whom I met in the woods, and who persuaded me to come there. He then asked me how old I was? I told him not fifteen. He asked me how I was supported before I met with this man? I answered, by the Lord Jesus Christ, which seemed to confound him. He turned round, and asked me if he lived where I came from? I answered, yes, and here also. He looked about the room, and said he did not see him; but I told him I felt him. The executioner fell upon his knees, and intreated the king, and told him what he had felt of the same Lord. At this instant the king's eldest daughter came into the chamber, a person about 19 years of age, and stood at my right-hand. I had a Bible in my hand, which she took out of it, and having opened it, she kissed it, and seemed much delighted with it. When she had put it into my hand again, the king asked me what it was? and I told him, the name of my God was recorded there; and, after several questions, he bid me read it, which I did, particularly the 53d chapter of Isaiah, in the most solemn manner I was able; and also the 26th chapter of Matthew's Gospel; and when I pronounced the name of Jesus, the particular effect it had upon me was observed by the king. When I had finished reading, he asked me why I read those names with so much reverence? I told him, because the Being to whom those names belonged made heaven and earth, and I and he; this he denied. I then pointed to the sun, and asked him who made the sun, and moon, and stars, and preserved them in their regular order? He said there was a man in their town that did it. I laboured as much as I could to convince him to the contrary. His daughter took the book out of my hand a second time; she opened it, and kissed it again; her father bid her give it to me, which she did; but said, with much sorrow, the book would not speak to her. The executioner then fell upon his knees, and begged the king to let me go to prayer, which being granted, we all went upon our knees, and now the Lord displayed his glorious power. In the midst of the prayer some of them cried out, particularly the king's daughter, and the man who ordered me to be executed, and several others seemed under deep conviction of sin: This made the king very angry; he called me a witch, and commanded me to be thrust into the prison, and to be executed the next morning. This was enough to make me think, as old Jacob once did, "All these things are against me;" for I was dragged away, and thrust into the dungeon with much indigna-tion; but God, who never forsakes his people, was with me. Though I was weak in body, yet was I strong in the spirit: The Lord works, and who shall let it? The executioner went to the king, and assured him, that if he put me to death, his daughter would never be well. They used the skill of all their doctors that afternoon and night; but physical prescriptions were useless. In the morning the executioner came to me, and, without opening the prison door, called to me, and hearing me answer, said, "Fear not, thy God who delivered thee yesterday, will deliver thee to-day." This comforted me very much, especially to find he could trust the Lord. Soon after I was fetched out; I thought it was to be executed; but they led me away to the king's chamber with much bodily weakness, having been without food two days. When I came into the king's presence, he said to me, with much anger, if I did not make his daughter and that man well, I should be laid down and chopped into pieces before him. I was not afraid, but the Lord tried my faith sharply. The king's daughter and the other person were brought out into the outer chamber, and we went to prayer; but the heavens were locked up to my petitions. I besought the Lord again, but received no answer: I cried again, and he was intreated. He said, "Be it to thee as thou wilt;" the Lord appeared most lovely and glorious; the king himself was awakened, and the other[1] set at liberty. A great change took place among the people; the king's house became God's house; the soldiers were ordered away, and the poor condemned prisoner had perfect liberty, and was treated like a prince. Now the Lord made all my enemies to become my great friends. I remained nine weeks in the king's palace, praising God day and night: I was never out but three days all the time. I had assumed the habit of the country, and was dressed much like the king, and nothing was too good for me. . . .

SUGGESTED ADDITIONAL READING

VanDerBeets, Richard, ed. *Held Captive by Indians: Selected Narratives, 1642–1836* (1973).

SELECTED REFERENCES

Pearce, Roy Harvey. "The Significance of the Captivity Narrative." *American Literature,* 19 (1947), 1–20.

VanDerBeets, Richard. "The Indian Captivity Narrative as Ritual." *American Literature,* 43 (1972), 548–62.

[1]Marrant himself.

PROJECTS AND PROBLEMS

Compare this selection with the earlier captivity narrative of Mrs. Mary Rowlandson or with incidents in fiction by James Fenimore Cooper, Robert Montgomery Bird, or William Gilmore Simms.

One reason that Marrant's work should not be classed, as it sometimes has been, as a "slave narrative" is that the author was a free man whose family had the means to provide him with an education. What are other reasons?

Marrant's narrative appeared in several editions, including one version in Welsh. See Dorothy B. Porter, "Early American Negro Writings, a Bibliographical Study," in the Bibliographical Society of America *Papers* for 1945. Compare Marrant's publication record with that of *The Interesting Narrative of the Life of Olaudah Equiano, or Gustavus Vassa, the African* (1789), a notable autobiography.

Does the incident described in the selection bear any resemblance to John Smith's account of his captivity and rescue by Pocahontas?

THOMAS JEFFERSON
(1743–1826)

Jefferson's literary works, like the many other accomplishments of his career, testify to the exceptional abilities of this "Renaissance man." But despite his vow of "eternal hostility against every form of tyranny over the mind of man," he was not unaffected by the racism of his time. Too often the judgments about race he expressed in *Notes on the State of Virginia* (1784–85), from which the following selection is taken, have been hailed as definitive truths or assailed as the rationalizations of a bigot. The complex problem of Jefferson's racial attitudes and his relations with blacks and Indians requires careful study of the full record, including his antislavery sentiments, his behavior as a slaveholder, and his performance as President of the United States.

RED MEN AND BLACK MEN

... The principles of their [Indian] society forbidding all compulsion, they are to be led to duty and to enterprise by personal influence and persuasion. Hence eloquence in council, bravery and address in war, become the foundations of all consequence with them. To these acquirements all their faculties are directed. Of their bravery and address in war we have multiplied proofs, because we have been the subjects on which they were exercised. Of their eminence in oratory we have fewer examples, because it is displayed chiefly in their own councils. Some, however, we have, of very superior lustre. I may challenge the whole orations of Demosthenes and Cicero, and of any more eminent orator, if Europe has furnished more eminent, to produce a single passage, superior to the speech of Logan, a Mingo chief, to Lord Dunmore, then governor of this State. And as a testimony of their talents in this line, I beg leave to introduce it, first stating the incidents necessary for understanding it.

In the spring of the year 1774, a robbery was committed by some Indians on certain land-adventurers on the river Ohio. The whites in that quarter, according to their custom, undertook to punish this outrage in a summary way. Captain Michael Cresap, and a certain Daniel Greathouse, leading on these parties, surprised, at different times, travelling and hunting parties of the Indians, having their women and children with them, and murdered many. Among these were unfortunately the family of Logan, a chief celebrated in peace and war, and long distinguished as the friend of the whites. This unworthy return provoked his vengeance. He accordingly signalized himself in the war which ensued. In the autumn of the same year a decisive battle was fought at the mouth of the Great Kanhaway, between the collected forces of the Shawanese, Mingoes and Delawares, and a detachment of the Virginia militia. The Indians were defeated and sued for peace. Logan, however, disdained to be seen among the suppliants. But lest the sincerity of a treaty should be disturbed, from which so distinguished a chief absented himself, he sent, by a messenger, the following speech, to be delivered to Lord Dunmore.

139

"I appeal to any white man to say, if ever he entered Logan's cabin hungry, and he gave him not meat; if ever he came cold and naked, and he clothed him not. During the course of the last long and bloody war Logan remained idle in his cabin, an advocate for peace. Such was my love for the whites, that my countrymen pointed as they passed, and said, "Logan is the friend of white men." I had even thought to have lived with you, but for the injuries of one man. Colonel Cresap, the last spring, in cold blood, and un-provoked, murdered all the relations of Logan, not even sparing my women and children. There runs not a drop of my blood in the veins of any living creature. This called on me for revenge. I have sought it: I have killed many: I have fully glutted my vengeance: for my country I rejoice at the beams of peace. But do not harbor a thought that mine is the joy of fear. Logan never felt fear. He will not turn on his heel to save his life. Who is there to mourn for Logan?—Not one."

*   *   *   *   *

Many of the laws which were in force during the monarchy being relative merely to that form of government, or inculcating princi-ples inconsistent with republicanism, the first assembly which met after the establishment of the commonwealth appointed a commit-tee to revise the whole code, to reduce it into proper form and volume, and report it to the assembly. This work has been executed by three gentlemen, and reported; but probably will not be taken up till a restoration of peace shall leave to the legislature leisure to go through such a work.

The plan of the revisal was this. The common law of England, by which is meant, that part of the English law which was anterior to the date of the oldest statutes extant, is made the basis of the work. It was thought dangerous to attempt to reduce it to a text; it was therefore left to be collected from the usual monuments of it. Nec-essary alterations in that, and so much of the whole body of the Brit-ish statutes, and of acts of assembly, as were thought proper to be retained, were digested into one hundred and twenty-six new acts, in which simplicity of style was aimed at, as far as was safe. The fol-lowing are the most remarkable alterations proposed:

To change the rules of descent, so as that the lands of any person dying intestate shall be divisible equally among all his children, or other representatives, in equal degree.

To make slaves distributable among the next of kin, as other movables.

To have all public expenses, whether of the general treasury, or of a parish or county, (as for the maintenance of the poor, building bridges, court-houses, &c.,) supplied by assessment on the citizens, in proportion to their property.

To hire undertakers for keeping the public roads in repair, and indemnify individuals through whose lands new roads shall be opened.

To define with precision the rules whereby aliens should become citizens, and citizens make themselves aliens.

To establish religious freedom on the broadest bottom.

To emancipate all slaves born after the passing the act. The bill reported by the revisers does not itself contain this proposition; but an amendment containing it was prepared, to be offered to the legislature whenever the bill should be taken up, and farther directing, that they should continue with their parents to a certain age, then to be brought up, at the public expense, to tillage, arts, or sciences, according to their geniuses, till the females should be eighteen, and the males twenty-one years of age, when they should be colonized to such place as the circumstances of the time should render most proper, sending them out with arms, implements of household and of the handicraft arts, seeds, pairs of the useful domestic animals, &c., to declare them a free and independent people, and extend to them our alliance and protection, till they have acquired strength; and to send vessels at the same time to other parts of the world for an equal number of white inhabitants; to induce them to migrate hither, proper encouragements were to be proposed. It will probably be asked, Why not retain and incorporate the blacks into the State, and thus save the expense of supplying by importation of white settlers, the vacancies they will leave? Deep-rooted prejudices entertained by the whites; ten thousand recollections, by the blacks, of the injuries they have sustained; new provocations; the real distinctions which nature has made; and many other circumstances, will divide us into parties, and produce convulsions, which will probably never end but in the extermination of the one or the other race. To these objections, which are political, may be added others, which are physical and moral. The first difference which strikes us is that of color. Whether the black of the negro resides in the reticular membrane between the skin and scarf-skin, or in the scarf-skin itself; whether it proceeds from the color of the blood, the color of the bile, or from that of some other secretion, the difference is fixed in nature, and is as real as if its seat and cause were better known to us. And is this difference of no importance? Is it not the foundation of a greater or less share of beauty in the two races? Are not the fine mixtures of red and white, the expressions of every passion by greater or less suffusions of color in the one, preferable to that eternal monotony, which reigns in the countenances, that immovable veil of black which covers the emotions of the other race? Add to these, flowing hair, a more elegant symmetry of form, their own judgment in favor of the whites, declared by their preference of them, as uniformly as is the preference of the Oranootan for the black woman over those of his own species. The circumstance of superior beauty, is thought worthy attention in the propagation of our horses, dogs, and other domestic animals; why not in that of man? Besides those of color, figure, and hair, there are other physical distinctions proving a difference of race. They have less hair on the face and body. They secrete less by the kidneys, and more by the glands of the skin, which gives them a very strong and disagreeable odor. This greater degree of transpiration, renders them more tolerant of heat, and less so of cold than the whites. Perhaps, too, a difference of structure in the pulminary apparatus, which a late ingenious° experimentalist has discovered to be the principal regulator of animal heat, may have disabled them from extricating, in the act of inspiration, so much of that fluid from the outer air, or obliged them in expiration, to part with more of it. They seem to require less sleep. A black after hard labor through the day, will be induced by the slightest amusements to sit up till midnight, or later, though knowing he must be out with the first dawn of the morning. They are at least as brave, and more adventuresome. But this may perhaps proceed from a want of forethought, which prevents their seeing a danger till it be present. When present, they do not go through it with more coolness or steadiness than the whites. They are more ar-

°Crawford. [Jefferson's note.]

dent after their female; but love seems with them to be more an
eager desire, than a tender delicate mixture of sentiment and sensation. Their griefs are transient. Those numberless afflictions, which
render it doubtful whether heaven has given life to us in mercy or in
wrath, are less felt, and sooner forgotten with them. In general, their
existence appears to participate more of sensation than reflection.
To this must be ascribed their disposition to sleep when abstracted
from their diversions, and unemployed in labor. An animal whose
body is at rest, and who does not reflect, must be disposed to sleep
of course. Comparing them by their faculties of memory, reason,
and imagination, it appears to me that in memory they are equal to
the whites; in reason much inferior, as I think one could scarcely be
found capable of tracing and comprehending the investigations of
Euclid; and that in imagination they are dull, tasteless, and anomalous. It would be unfair to follow them to Africa for this investigation. We will consider them here, on the same stage with the whites,
and where the facts are not apochryphal on which a judgment is to
be formed. It will be right to make great allowances for the difference of condition, of education, of conversation, of the sphere in
which they move. Many millions of them have been brought to, and
born in America. Most of them, indeed, have been confined to tillage, to their own homes, and their own society; yet many have been
so situated, that they might have availed themselves of the conversation of their masters; many have been brought up to the handicraft
arts, and from that circumstance have always been associated with
the whites. Some have been liberally educated, and all have lived in
countries where the arts and sciences are cultivated to a considerable degree, and all have had before their eyes samples of the best
works from abroad. The Indians, with no advantages of this kind,
will often carve figures on their pipes not destitute of design and
merit. They will crayon out an animal, a plant, or a country, so as to
prove the existence of a germ in their minds which only wants cultivation. They astonish you with strokes of the most sublime oratory; such as prove their reason and sentiment strong, their imagination glowing and elevated. But never yet could I find that a black
had uttered a thought above the level of plain narration; never saw
even an elementary trait of painting or sculpture. In music they are
more generally gifted than the whites with accurate ears for tune

and time, and they have been found capable of imagining a small catch.* Whether they will be equal to the composition of a more extensive run of melody, or of complicated harmony, is yet to be proved. Misery is often the parent of the most affecting touches in poetry. Among the blacks is misery enough, God knows, but no poetry. Love is the peculiar oestrum of the poet. Their love is ardent, but it kindles the senses only, not the imagination. Religion, indeed, has produced a Phyllis Whately; but it could not produce a poet. The compositions published under her name are below the dignity of criticism. The heroes of the Dunciad are to her, as Hercules to the author of that poem. Ignatius Sancho has approached nearer to merit in composition; yet his letters do more honor to the heart than the head.[1] They breathe the purest effusions of friendship and general philanthropy, and show how great a degree of the latter may be compounded with strong religious zeal. He is often happy in the turn of his compliments, and his style is easy and familiar, except when he affects a Shandean fabrication of words. But his imagination is wild and extravagant, escapes incessantly from every restraint of reason and taste, and, in the course of its vagaries, leaves a tract of thought as incoherent and eccentric, as is the course of a meteor through the sky. His subjects should often have led him to a process of sober reasoning; yet we find him always substituting sentiment for demonstration. Upon the whole, though we admit him to the first place among those of his own color who have presented themselves to the public judgment, yet when we compare him with the writers of the race among whom he lived and particularly with the epistolary class in which he has taken his own stand, we are compelled to enrol him at the bottom of the column. This criticism supposes the letters published under his name to be genuine, and to have received amendment from no other hand; points which would not be of easy investigation. The improvement of the blacks in body and mind, in the first instance of their mixture with the whites, has been observed by every one, and proves that their inferiority is not

*The instrument proper to them is the Banjar, which they brought hither from Africa, and which is the original of the guitar, its chords being precisely the four lower chords of the guitar. [Jefferson's note.]

[1]Born on a slave ship in 1729, Sancho was butler to the family of the Duke of Montague for over twenty years. His Letters appeared in 1782, two years after his death.

the effect merely of their condition of life. . . . Whether further observation will or will not verify the conjecture, that nature has been less bountiful to them in the endowments of the head, I believe that in those of the heart she will be found to have done them justice. That disposition to theft with which they have been branded, must be ascribed to their situation, and not to any depravity of the moral sense. The man in whose favor no laws of property exist, probably feels himself less bound to respect those made in favor of others. When arguing for ourselves, we lay it down as a fundamental, that laws, to be just, must give a reciprocation of right; that, without this, they are mere arbitrary rules of conduct, founded in force, and not in conscience; and it is a problem which I give to the master to solve, whether the religious precepts against the violation of property were not framed for him as well as his slave? And whether the slave may not as justifiably take a little from one who has taken all from him, as he may slay one who would slay him? That a change in the relations in which a man is placed should change his ideas of moral right or wrong, is neither new, nor peculiar to the color of the blacks. Homer tells us it was so two thousand six hundred years ago.

'Emisu, ger t' aretes apoainutai euruopa Zeus
Haneros, eut' an min kata doulion ema elesin.

Odd. 17, 323.

Jove fix'd it certain, that whatever day
Makes man a slave, takes half his worth away.

But the slaves of which Homer speaks were whites. Notwithstanding these considerations which must weaken their respect for the laws of property, we find among them numerous instances of the most rigid integrity, and as many as among their better instructed masters, of benevolence, gratitude, and unshaken fidelity. The opinion that they are inferior in the faculties of reason and imagination, must be hazarded with great diffidence. To justify a general conclusion, requires many observations, even where the subject may be submitted to the anatomical knife, to optical glasses, to analysis by fire or by solvents. How much more then where it is a faculty, not a substance, we are examining; where it eludes the research of all the senses; where the conditions of its existence are various and variously combined; where the effects of those which are present or absent bid defiance to calculation; let me add too, as a circumstance of great tenderness, where our conclusion would degrade a whole race of men from the rank in the scale of beings which their Creater may perhaps have given them. To our reproach it must be said, that though for a century and a half we have had under our eyes the races of black and of red men, they have never yet been viewed by us as subjects of natural history. I advance it, therefore, as a suspicion only, that the blacks, whether originally a distinct race, or made distinct by time and circumstances, are inferior to the whites in the endowments both of body and mind. It is not against experience to suppose that different species of the same genus, or varieties of the same species, may possess different qualifications. Will not a lover of natural history then, one who views the gradations in all the races of animals with the eye of philosophy, excuse an effort to keep those in the department of man as distinct as nature has formed them? This unfortunate difference of color, and perhaps of faculty, is a powerful obstacle to the emancipation of these people. Many of their advocates, while they wish to vindicate the liberty of human nature, are anxious also to preserve its dignity and beauty. Some of these, embarrassed by the question, "What further is to be done with them?" join themselves in opposition with those who are actuated by sordid avarice only. Among the Romans emancipation required but one effort. The slave, when made free, might mix with, without staining the blood of his master. But with us a second is necessary, unknown to history. When freed, he is to be removed beyond the reach of mixture.

BENJAMIN BANNEKER
Letter to Condorcet

August 30, 1791   *Philadelphia*

Dear Sir, I am to acknowledge the receipt of your favor on the subject of the element of measure adopted by France. Candor obliges me to confess that it is not what I would have approved. It is liable to the inexactitude of mensuration as to that part of the quadrant of the earth which is to be measured, that is to say as to one tenth of the quadrant, and as to the remaining nine tenths they are to be calculated on conjectural data, presuming the figure of the earth which has not yet been proved. It is liable too to the objection that no nation but your own can come at it; because yours is the only nation within which a meridian can be found of such extent crossing the 45th degree and terminating at both ends in a level. We may certainly say then that this measure is uncatholic, and I would rather have seen you depart from Catholicism in your religion than in your philosophy.

I am happy to be able to inform you that we have now in the United States a Negro, the son of a black man born in Africa, and of a black woman born in the United States, who is a very respectable mathematician.[2] I procured him to be employed under one of our chief directors in laying out the new federal city on the Potomac, and in the intervals of his leisure, while on that work, he made an almanac for the next year, which he sent me in his own handwriting, and which I enclose to you. I have seen very elegant solutions of geometrical problems by him. Add to this that he is a very worthy and respectable member of society. He is a free man. I shall be delighted to see these instances of moral eminence so multiplied as to prove that the want of talents observed in them is merely the effect of their degraded condition, and not proceeding from any difference in the structure of the parts on which intellect depends.

I am looking ardently to the completion of the glorious work[3] in

[1]Secretary of the Academy of Sciences, Paris.

[2]Benjamin Banneker.

[3]The French Revolution.

147

which your country is engaged. I view the general condition of Europe as hanging on the success or failure of France. Having set such an example of philosophical arrangement within, I hope it will be extended without your limits also, to your dependents and to your friends in every part of the earth.

TALENT IS NO MEASURE OF RIGHTS
Letter to Henri Grégoire

February 25, 1809   *Washington*

Sir, I have received the favor of your letter of August 17th, and with it the volume you were so kind as to send me on the "Literature of Negroes." Be assured that no person living wishes more sincerely than I do, to see a complete refutation of the doubts I have myself entertained and expressed on the grade of understanding allotted to them by nature, and to find that in this respect they are on a par with ourselves. My doubts were the result of personal observation on the limited sphere of my own State, where the opportunities for the development of their genius were not favorable, and those of exercising it still less so. I expressed them therefore with great hesitation; but whatever be their degree of talent, it is no measure of their rights. Because Sir Isaac Newton was superior to others in understanding, he was not therefore lord of the person or property of others. On this subject they are gaining daily in the opinions of nations, and hopeful advances are making towards their reestablishment on an equal footing with the other colors of the human family. I pray you, therefore, to accept my thanks for the many instances you have enabled me to observe of respectable intelligence in that race of men, which cannot fail to have effect in hastening the day of their relief.

VIRGINIA'S DEFINITION OF A MULATTO
Letter to Francis C. Gray

March 4, 1815   *Monticello*

You asked me in conversation, what constituted a mulatto by our law? And I believe I told you four crossings with the whites. I looked afterwards into our law, and found it to be in these words: "Every person, other than a Negro, of whose grandfathers or grandmothers anyone shall have been a Negro, shall be deemed a mulatto, and so every such person who shall have one-fourth part or more of Negro blood, shall in like manner be deemed a mulatto;" L. Virgà 1792, December 17: the case put in the first member of this paragraph of the law is *exempli gratiâ.* The latter contains the true canon, which is that one-fourth of Negro blood, mixed with any portion of white, constitutes the mulatto. As the issue has one-half of the blood of each parent, and the blood of each of these may be made up of a variety of fractional mixtures, the estimate of their compound in some cases may be intricate, it becomes a mathematical problem of the same class with those on the mixtures of different liquors or different metals; as in these, therefore, the algebraical notation is the most convenient and intelligible. Let us express the pure blood of the white in the capital letters of the printed alphabet, the pure blood of the Negro in the small letters of the printed alphabet, and any given mixture of either, by way of abridgment in MS. letters.

Let the first crossing be of a, pure Negro, with A, pure white. The unit of blood of the issue being composed of the half of that of each parent, will be $a/2 + A/2$. Call it, for abbreviation, h (half blood).

Let the second crossing be of h and B, the blood of the issue will be $h/2 + B/2$ or substituting for $h/2$ its equivalent, it will be $a/4 + A/4 + B/2$ call it q (quarteroon) being 1/4 Negro blood.

Let the third crossing be of q and C, their offspring will be $q/2 + C/2 = a/8 + A/8 + B/4 + C/2$, call this e (eighth), who having

150

less than 1/4 of a, or of pure Negro blood, to wit 1/8 only, is no longer a mulatto, so that a third cross clears the blood.

From these elements let us examine their compounds. For example, let h and q cohabit, their issue will be $h/2 + q/2 = a/4 + A/4 + a/8 + A/8 + B/4 = {}^3a/8 + {}^3A/8 + B/4$ wherein we find 3/8 of a, or Negro blood.

Let h and e cohabit, their issue will be $h/2 + e/2 = a/4 + A/4 + a/16 + A/16 + B/8 + c/4 = {}^5a/16 + {}^5A/16 + B/8 + c/4$, wherein 5/16 a makes still a mulatto.

Let q and e cohabit, the half of the blood of each will be $q/2 + e/2 = a/8 + A/8 + B/4 + a/16 + A/16 + B/8 + C/4 = {}^3a/16 + {}^3A/16 + {}^3B/8 + C/4$, wherein 3/16 of a is no longer a mulatto, and thus may every compound be noted and summed, the sum of the fractions composing the blood of the issue being always equal to unit. It is understood in natural history that a fourth cross of one race of animals with another gives an issue equivalent for all sensible purposes to the original blood, Thus a Merino ram being crossed, first with a country ewe, second with his daughter, third with his granddaughter, and fourth with the great-granddaughter, the last issue is deemed pure Merino, having in fact but 1/16 of the country blood. Our canon considers two crosses with the pure white, and a third with any degree of mixture, however small, as clearing the issue of the Negro blood. But observe, that this does not re-establish freedom, which depends on the condition of the mother, the principle of the civil law, *partus sequitur ventrem*, being adopted here. But if e emancipated, he becomes a free *white* man, and a citizen of the United States to all intents and purposes. So much for this trifle by way of correction.

AFRICAN COLONIZATION
Letter to Jared Sparks

February 4, 1824   *Monticello*

Dear Sir,—I duly received your favor of the 13th, and with it, the last number of the North American Review. This has anticipated the one I should receive in course, but have not yet received, under my subscription to the new series. The article on the African colonization of the people of color, to which you invite my attention, I have read with great consideration. It is, indeed, a fine one, and will do much good. I learn from it more, too, than I had before known, of the degree of success and promise of that colony.

In the disposition of these unfortunate people, there are two rational objects to be distinctly kept in view. First. The establishment of a colony on the coast of Africa, which may introduce among the aborigines the arts of cultivated life, and the blessings of civilization and science. By doing this, we may make to them some retribution for the long course of injuries we have been committing on their population. And considering that these blessings will descend to the *"nati natorum, et qui nascentur ab illis,"*[1] we shall in the long run have rendered them perhaps more good than evil. To fulfil this object, the colony of Sierra Leone promises well, and that of Mesurado adds to our prospect of success. Under this view, the colonization society is to be considered as a missionary society, having in view, however, objects more humane, more justifiable, and less aggressive on the peace of other nations, than the others of that appellation.

The second object, and the most interesting to us, as coming home to our physical and moral characters, to our happiness and safety, is to provide an asylum to which we can, by degrees, send the whole of that population from among us, and establish them under our patronage and protection, as a separate, free and independent people, in some country and climate friendly to human life and happiness. That any place on the coast of Africa should answer the latter purpose, I have ever deemed entirely impossible. And without repeating the other arguments which have been urged by others, I will appeal to figures only, which admit no controversy. I shall

[1]Children's children, and those who are born of them.

speak in round numbers, not absolutely accurate, yet not so wide from truth as to vary the result materially. There are in the United States a million and a half of people of color in slavery. To send off the whole of these at once, nobody conceives to be practicable for us, or expedient for them. Let us take twenty-five years for its accomplishment, within which time they will be doubled. Their estimated value as property, in the first place, (for actual property has been lawfully vested in that form, and who can lawfully take it from the possessors?) at an average of two hundred dollars each, young and old, would amount to six hundred millions of dollars, which must be paid or lost by somebody. To this, add the cost of their transportation by land and sea to Mesurado, a year's provision of food and clothing, implements of husbandry and of their trades, which will amount to three hundred millions more, making thirty-six millions of dollars a year for twenty-five years, with insurance of peace all that time, and it is impossible to look at the question a second time. I am aware that at the end of about sixteen years, a gradual detraction from this sum will commence, from the gradual diminution of breeders, and go on during the remaining nine years. Calculate this deduction, and it is still impossible to look at the enterprise a second time. I do not say this to induce an inference that the getting rid of them is forever impossible. For that is neither my opinion nor my hope. But only that it cannot be done in this way. There is, I think, a way in which it can be done; that is, by emancipating the afterborn, leaving them, on due compensation with their mothers, until their services are worth their maintenance, and then putting them to industrious occupations, until a proper age for deportation. This was the result of my reflections on the subject five and forty years ago, and I have never yet been able to conceive any other practicable plan. It was sketched in the Notes on Virginia, under the fourteenth query. The estimated value of the new-born infant is so low, (say twelve dollars and fifty cents,) that it would probably be yielded by the owner gratis, and would thus reduce the six hundred millions of dollars, the first head of expense, to thirty-seven millions and a half; leaving only the expenses of nourishment while with the mother, and of transportation. And from what fund are these expenses to be furnished? Why not from that of the lands which have been ceded by the very States now needing this relief?

And ceded on no consideration, for the most part, but that of the general good of the whole. These cessions already constitute one-fourth of the States of the Union. It may be said that these lands have been sold; are now the property of the citizens composing those States; and the money long ago received and expended. But an equivalent of lands in the territories since acquired, may be appropriated to that object, or so much, at least, as may be sufficient; and the object, although more important to the slave States, is highly so to the others also, if they were serious in their arguments on the Missouri question. The slave States, too, if more interested, would also contribute more by their gratuitous liberation, thus taking on themselves alone the first and heaviest item of expense.

In the plan sketched in the Notes on Virginia, no particular place of asylum was specified; because it was thought possible, that in the revolutionary state of America, then commenced, events might open to us some one within practicable distance. This has now happened. St. Domingo has become independent, and with a population of that color only; and if the public papers are to be credited, their Chief offers to pay their passage, to receive them as free citizens, and to provide them employment. This leaves, then, for the general confederacy, no expense but of nurture with the mother a few years, and would call, of course, for a very moderate appropriation of the vacant lands. Suppose the whole annual increase to be of sixty thousand effective births, fifty vessels, of four hundred tons burden each, constantly employed in that short run, would carry off the increase of every year, and the old stock would die off in the ordinary course of nature, lessening from the commencement until its final disappearance. In this way no violation of private right is proposed. Voluntary surrenders would probably come in as fast as the means to be provided for their care would be competent to it. Looking at my own State only, and I presume not to speak for the others, I verily believe that this surrender of property would not amount to more, annually, than half our present direct taxes, to be continued fully about twenty or twenty-five years, and then gradually diminishing for as many more until their final extinction; and even this half tax would not be paid in cash, but by the delivery of an object which they have never yet known or counted as part of their property; and those not possessing the object will be called on for nothing. I do not go into all the details of the burdens and benefits of this operation. And who could estimate its blessed effects? I leave this to those who will live to see their accomplishment, and to enjoy a beatitude forbidden to my age. But I leave it with this admonition, to rise and be doing. A million and a half are within their control; but six millions, (which a majority of those now living will see them attain,) and one million of these fighting men, will say, "we will not go."

I am aware that this subject involves some constitutional scruples. But a liberal construction, justified by the object, may go far, and an amendment of the Constitution, the whole length necessary. The separation of infants from their mothers, too, would produce some scruples of humanity. But this would be straining at a gnat, and swallowing a camel. . . .

SELECTED REFERENCES

Brodie, Fawn M. *Thomas Jefferson: An Intimate History* (1974).

Cohen, William. "Thomas Jefferson and the Problem of Slavery." *Journal of American History*, 56 (1969), 503–27.

Farrison, W. Edward. "Clotel, Thomas Jefferson, and Sally Hemmings." *CLA Journal*, 17 (1973), 147–74.

Greenfield, Thomas A. "Race and Passive Voice at Monticello." *Crisis*, April, 1975, pp. 146–47.

Jordan, Winthrop D. *White Over Black: American Attitudes Toward the Negro, 1550–1812* (1968).

Kohler, Max J. "Unpublished Correspondence Between Thomas Jefferson and Some American Jews." *Publications of the American Jewish Historical Society*, 20 (1911), 11–30.

Morris, Mabel. "Jefferson and the Language of the American Indians." *Modern Language Quarterly*, 6 (1945), 31–34.

Seeber, Edward D. "Critical Views on Logan's Speech." *Journal of American Folklore*, 60 (1947), 130–46.

Sheehan, B. W. "Paradise and the Noble Savage in Jeffersonian Thought." *William and Mary Quarterly*, 26 (1969), 327–59.

PROJECTS AND PROBLEMS

Jefferson's comments on slavery were deleted from the Declaration of Independence. Were they consistent with his other statements about slavery?

Consider Jefferson's correspondence with Benjamin Banneker, his letter to Joel Barlow of October 8, 1809, and selected other letters as documentation of his opinions about the intellectual capacities of blacks.

How did President Jefferson propose to deal with the Indians in order to maintain peace and to remove them from their lands? See his private letter to Governor Harrison, and other documents, in *Tecumseh: Fact and Fiction in Early Records* (1961), ed. by Carl F. Klinck.

Study Jefferson's views on African colonization as they appear in *Notes on Virginia* and, forty-five years later, in his letter to Jared Sparks. Did Hugh Henry Brackenridge hold similar views? Consider those views in connection with the career of Martin R. Delaney, black novelist and abolitionist, who advocated African colonization.

Read all the passages in Jefferson's *Notes on Virginia* pertaining to the Indian and compare his opinions with those of Franklin. Give special attention to their attitude toward Indian eloquence.

Compare Jefferson's definition of "mulatto" with Charles W. Chesnutt's "What Is a White Man?" See Carter G. Woodson's "The Beginnings of the Miscegenation of the Whites and Blacks," *Journal of Negro History*, 5 (1918), 335–53, and Maxwell Whiteman, "Black Genealogy,"*RQ* [Reference Quarterly of the American Library Association], 11 (1972), 311–19.

Discuss the relationship between William Wells Brown's *Clotel* and the allegations concerning Jefferson and Sally Hemings, one of his slaves. In addition to the references by Fawn M. Brodie and Winthrop D. Jordan, see in particular the essay by W. Edward Farrison.

BENJAMIN BANNEKER
(1731–1806)

Although he is not notable for contributions to belles
lettres, this exceptional black man assuredly had an
impact on American culture. Born free in Maryland,
Banneker won a reputation for inventiveness in making a
wooden clock and, later, for skill as mathematician and
astronomer. The almanacs he published were cited to
refute prevailing assumptions about the intellectual
inferiority of Africans, assumptions used as justification
for their enslavement. On the recommendation of
Thomas Jefferson, then Secretary of State, Banneker was
appointed to assist in the survey of the city of
Washington. His letter to Jefferson, below, and
Jefferson's reply were widely circulated.

157

A RACE UNDER ABUSE AND CENSURE
Letter to Thomas Jefferson

Maryland, Baltimore County
Near Ellicotts' Lower Mills,
August 19th, 1791

Thomas Jefferson, Secretary of State.

Sir:—I am fully sensible of the greatness of that freedom, which I take with you on the present occasion, a liberty which seemed to me scarcely allowable, when I reflected on that distinguished and dignified station in which you stand, and the almost general prejudice and prepossession which is so prevalent in the world against those of my complexion.

I suppose it is a truth too well attested to you, to need a proof here, that we are a race of beings who have long laboured under the abuse and censure of the world, that we have long been considered rather as brutish than human, and scarcely capable of mental endowments.

Sir, I hope I may safely admit, in consequence of that report which hath reached me, that you are a man far less inflexible in sentiments of this nature than many others, that you are measurably friendly and well disposed towards us, and that you are willing and ready to lend your aid and assistance to our relief, from those many distresses and numerous calamities, to which we are reduced.

Now, sir, if this is founded in truth, I apprehend you will readily embrace every opportunity to eradicate that train of absurd and false ideas and opinions, which so generally prevails with respect to us, and that your sentiments are concurrent with mine, which are that one universal Father hath given Being to us all, and that he hath not only made us all of one flesh, but that he hath also without partiality afforded us all the same sensations, and endued us all with the same faculties, and that however variable we may be in society or religion, however diversified in situation or colour, we are all of the same family, and stand in the same relation to him.

Sir, if these are sentiments of which you are fully persuaded, I

158

hope you cannot but acknowledge, that it is the indispensable duty
of those who maintain for themselves the rights of human nature,
and who profess the obligations of Christianity, to extend their
power and influence to the relief of every part of the human race,
from whatever burden or oppression they may unjustly labour
under, and this I apprehend a full conviction of the truth and obliga-
tion of these principles should lead all to.

Sir, I have long been convinced that if your love for yourselves
and for those inesteemable laws, which preserve to you the rights of
human nature, was found on sincerity, you could not but be solicit-
ous that every individual of whatever rank or distinction, might with
you equally enjoy the blessings thereof, neither could you rest satisfied, short of the most active diffusion of your exertions in order to
their promotions from any state of degradation to which the un-
justifiable cruelty and barbarism of men have reduced them.

Sir, I freely and cheerfully acknowledge that I am of the African
race, and in that colour which is natural to them of the deepest dye,
and it is under a sense of the most profound gratitude to the Supreme Ruler of the universe that I now confess to you that I am not
under that state of tyrannical thraldom and inhuman captivity to
which too many of my brethren are doomed; but that I have abundantly tasted of the fruition of those blessings which proceed from
that free and unequalled liberty with which you are favoured and
which, I hope you will willingly allow you have received from the
immediate hand of that Being, from whom proceedeth every good
and perfect gift.

Sir, suffer me to recall to your mind that time in which the arms
and tyranny of the British Crown were exerted with every powerful
effort in order to reduce you to a State of Servitude, look back I en-
treat you on the variety of dangers to which you were exposed; reflect on that time in which every human aid appeared unavailable,
and in which even hope and fortitude wore the aspect of inability to
the conflict and you cannot but be led to a serious and grateful sense
of your miraculous and providential preservation; you cannot but
acknowledge that the present freedom and tranquility which you
enjoy you have mercifully received and that it is the peculiar blessing of Heaven.

This sir, was a time in which you clearly saw into the injustice of a

state of slavery and in which you had just apprehensions of the horrors of its condition, it was now, sir, that your abhorrence thereof
was so excited, that you publickly held forth this true and valuable
doctrine, which is worthy to be recorded and remembered in all succeeding ages. "We hold these truths to be self-evident, that all men
are created equal, and that they are endowed by their creator with
certain unalienable rights, that among these are life, liberty and the
pursuit of happiness."

Here, sir, was a time in which your tender feelings for yourselves
had engaged you thus to declare, you were then impressed with
proper ideas of the great valuation of liberty and the free possession
of those blessings to which you were entitled by nature; but, sir, how
pitiable is it to reflect that although you were so fully convinced of
the benevolence of the Father of mankind and of his equal and im-
partial distribution of those rights and privileges which he had con-
ferred upon them, that you should at the same time counteract his
mercies in detaining by fraud and violence so numerous a part of my
brethren under groaning captivity and cruel oppression, that you
should at the same time be found guilty of that most criminal act
which you professedly detested in others with respect to yourselves.

Sir, I suppose that your knowledge of the situation of my brethren
is too extensive to need a recital here; neither shall I presume to pre-
scribe methods by which they may be relieved, otherwise than by
recommending to you and all others to wean yourselves from those
narrow prejudices which you have imbibed with respect to them and
as Job proposed to his friends, "put your souls in their souls stead,"
thus shall your hearts be enlarged with kindness and benevolence
towards them, and thus shall you need neither the direction of
myself or others, in what manner to proceed herein.

And now, sir, although my sympathy and affection for my brethren hath caused my enlargement thus far, I ardently hope that your
candour and generosity will plead with you in my behalf when I
make known to you that it was not originally my design; but that
having taken up my pen in order to direct to you as a present, a copy
of an almanac, which I have calculated for the succeeding year, I
was unexpectedly and unavoidably led thereto.

This calculation, sir, is the production of my arduous study in this
my advanced stage of life; for having long had unbounded desires to

become acquainted with the secrets of nature, I have had to gratify my curiosity herein through my own assiduous application to astronomical study, in which I need not to recount to you the many difficulties and disadvantages which I have had to encounter.

And although I had almost declined to make my calculation for the ensuing year, in consequence of that time which I had allotted therefor being taken up at the Federal Territory by the request of Mr. Andrew Ellicott, yet finding myself under several engagements to printers of this state, to whom I had communicated my design, on my return to my place of residence I industriously applied myself thereto which I hope I have accomplished with correctness and accuracy, a copy of which I have taken the liberty to direct to you and which I humbly request you will favorably receive. Although you may have the opportunity of perusing it after its publication yet I chose to send it to you in manuscript previous thereto that you might not only have an earlier inspection but that you might also view it in my own handwriting.

And now, sir, I shall conclude and subscribe myself, with the most profound respect, your most obedient humble servant,

B. Banneker

SELECTED REFERENCES

Baker, Henry E. "Benjamin Banneker, The Negro Mathematician and Astronomer." *Journal of Negro History,* 3 (1918), 99–118.
Bedini, Silvio A. *A Life of Benjamin Banneker* (1972).

PROJECTS AND PROBLEMS

Why did the first of Banneker's almanacs, published in 1791, contain an introduction testifying that the author had performed the calculations without assistance? Compare this introduction with the prefatory matter in Phillis Wheatley's *Poems on Various Subjects, Religious and Moral.*

In what sense were Banneker's almanacs equivalent to antislavery tracts? Why were his accomplishments, rather than achievements of other contemporary blacks of demonstrated intellectual capacity (e.g., Richard Allen and Absalom Jones), used to challenge Jefferson's notions of the inferiority of Africans?

Benjamin Franklin and Banneker both published almanacs. Discuss other parallels in their lives.

HUGH HENRY BRACKENRIDGE (1748–1816)

Poet, minister, lawyer, and journalist, Hugh Henry Brackenridge moved American literature forward with his novel, *Modern Chivalry* (1792–1815). This first selection is from Book V, Chapter 1 of this episodic narrative of the adventures of Captain Farrago and Teague O'Reagan, his Irish servant. "The Trial of Mamachtaga" appeared in Archibald Loudon's *Selection of Some of the Most Interesting Narratives of Outrages Committed by the Indians* (1808).

ON THE DIVERSITY OF THE
HUMAN SPECIES

There is no fact that has proved more stubborn than the diversity of the human species; especially that great extreme of diversity in the natives of Africa. How the descendants of Adam and Eve, both good looking people, should ever come to be a vile negro, or even a mulatto man or woman, is puzzling.

Some have conjectured, that a black complexion, frizzled hair, a flat nose, and bandy legs, were the mark set on Cain, for the murder of his brother Abel. But, as the deluge drowned the whole world and only one family was saved, the blacks must have all perished; like the Mammoth, whose bones are found on the Ohio, and other places, which was too big for Noah to get into the ark.

Some suppose, that it was the curse pronounced upon Canaan, the son of Noah, for looking at his father's nakedness. They got rid by this means of the difficulty of the flood; but by Moses' own account the Canaanites were the descendants of Canaan; and we do not hear of them being negroes; which, had it been the case, we cannot doubt would have been laid hold of by the Israelites, as a circumstance to justify their extirpating, or making slaves of them.

Lord Kames, in his Sketches of the History of Man, solves the difficulty, by supposing, that, at the building of Babel, there was a confusion of complexions, as well as languages. But, besides that it is not to be supposed that the historians would pass over so material a circumstance, without particularly mentioning it, it is introducing a miracle, which we are not warranted in doing, unless it had been expressly laid down to have been wrought.

The last theory, has been that of accounting for the change, from the climate, and accident of wind and weather; calling in aid, in the mean time, the imagination of the mothers. This does not appear altogether satisfactory. At least, there are those who would not be averse to hear some other solution of the difficulty. I have thought of one, which I would suggest with great diffidence; the authors of those before me being great men, and their hypothesis not to be lightly overthrown.

I am of opinion that Adam was a tall, straight limbed, red haired man, with a fair complexion, blue eyes, and an aquiline nose; and that Eve was a negro woman.

For what necessity to make them both of the same colour, feature, and form, when there is beauty in variety. Do not you see in a tulip, one leaf blue, and another white, and sometimes the same leaf white and red?

As God made Adam in his own likeness, so it is to be supposed, that Adam begat some in his; and these were red haired, fair complexioned, blue eyed, proportionably featured boys and girls; while, on the other hand, some took after the mother, and became negro men and women. From a mixture of complexion, the offspring, at other times, might be a shade darker, in one case, than the father; and a shade lighter, in another case, than the mother; and hence, a diversifyed progeny, with a variety of features; from the bottlenose to the mire-snipe; which is that of the people in the west of Ireland; and from the auburn of the Corsican hair, to the golden locks of the Caledonian beauty; and from the black eye to the hazle and the grey.

It may be asked, How at the flood? when Noah, his wife, his three sons, and their wives, eight persons, only were saved? It is but giving some of the sons negro wenches for their wives, and you have the matter all right.

THE TRIAL OF MAMACHTAGA, AN INDIAN, AT A COURT OF OYER AND TERMINER FOR THE COUNTY OF WESTMORELAND, IN THE YEAR 1784-5

I KNOW the particulars of the following story well, because one of the men (Smith) was shingling a house for me in the town of Pittsburgh, the evening before he was murdered by Mamachtaga, and for which murder, and some others, this Indian was tried. Smith had borrowed a blanket of me, saying that he was about to cross the river (Allegheny) to the Indian camp on the west side. Here a party of Indians, mostly Delawares, had come in, it being just after the war, and the greater part of these Indians having professed themselves friendly during the war, and their Chief, Killbuck, with his family and that of several others, having remained at the garrison, or on an island in the Ohio river, called Killbuck's Island, and under the reach of the guns of the fort. Mamachtaga had been at war against the settlements with others of the Delawares who were now at this encampment.

I went myself over to the encampment, the next morning, and found the Indians there. Two men had been murdered, Smith and another of the name of Evans, and two wounded, one of them a dwarf of the name of Freeman. According to the relation which I got from the wounded, there were four white men together in a cabin when Mamachtaga, without the least notice, rushed in and stabbed Smith mortally, and had stabbed Evans, who had seized the Indian who was entangled with the dwarf among his feet attempting to escape, and who had received wounds also in the scuffle; the other white man had also received a stab. It would appear that the Indian had been in liquor, according to the account of the other In-

166

dians and of the white men who escaped. Killbuck appeared greatly
cast down, and sat upon a log, silent. Mamachtaga made no attempt
to escape. He was now sober, and gave himself up to the guard that
came over, affecting not to know what had happened. The seat of
justice of Westmoreland county being 30 miles distant, and the jail
there not being secure, he was taken to the guard-house of the garrison, to be confined until a court of Oyer and Terminer should be
holden in the county. Living in the place and being of the profession
of the law, said I to the interpreter, Joseph Nicholas, one day, has
that Indian any fur or peltry, or has he any interest with his nation
that he could collect some and pay a lawyer to take up his defence
for this homicide? The interpreter said that he had some in the
hands of a trader in town, and that he could raise from his nation any
quantity of racoon or beaver, provided it would answer any purpose.
I was struck with the pleasantry of having an Indian for a client, and
getting a fee in this way, and told the interpreter to go to the Indian,
and explain the matter to him, who did so, and brought me an account that Mamachtaga had forty weight of Beaver, which he was
ready to make over, being with a trader in town, William Amber-
son, with whom he had left it, and that he had a brother who would
set off immediately to the Indian towns, and procure an hundred
weight or more if that would do any good, but the interpreter stipulated that he should have half of all that should be got, for his trouble in bringing about the contract. Accordingly he was dispatched to
the Indian, from whom he brought, in a short time, an order for the
beaver in the hand of the trader, with Mamachtaga (his mark). The
mark was something like a turkey's foot, as these people have no
idea of an hieroglyphic merely abstract, as a straight line or a curve,
but it must bear some resemblance to a thing in nature. After this, as
it behoved, I went to consult with my client and arrange his defense,
if it were possible to make one on which a probable face could be
put. Accompanied by the interpreter, I was admitted to the Indian,
so that I could converse with him; he was in what is called the black
hole, something resembling that kind of hole which is depressed in
the floor, and which the southern people have in their cabins, in
which to keep their esculent roots from the frost during the winter
season. Not going down into the hole as may be supposed, though it
was large enough to contain two or three, and was depressed about

eight feet, being the place in which delinquent or refractory soldiery had been confined occasionally for punishment, but standing on the floor above, I desired the interpreter to put his questions. This was done, explaining to him the object of the enquiry, that it was to serve him, and by knowing the truth, be prepared for his defense; he affected to know nothing about it, nor was he disposed to rely upon any defense that could be made. His idea was that he was giving the beaver as a commutation for his life. Under this impression it did not appear to me proper that I should take the beaver, knowing that I could do nothing for him; besides, seeing the manner in which the dark and squalid creature was accommodated with but a shirt and breech-clout on, humanity dictated that the beaver should be applied to procure him a blanket and food additional to the bread and water which he was allowed. Accordingly I returned the order to the interpreter, and desired him to procure and furnish these things. He seemed reluctant, and thought we ought to keep the perquisite we had got. On this, I thought it most advisable to retain the order and give it to a trader in town with directions to furnish these articles occasionally to the officer of the guard, which I did, taking the responsibility upon myself to the interpreter for his part of the beaver.

An Indian woman, known by the name of the Grenadier Squaw, was sitting doing some work by the trap-door of the cell, or hole in which he was confined, for the trap-door was kept open and a sentry at the outer door of the guard-house. The Indian woman was led by sympathy to sit by him. I had a curiosity to know the force of abstract sentiment, in preferring greater evils to what with us would seem to be less; or rather the force of opinion over pain. For knowing the idea of the Indians with regard to the disgrace of hanging, I proposed to the Indian woman, who spoke English as well as Indian, and was a Delaware herself, (Mamachtaga was of that nation.) to ask him which he would choose, to be hanged or burnt? Whether it was that the woman was struck with the inhumanity of introducing the idea of death, she not only declined to put the question, but her countenance expressed resentment. I then recollected, and have since attended to the circumstance, that amongst themselves, when they mean to put any one to death, they conceal the determination, and the time, until it is about to be put in execution, unless the blacking the prisoner, which is a mark upon such as are about to be burnt, may be called an intimation; but it is only by those who are accustomed to their manners that it can be understood. However, I got the question put by the interpreter, at which he seemed to hesitate for some time, but said he would rather be shot or be tomahawked. In a few days it made a great noise through the country that I was to appear for the Indian, and having acquired some reputation in the defense of criminals, it was thought possible by some that he might be acquitted by *the crooks of the law,* as the people expressed it; and it was talked of publickly to raise a party and come to town and take the interpreter and me both, and hang the interpreter, and exact an oath from me not to appear in behalf of the Indian. It was, however, finally concluded to come in to the garrison and demand the Indian, and hang him themselves. Accordingly, a party came, in a few days, and about break of day summoned the garrison, and demanded the surrender of the Indian; the commanding officer remonstrated, and prevailed with them to leave the Indian to the civil authority. Upon which they retired, firing their guns as they came through the town. The interpreter, hearing the alarm, sprang up in his shirt, and made for a hill above the town, called Grant's–hill. On seeing him run, he was taken for the Indian, who they supposed had been suffered to escape, and was pursued, until the people were assured that it was not the Indian. In the mean time he had run some miles, and swimming the river, lay in the Indian country until he thought it might be safe to return.

It was not without good reason that the interpreter was alarmed, for having been some years amongst the Indians, in early life a prisoner, and since a good deal employed in the Indian trade, and on all occasions of treaty, employed as an interpreter, he was associated in the public mind with an Indian, and on this occasion, considered as the abetter of the Indian, from the circumstance of employing council to defend him. And before this time a party had come from the Chartiers, a settlement south of the Monongahela, in the neighborhood of this town, and had attacked some friendly Indians on the Island in the Ohio, (Killbuck's Island) under the protection of the garrison, had killed several, and amongst them some that had been of essential service to the whites, in the expeditions against the Indian towns, and on scouting parties, in case of attacks upon the settlements. One to whom the whites had given the name of Wilson,

(Captain Wilson) was much regretted by the garrison. A certain Cisna had commanded the party that committed this outrage.

A day or two after his return, the interpreter came to me, and relinquished all interest in the beaver that was lodged with the trader, or expectant from the towns, that he might, to use his own language, wipe his hands of the affair, and be clear of the charge of supporting the Indian. The fact was, that as to beaver from the towns I expected none, having been informed in the mean time by the friendly Indians, that Mamachtaga was a bad man, and was thought so by his nation; that he had been a great warrior; but was mischievous in liquor, having killed two of his own people; that it would not be much regretted in the nation to hear of his death; and that, except his brother, no one would give any thing to get him off.

He had the appearance of great ferocity; was of tall stature, and fierce aspect. He was called Mamachtaga, which signifies trees blown across, as is usual in a hurricane or tempest by the wind, and this name had been given him from the ungovernable nature of his passion. Having, therefore, no expectation of peltry or fur in the case, it was no great generosity in me to press upon the interpreter the taking half the beaver, as his right in procuring the contract; but finding me obstinate in insisting upon it, he got a friend to speak to me, and at length I suffered myself to be prevailed upon to let him off and take all the beaver that could be got to myself.

It did not appear to me advisable to relinquish the defense of the Indian, fee or no fee, lest it should be supposed that I yielded to the popular impression, the fury of which, when it had a little spent itself, began to subside, and there were some who thought the Indian might be cleared, if it could be proved that the white men killed had made the Indian drunk, which was alleged to be the case; but which the wounded and surviving persons denied, particularly the dwarf, (William Freeman,) but his testimony, it was thought, would not be much regarded, as he could not be said to be *man grown*, and had been convicted at the quarter sessions of stealing a keg of whiskey some time before.

At a court of Oyer and Terminer holden for the county of Westmoreland, before Chief Justice M'Kean, and Bryan, Mamachtaga was brought to trial. The usual forms were pursued. An interpreter, not Nicholas, but a certain Handlyn, stood by him and interpreted, in the Delaware language, the indictment and the meaning of it, and the privilege he had to deny the charge, that is, the plea of "*not guilty.*" But he could not easily comprehend that it was matter of form, and that he must say "*not guilty*"; for he was unwilling to deny, as unbecoming a warrior to deny the truth. For though he did not confess, yet he did not like to say that he had not killed the men; only that he was drunk, and did not know what he had done; but "supposed he should know which he was under the ground." The court directed the plea to be entered for him, and he was put upon his trial.

He was called upon to make his challenges, which the interpreter explained to him, which he was left to make himself, and which he did as he liked the countenance of the jury, and challenged according to the sourness, or cheerfulness of the countenance, and what he thought indications of a mild temper. The jurors, as they were called to the book, being told in the usual form, "Prisoner, look upon the juror—juror, look upon the prisoner at the bar—are you related to the prisoner?" One of them, a German of a swarthy complexion, and being the first called, took the question amiss, thinking it a reflection, and said with some anger, that "he thought that an uncivil way to treat Dutch people, as if he could be the brother, or cousin, of an Indian"; but the matter being explained to him by another German on the jury, he was satisfied, and was sworn.

The meaning of the jury being on oath, was explained to the Indian, to give him some idea of the solemnity and fairness of the trial. The testimony was positive and put the homicide beyond a doubt; so that nothing remained for me, in opening his defence, but the offering to prove that he was in liquor, and that this had been given him by the white people, the traders in town. This testimony was overruled, and it was explained to the Indian that the being drunk could not by our law excuse the murder. The Indian said "he hoped the good man above would excuse it."

The jury gave their verdict, guilty, without leaving the bar. And the prisoner was remanded to jail. In the mean time there was tried at the same court another person, (John Bradly,) on a charge of homicide, but who was found guilty of *manslaughter* only. Towards the ending of the court, these were both brought up to receive sentence. The Indian was asked what he had to say, why sentence of death should not be pronounced upon him. This was interpreted to him, and he said that he would rather *run awhile*. This was under the idea of the custom among the Indians of giving time to the murderer, according to the circumstances of the case, to run, during which time if he can satisfy the relations of the deceased, by a commutation for his life, a gun, a horse, fur and the like, it is in their power to dispense with the punishment, but if this cannot be done, having not enough to give, or the relations not consenting to take a commutation, he must come at the end of the time appointed, to the spot assigned, and there, by a warrior of the nation, or some relative, son, brother, &c. of the deceased, be put to death, in which case the tomahawk is the usual instrument. No instance will occur in which the condemned will not be punctual to his engagement. And I think it very probable, or rather can have no doubt, but that if this Indian had been suffered to run at this time, that is, go to his nation, on the condition to return at a certain period, to receive the sentence of what he would call the council, he would have come, with as much fidelity, as a man challenged, would on a point of honour come to the place assigned, and at the time when, to risk himself to his adversary. Such is the force of opinion, from education, on the human mind.

Sentence having been pronounced upon the [man] convicted of manslaughter. (In this case, the first part of the sentence, as the law directs, was that of hanging, which is done until the *benefit of clergy is prayed by the prisoner;* but not understanding this, he was not prepared for the shock;—nothing could exceed the contortion of his muscles when a sentence, contrary to what he had expected, was pronounced. Being a simple man, he made a hideous outcry, gave a most woful look to the court, and country and begged for mercy; and it was not for some time after that, having the matter explained to him, and the benefit of clergy being allowed, he could be composed,) sentence of *burning in the hand* being now pronounced; at this moment the sheriff came in with a rope to bind up his hand to a beam of the low and wooden court-house in which we were, in order that the hot iron might be put upon it.

Sentence of hanging had been previously pronounced upon the Indian, on which he had said that he would prefer to be shot; but it being explained to him that this could not be done, he had the idea of hanging in his mind. Accordingly, by a side glance, seeing the sheriff coming in with a rope, which was a bed cord he had procured, having nothing else, in our then low state of trade and manufactures, Mamachtaga conceived that the sentence was about to be executed presently upon him, and that the rope was for this purpose, which coming unaware upon him, he lost the command of himself for a moment; his visage grew black, his features were screwed up, and he writhed with horror and aversion; the surprise not having given time to the mind to collect itself, and on the acquired principle of honour, to conceal its dismay, or on those of reason to bear with and compose itself to its fate. Even when undeceived and made acquainted that he was not to die then, he remained under a visible horror, the idea of immediate death, and especially of hanging, giving a tremor, like the refrigeration of cold upon the human frame.

Before he was taken from the bar, he wished to say something, which was to acknowledge, that his trial had been fair, and to express a wish, that his nation would not revenge his death, or come to war on his account. Being asked as he was taken off, by some of those accompanying the sheriff, in conducting him to jail, whom he thought the judges to be, before whom he had been tried, and who were on the bench in scarlet robes, which was the official custom of that time, and being of the Delaware nation, amongst whom Moravian missionaries had been a good deal, and as it would seem, mixing some recollections which he had derived from this source, he answered that the one, meaning the chief justice, was God, and the other Jesus Christ.

At the same court of Oyer and Terminer was convicted a man for the crime against nature, and at a court of Quarter Sessions a short time after, another, a young man of the name of Jack, had been convicted of larceny, and was now confined in the same jail, and in fact in the same room, for there was but one, with the Indian and the white man before-mentioned; and though, upon account of his youth and family connections, the jury in finding a verdict had recommended him to pardon, for which the supreme executive council of the State had been petitioned some time before; nevertheless he could not restrain the wickedness of his mind and had prevailed upon the white man, guilty of the crime against nature, as he had to die at any rate, to save the disgrace of being hanged, to consent to be murdered by the Indian. The creature was extremely simple, and had actually consented, and Jack had prepared a knife for the purpose, but the Indian refused, though solicited, and offered liquor, saying that he had killed white men enough already.

A child of the jailor had been taken sick, and had a fever. The Indian said he could cure it, if he had roots from the woods, which he knew. The jailor taking off his irons which he had on his feet, took his word that he would not make his escape, while he let him go to the woods to collect roots, telling him that if he did make his escape, the great council, the judges, would hang him, (the jailor,) in his place. But for greater security the jailor thought proper to accompany him to the woods, where roots were collected, which on their return were made use of in the cure of the child.

The warrant for the execution of the Indian and of the white man, came to hand, and the morning of the execution the Indian expressed a wish to be painted, that he might die like a warrior. The jailor, as before, unironed him, and took him to the woods to collect his usual paints, which having done, he returned, and prepared himself for the occasion, painting highly with the rouge which they use on great occasions.

A great body of people assembling at the place of execution, the white man was hung first, and afterwards the Indian ascended a ladder placed to the cross timber of the gibbet; the rope being fastened, when he was swung off it broke, and the Indian fell, and having swooned a little, he rose with a smile, and went up again, a stronger rope in the mean time having been provided, or rather two put about his neck together, so that his weight was supported, and he underwent the sentence of the law, and was hanged till he was dead.

This was during the Indian war, and the place on the verge of the settlement, so that if the Indian had taken a false step, and gone off from the jailor while he was looking for roots for the cure, or for painting, it would have been easy for him to have made his escape; but such is the force of opinion, as we have before said, resulting from the way of thinking amongst the Indians, that he did not seem to think that he had the physical power to go. It was nevertheless considered an imprudent thing in the jailor to run this risk. For if the Indian had made his escape, it is morally certain that in the then state of public mind, the jailor himself would have fallen a sacrifice to the resentment of the people.

SUGGESTED ADDITIONAL READINGS

"The Animals, Vulgarly Called Indians"
"Thoughts on the Enfranchisement of the Negroes"
"Farther and Concluding Thoughts on the Indian War"

SELECTED REFERENCE

Haims, Lynn. "Of Indians and Irishmen: A Note on Bracken-ridge's Use of Sources for Satire in *Modern Chivalry*." *Early American Literature*, X(1975), 88–92.
Marder, Daniel. *Hugh Henry Brackenridge* (1967).

PROJECTS AND PROBLEMS

Modern Chivalry reveals much about the status of minorities in Brackenridge's America. What were his attitudes toward blacks and Irish immigrants? Discuss Teague O'Reagan and the Irish stereo-type.

Compare Brackenridge's notions about Indians with those of Philip Freneau, his Princeton classmate. What are some explana-tions for their different views? See Brackenridge's letter on Indian rights in the Arno Press anthology, *Captivity Tales* (1974). *See also A Hugh Henry Brackenridge Reader: 1770–1815* (1970), ed. by Dan-iel Marder.

Compare the explanation of the origin of species given in the se-lection in this volume with the "oration" of the Guinea Negro which immediately precedes it in Book V of *Modern Chivalry*. Is Cuff's dialect carefully rendered?

Compare the story of Mamachtaga with the tale of another con-victed murderer, "Oakatibbe, or the Chocktaw Sampson," in *The Wigwam and the Cabin* (1845), by William Gilmore Simms.

PHILIP FRENEAU
(1752–1832)

An ardent nationalist, Freneau devoted his talents as poet and journalist to the American Revolution and the principle of independence. His poems show both neo–classic and romantic characteristics, but it is the doctrines of romantic literature that dominate his poems about Indian subjects. Some of these are among his best. He wrote "To Sir Toby" in 1784, when he was a master of a brig sailing in Caribbean waters.

TO SIR TOBY
A Sugar Planter in the Interior Parts of Jamaica, Near the City of San Jago De La Vega, (Spanish Town) 1784

> *The motions of his spirit are black as night,*
> *And his affections dark as Erebus.*
>
> SHAKESPEARE

If there exists a hell—the case is clear—
Sir Toby's slaves enjoy that portion here:
Here are no blazing brimstone lakes—'tis true;
But kindled Rum too often burns as blue;
In which some friend, whom nature must detest,
Steeps Toby's brand, and marks poor Cudjoe's breast.[1]
    Here whips on whips excite perpetual fears,
And mingled howlings vibrate on my ears:
Here nature's plagues abound, to fret and teaze,
Snakes, scorpions, despots, lizards, centipees—
No art, no care escapes the busy lash;
All have their dues—and all are paid in cash—
The eternal driver keeps a steady eye
On a black herd, who would his vengeance fly,
But chained, imprisoned, on a burning soil,
For the mean avarice of a tyrant, toil!
The lengthy cart-whip guards this monster's reign—
And cracks, like pistols, from the fields of cane.
    Ye powers! who formed these wretched tribes, relate,
What had they done, to merit such a fate!
What were they brought from Eboe's[2] sultry waste,
To see that plenty which they must not taste—

---

[1]This passage has a reference to the West India custom (sanctioned by law) of branding a newly imported slave on the breast, with a red hot iron, as an evidence of the purchaser's property. [Freneau's note.]

[2]A small negro kingdom near the river Senegal. [Freneau's note.]

Food, which they cannot buy, and dare not steal;
Yams and potatoes—many a scanty meal!—
    One, with a gibbet wakes his negro's fears,
One to the windmill nails him by the ears;
One keeps his slave in darkened dens, unfed,
One puts the wretch in pickle ere he's dead:
This, from a tree suspends him by the thumbs,
That, from his table grudges even the crumbs!
    O'er yond' rough hills a tribe of females go,
Each with her gourd, her infant, and her hoe;
Scorched by a sun that has no mercy here,
Driven by a devil, whom men call overseer—
In chains, twelve wretches to their labors haste;
Twice twelve I saw, with iron collars graced!—
    Are such the fruits that spring from vast domains?
Is wealth, thus got, Sir Toby, worth your pains!—
Who would your wealth on terms, like these, possess,
Where all we see is pregnant with distress—
Angola's natives scourged by ruffian hands,
And toil's hard product shipp'd to foreign lands.
    Talk not of blossoms, and your endless spring;
What joy, what smile, can scenes of misery bring?—
Though Nature, here, has every blessing spread,
Poor is the laborer—and how meanly fed!—
    Here Stygian paintings light and shade renew,
Pictures of hell, that Virgil's pencil drew:
Here, surly Charons make their annual trip,
And ghosts arrive in every Guinea ship,
To find what beasts these western isles afford,
Plutonian scourges, and despotic lords:—
    Here, they, of stuff determined to be free,
Must climb the rude cliffs of the Liguanee:[3]
Beyond the clouds, in sculking haste repair,
And hardly safe from brother traitors there.—[4]

[3]The mountains northward of Kingston. [Freneau's note.]

[4]Alluding to the *Independent negroes* in the blue mountains, who for a stipulated reward, deliver up every fugitive that falls into their hands, to the English Government. [Freneau's note.]

THE DEATH SONG OF A CHEROKEE INDIAN

The sun sets in night, and the stars shun the day,
But glory remains when their lights fade away.
Begin, ye tormentors: your threats are in vain
For the son of Alknomock can never complain.

Remember the woods, where in ambush he lay,
And the scalps which he bore from your nation away!
Why do ye delay?—'till I shrink from my pain?
Know the son of Alknomock can never complain.

Remember the arrows he shot from his bow,
Remember your chiefs by his hatchet laid low,
The flame rises high, you exult in my pain?
Know the son of Alknomock will never complain.

I go to the land where my father is gone:
His ghost shall rejoice in the fame of his son,
Death comes like a friend, he relieves me from pain
And thy son, O Alknomock, has scorned to complain.

THE PROPHECY OF KING TAMMANY

The Indian chief who, famed of yore,
   Saw Europe's sons adventuring here,
Looked, sorrowing, to the crowded shore,
   And sighing dropt a tear!
He saw them half his world explore,
He saw them draw the shining blade,
He saw their hostile ranks displayed,
And cannons blazing through that shade
   Where only peace was known before.

"Ah, what unequal arms!" he cried,
"How art thou fallen, my country's pride,
   The rural, sylvan reign!
Far from our pleasing shores to go
To western rivers, winding slow,
Is this the boon the gods bestow!
What have we done, great patrons, say,
That strangers seize our woods away,
   And drive us naked from our native plain?

"Rage and revenge inspire my soul,
And passion burns without controul;
   Hence, strangers, to your native shore!
Far from our Indian shades retire,
Remove these gods that vomit fire,
   And stain with blood these ravaged glades no more;
In vain I weep, in vain I sigh,
These strangers all our arms defy,
As they advance our chieftains die!—

   What can their hosts oppose!
The bow has lost its wonted spring,
The arrow faulters on the wing,
Nor carries ruin from the string
   To end their being and our woes.

"Yes, yes,—I see our nation bends;
The gods no longer are our friends;—
    But why these weak complaints and sighs?
Are there not gardens in the west,
Where all our far-famed Sachems rest?—
I'll go, an unexpected guest,
    And the dark horrors of the way despise.

"Even now the thundering peals draw nigh,
"Tis theirs to triumph, ours to die!
But mark me, Christian, ere I go—
Thou, too, shalt have thy share of woe;
The time rolls on, not moving slow,
When hostile squadrons for your blood shall come,
    And ravage all your shore!
Your warriors and your children slay,
And some in dismal dungeons lay,
Or lead them captive far away
    To climes unknown, through seas untried before.

"When struggling long, at last with pain
You break a cruel tyrant's chain,
That never shall be joined again,
    When half your foes are homeward fled,
    And hundreds maimed and thousands dead,
    A sordid race will then succeed,
        To slight the virtues of the firmer race,
        That brought your tyrant to disgrace,
Shall give your honours to an odious train,
Who shunned all conflicts on the main
And dared no battles on the bloody plain,
Whose little souls sunk in the gloomy day
When virtue only could support the fray
And sunshine friends kept off—or ran away."

So spoke the chief, and raised his funeral pyre—
    Around him soon the crackling flames ascend;

He smiled amid the fervours of the fire
  To think his troubles were so near their end,
'Till the freed soul, her debt to nature paid,
Rose from the ashes that her prison made,
And sought the world unknown, and dark oblivion's
    shade.

THE INDIAN BURYING
GROUND

In spite of all the learned have said,
   I still my old opinion keep;
The posture, that we give the dead,
   Points out the soul's eternal sleep.

Not so the ancients of these lands—
   The Indian, when from life released,
Again is seated with his friends,
   And shares again the joyous feast.°

His imaged birds, and painted bowl,
   And venison, for a journey dressed,
Bespeak the nature of the soul,
   Activity, that knows no rest.

His bow, for action ready bent,
   And arrows, with a head of stone,
Can only mean that life is spent,
   And not the old ideas gone.

Thou, stranger, that shalt come this way,
   No fraud upon the dead commit—
Observe the swelling turf, and say
   They do not lie, but here they sit.

Here still a lofty rock remains,
   On which the curious eye may trace
(Now wasted, half, by wearing rains)
   The fancies of a ruder race.

°The North American Indians bury their dead in a sitting posture; decorating the corpse with wampum, the images of birds, quadrupeds, &c.: and (if that of a warrior) with bows, arrows, tomahawks, and other military weapons. [Freneau's note.]

Here still an aged elm aspires,
   Beneath whose far-projecting shade
(And which the shepherd still admires)
   The children of the forest played!

There oft a restless Indian queen
   (Pale Shebah, with her braided hair)
And many a barbarous form is seen
   To chide the man that lingers there.

By midnight moons, o'er moistening dews;
   In habit for the chase arrayed,
The hunter still the deer pursues,
   The hunter and the deer, a shade!

And long shall timorous fancy see
   The painted chief, and pointed spear,
And Reason's self shall bow the knee
   To shadows and delusions here.

THE INDIAN CONVERT

An Indian, who lived at *Muskingum,* remote,
Was teazed by a parson to join his dear flock,
To throw off his blanket and put on a coat,
And of grace and religion to lay in a stock.

The Indian long slighted an offer so fair,
Preferring to preaching his fishing and fowling;
A *sermon* to him was a heart full of care,
And singing but little superior to howling.

At last by persuasion and constant harassing
Our Indian was brought to consent to be *good;*
He saw that the malice of *Satan* was pressing,
And the *means* to repel him not yet understood.

Of heaven, one day, when the parson was speaking,
And painting the beautiful things of the place,
The *convert,* who something substantial was seeking,
Rose up, and confessed he had doubts in the case.—

Said he, *Master Minister,* this place that you talk of,
Of things for the stomach, pray what has it got;
Has it liquors in plenty?—if so I'll soon walk off
And put myself down in the heavenly spot.

You fool (said the preacher) no liquors are there!
The place I'm describing is most like our meeting,
Good people, all singing, with preaching and prayer;
They live upon these without eating or drinking.

But the doors are all locked against folks that are
    wicked:
And you, I am fearful, will never get there:—
A life of REPENTANCE must purchase the ticket,
And few of you, Indians, can buy it, I fear.

Farewell (said the Indian) I'm none of your mess;
On victuals, so airy, I faintish should feel,
I cannot consent to be lodged in a place
Where there's nothing to eat and but little to steal.

THE INDIAN STUDENT
or, Force of Nature

From Susquehanna's farthest springs
Where savage tribes pursue their game,
(His blanket tied with yellow strings.)
A shepherd of the forest came.

Not long before, a wandering priest
Expressed his wish, with visage sad—
"Ah, why (he cried) in Satan's waste,
Ah, why detain so fine a lad?

"In white-man's land there stands a town
Where learning may be purchased low—
Exchange his blanket for a gown,
And let the lad to college go."—

From long debate the council rose,
And viewing Shalum's tricks with joy
To Cambridge Hall, o'er wastes of snows,
They sent the copper-colored boy.

One generous chief a bow supplied,
This gave a shaft, and that a skin;
The feathers, in vermillion dyed,
Himself did from a turkey win:

Thus dressed so gay, he took his way
O'er barren hills, alone, alone!
His guide a star, he wandered far,
His pillow every night a stone.

At last he came, with foot so lame
Where learned men talk heathen Greek,
And Hebrew lore is gabbled o'er,
To please the Muses,—twice a week.

Awhile he writ, awhile he read,
Awhile he conned their grammar rules—
(An Indian savage so well bred
Great credit promised to the schools.)

Some thought he would in law excel,
Some said in physic he would shine;
And one that knew him, passing well,
Beheld, in him, a sound Divine.

But those of more discerning eye
Even then could other prospects show,
And saw him lay his *Virgil* by
To wander with his dearer bow.

The tedious hours of study spent,
The heavy-molded lecture done,
He to the woods a-hunting went,
Through lonely wastes he walked, he run.

No mystic wonders fired his mind;
He sought to gain no learned degree,
But only sense enough to find
The squirrel in the hollow tree.

The shady bank, the purling stream,
The woody wild his heart possessed,
The dewy lawn, his morning dream
In fancy's gayest colors dressed.

"And why (he cried) did I forsake
My native wood for gloomy walls;
The silver stream, the limpid lake
For musty books and college halls.

"A little could my wants supply—
Can wealth and honor give me more;
Or, will the sylvan god deny
The humble treat he gave before?

"Let seraphs gain the bright abode,
And heaven's sublimest mansions see—
I only bow to Nature's God—
The land of shades will do for me.

"These dreadful secrets of the sky
Alarm my soul with chilling fear—
Do planets in their orbits fly?
And is the earth, indeed, a sphere?

"Let planets still their course pursue,
And comets to the Center run—
In Him my faithful friend I view,
The image of my God—the Sun.

"Where Nature's ancient forests grow,
And mingled laurel never fades,
My heart is fixed;—and I must go
To die among my native shades."

He spoke and to the western springs,
(His gown discharged, his money spent,
His blanket tied with yellow strings,)
The shepherd of the forest went.

SUGGESTED ADDITIONAL READINGS

"The Dying Indian: Tomo-Chequi"
"The American Village"
"Verses Written on Leaving a Great House of Much Ceremony"
Miscellaneous Works

SELECTED REFERENCE

Calverton, Victor F. "Philip Freneau: Apostle of Freedom." *Modern Monthly*, 7 (1933), 533–46.

PROJECTS AND PROBLEMS

Timothy Dwight, Freneau's contemporary, recognized slavery as an ugly blemish on the romantic picture of America he presented in his poetry. Compare Freneau's "To Sir Toby" with Part II of Dwight's *Greenfield Hill.*

See *Miscellaneous Works* for Freneau's many essays on Indians. Is his poetry or his prose more effective in criticizing white mistreatment of the Indian?

In connection with Freneau's "The Indian Student," consider the career of Samson Occum, the Indian schoolmaster and minister whose *Sermon Preached at the Execution of Moses Paul, an Indian,* was published in 1772. Take into account also Elias Boudinot, a full-blooded Cherokee educated at Andover Theological Seminary, who protested eloquently against the eviction of the Cherokees from their Georgia lands and died in 1839 at the hands of young Indians who resented his white ways. See "An Address to the Whites" in *The Dark and Tangled Path: Race in America* (1971), ed. by David D. Anderson and Robert L. Wright.

ROYALL TYLER
(1757–1826)

More successful as dramatist than as novelist, Royall Tyler is best known for *The Contrast* (1787), a social comedy that continues to please audiences as a stage production. This selection is from *The Algerine Captive* (1797), a picaresque novel about a physician who witnesses slavery in the South before becoming a surgeon on a vessel engaged in the slave trade. Captured by pirates and sold in Algiers, he spends six years in the torments of servitude. The brief verses preceding Tyler's chapter headings are omitted in the selection.

A BLACK SOUL IN A WHITE BODY

... The day after our arrival at Cacongo, several Portuguese and negro merchants, hardly distinguishable however by their manners, employments, or complexions, came to confer with the captain about the purchase of our cargo of slaves. They contracted to deliver him two hundred and fifty head of slaves in fifteen days' time. To hear these men converse upon the purchase of human beings, with the same indifference, and nearly in the same language, as if they were contracting for so many head of cattle or swine, shocked me exceedingly. But when I suffered my imagination to rove to the habitation of these victims to this infamous cruel commerce, and fancied that I saw the peaceful husbandman dragged from his native farm, the fond husband torn from the embraces of his beloved wife, the mother from her babes, the tender child from the arms of its parent, and all the tender endearing ties of natural and social affection rended by the hand of avaricious violence, my heart sunk within me. I execrated myself for even the involuntary part I bore in this execrable traffic: I thought of my native land, and blushed. When the captain kindly inquired of me how many slaves I thought my privilege in the ship entitled me to transport for my adventure, I rejected my privilege with horror, and declared I would sooner suffer servitude than purchase a slave. This observation was received in the great cabin with repeated bursts of laughter, and excited many a stroke of coarse ridicule. Captain Russell observed, that he would not insist upon my using my privilege if I had so much of the yankee about me. Here is my clerk, Ned Randolph, will jump at the chance, though the rogue has been rather unlucky in the trade. Out of five-and-twenty negroes he purchased, he never carried but one alive to port, and that poor devil was broken-winded; and he was obliged to sell him for half price in Antigua.

Punctual to the day of the delivery, the contractors appeared, and brought with them about one hundred and fifty negroes—men, women, and children. The men were fastened together in pairs by a bar of iron, with a collar to receive the neck at each extremity; a

192

long pole was passed over their shoulder, and between each two was bound by a staple and ring, through which the pole was thrust, and thus twenty, and sometimes thirty, were connected together; while their conductors incessantly applied the scourge to those who loitered, or sought to strangle themselves by lifting their feet from the ground in despair; which sometimes had been successfully attempted. The women and children were bound with cords, and driven forward by the whip. When they arrived at the factory the men were unloosed from the poles, but still chained in pairs, and turned into strong cells built for the purpose. The dumb sorrow of some, the phrensy of others, the sobbings and tears of the children, and shrieks of the women, when they were presented to our captain, so affected me, that I was hastening from this scene of barbarity on board the ship, when I was called by the mate, and discovered, to my surprise and horror, that, by my station in the ship, I had a principal and active part of this inhuman transaction imposed upon me. As surgeon, it was my duty to inspect the bodies of the slaves, to see, as the captain expressed himself, that our owners were not shammed off with unsound flesh. In this inspection I was assisted by Randolph the clerk, and two stout sailors. It was transacted with all that unfeeling insolence which wanton barbarity can inflict upon defenceless wretchedness. The man, the affrighted child, the modest matron, and the timid virgin, were alike exposed to this severe scrutiny, equally insulting to humanity and common decency.

I cannot even now reflect on this transaction without shuddering. I have deplored my conduct with tears of anguish; and I pray a merciful God, the common parent of the great family of the universe, who hath made of one flesh and one blood all nations of the earth, that the miseries, the insults, and cruel woundings, I afterwards received when a slave myself, may expiate for the inhumanity I was necessitated to exercise towards these MY BRETHREN OF THE HUMAN RACE.

CHAP. XXXI
ARGUMENT:
TREATMENT OF THE SLAVES ON BOARD THE SHIP.

Of one hundred and fifty Africans, we rejected seventeen as not merchantable. While I was doubting which to lament most—those who were about being precipitated into all the miseries of an American slavery, or those whom we had rejected as too wretched for slaves—captain Russell was congratulating the slave-contractors upon the immense good luck they had in not suffering more by this lot of human creatures. I understood that, what from wounds received by some of these miserable creatures at their capture, or in their violent struggles for liberty, or attempts at suicide, and what with the fatigue of a long journey, partly over the burning sands of a sultry climate, it was usual to estimate the loss in the passage to the sea-shore at twenty-five in a hundred.

No sooner was the purchase completed, than these wretched Africans were transported in herds aboard the ship, and immediately precipitated between decks, where a strong chain, attached to a staple in the lower deck, was rivetted to the bar before described; and then the men were chained in pairs and hand-cuffed, and two sailors with cutlasses guarded every twenty; while the women and children were tied together in pairs with ropes, and obliged to supply the men with provisions and the slush-bucket; or, if the young women were released, it was only to gratify the brutal lust of the sailors: for though I cannot say I ever was witness to an actual rape, yet the frequent shrieks of these forlorn females in the berths of the seamen left me little charity to doubt of the repeated commission of that degrading crime. The eve after we had received the slaves on board, all hands were piped on deck, and ordered to assist in manufacturing and knotting cat-o'nine-tails, the application of which, I was informed, was always necessary to bring the slaves to their appetite. The night after they came on board was spent by these wretched people in sobbings, groans, tears, and the most heart-rending bursts of sorrow and despair. The next morning all was still. Surprised by this unexpected silence, I almost hoped that Providence, in pity to these her miserable children, had permitted some kindly suffocation to put a period to their anguish. It was neither novel nor unexpected to the ship's crew. It is only the dumb fit come on, cried every one: we will cure them. After breakfast, the whole ship's crew went between decks, and carried with them the provisions for the slaves, which they one and all refused to eat. A more affecting group of misery was never seen. These injured Africans, preferring death to slavery, or perhaps buoyed above the fear of dissolution by their religion, which taught them to look with an eye of faith to a country beyond the grave, where they should again meet those friends and relatives from whose endearments they had been torn, and where no fiend should torment or Christian thirst for gold, had resolved to starve themselves, and every eye lowered the fixed resolve of this deadly intent. In vain were the men beaten. They refused to taste one mouthful; and, I believe, would have died under the operation, if the ingenious cruelty of the clerk, Randolph, had not suggested the plan of whipping the women and children in sight of the men; assuring the men they should be tormented until all had eaten. What the torments exercised on the bodies of these brave Africans failed to produce, the feelings of nature effected. The negro, who could undauntedly expire under the anguish of the lash, could not view the agonies of his wife, child, or mother; and though repeatedly encouraged by these female sufferers to persevere unto death, unmoved by their torments, yet, though the *man* dared to die, the *father* relented, and in a few hours they had all eaten their provisions, *mingled with their tears.*

Our slave-dealers being unable to fulfil their contract, unless we tarried three weeks longer, our captain concluded to remove to some other market. We accordingly weighed anchor, steered for Benin, and anchored in the river Formosa, where we took in one hundred and fifteen more slaves. The same process in the purchase was pursued here; and though I frequently assured the captain, as a physician, that it was impracticable to stow fifty more persons between decks without endangering health and life, yet the whole hundred and fifteen were thrust, with the rest, between decks. The stagnant confined air of this infernal hole, rendered more deleterious by the stench of the fæces and violent perspiration of such a crowd, occasioned putrid diseases; and, even while in the mouth of the Formosa, it was usual to throw one or two negro corpses over every day. It was in vain that I remonstrated to the captain. In vain I enforced the necessity of more commodious berths, and a more free influx of air for the slaves. In vain I represented that these miserable people had been used to the vegetable diet and pure air of a country life; that at home they were remarkable for cleanliness of person, the very rites of their religion consisting, almost entirely, in frequent ablutions. The captain was by this time prejudiced against me. He observed that he did not doubt my skill, and would be bound by my advice, as to the health of those on board his ship, when he found I was actuated by the interest of the owners; but he feared that I was now moved by some *yankee nonsense about humanity.*

Randolph the clerk blamed me in plain terms. He said he had made seven African voyages with as good surgeons as I was; and that it was their common practice, when an infectious disorder prevailed among the slaves, to make critical search for all those who had the slightest symptoms of it, or whose habits of body inclined them to it; to tie them up and cast them over the ship's side together, and thus at one dash to purify the ship. *What signifies,* added he, *the lives of the black devils? They love to die. You cannot please them better than by chucking them into the water.*

When we stood out to sea, the rolling of the vessel brought on the sea sickness, which increased the filth: the weather being rough, we were obliged to close some of the ports which ventilated the space between decks, and death raged dreadfully among the slaves. Above two thirds were diseased. It was affecting to observe the ghastly smile on the countenance of the dying African, as if rejoicing to escape the cruelty of his oppressors. I noticed one man, who gathered all his strength, and in one last effort spoke with great emphasis, and expired. I understood by the linguist, that with his dying breath he invited his wife and a boy and girl to follow him quickly, and slake their thirst with him at the cool streams of the fountain of their Great Father, beyond the reach of the wild white beasts. The captain was now alarmed for the success of his voyage; and, upon my urging the necessity of landing the slaves, he ordered the ship about, and we anchored near an uninhabited part of the Gold Coast—I conjecture, not far from Cape St. Paul.

Tents were erected on the shore, and the sick landed. Under my direction they recovered surprisingly. It was affecting to see the effect gentle usage had upon these hitherto sullen obstinate people. As I had the sole direction of the hospital, they looked on me as the source of this sudden transition from the filth and rigour of the ship to the cleanliness and kindness of the shore. Their gratitude was excessive. When they recovered so far as to walk out, happy was he who could, by picking a few berries, gathering the wild fruits of the country, or doing any menial services, manifest his affection for me.

Our linguist has told me, he has often heard them behind the bushes praying to their God for my prosperity, and asking him with earnestness, why he put my good *black* soul into a *white* body. . . .

SELECTED REFERENCES

Bontemps, Arna, ed. *Great Slave Narratives* (1969).
Cowie, Alexander. *The Rise of the American Novel* (1948).

PROJECTS AND PROBLEMS

Compare the middle passage scenes in Tyler's novel with those in *The Interesting Narrative of the Life of Olaudah Equiano, or Gustavus Vassa, the African,* first published in 1789. In his autobiography, a document useful to antislavery forces in both England and America, Equiano gives a vivid account of being kidnapped from his home in Nigeria as a boy and shipped to slavery in the West Indies.

In *Redburn,* Herman Melville describes the character and sufferings of hundreds of Irish immigrants who are steerage passengers on Redburn's ship on the voyage from Liverpool to New York. Compare Melville and Tyler as humanitarians and social critics on the basis of their middle passage scenes.

Compare Tyler's portrait of a Jewish merchant in *The Algerine Captive* with Charles Brockden Brown's treatment of Achsa Fielding in *Arthur Mervyn.*

CHARLES BROCKDEN BROWN
(1771–1810)

America's first professional writer, Charles Brockden
Brown was greatly influenced by William Godwin,
father of Mary Shelley and exponent of radical political
and philosophical views. Brown's four principal novels
are in the tradition of the Gothic romance and confuse
modern readers with their unconventional ideas and
extraordinary narrative devices. Earlier, in *Alcuin: A
Dialogue,* he argued for women's rights. "Portrait of an
Emigrant" is from *The Monthly Magazine and American
Review,* June, 1799.

PORTRAIT OF AN EMIGRANT
Extracted from a Letter

I called, as you desired, on Mrs. K———. We had considerable
conversation. Knowing, as you do, my character and her's, you may
be somewhat inquisitive as to the subject of our conversation. You
may readily suppose that my inquiries were limited to domestic and
every–day incidents. The state of her own family, and her servants
and children being discussed, I proceeded to inquire into the condition of her neighbours. It is not in large cities as it is in villages.
Those whose education does not enable and accustom them to look
abroad, to investigate the character and actions of beings of a distant age and country, are generally attentive to what is passing
under their own eye. Mrs. K——— never reads, not even a newspaper. She is unacquainted with what happened before she was born.
She is equally a stranger to the events that are passing in distant nations, and to those which ingross the attention and shake the passions of the statesmen and politicians of her own country; but her
mind, nevertheless, is far from being torpid or inactive. She specu-
lates curiously and even justly on the objects that occur within her
narrow sphere.

Were she the inhabitant of a village, she would be mistress of the
history and character of every family within its precincts; but being
in a large city,[1] her knowledge is confined chiefly to her immediate
neighbours; to those who occupy the house on each side and opposite. I will not stop to inquire into the reason of this difference in the
manners of villagers and citizens. The fact has often been remarked,
though seldom satisfactorily explained. I shall merely repeat the dialogue which took place on my inquiry into the state of the family
inhabiting the house on the right hand and next to her's.

"M'Culey," said she, "who used to live there, is gone."

"Indeed! and who has taken his place?"

"A Frenchman and his wife. His wife, I suppose her to be, though
he is a man of fair complexion, well formed, and of genteel appearance, and the woman is half negro. I suppose they would call her a

[1]Philadelphia. [Brown's note.]

199

mestee. They came last winter from the West-Indies, and miserably poor I believe; for when they came into this house they had scarcely any furniture besides a bed, and a chair or two, and a pine table. They shut up the lower rooms, and lived altogether in the two rooms in the second story."

"Of whom does the family consist?"

"The man and woman, and a young girl, whom I first took for their daughter, but I afterwards found she was an orphan child, whom, shortly after their coming here, they found wandering in the streets; and, though poor enough themselves, took her under their care."

"How do they support themselves?"

"The man is employed in the compting-house of a French merchant of this city. What is the exact sort of employment, I do not know, but it allows him to spend a great deal of his time at home. The woman is an actress in Lailson's pantomimes. In the winter she scarcely ever went out in the day-time, but now that the weather is mild and good she walks out a great deal."

"Can you describe their mode of life, what they eat and drink, and how they spend their time?"

"I believe I can. Most that they do can be seen from our windows and yard, and all that they say can be heard. In the morning every thing is still till about ten o'clock. Till that hour they lie a-bed. The first sign that they exist, is given by the man, who comes half dressed, to the back window; and lolling out of it, smokes two or three segars, and sometimes talks to a dog that lies on the out-side of the kitchen door. After some time passed in this manner he goes into the room over the kitchen, takes a loaf of bread from the closet, and pours out a tumbler of wine; with these he returns to the front room, but begins as soon as he has hold of them, to gnaw at one and sip from the other. This constitutes their breakfast. In half an hour they both re-appear at the window. They throw out crums of bread to the dog, who stands below with open mouth to receive it; and talk sometimes to him and sometimes to each other. Their tongues run incessantly; frequently they talk together in the loudest and shrillest tone imaginable. I thought, at first, they were quarrelsome; but every now and then they burst into laughter, and it was plain that they were in perfect good humour with each other.

"About twelve o'clock the man is dressed, and goes out upon his business. He returns at three. In the mean time the lady employs herself in washing every part of her body, and putting on a muslin dress, perfectly brilliant and clean. Then she either lolls at the window, and sings without intermission, or plays on a guitar. She is certainly a capital performer and singer. No attention is paid to house or furniture. As to rubbing tables, and sweeping and washing floors, these are never thought of. Their house is in a sad condition, but she spares no pains to make her person and dress clean.

"The man has scarcely entered the house, when he is followed by a black fellow, with bare head and shirt tucked up at his elbows, carrying on his head a tray covered with a white napkin. This is their dinner, and is brought from *Simonet's*. After dinner the man takes his flute, on which he is very skilful; and the woman either sings or plays in concert till evening approaches: some visitants then arrive, and they all go out together to walk. We hear no more of them till next morning."

"What becomes of the girl all this time?"

"She eats, sings, dresses, and walks with them. She often comes into our house, generally at meal times; if she spies any thing she likes, she never conceals her approbation. 'O my, how good *dat* must be! Me wish me had some: will you *gif* me some?' She is a pretty harmless little thing, and one cannot refuse what she asks.

"Next day after they came into this house, the girl, in the morning, while our servant was preparing breakfast, entered the kitchen —'O my!' said she to me, 'what you call dem tings?'

'Buckwheat cakes.'

'Ahah! buckawit cake! O my! how good dey must be! Me likes— will you give me one?'

"Next morning she came again, and we happened to be making *muffins*. 'O my!' cried she, 'you be always baking and baking! What you call dem dere?'

'Muffins.'

'Mofeen? O my! me wish for some, me do.'

"Afterwards she was pretty regular in her visits. She was modest, notwithstanding; and, seeming to be half-starved, we gave her entertainment as often as she claimed it."

"Are not these people very happy?"

"Very happy. When together they are for ever chattering and laughing, or playing and singing in concert. How the man is employed when separate we do not certainly know; but the woman, it seems, is continually singing, and her hands, if not employed in adorning her own person, are plying the guitar. I am apt to think the French are the only people that know how to live. These people, though exiles and strangers, and subsisting on scanty and precarious funds, move on smoothly and at ease. Household cares they know not. They breakfast upon bread and wine, without the ceremony of laying table, and arranging platters and cups. From the trouble of watching and directing servants they are equally exempt. Their cookery is performed abroad. Their clothes are washed in the same way. The lady knows no manual employment but the grateful one of purifying and embellishing her own person. The intervals are consumed in the highest as well as purest sensual enjoyments, in music, in which she appears to be an adept, and of which she is passionately enamoured. When the air is serene and bland, she repairs to the public walks, with muslin handkerchief in one hand, and particoloured *parasol* in the other. She is always accompanied by men anxious to please her, busy in supplying her with amusing topics, and listening with complacency and applause to her gay effusions and her ceaseless volubility.

"I have since taken some pains to discover the real situation of this family. I find that the lady was the heiress of a large estate in St. Domingo, that she spent her youth in France, where she received a polished education, and where she married her present companion, who was then in possession of rank and fortune, but whom the revolution has reduced to indigence. The insurrection in St. Domingo destroyed their property in that island. They escaped with difficulty to these shores in 1793, and have since subsisted in various modes and places, frequently pinched by extreme poverty, and sometimes obliged to solicit public charity; but retaining, in every fortune, and undiminished, their propensity to talk, laugh and sing— their flute and their guitar."

Nothing is more ambiguous than the motives that stimulate men to action. These people's enjoyments are unquestionably great. They are innocent: they are compatible, at least, with probity and wisdom, if they are not the immediate fruits of it. Constitutional gaiety may account for these appearances; but as they may flow, in one case, from the absence of reflection and foresight, they may likewise, in another instance, be the product of justice and benevolence.

It is our duty to make the best of our condition; to snatch the good that is within our reach, and to nourish no repinings on account of what is unattainable. The gratifications of sense, of conjugal union, and of social intercourse, are among the highest in the scale; and these are as much in the possession of *de Lisle* and his wife, as of the most opulent and luxuriant members of the community.

As to mean habitation and scanty furniture, their temper or their reason enables them to look upon these things as trifles. They are not among those who witnessed their former prosperity, and their friends and associates are unfortunate like themselves. Instead of humiliation and contempt, adversity has probably given birth to sympathy and mutual respect.

His profession is not laborious; and her's, though not respectable according to our notions, is easy and amusing. Her life scarcely produces any intermission of recreation and enjoyment. Few instances of more unmingled and uninterrupted felicity can be found; and yet these people have endured, and continue to endure, most of the evils which the imagination is accustomed to regard with most horror; and which would create ceaseless anguish in beings fashioned on the model of my character, or of yours. Let you and I grow wise by the contemplation of their example.

SUGGESTED ADDITIONAL READINGS

Alcuin: A Dialogue
Ormond
Arthur Mervyn
Edgar Huntly

SELECTED REFERENCES

Bennett, Charles E. "Charles Brockden Brown's 'Portrait of an Emigrant.'" *CLA Journal,* 14 (1970), 87–90.

Kimball, Arthur G. "Savages and Savagism: Brockden Brown's Dramatic Irony." *Studies in Romanticism,* 6 (1967), 214–25.

Morris, Mabel. "Charles Brockden Brown and the American Indian." *American Literature,* 18 (1946), 244–47.

Ringe, Donald A. *Charles Brockden Brown* (1966).

PROJECTS AND PROBLEMS

Does Brown use a stereotype of the Jew in *Arthur Mervyn?* If so, for what literary purpose?

Does the incidental treatment of the Indian in Brown's *Edgar Huntly* agree with that in *Arthur Mervyn?* Is the incidental treatment of blacks in *Ormond* stereotyped or otherwise?

WASHINGTON IRVING
(1783–1859)

The first American author to win a reputation in Europe was Washington Irving whose stories about Rip Van Winkle and the headless horseman have delighted generations of readers. In his works there are treatments of minorities ranging from the Dutch burghers of the Catskill region to the Indians beyond the Rocky Mountains. "Philip of Pokanoket" is from his most successful work, *The Sketch Book of Geoffrey Crayon, Gent.* (1819–20). "The Creole Village," first published in 1837, is one of the sketches in *Wolfert's Roost and Other Papers* (1855).

PHILIP OF POKANOKET
An Indian Memoir

As monumental bronze unchanged his look:
A soul that pity touch'd, but never shook:
Train'd from his tree-rock'd cradle to his bier,
The fierce extremes of good and ill to brook
Impassive—fearing but the shame of fear—
A stoic of the woods—a man without a tear.

CAMPBELL

It is to be regretted that those early writers, who treated of the discovery and settlement of America, have not given us more particular and candid accounts of the remarkable characters that flourished in savage life. The scanty anecdotes which have reached us are full of peculiarity and interest; they furnish us with nearer glimpses of human nature, and show what man is in a comparatively primitive state, and what he owes to civilization. There is something of the charm of discovery in lighting upon these wild and unexplored tracts of human nature; in witnessing, as it were, the native growth of moral sentiment, and perceiving those generous and romantic qualities which have been artificially cultivated by society, vegetating in spontaneous hardihood and rude magnificence.

In civilized life, where the happiness, and indeed almost the existence, of man depends so much upon the opinion of his fellow-men, he is constantly acting a studied part. The bold and peculiar traits of native character are refined away, or softened down by the levelling influence of what is termed good breeding; and he practises so many petty deceptions, and affects so many generous sentiments, for the purposes of popularity, that it is difficult to distinguish his real from his artificial character. The Indian, on the contrary, free from the restraints and refinements of polished life, and, in a great degree, a solitary and independent being, obeys the impulses of his inclination or the dictates of his judgment; and thus the attributes of his nature, being freely indulged, grow singly great and striking. Society is like a lawn, where every roughness is smoothed, every bramble eradi-

206

cated, and where the eye is delighted by the smiling verdure of a velvet surface; he, however, who would study nature in its wildness and variety, must plunge into the forest, must explore the glen, must stem the torrent, and dare the precipice.

These reflections arose on casually looking through a volume of early colonial history, wherein are recorded, with great bitterness, the outrages of the Indians, and their wars with the settlers of New England. It is painful to perceive even from these partial narratives, how the footsteps of civilization may be traced in the blood of the aborigines; how easily the colonists were moved to hostility by the lust of conquest; how merciless and exterminating was their warfare. The imagination shrinks at the idea, how many intellectual beings were hunted from the earth, how many brave and noble hearts of nature's sterling coinage, were broken down and trampled in the dust.

Such was the fate of PHILIP OF POKANOKET, an Indian warrior, whose name was once a terror throughout Massachusetts and Connecticut. He was the most distinguished of a number of contemporary Sachems who reigned over the Pequods, the Narragansets, the Wampanoags, and the other eastern tribes, at the time of the first settlement of New England; a band of native untaught heroes, who made the most generous struggle of which human nature is capable; fighting to the last gasp in the cause of their country, without a hope of victory or a thought of renown. Worthy of an age of poetry, and fit subjects for local story and romantic fiction, they have left scarcely any authentic traces on the page of history, but stalk, like gigantic shadows, in the dim twilight of tradition.[1]

When the pilgrims, as the Plymouth settlers are called by their descendants, first took refuge on the shores of the New World, from the religious persecutions of the Old, their situation was to the last degree gloomy and disheartening. Few in number, and that number rapidly perishing away through sickness and hardships; surrounded by a howling wilderness and savage tribes; exposed to the rigors of an almost arctic winter and the vicissitudes of an ever-shifting climate; their minds were filled with doleful forebodings, and nothing preserved them from sinking into despondency but the strong ex-

---

[1]While correcting the proof-sheets of this article, the author is informed that a celebrated English poet has nearly finished an heroic poem on the story of Philip of Pokanoket. [Irving's note.]

citement of religious enthusiasm. In this forlorn situation they were visited by Massasoit, chief Sagamore of the Wampanoags, a powerful chief, who reigned over a great extent of country. Instead of taking advantage of the scanty number of the strangers, and expelling them from his territories, into which they had intruded, he seemed at once to conceive for them a generous friendship, and extended towards them the rites of primitive hospitality. He came early in the spring to their settlement of New Plymouth, attended by a mere handful of followers, entered into a solemn league of peace and amity; sold them a portion of the soil, and promised to secure for them the good-will of his savage allies. Whatever may be said of Indian perfidy, it is certain that the integrity and good faith of Massasoit have never been impeached. He continued a firm and magnanimous friend of the white men; suffering them to extend their possessions, and to strengthen themselves in the land; and betraying no jealousy of their increasing power and prosperity. Shortly before his death he came once more to New Plymouth, with his son Alexander, for the purpose of renewing the covenant of peace, and of securing it to his posterity.

At this conference he endeavored to protect the religion of his forefathers from the encroaching zeal of the missionaries; and stipulated that no further attempt should be made to draw off his people from their ancient faith; but, finding the English obstinately opposed to any such condition, he mildly relinquished the demand. Almost the last act of his life was to bring his two sons, Alexander and Philip (as they had been named by the English), to the residence of a principal settler, recommending mutual kindness and confidence; and entreating that the same love and amity which had existed between the white men and himself might be continued afterwards with his children. The good old Sachem died in peace, and was happily gathered to his fathers before sorrow came upon his tribe; his children remained behind to experience the ingratitude of white men.

His eldest son, Alexander, succeeded him. He was of a quick and impetuous temper, and proudly tenacious of his hereditary rights and dignity. The intrusive policy and dictatorial conduct of the strangers excited his indignation; and he beheld with uneasiness their exterminating wars with the neighboring tribes. He was doomed soon to incur their hostility, being accused of plotting with the Narragansets to rise against the English and drive them from the land. It is impossible to say whether this accusation was warranted by facts or was grounded on mere suspicion. It is evident, however, by the violent and overbearing measures of the settlers, that they had by this time begun to feel conscious of the rapid increase of their power, and to grow harsh and inconsiderate in their treatment of the natives. They despatched an armed force to seize upon Alexander, and to bring him before their courts. He was traced to his woodland haunts, and surprised at a hunting-house, where he was reposing with a band of his followers, unarmed, after the toils of the chase. The suddenness of his arrest, and the outrage offered to his sovereign dignity, so preyed upon the irascible feelings of this proud savage, as to throw him into a raging fever. He was permitted to return home, on condition of sending his son as a pledge for his reappearance; but the blow he had received was fatal, and before he had reached his home he fell a victim to the agonies of a wounded spirit.

The successor of Alexander was Metacomet, or King Philip, as he was called by the settlers, on account of his lofty spirit and ambitious temper. These, together with his well-known energy and enterprise, had rendered him an object of great jealousy and apprehension, and he was accused of having always cherished a secret and implacable hostility towards the whites. Such may very probably, and very naturally, have been the case. He considered them as originally but mere intruders into the country, who had presumed upon indulgence, and were extending an influence baneful to savage life. He saw the whole race of his countrymen melting before them from the face of the earth; their territories slipping from their hands, and their tribes becoming feeble, scattered, and dependent. It may be said that the soil was originally purchased by the settlers; but who does not know the nature of Indian purchases, in the early periods of colonization? The Europeans always made thrifty bargains through their superior adroitness in traffic; and they gained vast accessions of territory by easily provoked hostilities. An uncultivated savage is never a nice inquirer into the refinements of law, by which an injury may be gradually and legally inflicted. Leading facts are all by which he judges; and it was enough for Philip to know that before the intrusion of the Europeans his countrymen were lords of the soil, and that now they were becoming vagabonds in the land of their fathers.

But whatever may have been his feelings of general hostility, and his particular indignation at the treatment of his brother, he suppressed them for the present, renewed the contract with the settlers, and resided peaceably for many years at Pokanoket, or, as it was called by the English, Mount Hope,[1] the ancient seat of dominion of his tribe. Suspicions, however, which were at first but vague and indefinite, began to acquire form and substance; and he was at length charged with attempting to instigate the various Eastern tribes to rise at once, and, by a simultaneous effort, to throw off the yoke of their oppressors. It is difficult at this distant period to assign the proper credit due to these early accusations against the Indians. There was a proneness to suspicion, and an aptness to acts of violence, on the part of the whites, that gave weight and importance to every idle tale. Informers abounded where tale-bearing met with countenance and reward, and the sword was readily unsheathed when its success was certain, and it carved out empire.

The only positive evidence on record against Philip is the accusation of one Sausaman, a renegado Indian, whose natural cunning had been quickened by a partial education which he had received among the settlers. He changed his faith and his allegiance two or three times, with a facility that evinced the looseness of his principles. He had acted for some time as Philip's confidential secretary and counsellor, and had enjoyed his bounty and protection. Finding, however, that the clouds of adversity were gathering round his patron, he abandoned his service and went over to the whites; and, in order to gain their favor, charged his former benefactor with plotting against their safety. A rigorous investigation took place. Philip and several of his subjects submitted to be examined, but nothing was proved against them. The settlers, however, had now gone too far to retract; they had previously determined that Philip was a dangerous neighbor; they had publicly evinced their distrust; and had done enough to insure his hostility; according, therefore, to the usual mode of reasoning in these cases, his destruction had become necessary to their security. Sausaman, the treacherous informer, was shortly afterwards found dead, in a pond, having fallen a victim to the venge-

[1] Now Bristol, Rhode Island. [Irving's note.]

ance of his tribe. Three Indians, one of whom was a friend and counsellor of Philip, were apprehended and tried, and, on the testimony
of one very questionable witness, were condemned and executed as
murderers.

This treatment of his subjects, and ignominious punishment of his
friend, outraged the pride and exasperated the passions of Philip.
The bolt which had fallen thus at his very feet awakened him to the
gathering storm, and he determined to trust himself no longer in the
power of the white men. The fate of his insulted and broken-hearted
brother still rankled in his mind; and he had a further warning in the
tragical story of Miantonimo, a great Sachem of the Narragansets,
who, after manfully facing his accusers before a tribunal of the colonists, exculpating himself from a charge of conspiracy, and receiving
assurances of amity, had been perfidiously despatched at their in-
stigation. Philip, therefore, gathered his fighting men about him;
persuaded all strangers that he could to join his cause; sent the
women and children to the Narragansets for safety; and wherever he
appeared, was continually surrounded by armed warriors.

When the two parties were thus in a state of distrust and irrita-
tion, the least spark was sufficient to set them in a flame. The Indians, having weapons in their hands, grew mischievous, and committed various petty depredations. In one of their maraudings a warrior
was fired on and killed by a settler. This was the signal for open hostilities; the Indians pressed to revenge the death of their comrade,
and the alarm of war resounded through the Plymouth colony.

In the early chronicles of these dark and melancholy times we
meet with many indications of the diseased state of the public mind.
The gloom of religious abstraction, and the wildness of their situation, among trackless forests and savage tribes, had disposed the
colonists to superstitious fancies, and had filled their imaginations
with the frightful chimeras of witchcraft and spectrology. They were
much given also to a belief in omens. The troubles with Philip and
his Indians were preceded, we are told, by a variety of those awful
warnings which forerun great and public calamities. The perfect
form of an Indian bow appeared in the air at New Plymouth, which
was looked upon by the inhabitants as a "prodigious apparition." At
Hadley, Northampton, and other towns in their neighborhood, "was
heard the report of a great piece of ordnance, with a shaking of the

earth and a considerable echo."[1] Others were alarmed on a still, sunshiny morning by the discharge of guns and muskets; bullets seemed to whistle past them, and the noise of drums resounded in the air, seeming to pass away to the westward; others fancied that they heard the galloping of horses over their heads; and certain monstrous births, which took place about the time, filled the superstitious in some towns with doleful forebodings. Many of these portentous sights and sounds may be ascribed to natural phenomena: to the northern lights which occur vividly in those latitudes; the meteors which explode in the air; the casual rushing of a blast through the top branches of the forest; the crash of fallen trees or disrupted rocks; and to those other uncouth sounds and echoes which will sometimes strike the ear so strangely amidst the profound stillness of woodland solitudes. These may have startled some melancholy imaginations, may have been exaggerated by the love for the marvellous, and listened to with that avidity with which we devour whatever is fearful and mysterious. The universal currency of these superstitious fancies, and the grave record made of them by one of the learned men of the day, are strongly characteristic of the times.

The nature of the contest that ensued was such as too often distinguishes the warfare between civilized men and savages. On the part of the whites it was conducted with superior skill and success; but with a wastefulness of the blood, and a disregard of the natural rights of their antagonists; on the part of the Indians it was waged with the desperation of men fearless of death, and who had nothing to expect from peace but humiliation, dependence, and decay.

The events of the war are transmitted to us by a worthy clergyman of the time; who dwells with horror and indignation on every hostile act of the Indians, however justifiable, whilst he mentions with applause the most sanguinary atrocities of the whites. Philip is reviled as a murderer and a traitor; without considering that he was a true-born prince, gallantly fighting at the head of his subjects to avenge the wrongs of his family; to retrieve the tottering power of his line; and to deliver his native land from the oppression of usurping strangers.

The project of a wide and simultaneous revolt, if such had really been formed, was worthy of a capacious mind, and, had it not been

[1]The Rev. Increase Mather's History, [Irving's note.]

prematurely discovered, might have been overwhelming in its consequences. The war that actually broke out was but a war of detail, a mere succession of casual exploits and unconnected enterprises. Still it sets forth the military genius and daring prowess of Philip; and wherever, in the prejudiced and passionate narrations that have been given of it, we can arrive at simple facts, we find him displaying a vigorous mind, a fertility of expedients, a contempt of suffering and hardship, and an unconquerable resolution that command our sympathy and applause.

Driven from his paternal domains at Mount Hope, he threw himself into the depths of those vast and tractless forests that skirted the settlements, and were almost impervious to anything but a wild beast, or an Indian. Here he gathered together his forces, like a storm accumulating its stores of mischief in the bosom of the thunder-cloud, and would suddenly emerge at a time and place least expected, carrying havoc and dismay into the villages. There were now and then indications of these impending ravages, that filled the minds of the colonists with awe and apprehension. The report of a distant gun would perhaps be heard from the solitary woodland, where there was known to be no white man; the cattle which had been wandering in the woods would sometimes return home wounded; or an Indian or two would be seen lurking about the skirts of the forests, and suddenly disappearing; as the lightning will sometimes be seen playing silently about the edge of the cloud that is brewing up the tempest.

Though sometimes pursued and even surrounded by the settlers, yet Philip as often escaped almost miraculously from their toils, and plunging into the wilderness, would be lost to all search or inquiry, until he again emerged at some far distant quarter, laying the country desolate. Among his strongholds were the great swamps or morasses, which extend in some parts of New England; composed of loose bogs of deep black mud; perplexed with thickets, brambles, rank weeds, the shattered and mouldering trunks of fallen trees, overshadowed by lugubrious hemlocks. The uncertain footing and the tangled mazes of these shaggy wilds rendered them almost impenetrable to the white man, though the Indian could thrid their labyrinths with the agility of a deer. Into one of these, the great swamp of Pocasset Neck, was Philip once driven with a band of his followers. The English did not dare to pursue him, fearing to venture into these dark and frightful recesses, where they might perish in fens and miry pits, or be shot down by lurking foes. They therefore invested the entrance to the Neck, and began to build a fort, with the thought of starving out the foe; but Philip and his warriors wafted themselves on a raft over an arm of the sea, in the dead of the night, leaving the women and children behind; and escaped away to the westward, kindling the flames of war among the tribes of Massachusetts and the Nipmuck country, and threatening the colony of Connecticut.

In this way Philip became a theme of universal apprehension. The mystery in which he was enveloped exaggerated his real terrors. He was an evil that walked in darkness, whose coming none could foresee, and against which none knew when to be on the alert. The whole country abounded with rumors and alarms. Philip seemed almost possessed of ubiquity; for, in whatever part of the widely extended frontier an irruption from the forest took place, Philip was said to be its leader. Many superstitious notions also were circulated concerning him. He was said to deal in necromancy, and to be attended by an old Indian witch or prophetess, whom he consulted, and who assisted him by her charms and incantations. This indeed was frequently the case with Indian chiefs; either through their own credulity, or to act upon that of their followers; and the influence of the prophet and the dreamer over Indian superstition has been fully evidenced in recent instances of savage warfare.

At the time that Philip effected his escape from Pocasset, his fortunes were in a desperate condition. His forces had been thinned by repeated fights, and he had lost almost the whole of his resources. In this time of adversity he found a faithful friend in Canonchet, chief Sachem of all the Narragansets. He was the son and heir of Miantonimo, the great Sachem who, as already mentioned, after an honorable acquittal of the charge of conspiracy, had been privately put to death at the perfidious instigations of the settlers. "He was the heir," says the old chronicler, "of all his father's pride and insolence, as well as of his malice towards the English";—he certainly was the heir of his insults and injuries, and the legitimate avenger of his murder. Though he had forborne to take an active part in this hopeless war, yet he received Philip and his broken forces with open arms, and gave them the most generous countenance and support. This at once drew upon him the hostility of the English; and it was determined to strike a signal blow that should involve both the Sachems in one common ruin. A great force was, therefore, gathered together from Massachusetts, Plymouth, and Connecticut, and was sent into the Narraganset country in the depth of winter, when the swamps, being frozen and leafless, could be traversed with comparative facility, and would no longer afford dark and impenetrable fastnesses to the Indians.

Apprehensive of attack, Canonchet had conveyed the greater part of his stores, together with the old, the infirm, the women and children of his tribe, to a strong fortress, where he and Philip had likewise drawn up the flower of their forces. This fortress, deemed by the Indians impregnable, was situated upon a rising mound, or kind of island, of five or six acres, in the midst of a swamp; it was constructed with a degree of judgment and skill vastly superior to what is usually displayed in Indian fortification, and indicative of the martial genius of these two chieftains.

Guided by a renegado Indian, the English penetrated through December snows, to this stronghold, and came upon the garrison by surprise. The fight was fierce and tumultuous. The assailants were repulsed in their first attack, and several of their bravest officers were shot down in the act of storming the fortress sword in hand. The assault was renewed with greater success. A lodgment was effected. The Indians were driven from one post to another. They disputed their ground inch by inch, fighting with the fury of despair. Most of their veterans were cut to pieces; and after a long and bloody battle, Philip and Canonchet, with a handful of surviving warriors, retreated from the fort, and took refuge in the thickets of the surrounding forest.

The victors set fire to the wigwams and the fort; the whole was soon in a blaze; many of the old men, the women, and the children perished in the flames. This last outrage overcame even the stoicism of the savage. The neighboring woods resounded with the yells of rage and despair, uttered by the fugitive warriors, as they beheld the destruction of their dwellings, and heard the agonizing cries of their wives and offspring. "The burning of the wigwams," says a contemporary writer, "the shrieks and cries of the women and children, and the yelling of the warriors, exhibited a most horrible and affecting scene, so that it greatly moved some of the soldiers." The same writer cautiously adds, "they were in *much doubt* then, and afterwards seriously inquired, whether burning their enemies alive could be consistent with humanity and the benevolent principles of the Gospel."[1]

The fate of the brave and generous Canonchet is worthy of particular mention: the last scene of his life is one of the noblest instances on record of Indian magnanimity.

Broken down in his power and resources by this signal defeat, yet faithful to his ally, and to the hapless cause which he had espoused, he rejected all overtures of peace, offered on condition of betraying Philip and his followers, and declared that "he would fight it out to the last man, rather than become a servant to the English." His home being destroyed; his country harassed and laid waste by the incursions of the conquerors; he was obliged to wander away to the banks of the Connecticut; where he formed a rallying point to the whole body of western Indians, and laid waste several of the English settlements.

Early in the spring he departed on a hazardous expedition, with only thirty chosen men, to penetrate to Seaconck, in the vicinity of Mount Hope, and to procure seed-corn to plant for the sustenance of his troops. This little band of adventurers had passed safely through the Pequod country, and were in the centre of the Narraganset, resting at some wigwams near Pawtucket River, when an alarm was given of an approaching enemy. Having but seven men by him at the time, Canonchet despatched two of them to the top of a neighboring hill, to bring intelligence of the foe.

Panic-struck by the appearance of a troop of English and Indians rapidly advancing, they fled in breathless terror past their chieftain, without stopping to inform him of the danger. Canonchet sent another scout, who did the same. He then sent two more, one of whom, hurrying back in confusion and affright, told him that the whole British army was at hand. Canonchet saw there was no choice but immediate flight. He attempted to escape round the hill, but was perceived and hotly pursued by the hostile Indians, and a few of

[1]MS. of the Rev. W. Ruggles. [Irving's note.]

the fleetest of the English. Finding the swiftest pursuer close upon his heels, he threw off, first his blanket, then his silver-laced coat and belt of peag, by which his enemies knew him to be Canonchet, and redoubled the eagerness of pursuit.

At length, in dashing through the river, his foot slipped upon a stone, and he fell so deep as to wet his gun. This accident so struck him with despair, that, as he afterwards confessed, "his heart and his bowels turned within him, and he became like a rotten stick, void of strength."

To such a degree was he unnerved, that, being seized by a Pequod Indian within a short distance of the river, he made no resistance, though a man of great vigor of body and boldness of heart. But on being made prisoner the whole pride of his spirit arose within him; and from that moment, we find, in the anecdotes given by his enemies, nothing but repeated flashes of elevated and prince-like heroism. Being questioned by one of the English who first came up with him, and who had not attained his twenty-second year, the proud-hearted warrior, looking with lofty contempt upon his youthful countenance, replied, "You are a child; you cannot understand matters of war; let your brother or your chief come,—him will I answer."

Though repeated offers were made to him of his life, on condition of submitting with his nation to the English, yet he rejected them with disdain, and refused to send any proposals of the kind to the great body of his subjects; saying, that he knew none of them would comply. Being reproached with his breach of faith towards the whites,—his boast that he would not deliver up a Wampanoag nor the paring of a Wampanoag's nail,—and his threat that he would burn the English alive in their houses,—he disdained to justify himself, haughtily answering that others were as forward for the war as himself, and "he desired to hear no more thereof."

So noble and unshaken a spirit, so true a fidelity to his cause and his friend, might have touched the feelings of the generous and the brave; but Canonchet was an Indian, a being towards whom war had no courtesy, humanity no law, religion no compassion;—he was condemned to die. The last words of him that are recorded are worthy the greatness of his soul. When sentence of death was passed upon him, he observed "that he liked it well, for he should die before his heart was soft, or he had spoken anything unworthy of himself." His enemies gave him the death of a soldier, for he was shot at Stoningham, by three young Sachems of his own rank.

The defeat at the Narraganset fortress, and the death of Canonchet, were fatal blows to the fortunes of King Philip. He made an ineffectual attempt to raise a head of war, by stirring up the Mohawks to take arms; but though possessed of the native talents of a statesman, his arts were counteracted by the superior arts of his enlightened enemies, and the terror of their warlike skill began to subdue the resolution of the neighboring tribes. The unfortunate chieftain saw himself daily stripped of power, and his ranks rapidly thinning around him. Some were suborned by the whites; others fell victims to hunger and fatigue, and to the frequent attacks by which they were harassed. His stores were all captured; his chosen friends were swept away from before his eyes; his uncle was shot down by his side; his sister was carried into captivity; and in one of his narrow escapes he was compelled to leave his beloved wife and only son to the mercy of the enemy. "His ruin," says the historian, "being thus gradually carried on, his misery was not prevented, but augmented thereby; being himself made acquainted with the sense and experimental feeling of the captivity of his children, loss of friends, slaughter of his subjects, bereavement of all family relations, and being stripped of all outward comforts, before his own life should be taken away."

To fill up the measure of his misfortunes, his own followers began to plot against his life, that by sacrificing him they might purchase dishonorable safety. Through treachery a number of his faithful adherents, the subjects of Wetamoe, an Indian princess of Pocasset, a near kinswoman and confederate of Philip, were betrayed into the hands of the enemy. Wetamoe was among them at the time, and attempted to make her escape by crossing a neighboring river: either exhausted by swimming, or starved by cold and hunger, she was found dead and naked near the water-side. But persecution ceased not at the grave. Even death, the refuge of the wretched, where the wicked commonly cease from troubling, was no protection to this outcast female, whose great crime was affectionate fidelity to her kinsman and her friend. Her corpse was the object of unmanly and dastardly vengeance; the head was severed from the body and set upon a pole, and was thus exposed at Taunton, to the view of her captive subjects. They immediately recognized the features of their unfortunate queen, and were so affected at this barbarous spectacle, that we are told they broke forth into the "most horrible and diabolical lamentations."

However Philip had borne up against the complicated miseries and misfortunes that surrounded him, the treachery of his followers seemed to wring his heart and reduce him to despondency. It is said that "he never rejoiced afterwards, nor had success in any of his designs." The spring of hope was broken,—the ardor of enterprise was extinguished,—he looked around, and all was danger and darkness; there was no eye to pity, nor any arm that could bring deliverance. With a scanty band of followers, who still remained true to his desperate fortunes, the unhappy Philip wandered back to the vicinity of Mount Hope, the ancient dwelling of his fathers. Here he lurked about, like a spectre, among the scenes of former power and prosperity, now bereft of home, of family and friend. There needs no better picture of his destitute and piteous situation than that furnished by the homely pen of the chronicler, who is unwarily enlisting the feelings of the reader in favor of the hapless warrior whom he reviles. "Philip," he says, "like a savage wild beast, having been hunted by the English forces through the woods, above a hundred miles backward and forward, at last was driven to his own den upon Mount Hope, where he retired, with a few of his best friends, into a swamp, which proved but a prison to keep him fast till the messengers of death came by divine permission to execute vengeance upon him."

Even in this last refuge of desperation and despair, a sullen grandeur gathers round his memory. We picture him to ourselves seated among his careworn followers, brooding in silence over his blasted fortunes, and acquiring a savage sublimity from the wildness and dreariness of his lurking-place. Defeated, but not dismayed—crushed to the earth, but not humiliated—he seemed to grow more haughty beneath disaster, and to experience a fierce satisfaction in draining the last dregs of bitterness. Little minds are tamed and subdued by misfortune; but great minds rise above it. The very idea of submission awakened the fury of Philip, and he smote to death one of his followers who proposed an expedient of peace. The brother of the victim made his escape, and in revenge betrayed the retreat of his chieftain. A body of white men and Indians were immediately despatched to the swamp where Philip lay crouched, glaring with fury and despair. Before he was aware of their approach, they had begun to surround him. In a little while he saw five of his trustiest followers laid dead at his feet; all resistance was vain; he rushed forth from his covert, and made a headlong attempt to escape, but was shot through the heart by a renegado Indian of his own nation.

Such is the scanty story of the brave, but unfortunate King Philip; persecuted while living, slandered and dishonored when dead. If, however, we consider even the prejudiced anecdotes furnished us by his enemies, we may perceive in them traces of amiable and lofty character sufficient to awaken sympathy for his fate, and respect for his memory. We find that, amidst all the harassing cares and ferocious passions of constant warfare, he was alive to the softer feelings of connubial love and paternal tenderness, and to the generous sentiment of friendship. The captivity of his "beloved wife and only son" are mentioned with exultation as causing him poignant misery: the death of any near friend is triumphantly recorded as a new blow on his sensibilities; but the treachery and desertion of many of his followers, in whose affections he had confided, is said to have desolated his heart, and to have bereaved him of all further comfort. He was a patriot attached to his native soil,—a prince true to his subjects, and indignant of their wrongs,—a soldier, daring in battle, firm in adversity, patient of fatigue, of hunger, of every variety of bodily suffering, and ready to perish in the cause he had espoused. Proud of heart, and with an untamable love of natural liberty, he preferred to enjoy it among the beasts of the forests or in the dismal and famished recesses of swamps and morasses, rather than bow his haughty spirit to submission, and live dependent and despised in the ease and luxury of the settlements. With heroic qualities and bold achievements that would have graced a civilized warrior, and have rendered him the theme of the poet and the historian, he lived a wanderer and a fugitive in his native land, and went down, like a lonely bark foundering amid darkness and tempest—without a pitying eye to weep his fall, or a friendly hand to record his struggle.

THE CREOLE VILLAGE
A Sketch from a Steamboat

In travelling about our motley country, I am often reminded of Ariosto's account of the moon, in which the good paladin Astolpho found every thing garnered up that had been lost on earth. So I am apt to imagine, that many things lost in the old world, are treasured up in the new; having been handed down from generation to generation, since the early days of the colonies. A European antiquary, therefore, curious in his researches after the ancient and almost obliterated customs and usages of his country, would do well to put himself upon the track of some early band of emigrants, follow them across the Atlantic, and rummage among their descendants on our shores.

In the phraseology of New England might be found many an old English provincial phrase, long since obsolete in the parent country; with some quaint relics of the roundheads; while Virginia cherishes peculiarities characteristic of the days of Elizabeth and Sir Walter Raleigh.

In the same way, the sturdy yeomanry of New Jersey and Pennsylvania keep up many usages fading away in ancient Germany; while many an honest, broad-bottomed custom, nearly extinct in venerable Holland, may be found flourishing in pristine vigor and luxuriance in Dutch villages, on the banks of the Mohawk and the Hudson.

In no part of our country, however, are the customs and peculiarities, imported from the old world by the earlier settlers, kept up with more fidelity than in the little, poverty-stricken villages of Spanish and French origin, which border the rivers of ancient Louisiana. Their population is generally made up of the descendants of those nations, married and interwoven together, and occasionally crossed with a slight dash of the Indian. The French character, however, floats on top, as, from its buoyant qualities, it is sure to do, whenever it forms a particle, however small, of an intermixture.

In these serene and dilapidated villages, art and nature stand still, and the world forgets to turn round. The revolutions that distract other parts of this mutable planet, reach not here, or pass over without leaving any trace. The fortunate inhabitants have none of that public spirit which extends its cares beyond its horizon, and imports trouble and perplexity from all quarters in newspapers. In fact, newspapers are almost unknown in these villages, and as French is the current language, the inhabitants have little community of opinion with their republican neighbors. They retain, therefore, their old habits of passive obedience to the decrees of government, as though they still lived under the absolute sway of colonial commandants, instead of being part and parcel of the sovereign people, and having a voice in public legislation.

A few aged men, who have grown gray on their hereditary acres, and are of the good old colonial stock, exert a patriarchal sway in all matters of public and private import; their opinions are considered oracular, and their word is law.

The inhabitants, moreover, have none of that eagerness for gain, and rage for improvement, which keep our people continually on the move, and our country towns incessantly in a state of transition. There the magic phrases, "town lots," "water privileges," "railroads," and other comprehensive and soul-stirring words, from the speculator's vocabulary, are never heard. The residents dwell in the houses built by their forefathers, without thinking of enlarging or modernizing them, or pulling them down and turning them into granite stores. The trees, under which they have been born, and have played in infancy, flourish undisturbed; though, by cutting them down, they might open new streets, and put money in their pockets. In a word, the almighty dollar, that great object of universal devotion throughout our land, seems to have no genuine devotees in these peculiar villages; and unless some of its missionaries penetrate there, and erect banking houses and other pious shrines, there is no knowing how long the inhabitants may remain in their present state of contented poverty.

In descending one of our great western rivers in a steamboat, I met with two worthies from one of these villages, who had been on a distant excursion, the longest they had ever made, as they seldom ventured far from home. One was the great man, or Grand Seigneur of the village; not that he enjoyed any legal privileges or power there, every thing of the kind having been done away when the province was ceded by France to the United States. His sway over

his neighbors was merely one of custom and convention, out of deference to his family. Beside, he was worth full fifty thousand dollars,
an amount almost equal, in the imaginations of the villagers, to the
treasures of King Solomon.

This very substantial old gentleman, though of the fourth or fifth
generation in this country, retained the true Gallic feature and deportment, and reminded me of one of those provincial potentates,
that are to be met with in the remote parts of France. He was of a
large frame, a ginger-bread complexion, strong features, eyes that
stood out like glass knobs, and a prominent nose, which he frequently regaled from a gold snuff-box, and occasionally blew with a
colored handkerchief, until it sounded like a trumpet.

He was attended by an old negro, as black as ebony, with a huge
mouth, in a continual grin; evidently a privileged and favorite servant, who had grown up and grown old with him. He was dressed in
creole style—with white jacket and trousers, a stiff shirt collar, that
threatened to cut off his ears, a bright madras handkerchief tied
round his head, and large gold ear-rings. He was the politest negro I
met with in a western tour; and that is saying a great deal, for, ex-
cepting the Indians, the negroes are the most gentlemanlike personages to be met with in those parts. It is true, they differ from the
Indians in being a little extra polite and complimentary. He was also
one of the merriest; and here, too, the negroes, however we may de-
plore their unhappy condition, have the advantage of their masters.
The whites are, in general, too free and prosperous to be merry. The
cares of maintaining their rights and liberties, adding to their
wealth, and making presidents, engross all their thoughts, and dry up
all the moisture of their souls. If you hear a broad, hearty, devil-
may-care laugh, be assured it is a negro's.

Beside this African domestic, the seigneur of the village had another no less cherished and privileged attendant. This was a huge
dog, of the mastiff breed, with a deep, hanging mouth, and a look of
surly gravity. He walked about the cabin with the air of a dog perfectly at home, and who had paid for his passage. At dinner time he
took his seat beside his master, giving him a glance now and then
out of a corner of his eye, which bespoke perfect confidence that he
would not be forgotten. Nor was he—every now and then a huge
morsel would be thrown to him, peradventure the half-picked leg of

a fowl, which he would receive with a snap like the springing of a steel-trap—one gulp, and all was down; and a glance of the eye told his master that he was ready for another consignment.

The other village worthy, travelling in company with the seigneur, was of a totally different stamp. Small, thin, and weazenfaced, as Frenchmen are apt to be represented in caricature, with a bright, squirrel-like eye, and a gold ring in his ear. His dress was flimsy, and sat loosely on his frame, and he had altogether the look of one with but little coin in his pocket. Yet, though one of the poorest, I was assured he was one of the merriest and most popular personages in his native village.

Compere Martin, as he was commonly called, was the factotum of the place—sportsman, schoolmaster, and land-surveyor. He could sing, dance, and, above all, play on the fiddle, an invaluable accomplishment in an old French creole village, for the inhabitants have a hereditary love for balls and fêtes; if they work but little, they dance a great deal, and a fiddle is the joy of their heart.

What had sent Compere Martin travelling with the Grand Seigneur I could not learn; he evidently looked up to him with great deference, and was assiduous in rendering him petty attentions; from which I concluded that he lived at home upon the crumbs which fell from his table. He was gayest when out of his sight; and had his song and his joke when forward, among the deck passengers; but altogether Compere Martin was out of his element on board of a steamboat. He was quite another being, I am told, when at home, in his own village.

Like his opulent fellow-traveller, he too had his canine follower and retainer—and one suited to his different fortunes—one of the civilest, most unoffending little dogs in the world. Unlike the lordly mastiff, he seemed to think he had no right on board of the steamboat; if you did but look hard at him, he would throw himself upon his back, and lift up his legs, as if imploring mercy.

At table he took his seat a little distance from his master; not with the bluff, confident air of the mastiff, but quietly and diffidently; his head on one side, with one ear dubiously slouched, the other hopefully cocked up; his under teeth projecting beyond his black nose, and his eye wistfully following each morsel that went into his master's mouth.

If Compere Martin now and then should venture to abstract a morsel from his plate, to give to his humble companion, it was edifying to see with what diffidence the exemplary little animal would take hold of it, with the very tip of his teeth, as if he would almost rather not, or was fearful of taking too great a liberty. And then with what decorum would he eat it! How many efforts would he make in swallowing it, as if it stuck in his throat; with what daintiness would he lick his lips; and then with what an air of thankfulness would he resume his seat, with his teeth once more projecting beyond his nose, and an eye of humble expectation fixed upon his master.

It was late in the afternoon when the steamboat stopped at the village which was the residence of these worthies. It stood on the high bank of the river, and bore traces of having been a frontier trading post. There were the remains of stockades that once protected it from the Indians, and the houses were in the ancient Spanish and French colonial taste, the place having been successively under the domination of both those nations prior to the cession of Louisiana to the United States.

The arrival of the seigneur of fifty thousand dollars, and his humble companion, Compere Martin, had evidently been looked forward to as an event in the village. Numbers of men, women, and children, white, yellow, and black, were collected on the river bank; most of them clad in old-fashioned French garments, and their heads decorated with colored handkerchiefs, or white nightcaps. The moment the steamboat came within sight and hearing, there was a waving of handkerchiefs, and a screaming and bawling of salutations, and felicitations, that baffle all description.

The old gentleman of fifty thousand dollars was received by a train of relatives, and friends, and children, and grandchildren, whom he kissed on each cheek, and who formed a procession in his rear, with a legion of domestics, of all ages, following him to a large, old-fashioned French house, that domineered over the village.

His black valet de chambre, in white jacket and trousers, and gold ear-rings, was met on the shore by a boon, though rustic companion, a tall negro fellow, with a long, good-humored face, and the profile of a horse, which stood out from beneath a narrow-rimmed straw hat, stuck on the back of his head. The explosions of laughter of these two varlets on meeting and exchanging compliments, were enough to electrify the country round.

The most hearty reception, however, was that given to Compere Martin. Every body, young and old, hailed him before he got to land. Every body had a joke for Compere Martin, and Compere Martin had a joke for every body. Even his little dog appeared, to partake of his popularity, and to be caressed by every hand. Indeed, he was quite a different animal the moment he touched the land. Here he was at home; here he was of consequence. He barked, he leaped, he frisked about his old friends, and then would skim round the place in a wide circle, as if mad.

I traced Compere Martin and his little dog to their home. It was an old ruinous Spanish house, of large dimensions, with verandas overshadowed by ancient elms. The house had probably been the residence, in old times, of the Spanish commandant. In one wing of this crazy, but aristocratical abode, was nestled the family of my fellow-traveller; for poor devils are apt to be magnificently clad and lodged, in the cast-off clothes and abandoned palaces of the great and wealthy.

The arrival of Compere Martin was welcomed by a legion of women, children, and mongrel curs; and, as poverty and gayety generally go hand in hand among the French and their descendants, the crazy mansion soon resounded with loud gossip and lighthearted laughter.

As the steamboat paused a short time at the village, I took occasion to stroll about the place. Most of the houses were in the French taste, with casements and rickety verandas, but most of them in flimsy and ruinous condition. All the waggons, ploughs, and other utensils about the place were of ancient and inconvenient Gallic construction, such as had been brought from France in the primitive days of the colony. The very looks of the people reminded me of the villages of France.

From one of the houses came the hum of a spinning wheel, accompanied by a scrap of an old French chanson, which I have heard many a time among the peasantry of Languedoc, doubtless a traditional song, brought over by the first French emigrants, and handed down from generation to generation.

Half a dozen young lasses emerged from the adjacent dwellings, reminding me, by their light step and gay costume, of scenes in ancient France, where taste in dress comes natural to every class of females. The trim bodice and colored petticoat, and little apron, with its pockets to receive the hands when in an attitude for conversation; the colored kerchief wound tastefully round the head, with a coquettish knot perking above one ear; and the neat slipper and tight drawn stocking, with its braid of narrow ribbon embracing the ancle where it peeps from its mysterious curtain. It is from this ambush that Cupid sends his most inciting arrows.

While I was musing upon the recollections thus accidentally summoned up, I heard the sound of a fiddle from the mansion of Compere Martin, the signal, no doubt, for a joyous gathering. I was disposed to turn my steps thither, and witness the festivities of one of the very few villages I had met with in my wide tour, that was yet poor enough to be merry; but the bell of the steamboat summoned me to re-embark.

As we swept away from the shore, I cast back a wistful eye upon the moss-grown roofs and ancient elms of the village, and prayed that the inhabitants might long retain their happy ignorance, their absence of all enterprise and improvement, their respect for the fiddle, and their contempt for the almighty dollar.° I fear, however, my prayer is doomed to be of no avail. In a little while, the steamboat whirled me to an American town, just springing into bustling and prosperous existence.

The surrounding forest had been laid out in town lots; frames of wooden buildings were rising from among stumps and burnt trees. The place already boasted a court-house, a jail, and two banks, all built of pine boards, on the model of Grecian temples. There were rival hotels, rival churches, and rival newspapers; together with the usual number of judges, and generals, and governors; not to speak of doctors by the dozen, and lawyers by the score.

The place, I was told, was in an astonishing career of improvement, with a canal and two railroads in embryo. Lots doubled in price every week; every body was speculating in land; every body

°This phrase used for the first time, in this sketch, has since passed into current circulation, and by some has been questioned as savoring of irreverence. The author, therefore, owes it to his orthodoxy to declare that no irreverence was intended even to the dollar itself; which he is aware is daily becoming more and more an object of worship. [Irving's note.]

was rich; and every body was growing richer. The community, how-, ever, was torn to pieces by new doctrines in religion and in political economy; there were camp meetings, and agrarian meetings; and an election was at hand, which, it was expected, would throw the whole country into a paroxysm.

Alas! with such an enterprising neighbor, what is to become of the poor little creole village!

SUGGESTED ADDITIONAL READINGS

Tales of a Traveller
A Tour on the Prairies
Astoria
The Adventures of Captain Bonneville
Salmagundi

SELECTED REFERENCES

Benson, A.B. "Scandinavians in the Works of Washington Irving." *Scandinavian Studies*, 9 (1927), 207–23.

Hoffman, Daniel G. "Irving's Use of American Folklore in 'The Legend of Sleepy Hollow.'" *PMLA*, 68 (1953), 425–35.

Hough, Robert L. "Washington Irving, Indians, and the West." *South Dakota Review*, Winter, 1968–69, pp. 27–39.

Reed, Kenneth T. "Washington Irving and the Negro." *Negro American Literature Forum*, 4 (1970), 43–44.

PROJECTS AND PROBLEMS

Are Irving's exaggerated character descriptions racially motivated? In "The Legend of Sleepy Hollow" he describes a black musician and his companions "rolling their white eye-balls and showing grinning rows of ivory from ear to ear," and black Tucky Squash in *Salmagundi* has a face that "shone like a kettle." But Ichabod Crane, the white schoolmaster in "The Legend of Sleepy Hollow," has a flat head and "feet that might have served as shovels." What are other possible explanations for these descriptions?

Irving once said that Europeans did not know what an American is and were prone to assume that all Americans are Creoles. Consider the various current uses of "Creole" and study applications of the term in literary history. Which definition fits Irving's use in "The Creole Village"?

In Chapter V, Book I of *Knickerbocker's History of New York*, Irving offers a mock defense of white seizure of Indian land and a satire on prejudice in general. Can this piece be applied to contemporary world affairs?

John James Audubon, the artist and naturalist who was the son of a French sea captain and his Creole mistress, wrote perceptively of life on the Upper Mississippi shortly after Irving visited that area. Compare Irving's treatment of the scene with Audubon's "The Prairie" in his *Ornithological Biography*.

Did Irving react to the Indians of the plains in much the same way he did to those of the northeast? Compare "Traits of Indian Character" in *The Sketch Book* with "The Camp of Wild Horse" in *A Tour on the Prairies*.

Find in "The Devil and Tom Walker" an expression of Irving's opinion of the slave trader.

Compare Irving's treatment of the Dutch of New York State with that in *The Dutchman's Fireside* by his friend James Kirke Paulding.

WILLIAM CULLEN BRYANT
(1794–1878)

Although Bryant's literary reputation rests on his poetry, most of his writing was of another kind. For almost fifty years he was editor of the New York *Evening Post* and a consistent spokesman for liberal causes. In prose he supported improved working conditions for labor and the right of collective bargaining, and he urged the abolition of slavery. His verse celebrates nature in a style distinguished by simple dignity.

AN INDIAN AT THE BURIAL-PLACE OF HIS FATHERS

It is the spot I came to seek—
    My father's ancient burial-place,
Ere from these vales, ashamed and weak,
    Withdrew our wasted race.
It is the spot—I know it well—
Of which our old traditions tell.

For here the upland bank sends out
    A ridge toward the river-side;
I know the shaggy hills about,
    The meadows smooth and wide,
The plains, that, toward the southern sky,
Fenced east and west by mountains lie.

A white man, gazing on the scene,
    Would say a lovely spot was here,
And praise the lawns, so fresh and green,
    Between the hills so sheer.
I like it not—I would the plain
Lay in its tall old groves again.

The sheep are on the slopes around,
    The cattle in the meadows feed,
And laborers turn the crumbling ground,
    Or drop the yellow seed,
And prancing steeds, in trappings gay,
Whirl the bright chariot o'er the way.

Methinks it were a nobler sight
    To see these vales in woods arrayed,
Their summits in the golden light,
    Their trunks in grateful shade,

And herds of deer that bounding go
O'er hills and prostrate trees below.

And then to mark the lord of all,
    The forest hero, trained to wars,
Quivered and plumed, and lithe and tall,
    And seamed with glorious scars,
Walk forth, amid his reign, to dare
The wolf, and grapple with the bear.

This bank, in which the dead were laid,
    Was sacred when its soil was ours;
Hither the silent Indian maid
    Brought wreaths of beads and flowers,
And the gray chief and gifted seer
Worshipped the god of thunders here.

But now the wheat is green and high
    On clods that hid the warrior's breast,
And scattered in the furrows lie
    The weapons of his rest;
And there, in the loose sand, is thrown
Of his large arm the mouldering bone.

Ah, little thought the strong and brave
    Who bore their lifeless chieftain forth—
Or the young wife that weeping gave
    Her first-born to the earth,
That the pale race, who waste us now,
Among their bones should guide the plough.

They waste us—ay—like April snow
    In the warm noon, we shrink away;
And fast they follow, as we go
    Toward the setting day—
Till they shall fill the land, and we
Are driven into the Western sea.

But I behold a fearful sign,
   To which the white men's eyes are blind;
Their race may vanish hence, like mine,
   And leave no trace behind,
Save ruins o'er the region spread,
And the white stones above the dead.

Before these fields were shorn and tilled,
   Full to the brim our rivers flowed;
The melody of waters filled
   The fresh and boundless wood;
And torrents dashed and rivulets played,
And fountains spouted in the shade.

Those grateful sounds are heard no more,
   The springs are silent in the sun;
The rivers, by the blackened shore,
   With lessening current run;
The realm our tribes are crushed to get
May be a barren desert yet.

THE AFRICAN CHIEF

Chained in the market–place he stood,
　A man of giant frame,
Amid the gathering multitude
　That shrunk to hear his name—
All stern of look and strong of limb,
　His dark eye on the ground:—
And silently they gazed on him,
　As on a lion bound.

Vainly, but well that chief had fought,
　He was a captive now,
Yet pride, that fortune humbles not,
　Was written on his brow.
The scars his dark broad bosom wore
　Showed warrior true and brave;
A prince among his tribe before,
　He could not be a slave.

Then to his conqueror he spake:
　"My brother is a king;
Undo this necklace from my neck,
　And take this bracelet ring,
And send me where my brother reigns,
　And I will fill thy hands
With store of ivory from the plains,
　And gold-dust from the sands."

"Not for thy ivory nor thy gold
　Will I unbind thy chain;
That bloody hand shall never hold
　The battle-spear again.
A price that nation never gave
　Shall yet be paid for thee;
For thou shalt be the Christian's slave,
　In lands beyond the sea."

Then wept the warrior chief, and bade
   To shred his locks away;
And one by one, each heavy braid
   Before the victor lay.
Thick were the platted locks, and long,
   And closely hidden there
Shone many a wedge of gold among
   The dark and crispèd hair.

"Look, feast thy greedy eye with gold
   Long kept for sorest need;
Take it—thou askest sums untold—
   And say that I am freed.
Take it—my wife, the long, long day,
   Weeps by the cocoa-tree,
And my young children leave their play,
And ask in vain for me."

"I take thy gold, but I have made
   Thy fetters fast and strong,
And ween that by the cocoa-shade
   Thy wife will wait thee long."
Strong was the agony that shook
   The captive's frame to hear,
And the proud meaning of his look
   Was changed to mortal fear.

His heart was broken—crazed his brain:
   At once . 'ς eye grew wild;
He struggled fiercely with his chain,
   Whispered, and wept, and smiled;
Yet wore not long those fatal bands,
   And once, at shut of day,
They drew him forth upon the sands,
   The foul hyena's prey.

SUGGESTED ADDITIONAL READINGS

"The Indian Girl's Lament"
"An Indian Story"
"The Disinterred Warrior"
"The Death of Slavery"
"The White-Footed Deer"
Letters of a Traveller

SELECTED REFERENCES

Crapo, Paul. "Bryant on Slavery, Copyright, and Capital Punishment." *Emerson Society Quarterly*, 47 (1967), 139–40.

Dykes, Eva B. "William Cullen Bryant, Apostle of Freedom." *Negro History Bulletin*, 6 (1942), 29–32.

Freimarck, Vincent, and Bernard Rosenthal, eds. *Race and the American Romantics* (1971).

PROJECTS AND PROBLEMS

Do Bryant's poems about Indians show more genuine understanding of Indian culture than Philip Freneau's, or less?

Compare Bryant's "The African Chief" with Longfellow's "The Slave's Dream." Which poem is less patronizing?

Bryant wrote after a visit to South Carolina, "The blacks of this region are a cheerless, careless, dirty race, not hard worked, and in many respects indulgently treated." How might his opinion have been affected by the fact that William Gilmore Simms was his host at the cornshucking he observed there in 1843?

JAMES FENIMORE COOPER
(1789–1851)

The popular concepts of the frontiersman, the noble
American savage, and the villainous aborigine may be
traced to the enormous influence of the romantic fiction
of James Fenimore Cooper. The first selection is from
Chapter III of *The Last of the Mohicans* (1826), probably
the best of his border epics. It is followed by passages
from *Notions of the Americans, Picked Up by a
Travelling Bachelor* (1828), one of the volumes in which
the contentious Cooper lectured his readers about
controversial matters. The description of the Pinkster
frolic comes from *Satanstoe* (1845).

CHINGACHGOOK,
A NOBLE SAVAGE

"Before these fields were shorn and tilled,
Full to the brim our rivers flowed;
The melody of waters filled
The fresh and boundless wood;
And torrents dashed, and rivulets played,
And fountains spouted in the shade."

BRYANT.

Leaving the unsuspecting Heyward and his confiding companions to penetrate still deeper into a forest that contained such treacherous inmates, we must use an author's privilege, and shift the scene a few miles to the westward of the place where we have last seen them.

On that day, two men were lingering on the banks of a small but rapid stream, within an hour's journey of the encampment of Webb, like those who awaited the appearance of an absent person, or the approach of some expected event. The vast canopy of woods spread itself to the margin of the river overhanging the water, and shadowing its dark current with a deeper hue. The rays of the sun were beginning to grow less fierce, and the intense heat of the day was lessened, as the cooler vapors of the springs and fountains rose above their leafy beds, and rested in the atmosphere. Still that breathing silence, which marks the drowsy sultriness of an American landscape in July, pervaded the secluded spot, interrupted only by the low voices of the men, the occasional and lazy tap of a woodpecker, the discordant cry of some gaudy jay, or a swelling on the ear, from the dull roar of a distant waterfall.

These feeble and broken sounds were, however, too familiar to the foresters, to draw their attention from the more interesting matter of their dialogue. While one of these loiterers showed the red skin and wild accoutrements of a native of the woods, the other exhibited, through the mask of his rude and nearly savage equipments, the brighter, though sunburnt and long-faded complexion of one who might claim descent from a European parentage. The former

238

was seated on the end of a mossy log, in a posture that permitted him to heighten the effect of his earnest language, by the calm but expressive gestures of an Indian engaged in debate. His body, which was nearly naked, presented a terrific emblem of death, drawn in intermingled colors of white and black. His closely shaved head, on which no other hair than the well known and chivalrous scalping tuft[1] was preserved, was without ornament of any kind, with the exception of a solitary eagle's plume, that crossed his crown, and depended over the left shoulder. A tomahawk and scalping-knife, of English manufacture, were in his girdle; while a short military rifle, of that sort with which the policy of the whites armed their savage allies, lay carelessly across his bare and sinewy knee. The expanded chest, full formed limbs, and grave countenance of this warrior, would denote that he had reached the vigor of his days, though no symptoms of decay appeared to have yet weakened his manhood.

The frame of the white man, judging by such parts as were not concealed by his clothes, was like that of one who had known hardships and exertion from his earliest youth. His person, though muscular, was rather attenuated than full; but every nerve and muscle appeared strung and indurated by unremitted exposure and toil. He wore a hunting-shirt of forest green, fringed with faded yellow,[2] and a summer cap of skins which had been shorn of their fur. He also bore a knife in a girdle of wampum, like that which confined the scanty garments of the Indian, but no tomahawk. His moccasins were ornamented after the gay fashion of the natives, while the only part of his under-dress which appeared below the hunting-frock, was a pair of buckskin leggings, that laced at the sides, and which were gartered above the knees with the sinews of a deer. A

---

[1]The North American warrior caused the hair to be plucked from his whole body; a small tuft, only, was left on the crown of his head in order that his enemy might avail himself of it, in wrenching off the scalp in the event of his fall. The scalp was the only admissible trophy of victory. Thus, it was deemed more important to obtain the scalp than to kill the man. Some tribes lay great stress on the honor of striking a dead body. These practices have nearly disappeared among the Indians of the Atlantic States. [Cooper's note.]

[2]The hunting-shirt is a picturesque smock frock, being shorter, and ornamented with fringes and tassels. The colors are intended to imitate the hues of the wood with a view to concealment. Many corps of American riflemen have been thus attired; and the dress is one of the most striking of modern times. The hunting-shirt is frequently white. [Cooper's note.]

pouch and horn completed his personal accoutrements, though a rifle of great length,[3] which the theory of the more ingenious whites had taught them was the most dangerous of all fire-arms leaned against a neighboring sapling. The eye of the hunter, or scout, whichever he might be, was small, quick, keen, and restless, roving while he spoke, on every side of him, as if in quest of game, or distrusting the sudden approach of some lurking enemy. Notwithstanding the symptoms of habitual suspicion, his countenance was not only without guile, but at the moment at which he is introduced, it was charged with an expression of sturdy honesty.

"Even your traditions make the case in my favor, Chingachgook," he said, speaking in the tongue which was known to all the natives who formerly inhabited the country between the Hudson and the Potomac, and of which we shall give a free translation for the benefit of the reader; endeavoring, at the same time, to preserve some of the peculiarities, both of the individual and of the language. "Your fathers came from the setting sun, crossed the big river,[4] fought the people of the country, and took the land; and mine came from the red sky of the morning, over the salt lake, and did their work much after the fashion that had been set them by yours; then let God judge the matter between us, and friends spare their words!"

"My fathers fought with the naked redmen!" returned the Indian sternly, in the same language. "Is there no difference, Hawkeye, between the stone–headed arrow of the warrior, and the leaden bullet with which you kill?"

"There is reason in an Indian, though nature has made him with a red skin!" said the white man, shaking his head like one on whom such an appeal to his justice was not thrown away. For a moment he appeared to be conscious of having the worst of the argument, then, rallying again, he answered the objection of his antagonist in the best manner his limited information would allow: "I am no scholar, and I care not who knows it; but judging from what I have seen, at deer chases and squirrel hunts, of the sparks below, I should think a

---

[3]The rifle of the army is short; that of the hunter is always long. [Cooper's note.]

[4]The Mississippi. The scout alludes to a tradition which is very popular among the tribes of the Atlantic States. Evidence of their Asiatic origin is deduced from the circumstances, though great uncertainty hangs over the whole history of the Indians. [Cooper's note.]

rifle in the hands of their grandfathers was not so dangerous as a hickory bow and a good flint-head might be, if drawn with Indian judgment, and sent by an Indian eye."

"You have the story told by your fathers," returned the other, coldly waving his hand. "What say your old men? do they tell the young warriors, that the pale-faces met the redmen, painted for war and armed with the stone hatchet and wooden gun?"

"I am not a prejudiced man, nor one who vaunts himself on his natural privileges, though the worst enemy I have on earth, and he is an Iroquois, daren't deny that I am genuine white," the scout replied, surveying, with secret satisfaction, the faded color of his bony and sinewy hand; "and I am willing to own that my people have many ways, of which, as an honest man, I can't approve. It is one of their customs to write in books what they have done and seen, instead of telling them in their villages, where the lie can be given to the face of a cowardly boaster, and the brave soldier can call on his comrades to witness for the truth of his words. In consequence of this bad fashion, a man who is too conscientious to misspend his days among the women, in learning the names of black marks, may never hear of the deeds of his fathers, nor feel a pride in striving to outdo them. For myself, I conclude the Bumppos could shoot, for I have a natural turn with a rifle, which must have been handed down from generation to generation, as, our holy commandments tell us, all good and evil gifts are bestowed; though I should be loth to answer for other people in such a matter. But every story has its two sides; so I ask you, Chingachgook, what passed, according to the traditions of the redmen, when our fathers first met?"

A silence of a minute succeeded, during which the Indian sat mute; then, full of the dignity of his office, he commenced his brief tale, with a solemnity that served to heighten its appearance of truth.

"Listen, Hawkeye, and your ear shall drink no lie. 'Tis what my fathers have said, and what the Mohicans have done." He hesitated a single instant, and bending a cautious glance toward his companion, he continued, in a manner that was divided between interrogation and assertion, "Does not this stream at our feet run towards the summer, until its waters grow salt, and the current flows upward?"

"It can't be denied that your traditions tell you true in both these matters," said the white man; "for I have been there, and have seen them; though, why water, which is so sweet in the shade, should become bitter in the sun, is an alteration for which I have never been able to account."

"And the current!" demanded the Indian, who expected his reply with that sort of interest that a man feels in the confirmation of testimony, at which he marvels even while he respects it; "the fathers of Chingachgook have not lied!"

"The Holy Bible is not more true, and that is the truest thing in nature. They call this up-stream current the tide, which is a thing soon explained, and clear enough. Six hours the waters run in, and six hours they run out, and the reason is this: when there is higher water in the sea than in the river, they run in, until the river gets to be highest, and then it runs out again."

"The waters in the woods, and on the great lakes, run downward until they lie like my hand," said the Indian, stretching the limb horizontally before him, "and then they run no more."

"No honest man will deny it," said the scout, a little nettled at the implied distrust of his explanation of the mystery of the tides; "and I grant that it is true on the small scale, and where the land is level. But everything depends on what scale you look at things. Now, on the small scale, the 'arth is level; but on the large scale it is round. In this manner, pools and ponds, and even the great fresh-water lake, may be stagnant, as you and I both know they are, having seen them; but when you come to spread water over a great tract, like the sea, where the earth is round, how in reason can the water be quiet? You might as well expect the river to lie still on the brink of those black rocks a mile above us, though your own ears tell you that it is tumbling over them at this very moment!"

If unsatisfied by the philosophy of his companion, the Indian was far too dignified to betray his unbelief. He listened like one who was convinced, and resumed his narrative in his former solemn manner.

"We came from the place where the sun is hid at night, over great plains where the buffaloes live, until we reached the big river. There we fought the Alligewi, till the ground was red with their blood. From the banks of the big river to the shores of the salt lake, there was none to meet us. The Maquas followed at a distance. We said the country should be ours from the place where the water runs up no longer on this stream, to a river twenty suns' journey toward the summer. The land we had taken like warriors, we kept like men. We drove the Maquas into the woods with the bears. They only tasted salt at the licks; they drew no fish from the great lake; we threw them the bones."

"All this I have heard and believe," said the white man, observing that the Indian paused: "but it was long before the English came into the country."

"A pine grew then where this chestnut now stands. The first pale-faces who came among us spoke no English. They came in a large canoe, when my fathers had buried the tomahawk with the redmen around them. Then, Hawkeye," he continued, betraying his deep emotion only by permitting his voice to fall to those low, guttural tones, which rendered his language, as spoken at times, so very musical; "then, Hawkeye, we were one people, and we were happy. The salt lake gave us its fish, the wood its deer, and the air its birds. We took wives who bore us children; we worshipped the Great Spirit; and we kept the Maquas beyond the sound of our songs of triumph!"

"Know you anything of your own family at that time?" demanded the white. "But you are a just man, for an Indian! and, as I suppose you hold their gifts, your fathers must have been brave warriors, and wise men at the council fire."

"My tribe is the grandfather of nations, but I am an unmixed man. The blood of chiefs is in my veins, where it must stay forever. The Dutch landed, and gave my people the fire-water; they drank until the heavens and the earth seemed to meet, and they foolishly thought they had found the Great Spirit. Then they parted with their land. Foot by foot, they were driven back from the shores, until I, that am a chief and a sagamore, have never seen the sun shine but through the trees, and have never visited the graves of my fathers!"

"Graves bring solemn feelings over the mind," returned the scout, a good deal touched at the calm suffering of his companion; "and they often aid a man in his good intentions; though, for myself, I expect to leave my own bones unburied, to bleach in the woods, or to be torn asunder by the wolves. But where are to be found those of your race who came to their kin in the Delaware country, so many summers since?"

"Where are the blossoms of those summers!—fallen, one by one: so all of my family departed, each in his turn, to the land of spirits. I am on the hill-top, and must go down into the valley; and when Uncas follows in my footsteps, there will no longer be any of the blood of the sagamores, for my boy is the last of the Mohicans."

AN HUMBLED AND MUCH DEGRADED RACE

As a rule, the red man disappears before the superior moral and physical influence of the white, just as I believe the black man will eventually do the same thing, unless he shall seek shelter in some other region. In nine cases in ten, the tribes have gradually removed west; and there is now a confused assemblage of nations and languages collected on the immense hunting grounds of the Prairies. . . .

The ordinary manner of the disappearance of the Indian, is by a removal deeper into the forest. Still, many linger near the graves of their fathers, to which their superstitions, no less than a fine natural feeling, lend a deeper interest. The fate of the latter is inevitable; they become victims to the abuses of civilization, without ever attaining to any of its moral elevation.

As might be supposed, numberless divisions of these people, when the country was discovered, were found in possession of districts along the coast, and deriving a principal means of support from the ocean. They were fishermen rather than hunters, though the savage state ordinarily infers a resort to both pursuits. Most of these people, too, retired reluctantly from a view of "the great salt lake," but some were environed by the whites before they were properly aware of the blighting influence of the communion; and, getting gradually accustomed to their presence, they preferred remaining near the places where they had first drawn breath. Trifling districts of territory have been, in every instance in which they were sufficiently numerous to make such a provision desirable, secured to them, and on these little tracts of land many of them still remain. I have visited one or two of their establishments.

In point of civilization, comforts, and character, the Indians, who remain near the coasts, are about on a level with the lowest classes of European peasantry. Perhaps they are somewhat below the English, but I think not below the Irish peasants. They are much below the condition of the mass of the slaves. It is but another proof of the wayward vanity of man, that the latter always hold the Indians in

245

contempt, though it is some proof that they feel their own condition to be physically better: morally, in one sense, it certainly is not.

Many of these Atlantic Indians go to sea. They are quite often found in the whalers, and, in some instances, in the vessels of war. An officer in the navy has told me that he once knew a Montauk Indian who was a captain of the main-top in a sloop of war; and in another instance, a flag officer had his gig manned by Indians. They make active and very obedient seamen, but are never remarkable for strength. The whole number of them who now go to sea, does not, however, probably exceed a hundred or two.[1]

I accompanied Cadwallader on a visit to a connexion, who lives within forty miles of New-York, on the adjacent island of Nassau (Long Island). The uncle of my friend was a man of extensive hereditary estate, on which there might have been a reservation of a few thousand acres of woods. While shooting over this forest, one day, the proprietor asked me if I felt any desire to see an Indian king. Surprised at such a question, in such a place, an explanation was requested. He told me that an Indian, who claimed to be a descendant of the ancient Sachems, then held his court in his woods, and that a walk of fifteen minutes would bring us into the presence of King Peter. We went.

I found this Indian, dwelling with his family, in a wigwam of a most primitive construction. It was in the form of a bee-hive, or rather of a very high dome. The covering was made of a long, tough grass, that grows near the sea, and the texture was fine and even

---

[1]The writer, while in America, heard an anecdote which may give some idea of the notions of retributive justice which linger so long in the philosophy of an Indian, and which is, probably, the basis of his desire for revenge, since he is well known to be as eminently grateful as he is vindictive. The whalers always take their reward in a portion of the profits of the voyage. An Indian made several voyages in succession, in the same ship; he found, at his return, that bad luck, advances, and the supplies of an extravagant family at home, left him always in debt. "What shall I do?" was the question put to his owner, as each unfortunate balance was exhibited. "You must go to sea." To sea he went, and, as stated, for four or five years, always with the same result. At length, good fortune, with a proper amount of preventive castigation on his improvident wife, before he sailed, brought the balance on his side. The money was of course tendered; but for a long time he refused to receive it, insisting that justice required that his owners should now go to sea, where it would seem he had not enjoyed himself quite as much as he believed the other party to the contract had done on shore. [Cooper's note.]

beautiful. A post in the centre supported the fabric, which was shaped by delicate curving poles. A hole in the top admitted the light, and allowed the smoke to pass out; and the fire was near enough to the upright post to permit a kettle to be suspended from one of its knots (or cut branches) near enough to feel the influence of the heat. The door was a covering of mats, and the furniture consisted of a few rude chairs, baskets, and a bed, that was neither savage, nor yet such as marks the civilized man. The attire of the family was partly that of the one condition, and partly that of the other. The man himself was a full-blooded Indian, but his manner had that species of sullen deportment that betrays the disposition without the boldness of the savage. He complained that "basket stuff" was getting scarce, and spoke of an intention of removing his wigwam shortly to some other estate.

The manufacture of baskets and brooms is a common employment of all the Indians who reside near the settlements. They feed on game, and, sometimes, like the gypsies, they make free with poultry, though in common they are rigidly honest; nearly always so, unless corrupted by much intercourse with the whites. With the proceeds of their labour they purchase blankets, powder, and such other indulgences as exceed their art to manufacture. King Peter, I was told, claimed a right, in virtue of his royal descent, to cut saplings to supply his materials, on any estate in the island. He was permitted to enjoy this species of feudal privilege in quiet, it being well understood that he was not to exceed a certain discretion in its exercise.

In the more interior parts of the country, I frequently met families of the Indians, either travelling, or proceeding to some village, with their wares. They were all alike, a stunted, dirty, and degraded race. Sometimes they encamped in the forests, lighted their fires, and remained for weeks in a place; and at others, they kept roaming daily, until the time arrived when they should return to their reservations.

The reservations in the old States, and with tribes that cannot aspire to the dignity of nations, are managed on a sufficiently humane principle. The laws of the State, or of the United States, have jurisdiction there, in all matters between white men, or between a white man and an Indian; but the Indians themselves are commonly permitted to control the whole of their own internal policy. Bargains, exceeding certain amounts, are not valid between them and the whites, who cannot, for instance, purchase their lands. Schools are usually provided, in the more important tribes, by the general government, and in the less, by charity. Religious instruction is also furnished by the latter means.

I saw reservations in which no mean advances had been made in civilization. Farms were imperfectly tilled, and cattle were seen grazing in the fields. Still, civilization, advances slowly among a people who consider labour a degradation, in addition to the bodily dislike that all men have to its occupations.

There are many of these tribes, however, who fill a far more important, and altogether a remarkable position. There is certainly no portion of country within the admitted boundaries of the United States, in which their laws are not paramount, if they choose to exert them. Still, savage communities do exist within these limits, with whom they make treaties, against whom they wage open war, and with whom they make solemn peace. As a treaty is, by the constitution, the paramount law of the land, the several States are obliged to respect their legal provisions.

That neither the United States, nor any individual State, has ever taken possession of any land that, by usage or construction, might be decreed the property of the Indians, without a treaty and a purchase, is, I believe, certain. How far an equivalent is given, is another question: though I fancy that these bargains are quite as just as any that are ever driven between the weak and the strong, the intelligent and the ignorant. It is not pretended that the value of the territory gained is paid for; but the purchase is rather a deference to general principles of justice and humanity, than a concession to a right in the Indians, which itself might admit of a thousand legal quibbles. The treaties are sufficiently humane, and, although certain borderers, who possess the power of the white man with the disposition of the savage, do sometimes violate their conditions, there is no just reason to distrust the intentions or the conduct of the government. . . .

There is a bureau of the war department that is called the "office of the Indian affairs." A humane and discreet individual is at its head, and a good deal is endeavoured to be done in mitigating the sufferings and in meliorating the condition of the Indians, though, owing to the peculiar habits and opinions of these people, but little, I fear, is effected. I see by the report of the current year, (1827) that, in nine months, requisitions towards the support of the objects of this bureau, were made to the amount of 759,116 dollars, or at the rate of a little more than a million of dollars a year. This, you will remember, is one–tenth of the current expenditure of the whole government, and nearly as much as is paid for the support of the whole civil list, strictly speaking. . . .

The government, it would appear by the reports, puts the utmost latitude on the construction of their constitutional powers, by even paying money for the support of missionaries among the Indians. I believe, however, that the alleged and legal object of this charge, is for general instruction, though in point of fact, the teachers are missionaries. They are of all sects, Protestant and Catholic, the question of creed being never discussed at all. I see by the reports, that (in 1827) there were 1291 scholars in the different schools that come under the superintendence of the government. It is not probable that all the Indians belonging to the tribes that receive this instruction much exceed, if indeed they reach, the total number of 30,000. I think it is therefore apparent, that quite as good provision for elementary instruction is made in behalf of the Indians, as is commonly made for the people of any country, except those of the United States themselves. There is no reason to suppose that all the children who present themselves, are not taught; and there is much reason for believing that efforts are constantly making to induce all to come. The number of teachers is 293, which is quite enough to instruct ten times the number. You are not to suppose, however, that all these teachers are men hired expressly for that purpose. They are the missionaries, their wives and families, and some of them are for the purpose of instructing in the arts of life, as well as in reading and writing. Much of the expense is defrayed by charitable associations. The sum actually paid by the government for the express object of instruction, is 7,150 dollars, or enough to maintain rather more than forty teachers of stipends of 150 dollars each. It is probable that some receive more, and some less. It is said that the schools are generally in a flourishing condition.

Where there is much intercourse between the very strong and very weak, there is always a tendency in the human mind to suspect abuses of power. I shall not descend into the secret impulses that give rise to these suspicions; but in this stage of the world, there is no necessity for suspecting a nation like this of any unprovoked wrongs against a people like the savages. The inroad of the whites of the United States has never been marked by the gross injustice and brutality that have distinguished similar inroads elsewhere. The Indians have never been slain except in battle, unless by lawless individuals; never hunted by blood-hounds, or in any manner aggrieved, except in the general, and, perhaps, in some degree, justifiable invasion of a territory that they did not want, nor could not use. If the government of the United States was poor and necessitous, one might suspect it of an unjust propensity; but not only the facts, but the premises, would teach us to believe the reverse.

A great, humane, and, I think, rational project, is now in operation to bring the Indians within the pale of civilization. I shall furnish you with its outline as it is detailed in a recent report of the head of the Indian office.

Most, if not all of the Indians who reside east of the Mississippi, live within the jurisdiction of some State or of some territory. In most cases they are left to the quiet enjoyment of the scanty rights which they retain, but the people of their vicinity commonly wish to get rid of neighbours that retard civilization, and who are so often troublesome. The policy of States is sometimes adverse to their continuance. Though there is no power, except that of the United States, which can effect their removal without their own consent, the State authorities can greatly embarrass the control of the general government. A question of policy, and, perhaps, of jurisdiction, lately arose on this subject between Georgia and the general government. In the course of its disposal, the United States, in order to secure the rights of the Indians more effectually, and to prevent any future question of this sort, appear to have hit on the following plan.

West of the Mississippi they still hold large regions that belong to no State or territory. They propose to several tribes (Choctaws, Chickasaws, Cherokees, &c.) to sell their present possessions, improvements, houses, fences, stock, &c., and to receive, in return, acre for acre, with the same amount of stock, fences, and every other auxiliary of civilization they now possess. The inducements to make this exchange are as follows:—Perpetuity to their establishments, since a pledge is given that no title shall ever be granted that may raise a pretext for another removal; an organization of a republican, or, as it is termed, a territorial government for them, such as now exist in Florida, Arkansas, and Michigan; protection, by the presence of troops; and a right to send delegates to Congress, similar to that now enjoyed by the other territories.

If the plan can be effected, there is reason to think that the constant diminution in the numbers of the Indians will be checked, and that a race about whom there is so much that is poetic and fine in recollection, will be preserved. Indeed, some of the southern tribes have already endured the collision with the white man, and are still slowly on the increase. As one of these tribes, at least, (the Chickasaws,) is included in this plan, there is just ground to hope that the dangerous point of communication has been passed, and that they may continue to advance in civilization to maturity. The chief of the bureau on Indian affairs gives it as his opinion that they (the Chickasaws) have increased about ten per cent within six years. Their whole number is computed at four thousand souls.

Should such a territory be formed, a nucleus will be created, around which all the savages of the west, who have any yearnings for a more meliorated state of existence, can rally. As there is little reluctance to mingle the white and red blood, (for the physical difference is far less than in the case of the blacks, and the Indians have never been menial slaves,) I think an amalgamation of the two races would in time occur. Those families of America who are thought to have any of the Indian blood, are rather proud of their descent, and it is a matter of boast among many of the most considerable persons of Virginia, that they are descended from the renowned Pocahontas.

The character of the American Indian has been too often faithfully described to need any repetition here. The majority of them, in or near the settlements, are an humbled and much degraded race. As you recede from the Mississippi, the finer traits of savage life become visible; and, although most of the natives of the Prairies, even there, are far from being the interesting and romantic heroes that poets love to paint, there are specimens of loftiness of spirit, of bearing, and of savage heroism, to be found among the chiefs, that might embarrass the fertility of the richest invention to equal. I met one of those heroes of the desert, and a finer physical and moral man, allowing for peculiarity of condition, it has rarely been my good fortune to encounter.

FROLICKING BLACKS IN
OLD MANHATTAN

... We proceeded along the wharves in a body, admiring the different vessels that lined them. About nine o'clock, all three of us passed up Wall street, on the stoops of which, no small portion of its tenants were already seated, enjoying the sight of the negroes, as, with happy "shining" faces they left the different dwellings, to hasten to the Pinkster field. Our passage through the street attracted a good deal of attention; for, being all three strangers, it was not to be supposed we could be thus seen in a body, without exciting a remark. Such a thing could hardly have been expected in London itself.

After showing Jason the City Hall, Trinity Church, and the City Tavern, we went out of town, taking the direction of a large common that the king's officers had long used for a parade ground, and which has since been called the Park, though it would be difficult to say why, since it is barely a paddock in size, and certainly has never been used to keep any animals wilder than the boys of the town. A park, I suppose, it will one day become, though it has little at present that comports with my ideas of such a thing. On this common, then, was the Pinkster ground, which was now quite full of people, as well as of animation.

There was nothing new in a Pinkster frolic, either to Dirck, or to myself; though Jason gazed at the whole procedure with wonder. He was born within seventy miles of that very spot, but had not the smallest notion before, of such a holiday as Pinkster. There are few blacks in Connecticut, I believe; and those that are there, are so ground down in the Puritan mill, that they are neither fish, flesh, nor red-herring, as we say of a nondescript. No man ever heard of a festival in New England that had not some immediate connection with the saints, or with politics.

Jason was at first confounded with the noises, dances, music, and games that were going on. By this time, nine-tenths of the blacks of the city, and of the whole country within thirty or forty miles, indeed, were collected in thousands in those fields, beating banjoes, singing African songs, drinking, and worst of all, laughing in a way that seemed to set their very hearts rattling within their ribs. Every thing wore the aspect of good-humor, though it was good-humor in its broadest and coarsest forms. Every sort of common game was in requisition, while drinking was far from being neglected. Still, not a man was drunk. A drunken negro, indeed, is by no means a common thing. The features that distinguish a Pinkster frolic from the usual scenes at fairs, and other merry-makings, however, were of African origin. It is true, there are not now, nor were there then, many blacks among us of African birth; but the traditions and usages of their original country were so far preserved as to produce a marked difference between this festival, and one of European origin. Among other things, some were making music, by beating on skins drawn over the ends of hollow logs, while others were dancing to it, in a manner to show that they felt infinite delight. This, in particular, was said to be a usage of their African progenitors.

Hundreds of whites were walking through the fields, amused spectators. Among these last were a great many children of the better class, who had come to look at the enjoyment of those who attended them, in their own ordinary amusements. Many a sable nurse did I see that day, chaperoning her young master, or young mistress, or both together, through the various groups; demanding of all, and receiving from all, the respect that one of these classes was accustomed to pay to the other.

A great many young ladies between the ages of fifteen and twenty were also in the field, either escorted by male companions, or, what was equally as certain of producing deference, under the care of old female nurses, who belonged to the race that kept the festival. We had been in the field ourselves two hours, and even Jason was beginning to condescend to be amused, when, unconsciously, I got separated from my companions, and was wandering through the groups by myself, as I came on a party of young girls, who were under the care of two or three wrinkled and gray-headed negresses, so respectably attired, as to show at once they were confidential servants in some of the better families. . . .

SUGGESTED ADDITIONAL READINGS

The Leatherstocking Tales (*The Pioneers, The Last of the Mohicans, The Prairie, The Pathfinder, The Deerslayer*)
The Bravo
The American Democrat
The Littlepage Manuscripts (*Satanstoe, The Chainbearer, The Redskins*)
The Oak-Openings

SELECTED REFERENCES

Baym, Nina. "The Women of Cooper's Leatherstocking Tales." *American Quarterly*, 23 (1971), 696–709.

Fackler, Herbert V. "Cooper's Pawnees." *American Notes and Queries*, 6 (1967), 325–34.

Frederick, John T. "Cooper's Eloquent Indians." *PMLA*, 71 (1956), 1004–17.

Fussell, Edwin. *Frontier: American Literature and the American West* (1965).

House, Kay Seymour. *Cooper's Americans* (1966).

Keiser, Albert. *The Indian in American Literature* (1933).

Noble, David W. "Cooper, Leatherstocking and the Death of the American Adam." *American Quarterly*, 16 (1964), 419–31.

O'Daniel, Therman B. "Cooper's Treatment of the Negro." *Phylon*, 8 (1947), 164–76.

Paine, Gregory L. "The Indians of the Leatherstocking Tales." *Studies in Philology*, 23 (1926), 16–39.

Pound, Louise. "The Dialects of Cooper's Leather-Stocking." *American Speech*, 2 (1927), 479.

Ringe, Donald A. "Cooper's Littlepage Novels: Change and Stability in American Society." *American Literature*, 32 (1960), 280–90.

Russell, Jason Almus. "Cooper: Interpreter of the Real and the Historical Indian." *Journal of American History*, 23 (1929), 41–71.

Spiller, Robert E. "Fenimore Cooper's Defense of Slave-Owning America." *American Historical Review*, 35 (1930), 575–82.

PROJECTS AND PROBLEMS

Consider the justice of the criticism of Cooper by other writers, among them Francis Parkman, whose anonymous appraisal of Cooper's portrait of the Indian appeared in *North American Review* in January, 1852, and Mark Twain, whose "Fenimore Cooper's Literary Offenses" was published in that journal in July, 1895.

For a provocative English estimate, see the two chapters on Cooper in D. H. Lawrence's *Studies in Classic American Literature.* Compare Lawrence's views with those of Leslie Fiedler in *An End to Innocence* and *The Return of the Vanishing American.*

In both *Satanstoe* and *The Redskins* Cooper offers an Indian chief and a black slave as contrasting characters. Which race does he seem to regard as the more likely to survive? Which seems to him more admirable?

Compare Cooper's picture of the Pawnee Indians in *The Prairie* with that of the Delaware Indians in *The Last of the Mohicans.*

Analyze the attitude toward miscegenation presented in *The Last of the Mohicans.* Explain the significance of the responses of Alice and Cora to their Indian and white admirers. Why is Cora denied an alliance with either Duncan Heyward or Uncas? Consider the treatment of this subject in the first "dime novel," *Malaeska: The Indian Wife of the White Hunter* (1860), by Ann S. Stephens.

Compare Cooper's portrait of black sailors who are minor characters in *The Pilot* with Herman Melville's treatment of similar incidental figures in *Redburn* or *White-Jacket.* See also Cooper's Scipio Africa in *The Red Rover.*

Is Cooper's image of the Indian based entirely on the concept of the Noble Savage?

Compare Cooper's treatment of the Dutch in The Littlepage Manuscripts with that of Irving.

In *The Indian in American Literature,* Albert Keiser says, "The general truthfulness of Cooper's Indian portraits has been accepted by posterity and has not been successfully challenged." Is this judgment, originally published in 1933, valid?

See Cooper's discussions of slavery in *The American Democrat* and relate his position on this issue to his political and social philosophy. Does "On Prejudice," in that same volume, take into account prejudice against blacks?

Is the Jewish money-lender in *The Bravo* entirely stereotyped? In *The Oak-Openings,* what is the Indian response to the missionary's notion that "the red man is a Jew: a Jew is a red man"?

JOHN PENDLETON KENNEDY
(1795–1870)

Born and reared in Baltimore, Kennedy was active there in society and politics. He married a Southern aristocrat in 1829 and three years later published *Swallow Barn*, a novel that defended slavery and established the Plantation Tradition in literature. Though he wrote other novels and had a career in public service, it is for *Swallow Barn* and his assistance to Edgar Allan Poe that Kennedy is remembered. This selection is from Chapter XLVI.

THE HAPPY SLAVES AT SWALLOW BARN

Having despatched these important matters at the stable, we left our horses in charge of the servants, and walked towards the cabins, which were not more than a few hundred paces distant. These hovels, with their appurtenances, formed an exceedingly picturesque landscape. They were scattered, without order, over the slope of a gentle hill; and many of them were embowered under old and majestic trees. The rudeness of their construction rather enhanced the attractiveness of the scene. Some few were built after the fashion of the better sort of cottages; but age had stamped its heavy traces upon their exterior: the green moss had gathered upon the roofs, and the coarse weatherboarding had broken, here and there, into chinks. But the more lowly of these structures, and the most numerous, were nothing more than plain log-cabins, compacted pretty much on the model by which boys build partridge-traps; being composed of the trunks of trees, still clothed with their bark, and knit together at the corners with so little regard to neatness that the timbers, being of unequal lengths, jutted beyond each other, sometimes to the length of a foot. Perhaps, none of these latter sort were more than twelve feet square, and not above seven in height. A door swung upon wooden hinges, and a small window of two narrow panes of glass were, in general, the only openings in the front. The intervals between the logs were filled with clay; and the roof, which was constructed of smaller timbers, laid lengthwise along it and projecting two or three feet beyond the side or gable walls, heightened, in a very marked degree, the rustic effect. The chimneys communicated even a droll expression to these habitations. They were, oddly enough, built of billets of wood, having a broad foundation of stone, and growing narrower as they rose, each receding gradually from the house to which it was attached, until it reached the height of the roof. These combustible materials were saved from the access of the fire by a thick coating of mud; and the whole structure, from its tapering form, might be said to bear some resemblance to the spout of a tea kettle; indeed, this domestic implement would furnish no unapt type of the complete cabin.

259

From this description, which may serve to illustrate a whole species of habitations very common in Virginia, it will be seen, that on the score of accommodation, the inmates of these dwellings were furnished according to a very primitive notion of comfort. Still, however, there were little garden-patches attached to each, where cymblings, cucumbers, sweet potatoes, water-melons and cabbages flourished in unrestrained luxuriance. Add to this, that there were abundance of poultry domesticated about the premises, and it may be perceived that, whatever might be the inconveniences of shelter, there was no want of what, in all countries, would be considered a reasonable supply of luxuries.

Nothing more attracted my observation than the swarms of little negroes that basked on the sunny sides of these cabins, and congregated to gaze at us as we surveyed their haunts. They were nearly all in that costume of the golden age which I have heretofore described; and showed their slim shanks and long heels in all varieties of their grotesque natures. Their predominant love of sunshine, and their lazy, listless postures, and apparent content to be silently looking abroad, might well afford a comparison to a set of terrapins luxuriating in the genial warmth of summer, on the logs of a mill-pond.

And there, too, were the prolific mothers of this redundant brood, —a number of stout negro-women who thronged the doors of the huts, full of idle curiosity to see us. And, when to these are added a few reverend, wrinkled, decrepit old men, with faces shortened as if with drawing-strings, noses that seemed to have run all to nostril, and with feet of the configuration of a mattock, my reader will have a tolerably correct idea of this negro-quarter, its population, buildings, external appearance, situation and extent.

Meriwether, I have said before, is a kind and considerate master. It is his custom frequently to visit his slaves, in order to inspect their condition, and, where it may be necessary, to add to their comforts or relieve their wants. His coming amongst them, therefore, is always hailed with pleasure. He has constituted himself into a high court of appeal, and makes it a rule to give all their petitions a patient hearing, and to do justice in the premises. This, he tells me, he considers as indispensably necessary;—he says, that no overseer is entirely to be trusted; that there are few men who have the temper to administer wholesome laws to any population, however small, without some omissions or irregularities; and that this is more emphatically true of those who administer them entirely at their own will. On the present occasion, in almost every house where Frank entered, there was some boon to be asked; and I observed, that in every case, the petitioner was either gratified or refused in such a tone as left no occasion or disposition to murmur. Most of the women had some bargains to offer, of fowls or eggs or other commodities of household use, and Meriwether generally referred them to his wife, who, I found, relied almost entirely on this resource, for the supply of such commodities; the negroes being regularly paid for whatever was offered in this way.

One old fellow had a special favour to ask,—a little money to get a new padding for his saddle, which, he said, "galled his cretur's back." Frank, after a few jocular passages with the veteran, gave him what he desired, and sent him off rejoicing.

"That, sir," said Meriwether, "is no less a personage than Jupiter. He is an old bachelor, and has his cabin here on the hill. He is now near seventy, and is a kind of King of the Quarter. He has a horse, which he extorted from me last Christmas; and I seldom come here without finding myself involved in some new demand, as a consequence of my donation. Now he wants a pair of spurs which, I suppose, I must give him. He is a preposterous coxcomb, and Ned has administered to his vanity by a present of a *chapeau de bras*—a relic of my military era, which he wears on Sundays with a conceit that has brought upon him as much envy as admiration—the usual condition of greatness."

The air of contentment and good humor and kind family attachment, which was apparent throughout this little community, and the familiar relations existing between them and the proprietor struck me very pleasantly. I came here a stranger, in great degree, to the negro character, knowing but little of the domestic history of these people, their duties, habits or temper, and somewhat disposed, indeed, from prepossessions, to look upon them as severely dealt with, and expecting to have my sympathies excited towards them as objects of commiseration. I have had, therefore, rather a special interest in observing them. The contrast between my preconceptions of their condition and the reality which I have witnessed, has brought me a most agreeable surprise. I will not say that, in a high state of cultivation and of such self-dependence as they might possibly attain in a separate national existence, they might not become a more respectable people; but I am quite sure they never could become a happier people than I find them here. Perhaps they are destined, ultimately, to that national existence, in the clime from which they derive their origin—that this is a transition state in which we see them in Virginia. If it be so, no tribe of people have ever passed from barbarism to civilization whose middle stage of progress has been more secure from harm, more genial to their character, or better supplied with mild and beneficent guardianship, adapted to the actual state of their intellectual feebleness, than the negroes of Swallow Barn. And, from what I can gather, it is pretty much the same on the other estates in this region. I hear of an unpleasant exception to this remark now and then; but under such conditions as warrant the opinion that the unfavorable case is not more common than that which may be found in a survey of any other department of society. The oppression of apprentices, of seamen, of soldiers, of subordinates, indeed, in every relation, may furnish elements for a bead-roll of social grievances quite as striking, if they were diligently noted and brought to view.

What the negro is finally capable of, in the way of civilization, I am not philosopher enough to determine. In the present stage of his existence, he presents himself to my mind as essentially parasitical in his nature. I mean that he is, in his moral constitution, a dependant upon the white race; dependant for guidance and direction even to the procurement of his most indispensable necessaries. Apart from this protection he has the helplessness of a child,—without foresight, without faculty of contrivance, without thrift of any kind. We have instances, in the neighborhood of this estate, of individuals of the tribe falling into the most deplorable destitution from the want of that constant supervision which the race seems to require. This helplessness may be the due and natural impression which two centuries of servitude have stamped upon the tribe. But it is not the less a present and insurmountable impediment to that most cruel of all projects—the direct, broad emancipation of these people;—an act of legislation in comparison with which the revocation of the edict of Nantes would be entitled to be ranked among political benefactions. Taking instruction from history, all organized slavery is inevitably but a temporary phase of human condition. Interest, necessity and instinct, all work to give progression to the relations of mankind, and finally to elevate each tribe or race to its maximum of refinement and power. We have no reason to suppose that the negro will be an exception to this law.

At present, I have said, he is parasitical. He grows upward, only as the vine to which nature has supplied the sturdy tree as a support. He is extravagantly imitative. The older negroes here have—with some spice of comic mixture in it—that formal, grave and ostentatious style of manners, which belonged to the gentlemen of former days; they are profuse of bows and compliments, and very aristocratic in their way. The younger ones are equally to be remarked for aping the style of the present time, and especially for such tags of dandyism in dress as come within their reach. Their fondness for music and dancing is a predominant passion. I never meet a negro man—unless he is quite old—that he is not whistling; and the women sing from morning till night. And as to dancing, the hardest day's work does not restrain their desire to indulge in such pastime. During the harvest, when their toil is pushed to its utmost—the time being one of recognized privileges—they dance almost the whole night. They are great sportsmen, too. They angle and haul the seine, and hunt and tend their traps, with a zest that never grows weary. Their gayety of heart is constitutional and perennial, and when they are together they are as voluble and noisy as so many blackbirds. In short, I think them the most good-natured, careless, light-hearted, and happily-constructed human beings I have ever seen. Having but few and simple wants, they seem to me to be provided with every comfort which falls within the ordinary compass of their wishes; and, I might say, that they find even more enjoyment,—as that word may be applied to express positive pleasures scattered through the course of daily occupation—than any other laboring people I am acquainted with.

SELECTED REFERENCES

Gaines, Francis Pendleton. *The Southern Plantation: A Study in the Development and Accuracy of a Tradition* (1924).
Ridgely, J. V. *John Pendleton Kennedy* (1966).

PROJECTS AND PROBLEMS

Compare the first edition of *Swallow Barn* with the version published twenty years later. Do changes show that the author grew more enlightened about race and more realistic about slavery? Do changes suit the book to the developments that had taken place over the twenty-year period? Which version has more literary merit?

Was Kennedy's support for the Union during the Civil War evidence that he had altered his opinions about race and slavery?

Is Isaac, the black gardener in Kennedy's *Horse Shoe Robinson*, portrayed in accordance with the racial concepts pronounced in *Swallow Barn?*

DAVY CROCKETT
(1786–1836)

The life and legend of Davy Crockett fit the image of the classic frontier hero of American mythology. Born in Tennessee, Crockett became a backwoods politician of national importance, partly because of books that were written about his border exploits and pioneer spirit. In the war for the independence of Texas he died at the Alamo, closing his career on a characteristic dramatic note. The selection here is from *A Narrative of the Life of David Crockett* (1834), generally accepted as his autobiography.

BACKWOODS INCIDENTS

... I told the men we had set out to hunt a fight, and I wouldn't go back in that way; that we must go ahead, and see what the red men were at. We started and went to a Cherokee town about twenty miles off; and after a short stay there, we pushed on to the house of a man by the name of Radcliff. He was a white man, but had married a Creek woman, and lived just in the edge of the Creek nation. He had two sons, large likely fellows, and a great deal of potatoes and corn, and, indeed, almost every thing else to go on; so we fed our horses and got dinner with him, and seemed to be doing mighty well. But he was bad scared all the time. He told us that there had been ten painted warriors at his house only an hour before, and if we were discovered there, they would kill us and his family with us. I replied to him, that my business was to hunt for just such fellows as he had described, and I was determined not to go back until I had done it. Our dinner being over, we saddled up our horses, and made ready to start. But some of my small company I found were disposed to return. I told them, if we were to go back then, we should never hear the last of it: and I was determined to go ahead. I knowed some of them would go with me, and that the rest were afraid to go back by themselves; and so we pushed on to the camp of some friendly Creeks, which was distant about eight miles. The moon was about the full, and the night was clear; we therefore had the benefit of her light from night to morning, and I knew if we were placed in such danger as to make a retreat necessary, we could travel by night as well as in the day time.

We had not got very far when we met two negroes, well mounted on Indian ponies, and each with a good rifle. They had been taken from their owners by the Indians, and were running away from them, and trying to get back to their masters again. They were brothers, both very large and likely: and could talk Indian as well as English. One of them I sent on to Ditto's Landing, the other I took back with me. It was after dark when we got to the camp, where we found about forty men, women, and children.

They had bows and arrows, and I turned in to shooting with their boys by a pine light. In this way we amused ourselves very well for a

266

while, but at last the negro, who had been talking to the Indians, came to me and told me they were very much alarmed, for the "red sticks," as they called the war party of the Creeks, would come and find us there; and, if so, we should all be killed. I directed him to tell them that I would watch, and if one would come that night, I would carry the skin of his head home to make me a moccasin. When he made this communication, the Indians laughed aloud. At about ten o'clock at night we all concluded to try to sleep a little; but that our horses might be ready for use, as the treasurer said of the drafts on the United States' bank, on certain "contingencies," we tied them up with our saddles on them, and every thing to our hand, if in the night our quarters should get uncomfortable. We lay down with our guns in our arms, and I had just gotten into a doze of sleep, when I heard the sharpest scream that ever escaped the throat of a human creature. It was more like a wrathy painter than any thing else. The negro understood it, and he sprang to me; for tho' I heard the noise well enough, yet I wasn't wide awake enough to get up. So the negro caught me, and said the red sticks was coming. I rose quicker then, and asked what was the matter? Our negro had gone and talked with the Indian who had just fetched the scream, as he came into camp, and learned from him, that the war party had been cross-ing the Coosa river all day at the Ten Islands; and were going on to meet Jackson, and this Indian had come as a runner. This news very much alarmed the friendly Indians in camp, and they were all off in a few minutes. I felt bound to make this intelligence known as soon as possible to the army we had left at the landing; and so we all mounted our horses, and put out in a long lope to make our way back to that place. We were about sixty-five miles off. We went on to the same Cherokee town we had visited on our way out, having first called at Radcliff's who was off with his family; and at the town we found large fires burning, but not a single Indian was to be seen. They were all gone. These circumstances were calculated to lay our dander a little, as it appeared we must be in great danger; though we could easily have licked any force of not more than five to one. But we expected the whole nation would be on us, and against such fear-ful odds we were not so rampant for a fight.

o   o   o   o   o

The evening preceding my departure from Natchitoches, a gentleman, with a good horse and a light wagon, drove up to the tavern where I lodged. He was accompanied by a lady who carried an infant in her arms. As they alighted I recognized the gentleman to be the politician at whom I had discharged my last political speech, on board the boat coming down the Red river. We had let him out in our passage down, as he said he had some business to transact some distance above Natchitoches. He entered the tavern, and seemed to be rather shy of me, so I let him go, as I had no idea of firing two shots at such small game.

The gentleman had a private room, and called for supper; but the lady, who used every precaution to keep the child concealed from the view of any one refused to eat supper, saying she was unwell. However, the gentleman made a hearty meal, and excused the woman, saying, "My wife is subject to a pain in the stomach, which had deprived her of her food." Soon after supper the gentleman desired a bed to be prepared, which being done, they immediately retired to rest.

About an hour before daybreak, next morning, the repose of the whole inn was disturbed by the screams of the child. This continued for some time, and at length the landlady got up to see what it was ailed the noisy bantling. She entered the chamber without a light, and discovered the gentleman seated in the bed alone, rocking the infant in his arms, and endeavoring to quiet it by saying, "Hush, my dear—mamma will soon return." However the child still squalled on, and the long absence of the mother rendered it necessary that something should be done to quiet it.

The landlady proposed taking up the child, to see what was the reason of its incessant cries. She approached the bed, and requested the man to give her the infant, and tell her whether it was a son or daughter; but this question redoubled his consternation, for he was entirely ignorant which sex the child belonged to; however, with some difficulty, he made the discovery, and informed the landlady it was a son.

She immediately called for a light, which was no sooner brought than the landlady began to unfold the wrapper from the child, and exclaim, "O, what a fine big son you have got!" But on a more minute examination they found to their great astonishment, and to the mortification and vexation of the supposed father, that the child was a mulatto.

The wretched man, having no excuse to offer, immediately divulged the whole matter without reserve. He stated that he had fell in with her on the road to Natchitoches the day before, and had offered her a seat in his vehicle. Soon perceiving that she possessed an uncommon degree of assurance, induced him to propose that they should pass as man and wife. No doubt she had left her own home in order to rid herself of the stigma which she had brought on herself by her lewd conduct; and at midnight she had eloped from the bed, leaving the infant to the paternal care of her pretended husband.

Immediate search was made for the mother of the child, but in vain. And, as the song says, "Single misfortunes ne'er come alone," to his great consternation and grief, she had taken his horse, and left the poor politician destitute of everything except a fine *yellow boy*. . . .

SELECTED REFERENCE

Rourke, Constance. *Davy Crockett* (1934).

PROJECTS AND PROBLEMS

The popular book reputed to be Crockett's autobiography has a place in the tradition of frontier humor and the rise of the realistic movement in American literature. Does Crockett's version of life on the frontier seem more accurate than the work of writers like Cooper and Robert Montgomery Bird?

Compare John Filson's picture of Indians and Kentucky frontiersmen in "The Adventures of Col. Daniel Boon" with the treatment of Tennessee and Texas warriors in Crockett's narrative.

THOMAS CHANDLER HALIBURTON
(1796–1865)

The first Canadian writer to win an international reputation, Haliburton greatly influenced American humorists through his creation of Sam Slick, an itinerant Yankee clockmaker and peddler whose boasts and shrewd comments were rendered in Down East dialect. This selection is Chapter III of *The Clockmaker: Sayings and Doings of Samuel Slick of Slickville,* first published in 1837.

THE WHITE NIGGER

One of the most amiable, and at the same time most amusing traits, in the Clockmaker's character, was the attachment and kindness with which he regarded his horse. He considered "Old Clay" as far above a Provincial horse, as he did one of his "free and enlightened citizens" superior to a Bluenose. He treated him as a travelling companion, and when conversation flagged between us, would often soliloquize to him, a habit contracted from pursuing his journeys alone.

"Well, now," he would say, "Old Clay, I guess you took your time agoin' up that 'ere hill—s'pose we progress now. Go along, you old sculpin, and turn out your toes. I reckon you are as deff as a shad, do you hear there? Go ahead! Old Clay. There now," he'd say, " 'Squire, ain't that dreadful pretty? There's action. That looks about right: legs all under him—gathers all up snug—no bobbin' of his head—no rollin' of his shoulders—no wabblin' of his hind parts, but steady as a pump bolt, and the motion all underneath. When he fairly lays himself to it, he trots like all vengeance. Then look at his ear—jist like rabbit's; none o'your flopears like them Amherst beasts, half horses, half pigs, but straight up and p'inted, and not too near at the tips; for that 'ere, I consait, always shows a horse ain't true to draw. *There are only two things, 'Squire, worth lookin' at in a horse, action and soundness; for I never saw a critter that had good action that was a bad beast.* Old Clay puts me in mind of one of our free and enlightened"—

"Excuse me," said I, "Mr. Slick, but really you appropriate that word 'free' to your countrymen, as if you thought no other people in the world were entitled to it but yourselves."

"Neither be they," said he. "We first sot the example. Look at our Declaration of Independence. It was writ by Jefferson, and he was the first man of the age; perhaps the world never seed his ditto. It's a beautiful piece of penmanship that; he gave the British the but–eend of his mind there. I calculate you couldn't fault it in no particular; its generally allowed to be his cap-sheaf. In the first page of it, second section, and first varse, are these words: 'We hold this truth to be self-evident, that all men are created equal.' I guess King

271

George turned his quid when he read that. It was somethin' to chaw on, he hadn't been used to the flavor of, I reckon."

"Jefferson forgot to insert one little word," said I; "he should have said, 'all white men;' for as it now stands, it is a practical un-truth in a country which tolerates domestic slavery in its worst and most forbidding form. It is a declaration of *shame*, and not of *inde-pendence*. It is as perfect a misnomer as ever I knew."

"Well," said he, "I must admit there is a screw loose somewhere thereabouts, and I wish it would convene to Congress to do somethin' or another about our niggers, but I am not quite certified how that is to be sot to rights; I consait that you don't understand us. But," said he, evading the subject with his usual dexterity, "we deal only in niggers,—and those thick-skulled, crooked-shanked, flat-footed, long-heeled, woolly-headed gentlemen don't seem fit for much else but slavery, I do suppose; they ain't fit to contrive for themselves. They are just like grasshoppers; they dance and sing all summer, and when winter comes they have nothin' provided for it, and lay down and die. They require some one to see arter them. Now, we deal in black niggers only, but the Bluenoses sell their own species—they trade in white slaves."

"Thank God!" said I, "slavery does not exist in any part of his Ma-jesty's dominions now; we have at last wiped off that national stain."

"Not quite, I guess," said he, with an air of triumph, "it ain't done with in Nova Scotia, for I have seed these human cattle sales with my own eyes; I was availed of the truth of it up here to old Furlong's last November. I'll tell you the story," said he; and as this story of the Clockmaker's contained some extraordinary statements which I had never heard of before, I noted it in my journal, for the purpose of ascertaining their truth; and, if founded on fact, of laying them before the proper authorities.

"Last fall," said he, "I was on my way to Partridge Island, to ship off some truck and *produce* I had taken in, in the way of trade; and as I neared old Furlong's house, I seed an amazin' crowd of folks about the door; I said to myself, says I, Who's dead, and what's to pay now? what on airth is the meanin' of all this? Is it a vandew, or a weddin', or a rollin' frolic, or a religious stir, or what is it? Thinks I, I'll see; so I hitches Old Clay to the fence, and walks in. It was some time afore I was able to wiggle my way through the crowd, and get

into the house. And when I did, who should I see but Deacon Westfall, a smooth-faced, slick-haired, meechin' lookin' chap as you'd see
in a hundred, a standin' on a stool, with an auctioneer's hammer in
his hand; and afore him was one Jerry Oaks and his wife, and two
little orphan children, the prettiest little toads I ever beheld in all
my born days. 'Gentlemen,' said he, 'I will begin the sale by putting
up Jerry Oaks, of Apple River; he's a considerable of a smart man
yet, and can do many little chores besides feedin' the children and
pigs; I guess he's near about worth his keep.' 'Will you warrant him
sound, wind and limb?' says a tall, ragged lookin' countryman, 'for
he looks to me as if he was foundered in both feet, and had a string
halt into the bargain.' 'When you are as old as I be,' says Jerry, 'may-
hap you may be foundered too, young man; I have seen the day
when you wouldn't dare to pass that joke on me, big as you be.'
'Will any gentleman bid for him,' says the Deacon, 'he's cheap at 7s.
6d.' 'Why Deacon,' said Jerry, 'why surely your honor isn't agoin' for
to sell me separate from my poor old wife, are you? Fifty years have
we lived together as man and wife, and a good wife has she been to
me, through all my troubles and trials, and God knows I have had
enough of 'em. No one know my ways and my ailments but her; and
who can tend me so kind, or who will bear with the complaints of a
poor old man but his wife? Do, Deacon, and Heaven bless you for it,
and yours, do sell us together; we have but a few days to live now,
death will divide us soon enough. Leave her to close my old eyes,
when the struggle comes, and when it comes to you, Deacon, as
come it must to us all, may this good deed rise up for you, as a memorial before God. I wish it had pleased Him to have taken us afore
it came to this, but his will be done;' and he hung his head, as if he
felt he had drained the cup of degradation to its dregs. 'Can't afford
it, Jerry—can't afford it, old man,' said the Deacon, with such a smile
as a November sun gives, a passin' atween clouds. 'Last year they
took oats for rates, now nothin' but wheat will go down, and that's
as good as cash; and you'll hang on, as most of you do, yet these
many years. There's old Joe Crowe, I believe in my conscience he
will live forever.' The biddin' then went on, and he was sold for six
shillings a week. Well, the poor critter gave one long, loud, deep
groan, and then folded his arms over his breast, so tight that he
seemed tryin' to keep in his heart from bustin'. I pitied the misfor-

tunate wretch from my soul; I don't know as I ever felt so streaked afore. Not so his wife,—she was all tongue. She begged, and prayed, and cried, and scolded, and talked at the very tip eend of her voice, till she became, poor critter, exhausted, and went off in a faintin' fit, and they ketched her up and carried her out to the air, and she was sold in that condition.

"Well, I couldn't make head or tail of all this, I could hardly believe my eyes and ears; so says I to John Porter,—him that has that catamount of a wife, that I had such a touse with,—'John Porter,' says I, 'who ever seed or heerd tell of the like of this? what under the sun does it all mean? What has that 'ere critter done that he should be sold arter that fashion?' 'Done?' said he, 'why nothin', and that's the reason they sell him. This is town-meetin' day, and we always sell the poor for the year, to the lowest bidder. Them that will keep them for the lowest sum, gets them.' 'Why,' says I, 'that feller that bought him is a pauper himself, to my sartin knowledge. If you were to take him up by the heels and shake him for a week, you couldn't shake sixpence out of him. How can he keep him? it appears to me the poor buy the poor here, and that they all starve together.' Says I, 'there was a very good man once lived to Liverpool, so good, he said he hadn't sinned for seven years: well, he put a mill-dam across the river, and stopped all the fish from goin' up, and the court fined him fifty pounds for it; and this good man was so wrathy, he thought he should feel better to swear a little, but conscience told him it was wicked. So he compounded with conscience, and cheated the devil, by calling it a "dam fine business." Now, friend Porter, if this is your poor-law, it is a damn poor law, I tell you, and no good can come of such hard-hearted doins. It's no wonder your country don't prosper, for who ever heerd of a blessin' on such carryins on as this?' Says I, 'Did you ever hear tell of sartain rich man, that had a beggar called Lazarus laid at his gate, and how the dogs had more compassion than he had, and came and licked his sores? cause if you have, look at that forehanded and 'sponsible man there, Deacon Westfall, and you see the rich man. And then look at that 'ere pauper, dragged away in that ox-cart from his wife forever, like a feller to States' Prison, and you see Lazarus. Recollect what follered, John Porter, and have neither art nor part in it, as you are a Christian man.'

"It fairly made me sick all day. John Porter follered me out of the house, and as I was a turnin' Old Clay, said he, 'Mr. Slick,' says he, 'I never seed it in that 'ere light afore, for it's our custom, and custom, you know, will reconcile one to 'most anything. I must say, it does appear, as you lay it out, an unfeelin' way of providin' for the poor; but, as touchin' the matter of dividin' man and wife, why' (and he peered all round to see that no one was within hearin'), 'why, I don't know, but if it was my allotment to be sold, I'd as lieves they'd sell me separate from Jane as not, for it appears to me it's about the best part of it.'

"Now, what I have told you, Squire, said the Clockmaker, "is the truth; and if members, instead of their everlastin' politics, would only look into these matters a little, I guess it would be far better for the country. So, as for our Declaration of Independence, I guess you needn't twit me with our slave-sales, for we deal only in blacks; but Bluenose approbates no distinction in colors, and when reduced to poverty, is reduced to slavery, and is sold—*a white nigger.*"

SELECTED REFERENCES

Chattick, V. L. O. *Thomas Chandler Haliburton* (1924).
Rourke, Constance. *American Humor: A Study of the National Character* (1931).

PROJECTS AND PROBLEMS

Sam Slick's attitude toward Nova Scotians is suggestive of the current Ontario practice of calling residents of Newfoundland "Newfies" and telling "Newfie jokes" that are comparable to the "Polish jokes" in circulation in the United States. Is his use of "Bluenose" for the residents of Nova Scotia equivalent to his use of "nigger"?

Consider the relationship between Haliburton's work and *The Biglow Papers*, in which James Russell Lowell says:

"Chaps that make black slaves o' niggers
Want to make wite slaves o' you."

Compare Haliburton's use of the dialect of a Yankee peddler with Finley Peter Dunne's later handling of the brogue of a saloon keeper. Do they use dialect as a device to make social criticism more acceptable to their readers?

Relate Sam Slick to the tradition of frontier humor, with reference to the works of such men as Davy Crockett, Augustus B. Longstreet, Johnson Jones Hooper, George W. Harris, and Mark Twain. See *Humor of the Old Southwest* (1964), ed. by Hennig Cohen and William B. Dillingham.

Compare Haliburton's satire on a slave auction in "The White Nigger" with auction scenes in serious antislavery literature. See the auction scene by William Wells Brown in this volume and consider Frederick Law Olmstead's account of an auction in Richmond, Virginia, in *A Journey in the Seabord Slave States* (1856).

ROBERT MONTGOMERY BIRD
(1806-1854)

Nick of the Woods (1837), from which the following selection is taken, is the best known novel by a physician and playwright whose treatment of the Indian was more sensational and less sympathetic than that of James Fenimore Cooper. Nick, or the Jibbenainosay, is an odd Quaker who pretends to be peaceful but wreaks a bloody vengeance on his foes. The characters in the selection include Roland and Edith, conventional young lovers, and Telie Doe, supposedly the daughter of a renegade white man.

INDIAN WARFARE ON THE KENTUCKY BORDER

... His gaze fell upon a naked Indian stretched under a tree hard by, and sheltered from view only by a dead bough lately fallen from its trunk, yet lying so still and motionless that he might easily have been passed by without observation in the growing dusk and twilight of the woods, had it not been for the instinctive terrors of the pony, which, like other horses, had, and indeed, all other domestic beasts in the settlements, often thus pointed out to their masters the presence of an enemy.

The rifle of the soldier was in an instant cocked and at his shoulder, while the pedler and Emperor, as it happened, were too much discomposed at the spectacle to make any such show of battle. They gazed blankly upon the leader, whose piece, settling down into an aim that must have been fatal, suddenly wavered, and then to their surprise, was withdrawn.

"The slayer has been here before us," he exclaimed; "the man is dead and scalped already!"

With these words he advanced to the tree, and the others following, they beheld with horror the body of a savage of vast and noble proportions, lying on its face across the roots of the tree, and glued, it might almost be said, to the earth by a mass of coagulated blood, that had issued from the scalped and axe-cloven skull. The fragments of a rifle, shattered, as it seemed, by a violent blow against the tree under which it lay, were scattered at his side, with a broken powder-horn, a splintered knife, the helve of a tomahawk, and other equipments of a warrior, all in like manner shivered to pieces by the unknown assassin. The warrior seemed to have perished only after a fearful struggle; the earth was torn where he lay, and his hands, yet grasping the soil, were dyed a double red in the blood of his antagonist, or perhaps in his own.

While Roland gazed upon the spectacle, amazed, and wondering how the wretched being had met his death, which must have been very recently, and whilst his party was within the sound of a rifle-shot, he observed a shudder to creep over the apparently life-

278

less frame; the fingers relaxed their grasp of the earth, and then clutched it again with violence; a broken, strangling rattle came from the throat; and a spasm of convulsion seizing upon every limb, it was suddenly raised a little upon one arm, so as to display the countenance, covered with blood, the eyes retroverted into their orbits, and glaring with the sightless whites. It was a horrible spectacle,—the last convulsion of many that had shaken the wretched and insensible, yet still suffering clay, since it had received its death-stroke.

The spasm was the last, and but momentary; yet it sufficed to raise the body of the mangled barbarian so far, that when the pang that excited it suddenly ceased, and with it the life of the sufferer, the body rolled over on the back, and thus lay, exposing to the eyes of the lookers-on two gashes wide and gory on the breast, traced by a sharp knife and a powerful hand, and, as it seemed, in the mere wantonness of a malice and lust of blood, which even death could not satisfy. The sight of these gashes answered the question Roland had asked of his own imagination; they were in the form of a *cross;* and as the legend, so long derided, of the forest-fiend recurred to his memory, he responded, almost with a feeling of superstitious awe, to the trembling cry of Telie Doe:—

"It is the Jibbenainosay!" she exclaimed, staring upon the corpse with mingled horror and wonder; "Nick of the Woods is up again in the forest!"

°   °   °   °   °

The chief then pointed to a keg of the fire–water, and this was also given to the Piankeshaw, who received it with a grin of ecstasy, embraced it, snuffed at its odoriferous contents, and then passed it in like manner to his second follower. The chief made yet another signal, and the deputy, taking Roland by the arm, and giving him a piercing, perhaps even a pitying look, delivered him likewise into the hands of the Piankeshaw, who, as if his happiness were now complete, received him with a yell of joy, that was caught up by his two companions, and finally joined in by all the savages present.

This shout seemed to be the signal for the breaking up of the convention. All rose to their feet, iterating and reiterating the savage cry, while the Piankeshaw, clutching his prize, and slipping a noose around the thong that bound his arms, endeavored to drag him to the horse, on which the young men had already secured the keg of liquor, and which they were holding in readiness for the elder barbarian to mount.

At that conjecture, and while Roland was beginning to suspect that even the wretched consolation of remaining in captivity by his kinswoman's side was about to be denied him, and while the main body of savages were obviously bidding farewell to the little bands of Piankeshaws, some shaking them by the hands, while others made game of the prisoner's distress in sundry Indian ways, and all uttering yells expressive of their different feelings, there appeared rushing from the copse, and running among the barbarians, the damsel Telie Doe, who, not a little to the surprise even of the ill-fated Roland himself, ran to his side, caught the rope by which he was held, and endeavored frantically to snatch it from the hands of the Piankeshaw.

The act, for one of her peculiarly timorous spirit, was surprising enough; but a great transformation seemed to have suddenly taken place in her character and even her appearance, which was less that of a feeble woman engaged in a work of humanity, than of a tigress infuriated by the approach of hunters against the lair of her sleeping young. She grasped the cord with unexpected strength, and her eyes flashed fire as they wandered around, until they met those of the supposed half-breed, to whom she called, with tones of the most vehement indignation,—"Oh, father, father! what are you doing? You won't give him up to the murderers? You promised, you promised——"

"Peace, fool!" interrupted the man thus addressed, taking her by the arm, and endeavoring to jerk her from the prisoner; "away with you to your place, and be silent."

"I will not, father;—I will not be silent, I will not away!" cried the girl, resisting his efforts, and speaking with a voice that mingled the bitterest reproach with imploring entreaty; "you are a white man, father, and not an Indian; yes, father, you are no Indian, and you promised no harm should be done,—you did, father, you *did* promise!"

"Away, gal, I tell you!" thundered the renegade parent; and he again strove to drag her from the prisoner. But Telie, as driven frantic by the act, flung her arms round Roland's body, from which she was drawn only by an effort of strength which her weaker powers were unable to resist. But even then she did not give over her purpose; but starting from her father's arm, she ran screaming back to Roland, and would have again clasped him in her own; when the renegade, driven to fury by her opposition, arrested her with one hand, and with the other catching up a knife that lay in the grass, he made as if, in his fit of passion, he would have actually plunged it into her breast. His malevolent visage and brutal threat awoke the terrors of the woman in her heart, and she sank on her knees, crying, with a piercing voice,—"Oh, father, don't kill me! don't kill your own daughter!"

"Kill you, indeed!" muttered the outlaw, with a laugh of scorn; "even Injuns don't kill their own children;" and, taking advantage of her terror, he beckoned to the Piankeshaw, who, as well as all the other Indians, seemed greatly astounded and scandalized at the indecorous interference of a female in the affairs of warriors, to remove the prisoner; which he did by immediately beginning to drag him down the hill. The action was not unobserved by the girl, whose struggles to escape from her father's arms, to pursue, as it seemed, after the soldier, Roland could long see, while her wild and piteous cries were still longer brought to his ears . . . .

SUGGESTED ADDITIONAL READING

Sheppard Lee

SELECTED REFERENCE

Dahl, Curtis. Robert Montgomery Bird (1963).

PROJECTS AND PROBLEMS

Discuss similarities between John Smith's rescue by Pocahontas and Telie Doe's heroic efforts to save Roland.

Compare Bird's portrayal of Indians in *Nick of the Woods* with that of William Gilmore Simms in *The Yemassee.*

Discuss the use of black stereotypes for antislavery purposes in *Sheppard Lee*, in which the white protagonist lives for a time as a contented slave.

NATHANIEL HAWTHORNE
(1804–1864)

The stories and novels of Nathaniel Hawthorne are classics of American romanticism, but, whether they are set in his own time or depict the New England of the Puritan Age, they give little attention to the minority presence. The first selection is from *The American Notebooks*. The second is an essay written about a decade later, when he was editing a magazine for children.

THE COMMENCEMENT
CROWD AT WILLIAMS
COLLEGE, 1838

Wednesday, August 15th.—I went to Commencement at Williams College,—five miles distant. At the tavern were students with ribbons, pink or blue, fluttering from their buttonholes, these being the badges of rival societies. There was a considerable gathering of people, chiefly arriving in wagons or buggies, some in barouches, and very few in chaises. The most characteristic part of the scene was where the pedlers, gingerbread-sellers, etc., were collected, a few hundred yards from the meeting-house. . . .

There were a good many blacks among the crowd. I suppose they used to emigrate across the border, while New York was a slave State. There were enough of them to form a party, though greatly in the minority; and, a squabble arising, some of the blacks were knocked down, and otherwise maltreated. I saw one old negro, a genuine specimen of the slave negro, without any of the foppery of the race in our part of the State,—an old fellow, with a bag, I suppose of broken victuals, on his shoulder, and his pockets stuffed out at his hips with the like provender; full of grimaces and ridiculous antics, laughing laughably, yet without affectation; then talking with a strange kind of pathos about the whippings he used to get while he was a slave;—a singular creature, of mere feeling, with some glimmering of sense. Then there was another gray old negro, but of a different stamp, politic, sage, cautious, yet with boldness enough, talking about the rights of his race, yet so as not to provoke his audience; discoursing of the advantage of living under laws, and the wonders that might ensue, in that very assemblage, if there were no laws; in the midst of this deep wisdom, turning off the anger of a half-drunken fellow by a merry retort, a leap in the air, and a negro's laugh. I was interested—there being a drunken negro ascending the meeting-house steps, and near him three or four well-dressed and decent negro wenches—to see the look of scorn and shame and sorrow and painful sympathy which one of them assumed at this disgrace of her color.

THE DUSTON FAMILY

Goodman Duston and his wife, somewhat less than a century and a half ago, dwelt in Haverhill, at that time a small frontier settlement in the province of Massachusetts Bay. They had already added seven children to the King's liege subjects in America; and Mrs. Duston about a week before the period of our narrative, had blessed her husband with an eighth. One day in March, 1698, when Mr. Duston had gone forth about his ordinary business, there fell out an event, which had nearly left him a childless man, and a widower besides. An Indian war party, after traversing the trackless forest all the way from Canada, broke in upon their remote and defenceless town. Goodman Duston heard the war whoop and alarm, and, being on horseback, immediately set off full speed to look after the safety of his family. As he dashed along, he beheld dark wreaths of smoke eddying from the roofs of several dwellings near the road side; while the groans of dying men,—the shrieks of affrighted women, and the screams of children, pierced his ear, all mingled with the horrid yell of the raging savages. The poor man trembled yet spurred on so much the faster, dreading that he should find his own cottage in a blaze, his wife murdered in her bed, and his little ones tossed into the flames. But, drawing near the door, he saw his seven elder children, of all ages between two years and seventeen, issuing out together, and running down the road to meet him. The father only bade them make the best of their way to the nearest garrison, and, without a moment's pause, flung himself from his horse, and rushed into Mrs. Duston's bedchamber.

The good woman, as we have before hinted, had lately added an eighth to the seven former proofs of her conjugal affection; and she now lay with the infant in her arms, and her nurse, the widow Mary Neff, watching by her bedside. Such was Mrs. Duston's helpless state, when her pale and breathless husband burst into the chamber, bidding her instantly to rise and flee for her life. Scarcely were the words out of his mouth, when the Indian yell was heard: and staring wildly out of the window, Goodman Duston saw that the blood-thirsty foe was close at hand. At this terrible instant, it appears that the thought of his children's danger rushed so powerfully upon his heart, that he quite forgot the still more perilous situation of his wife; or, as is not improbable, he had such knowledge of the good lady's character, as afforded him a comfortable hope that she would hold her own, even in a contest with a whole tribe of Indians. However that might be, he seized his gun and rushed out of doors again, meaning to gallop after his seven children, and snatch up one of them in his flight, lest his whole race and generation should be blotted from the earth, in that fatal hour. With this idea, he rode up behind them, swift as the wind. They had, by this time, got about forty rods from the house, all pressing forward in a group; and though the younger children tripped and stumbled, yet the elder ones were not prevailed upon, by the fear of death, to take to their heels and leave these poor little souls to perish. Hearing the tramp of hoofs in their rear, they looked round, and espying Goodman Duston, all suddenly stopped. The little ones stretched out their arms; while the elder boys and girls, as it were, resigned their charge into his hands; and all the seven children seemed to say—"Here is our father! Now we are safe!"

But if ever a poor mortal was in trouble, and perplexity, and anguish of spirit, that man was Mr. Duston! He felt his heart yearn towards these seven poor helpless children, as if each were singly possessed of his whole affections; for not one among them all, but had some peculiar claim to their dear father's love. There was his first-born; there, too, the little one who, till within a week past, had been the baby; there was a girl with her mother's features, and a boy, the picture of himself, and another in whom the looks of both parents were mingled; there was one child, whom he loved for his mild, quiet, and holy disposition, and destined him to be a minister; and another, whom he loved not less for his rough and fearless spirit, and who, could he live to be a man, would do a man's part against these bloody Indians. Goodman Duston looked at the poor things, one by one; and with yearning fondness, he looked at them all, together; then he gazed up to Heaven for a moment, and finally waved his hand to his seven beloved ones. "Go on, my children," said he, calmly. "We will live or die together!"

He reined in his horse, and caused him to walk behind the children, who, hand in hand, went onward, hushing their sobs and wailings, lest these sounds should bring the savages upon them. Nor was it long, before the fugitives had proof that the red devils had found their track. There was a curl of smoke from behind the huge trunk of a tree—a sudden and sharp report echoed through the woods—and a bullet hissed over Goodman Duston's shoulder, and passed above the children's heads. The father, turning half round on his horse, took aim and fired at the skulking foe, with such effect as to cause a momentary delay of the pursuit. Another shot—and another— whistled from the covert of the forest; but still the little band pressed on, unharmed; and the stealthy nature of the Indians forbade them to rush boldly forward, in the face of so firm an enemy as Goodman Duston. Thus he and his seven children continued their retreat, creeping along, as Cotton Mather observes, "at the pace of a child of five years old," till the stockades of a little frontier fortress appeared in view, and the savages gave up the chase.

We must not forget Mrs. Duston, in her distress. Scarcely had her husband fled from the house, ere the chamber was thronged with the horrible visages of the wild Indians, bedaubed with paint and besmeared with blood, brandishing their tomahawks in her face, and threatening to add her scalp to those that were already hanging at their girdles. It was, however, their interest to save her alive, if the thing might be, in order to exact a ransom. Our great–great–grand-mothers, when taken captive in the old times of Indian warfare, ap-pear, in nine cases out of ten, to have been in pretty much such a delicate situation as Mrs. Duston; notwithstanding which, they were wonderfully sustained through long, rough, and hurried marches, amid toil, weariness, and starvation, such as the Indians themselves could hardly endure. Seeing that there was no help for it, Mrs. Dus-ton rose, and she and the widow Neff, with the infant in her arms, followed their captors out of doors. As they crossed the threshold, the poor babe set up a feeble wail; It was its death cry. In an instant, an Indian seized it by the heels, swung it in the air, dashed out its brains against the trunk of the nearest tree, and threw the little corpse at the mother's feet. Perhaps it was the remembrance of that moment, that hardened Hannah Duston's heart, when her time of vengeance came. But now, nothing could be done, but to stifle her grief and rage within her bosom, and follow the Indians into the dark gloom of the forest, hardly venturing to throw a parting glance at the blazing cottage, where she had dwelt happily with her husband, and had borne him eight children—the seven, of whose fate she knew nothing, and the infant, whom she had just seen murdered. The first day's march was fifteen miles; and during that, and many succeeding days, Mrs. Duston kept pace with her captors; for, had she lagged behind, a tomahawk would at once have been sunk into her brains. More than one terrible warning was given her; more than one of her fellow captives,—of whom there were many,—after tottering feebly, at length sank upon the ground; the next moment, the death groan was breathed, and the scalp was reeking at an Indian's girdle. The unburied corpse was left in the forest, till the rites of sepulture should be performed by the autumnal gales, strewing the withered leaves upon the whitened bones. When out of danger of immediate pursuit, the prisoners, according to Indian custom, were divided among different parties of the savages, each of whom were to shift for themselves. Mrs. Duston, the widow Neff, and an English lad, fell to the lot of a family, consisting of two stout warriours, three squaws, and seven children. These Indians, like most with whom the French had held intercourse, were Catholics; and Cotton Mather affirms, on Mrs. Duston's authority, that they prayed at morning, noon, and night, nor ever partook of food without a prayer; nor suffered their children to sleep, till they had prayed to the Christian's God. Mather, like an old hard-hearted, pedantic bigot, as he was, seems trebly to exult in the destruction of these poor wretches, on account of their Popish superstitions. Yet what can be more touching than to think of these wild Indians, in their loneliness and their wanderings, wherever they went among the dark, mysterious woods, still keeping up domestic worship, with all the regularity of a household at its peaceful fireside.

They were travelling to a rendezvous of the savages, somewhere in the northeast. One night, being now above a hundred miles from Haverhill, the red men and women, and the little red children, and the three pale faces, Mrs. Duston, the widow Neff, and the English lad, made their encampment, and kindled a fire beneath the gloomy old trees, on a small island in Contocook river. The barbarians sat down to what scanty food Providence had sent them, and shared it with their prisoners, as if they had all been the children of one wigwam, and had grown up together on the margin of the same river within the shadow of the forest. Then the Indians said their prayers

—the prayers that the Romish priests had taught them—and made the sign of the cross upon their dusky breasts, and composed themselves to rest. But the three prisoners prayed apart; and when their petitions were ended, they likewise lay down, with their feet to the fire. The night wore on; and the light and cautious slumbers of the red men were often broken, by the rush and ripple of the stream, or the groaning and moaning of the forest, as if nature were wailing over her wild children; and sometimes, too, the little red skins cried in sleep, and the Indian mothers awoke to hush them. But, a little before break of day, a deep, dead slumber fell upon the Indians. "See," cries Cotton Mather, triumphantly, "if it prove not so!"

Up rose Mrs. Duston, holding her own breath, to listen to the long, deep breathing of her captors. Then she stirred the widow Neff, whose place was by her own, and likewise the English lad; and all three stood up, with the doubtful gleam of the decaying fire hovering upon their ghastly visages, as they stared round at the fated slumberers. The next instant, each of the three captives held a tomahawk. Hark! that low moan, as of one in a troubled dream—it told a warriour's death pang! Another!—Another!—and the third half-uttered groan was from a woman's lips. But, Oh, the children! their skins are red; yet spare them, Hannah Duston, spare those seven little ones, for the sake of the seven that have fed at your own breast. "Seven," quoth Mrs. Duston to herself. "Eight children have I borne —and where are the seven, and where is the eighth!" The thought nerved her arm; and the copper coloured babes slept the same dead sleep with their Indian mothers. Of all that family, only one woman escaped, dreadfully wounded, and fled shrieking into the wilderness! and a boy, whom, it is said, Mrs. Duston had meant to save alive. But he did well to flee from the raging tigress! There was little safety for a red skin, when Hannah Duston's blood was up.

The work being finished, Mrs. Duston laid hold of the long black hair of the warriours, and the women, and the children, and took all their ten scalps, and left the island, which bears her name to this very day. According to our notion, it should be held accursed, for her sake. Would that the bloody old hag had been drowned in crossing Contocook river, or that she had sunk over head and ears in a swamp, and been there buried, till summoned forth to confront her victims at the Day of Judgment; or that she had gone astray and been starved to death in the forest, and nothing ever seen of her again, save her skeleton, with the ten scalps twisted round it for a girdle! But, on the contrary, she and her companions came safe home, and received the bounty on the dead Indians, besides liberal presents from private gentlemen, and fifty pounds from the Governour of Maryland. In her old age, being sunk into decayed circumstances, she claimed, and, we believe, received a pension, as a further price of blood.

This awful woman, and that tender hearted, yet valiant man, her husband, will be remembered as long as the deeds of old times are told round a New England fireside. But how different is her renown from his!

SUGGESTED ADDITIONAL READINGS

"Ethan Brand"
"The Gentle Boy"
"Young Goodman Brown"
The Scarlet Letter
The Marble Faun

SELECTED REFERENCES

Carpenter, F. I. "Puritans Preferred Blondes: The Heroines of Melville and Hawthorne." *New England Quarterly,* 9 (1936), 253–72.

Doubleday, Neal Frank. "Hawthorne's Hester and Feminism." *PMLA,* 54 (1939), 825–28.

Fass, Barbara. "Rejection of Paternalism: Hawthorne's 'My Kinsman Molineaux' and Ellison's *Invisible Man.*" *CLA Journal,* 14 (1971), 317–23.

Stewart, Randall. "Hawthorne and the Civil War." *Studies in Philology,* 34 (1937), 91–106.

Turner, Arlin. "Hawthorne and Reform." *New England Quarterly,* 15 (1942), 700–14.

Voight, Gilbert P. "Hawthorne and the Roman Catholic Church." *New England Quarterly,* 19 (1946), 394–98.
Harap, Louis. *The Image of the Jew in American Literature* (1974).

PROJECTS AND PROBLEMS

Contrast Hawthorne's picture of sin in Puritan New England (*The Scarlet Letter*) and sin in Catholic Italy (*The Marble Faun*).

Compare Hawthorne's "The Duston Family" with Thoreau's account of Hannah Duston's encounter with Indians in *A Week on the Concord and Merrimack Rivers.*

In his *Life of Franklin Pierce,* Hawthorne expressed the view that slavery was an evil that divine Providence would someday cause to "vanish like a dream" and that should not be subjected to the reformer's zeal. Was this opinion his own as well as Pierce's?

Compare Hawthorne's position on John Brown, as stated in his essay "Chiefly about War Matters" in *Atlantic Monthly* in 1862, with that of Frederick Douglass and William Dean Howells. Consider also Hawthorne's comments on Lincoln in that journal's July issue.

Do Hawthorne's casual references to minorities in his journals, and do the Indians, Jews, Quakers, and Italians in his fiction, tend to support the stereotypes or to challenge them? Consider, for instance, the Indian references in *The Scarlet Letter,* the Jew in "Ethan Brand," and Miriam in *The Marble Faun.*

EDGAR ALLAN POE
(1809–1849)

Most of the poetry, criticism, and fiction of Edgar Allan Poe has little to do with the particulars of American experience. This selection is from Chapters IV and V of "The Journal of Julius Rodman," first published in 1840 in *Burton's Gentleman's Magazine*, of which he was then co-editor. The story, which purports to be an account of the first passage across the Rocky Mountains by a party of white men, is based on Poe's reading and shows his acquaintance with Washington Irving's *Astoria*. In its use of a diary and certain other narrative devices, it is characteristic of Poe's fiction.

THE SIOUX AND OLD TOBY

... *Sioux* is the French term for the Indians in question—the English have corrupted it into *Sues*. Their primitive name is said to be *Darcotas*. Their original seats were on the Mississippi, but they had gradually extended their dominions, and, at the date of the Journal, occupied almost the whole of that vast territory circumscribed by the Mississippi, the Saskatchawine, the Missouri, and the Red River of Lake Winnipeg. They were subdivided into numerous clans. The Darcotas proper were the Winowacants, called the Gens du Lac by the French—consisting of about five hundred warriors, and living on both sides of the Mississippi, in the vicinity of the Falls of St. Anthony. Neighbors of the Winowacants, and residing north of them on the river St. Peter's, were the Wappatomies, about two hundred men. Still farther up the St. Peter's lived a band of one hundred, called the Wappytooties, among themselves, and by the French the Gens des Feuilles. Higher up the river yet, and near its source, resided the Sissytoonies, in number two hundred or thereabouts. On the Missouri dwelt the Yanktons and the Tetons. Of the first tribe there were two branches, the northern and southern, of which the former led an Arab life in the plains at the sources of the Red, Sioux, and Jacques rivers, being in number about five hundred. The southern branch kept possession of the tract lying between the river Des Moines on the one hand, and the rivers Jacques and Sioux on the other. But the Sioux most renowned for deeds of violence are the Tetons; and of these there were four tribes—the Saonies, the Minnakenozzies, the Okydandies, and the Bois-Brûlés. These last, a body of whom were now lying in wait to intercept the voyagers, were the most savage and formidable of the whole race, numbering about two hundred men, and residing on both sides of the Missouri near the rivers called by Captains Lewis and Clark, the White and Teton. Just below the Chayenne river were the Okydandies, one hundred and fifty. The Minnakenozzies—two hundred and fifty—occupied a tract between the Chayenne and the Watarhoo; and the Saonies, the largest of the Teton bands, counting as many as three hundred warriors, were found in the vicinity of the Warreconne.

Besides these four divisions—the regular Sioux—there were five tribes of seceders called Assiniboins; the Menatopae Assiniboins, two hundred, on Mouse river, between the Assiniboin and the Missouri; the Gens de Feuilles Assiniboins, two hundred and fifty, occupying both sides of White river; the Big Devils, four hundred and fifty, wandering about the heads of Porcupine and Milk rivers; with two other bands whose names are not mentioned, but who roved on the Saskatchawine and numbered together, about seven hundred men. These seceders were often at war with the parent or original Sioux.

In person, the Sioux generally are an ugly ill-made race, their limbs being much too small for the trunk, according to our ideas of the human form—their cheek bones are high, and their eyes protruding and dull. The heads of the men are shaved, with the exception of a small spot on the crown, whence a long tuft is permitted to fall in plaits upon the shoulders; this tuft is an object of scrupulous care, but is now and then cut off, upon an occasion of grief or solemnity. A full dressed Sioux chief presents a striking appearance. The whole surface of the body is painted with grease and coal. A shirt of skins is worn as far down as the waist, while round the middle is a girdle of the same material, and sometimes of cloth, about an inch in width; this supports a piece of blanket or fur passing between the thighs. Over the shoulders is a white-dressed buffalo mantle, the hair of which is worn next the skin in fair weather, but turned outwards in wet. This robe is large enough to envelop the whole body, and is frequently ornamented with porcupine quills (which make a rattling noise as the warrior moves) as well as with a great variety of rudely painted figures, emblematical of the wearer's military character. Fastened to the top of the head is worn a hawk's feather, adorned with porcupine quills. Leggings of dressed antelope skin serve the purpose of pantaloons, and have seams at the sides, about two inches wide, and bespotted here and there with small tufts of human hair, the trophies of some scalping excursion. The moccasins are of elk or buffalo skin, the hair worn inwards; on great occasions the chief is seen with the skin of a polecat dangling at the heel of each boot. The Sioux are indeed partial to this noisome animal; whose fur is in high favor for tobacco-pouches and other appendages.

The dress of a chieftain's squaw is also remarkable. Her hair is suffered to grow long, is parted across the forehead, and hangs loosely behind, or is collected into a kind of net. Her moccasins do not differ from her husband's; but her leggings extend upwards only as far as the knee, where they are met by an awkward shirt of elk–skin depending to the ancles, and supported above by a string going over the shoulders. This shirt is usually confined to the waist by a girdle, and over all is thrown a buffalo mantle like that of the men. The tents of the Teton Sioux are described as of neat construction, being formed of white-dressed buffalo hide, well secured and sup-ported by poles.

o   o   o   o   o

May 5. As we were getting under way very early this morning, a large party of Assiniboins suddenly rushed upon the boats, and suc-ceeded in taking possession of the piroque before we could make any effectual resistance. No one was in it at the time except Jules, who escaped by throwing himself into the river, and swimming to the large boat, which we had pushed out into the stream. These In-dians had been brought upon us by the two who had visited us the day before, and the party must have approached us in the most stealthy manner imaginable, as we had our sentries regularly posted, and even Neptune failed to give any token of their vicinity.

We were preparing to fire upon the enemy when Misquash (the new interpreter—son of Waukerassah) gave us to understand that the Assiniboins were friends and were now making signals of amity. Although we could not help thinking that the highway robbery of our boat was but an indifferent way of evincing friendship, still we were willing to see what these people had to say, and desired Mis-quash to ask them why they had behaved as they did. They replied with many protestations of regard; and we at length found that they really had no intention of molesting us any farther than to satisfy an ardent curiosity which consumed them, and which they now entreated us to appease. It appeared that the two Indians of the day before, whose singular conduct had so surprised us, had been struck with sudden amazement at the sooty appearance of our negro, Toby. They had never before seen or heard of a blackamoor, and it must therefore be confessed that their astonishment was not altogether causeless. Toby, moreover, was as ugly an old gentleman as ever spoke—having all the peculiar features of his race; the swollen lips, large white protruding eyes, flat nose, long ears, double head, pot-belly, and bow legs. Upon relating their adventure to their companions, the two savages could obtain no credit for the wonderful story, and were about losing caste for ever, as liars and double-dealers, when they proposed to conduct the whole band to the boats by way of vindicating their veracity. The sudden attack seemed to have been the mere result of impatience on the part of the still incredulous Assiniboins; for they never afterwards evidenced the slightest hostility, and yielded up the piroque as soon as we made them understand that we would let them have a good look at old Toby. The latter personage took the matter as a very good joke, and went ashore at once, *in naturalibus,* that the inquisitive savages might observe the whole extent of the question. Their astonishment and satisfaction were profound and complete. At first they doubted the evidence of their own eyes, spitting upon their fingers and rubbing the skin of the negro to be sure that it was not painted. The wool on the head elicited repeated shouts of applause, and the bandy legs were the subject of unqualified admiration. A jig dance on the part of our ugly friend brought matters to a climax. Wonder was now at its height. Approbation could go no farther. Had Toby but possessed a single spark of ambition he might then have made his fortune for ever by ascending the throne of the Assiniboins, and reigning as King Toby the First. . . .

SUGGESTED ADDITIONAL READINGS

"The Gold-Bug"
The Narrative of Arthur Gordon Pym

SELECTED REFERENCES

Campbell, Killis. "Poe's Treatment of the Negro and the Negro Dialect." *University of Texas Studies in English,* 16 (1936), 107–14.

Levin, Harry. *The Power of Blackness* (1958).

Marchand, Ernest. "Poe as Social Critic." *American Literature*, 6 (1934), 28–43.

Parkes, Henry Bamford. "Poe, Hawthorne, Melville: An Essay in Sociological Criticism." *Partisan Review*, 16 (1949), 157–65.

Stockton, Eric. "Poe's Use of Negro Dialect in 'The Gold-Bug.'" *Studies in Language and Linguistics in Honor of Charles C. Fries*, ed. by Albert H. Marckwardt (1964). Reprinted in *A Various Language: Perspectives in American Dialects*, ed. by Virginia V. Williamson and Virginia M. Burke (1971).

PROJECTS AND PROBLEMS

The review of James Kirke Paulding's *Slavery in the United States* that was once attributed to Poe is now known to be the work of Beverley Tucker. What was Poe's opinion of slavery?

Does Poe's picture of Jupiter in "The Gold-Bug" fit the stereotypes of the Plantation Tradition presented by his friend J. P. Kennedy in *Swallow Barn?* Take into account Poe's racial references in "How to Write a Blackwood Article," "A Predicament," "The Man Who Was Used Up," "The Oblong Box," "The Journal of Julius Rodman," and "The Elk." Note that in his essay on Catherine M. Sedgwick he criticized her for the dialogue she gave a black female character, remarking, "Who would suppose this graceful eloquence to proceed from the mouth of a negro woman?"

Compare Poe's treatment of the Indian in "The Journal of Julius Rodman" and *The Narrative of Arthur Gordon Pym* with his comment in "Marginalia" that to rename the United States "Appalachia" would be to "do honor to the Aborigines, whom, hitherto, we have at all points unmercifully despoiled, assassinated and dishonored."

Which color, black or white, is the symbol for evil in *The Narrative of Arthur Gordon Pym?* Include in your study Harry Levin's *The Power of Blackness* and Sidney Kaplan's introduction to the 1960 edition of the tale.

RICHARD HENRY DANA, JR.
(1815–1882)

The next selection is Chapter 21 of *Two Years Before the Mast*, published anonymously in 1840 by a Boston Brahmin who later earned distinction as a lawyer and humanitarian laboring in defense of the fugitive slave and the common seaman. Dana's health led him to interrupt his undergraduate studies at Harvard for a voyage on the brig *Pilgrim*. The journal in which he recorded his experiences and observations served as the basis for his book.

CALIFORNIA AND ITS INHABITANTS

We kept up a constant connection with the presidio, and by the close of the summer I had added much to my vocabulary, beside having made the acquaintance of nearly everybody in the place, and acquired some knowledge of the character and habits of the people, as well as of the institutions under which they live.

California was first discovered in 1536, by Cortes, and was subsequently visited by numerous other adventurers, as well as commissioned voyagers of the crown. It was found to be inhabited by numerous tribes of Indians, and to be in many parts extremely fertile; to which, of course, was added rumors of gold mines, pearl fishery, etc. No sooner was the importance of the country known, than the Jesuits obtained leave to establish themselves in it, to christianize and enlighten the Indians. They established missions in various parts of the country toward the close of the seventeenth century, and collected the natives about them, baptizing them into the church, and teaching them the arts of civilized life. To protect the Jesuits in their missions, and at the same time to support the power of the crown over the civilized Indians, two forts were erected and garrisoned, one at San Diego, and the other at Monterey. These were called Presidios, and divided the command of the whole country between them. Presidios have since been established at Santa Barbara and San Francisco; thus dividing the country into four large districts, each with its presidio, and governed by the commandant. The soldiers, for the most part, married civilized Indians; and thus, in the vicinity of each presidio, sprung up, gradually, small towns. In the course of time, vessels began to come into the ports to trade with the missions, and received hides in return; and thus began the great trade of California. Nearly all the cattle in the country belonged to the missions, and they employed their Indians, who became, in fact, their slaves, in tending their vast herds. In the year 1793, when Vancouver visited San Diego, the mission had obtained great wealth and power, and are accused of having depreciated the country with the sovereign, that they might be allowed to retain their possessions. On the expulsion of the Jesuits from the Spanish dominions, the missions passed into the hands of the Franciscans, though without any essential change in their management. Ever since the independence of Mexico, the missions have been going down; until, at last, a law was passed, stripping them of all their possessions, and confining the priests to their spiritual duties; and at the same time declaring all the Indians free and independent *Rancheros*. The change in the condition of the Indians was, as may be supposed, only nominal: they are virtually slaves, as much as they ever were. But in the missions, the change was complete. The priests have now no power, except in their religious character, and the great possessions of the missions are given over to be preyed upon by the harpies of the civil power, who are sent there in the capacity of *administradores*, to settle up the concerns; and who usually end, in a few years, by making themselves fortunes, and leaving their stewardships worse than they found them. The dynasty of the priests was much more acceptable to the people of the country, and, indeed, to every one concerned with the country, by trade or otherwise, than that of the administradores. The priests were attached perpetually to one mission, and felt the necessity of keeping up its credit. Accordingly, their debts were regularly paid, and the people were, in the main, well treated, and attached to those who had spent their whole lives among them. But the administradores are strangers sent from Mexico, having no interest in the country; not identified in any way with their charge, and, for the most part, men of desperate fortunes—broken down politicians and soldiers—whose only object is to retrieve their condition in as short a time as possible. The change had been made but a few years before our arrival upon the coast, yet, in that short time, the trade was much diminished, credit impaired, and the venerable missions going rapidly to decay. The external arrangements remain the same. There are four presidios, having under their protection the various missions, and pueblos, which are towns formed by the civil power, and containing no mission or presidio. The most northerly presidio is San Francisco; the next Monterey; the next Santa Barbara, including the mission of the same, St. Louis Obispo, and St. Buenaventura, which is the finest mission in the whole country, having very fertile soil and rich vineyards. The last, and most southerly, is San Diego, including the mission of the same, San Juan Campestraño, the Pueblo de los Angelos, the largest town in California, with the neighboring mission of San Gabriel. The priests in spiritual matters are subject to the Archbishop of Mexico, and in temporal matters to the governor–general, who is the great civil and military head of the country.

The government of the country is an arbitrary democracy; having no common law, and no judiciary. Their only laws are made and unmade at the caprice of the legislature, and are as variable as the legislature itself. They pass through the form of sending representatives to the congress at Mexico, but as it takes several months to go and return, and there is very little communication between the capital and this distant province, a member usually stays there, as permanent member, knowing very well that there will be revolutions at home before he can write and receive an answer; and if another member should be sent, he has only to challenge him, and decide the contested election in that way.

Revolutions are matters of constant occurrence in California. They are got up by men who are at the foot of the ladder and in desperate circumstances, just as a new political party is started by such men in our own country. The only object, of course, is the loaves and fishes; and instead of caucusing, paragraphing, libelling, feasting, promising, and lying, as with us, they take muskets and bayonets, and seizing upon the presidio and custom-house, divide the spoils, and declare a new dynasty. As for justice, they know no law but will and fear. A Yankee, who had been naturalized, and become a Catholic, and had married in the country, was sitting in his house at the Pueblo de los Angelos, with his wife and children, when a Spaniard, with whom he had had a difficulty, entered the house, and stabbed him to the heart before them all. The murderer was seized by some Yankees who had settled there, and kept in confinement until a statement of the whole affair could be sent to the governor-general. He refused to do anything about it, and the countrymen of the murdered man, seeing no prospect of justice being administered, made known that if nothing was done, they should try the man themselves. It chanced that, at this time, there was a company of forty trappers and hunters from Kentucky, with their rifles, who had made their head-quarters at the Pueblo; and these, together with the Americans and the Englishmen in the place, who were between twenty and thirty in number, took possession of the town, and waiting a reasonable time, proceeded to try the man according to the forms in their own country. A judge and jury were appointed, and he was tried, convicted, sentenced to be shot, and carried out before the town with his eyes blindfolded. The names of all the men were then put into a hat, and each one pledging himself to perform his duty, twelve names were drawn out, and the men took their stations with their rifles, and firing at the word, laid him dead. He was decently buried, and the place was restored quietly to the proper authorities. A general, with titles enough for an hidalgo, was at San Gabriel, and issued a proclamation as long as the foretop-bowline, threatening destruction to the rebels, but never stirred from his fort; for forty Kentucky hunters, with their rifles, were a match for a whole regiment of hungry, drawling, lazy half-breeds. This affair happened while we were at San Pedro, (the port of the Pueblo,) and we had all the particulars directly from those who were on the spot. A few months afterwards, another man, whom we had often seen in San Diego, murdered a man and his wife on the high road between the Pueblo and San Louis Rey, and the foreigners not feeling themselves called upon to act in this case, the parties being all natives, nothing was done about it; and I frequently afterwards saw the murderer in San Diego, where he was living with his wife and family.

When a crime has been committed by Indians, justice, or rather vengeance, is not so tardy. One Sunday afternoon, while I was at San Diego, an Indian was sitting on his horse, when another, with whom he had had some difficulty, came up to him, drew a long knife, and plunged it directly into the horse's heart. The Indian sprang from his falling horse, drew out the knife, and plunged it into the other Indian's breast, over his shoulder, and laid him dead. The poor fellow was seized at once, clapped into the calabozo, and kept there until an answer could be received from Monterey. A few weeks afterwards, I saw the poor wretch, sitting on the bare ground, in front of the calabozo, with his feet chained to a stake, and handcuffs about his wrists. I knew there was very little hope for him. Although the deed was done in hot blood, the horse on which he was sitting being his own, and a great favorite, yet he was an Indian, and that was enough. In about a week after I saw him, I heard that he had been shot. These few instances will serve to give one a notion of the distribution of justice in California.

In their domestic relations, these people are no better than in their public. The men are thriftless, proud, and extravagant, and very much given to gaming; and the women have but little education, and good deal of beauty, and their morality, of course, is none of the best; yet the instances of infidelity are much less frequent than one would at first suppose. In fact, one vice is set over against another; and thus, something like a balance is obtained. The women have but little virtue, but then the jealousy of their husbands is extreme, and their revenge deadly and almost certain. A few inches of cold steel has been the punishment of many an unwary man, who has been guilty, perhaps, of nothing more than indiscretion of manner. The difficulties of the attempt are numerous, and the consequences of discovery fatal. With the unmarried women, too, great watchfulness is used. The main object of the parents is to marry their daughters well, and to this, the slightest slip would be fatal. The sharp eyes of a dueña, and the cold steel of a father or brother, are a protection which the characters of most of them—men and women—render by no means useless; for the very men who would lay down their lives to avenge the dishonor of their own family, would risk the same lives to complete the dishonor of another.

Of the poor Indians, very little care is taken. The priests, indeed, at the missions, are said to keep them very strictly, and some rules are usually made by the alcaldes to punish their misconduct; but it all amounts to but little. Indeed, to show the entire want of any sense of morality or domestic duty among them, I have frequently known an Indian to bring his wife, to whom he was lawfully married in the church, down to the beach, and carry her back again, dividing with her the money which she had got from the sailors. If any of the girls were discovered by the alcalde to be open evil–livers, they were whipped, and kept at work sweeping the square of the presidio, and carrying mud and bricks for the buildings; yet a few reáls would generally buy them off. Intemperance, too, is a common vice among the Indians. The Spaniards, on the contrary, are very abstemious, and I do not remember ever having seen a Spaniard intoxicated.

Such are the people who inhabit a country embracing four or five hundred miles of sea-coast, with several good harbors; with fine forests in the north; the waters filled with fish, and the plains covered with thousands of herds of cattle; blessed with a climate, than which there can be no better in the world; free from all manner of diseases, whether epidemic or endemic; and with a soil in which corn yields from seventy to eighty fold. In the hands of an enterprising people, what a country this might be! we are ready to say. Yet how long would a people remain so, in such a country? The Americans (as those from the United States are called) and Englishmen, who are fast filling up the principal towns, and getting the trade into their hands, are indeed more industrious and effective than the Spaniards; yet their children are brought up Spaniards, in every respect, and if the "California fever" (laziness) spares the first generation, it always attacks the second.

SELECTED REFERENCES

Gale, Robert L. *Richard Henry Dana* (1969).
Lader, Lawrence. *The Bold Brahmins* (1961).

PROJECTS AND PROBLEMS

Dana's efforts to end cruelty to seamen anticipated similar work by Herman Melville, whom he influenced. Compare *Two Years Before the Mast* with Melville's *White-Jacket* for their treatment of brutalities in the United States Navy.

For Dana's services in defense of one runaway slave in the historic case of Anthony Burns, see the biography published by Charles Francis Adams in 1890.

Did Dana's opinion of Californians change as the years passed? Consider the chapter, "Twenty-Four Years After," that was added to some editions of the book after the author revisited California in 1859.

Numerous minorities are represented in Dana's travel narrative, the population of the *Pilgrim* being almost as cosmopolitan as that of Melville's *Pequod.* Compare the attitude of the two authors toward their polyglot crews.

HENRY WADSWORTH LONGFELLOW (1807–1882)

Longfellow's antislavery interests led to the writing of *Poems on Slavery* (1842), which included the following first two poems. "The Jewish Cemetery at Newport" came ten years later. "Hiawatha's Wooing" is Canto X of *The Song of Hiawatha*, published in 1855, when he was at the height of his popularity. Like his other narrative poems, recitation pieces for generations of school children but now in decline among critics, his Indian Edda is highly sentimental.

THE SLAVE'S DREAM

Beside the ungathered rice he lay,
　　His sickle in his hand;
His breast was bare, his matted hair
　　Was buried in the sand.
Again, in the mist and shadow of sleep,
　　He saw his Native Land.

Wide through the landscape of his dreams
　　The lordly Niger flowed;
Beneath the palm-trees on the plain
　　Once more a king he strode;
And heard the tinkling caravans
　　Descend the mountain road.

He saw once more his dark–eyed queen
　　Among her children stand;
They clasped his neck, they kissed his
　　　cheeks,
　　They held him by the hand!—
A tear burst from the sleeper's lids
　　And fell into the sand.

And then at furious speed he rode
　　Along the Niger's bank:
His bridle-reins were golden chains,
　　And, with a martial clank,
At each leap he could feel his scabbard of
　　　steel
　　Smiting his stallion's flank.

Before him, like a blood–red flag,
　　The bright flamingoes flew;
From morn till night he followed their
　　　flight,
　　O'er plains where the tamarind grew,

Till he saw the roofs of Caffre huts,
  And the ocean rose to view.

At night he heard the lion roar,
  And the hyena scream,
And the river-horse, as he crushed the
    reeds
  Beside some hidden stream;
And it passed, like a glorious roll of drums,
  Through the triumph of his dream.

The forests, with their myriad tongues,
  Shouted of liberty;
And the Blast of the Desert cried aloud,
  With a voice so wild and free,
That he started in his sleep and smiled
  At their tempestuous glee.

He did not feel the driver's whip,
  Nor the burning heat of day;
For Death had illumined the Land of
    Sleep,
  And his lifeless body lay
A worn-out fetter, that the soul
  Had broken and thrown away!

THE QUADROON GIRL

The Slaver in the broad lagoon
　　Lay moored with idle sail;
He waited for the rising moon,
　　And for the evening gale.

Under the shore his boat was tied,
　　And all her listless crew
Watched the gray alligator slide
　　Into the still bayou.

Odors of orange-flowers, and spice,
　　Reached them from time to time,
Like airs that breathe from Paradise
　　Upon a world of crime.

The Planter, under his roof of thatch,
　　Smoked thoughtfully and slow;
The Slaver's thumb was on the latch,
　　He seemed in haste to go.

He said, "My ship at anchor rides
　　In yonder broad lagoon;
I only wait the evening tides,
　　And the rising of the moon."

Before them, with her face upraised,
　　In timid attitude,
Like one half curious, half amazed,
　　A Quadroon maiden stood.

Her eyes were large, and full of light,
　　Her arms and neck were bare;
No garment she wore save a kirtle bright,
　　And her own long, raven hair.

And on her lips there played a smile
   As holy, meek, and faint,
As lights in some cathedral aisle
   The features of a saint.

"The soil is barren,—the farm is old,"
   The thoughtful planter said;
Then looked upon the Slaver's gold,
   And then upon the maid.

His heart within him was at strife
   With such accursèd gains:
For he knew whose passions gave her life,
   Whose blood ran in her veins.

But the voice of nature was too weak;
   He took the glittering gold!
Then pale as death grew the maiden's cheek,
   Her hands as icy cold.

The Slaver led her from the door,
   He led her by the hand,
To be his slave and paramour
   In a strange and distant land!

THE JEWISH CEMETERY AT NEWPORT

How strange it seems! These Hebrews in their graves,
　　Close by the street of this fair seaport town,
Silent beside the never-silent waves,
　　At rest in all this moving up and down!

The trees are white with dust, that o'er their sleep
　　Wave their broad curtains in the south-wind's breath,
While underneath these leafy tents they keep
　　The long, mysterious Exodus of Death.

And these sepulchral stones, so old and brown,
　　That pave with level flags their burial-place,
Seem like the tablets of the Law, thrown down
　　And broken by Moses at the mountain's base.

The very names recorded here are strange,
　　Of foreign accent, and of different climes;
Alvares and Rivera interchange
　　With Abraham and Jacob of old times.

"Blessed be God, for he created Death!"
　　The mourners said, "and Death is rest and peace;"
Then added, in the certainty of faith,
　　"And giveth Life that nevermore shall cease."

Closed are the portals of their Synagogue,
　　No Psalms of David now the silence break,
No Rabbi reads the ancient Decalogue
　　In the grand dialect the Prophets spake.

Gone are the living, but the dead remain,
　　And not neglected; for a hand unseen,
Scattering its bounty, like a summer rain,
　　Still keeps their graves and their remembrance green.

How came they here? What burst of Christian hate,
   What persecution, merciless and blind,
Drove o'er the sea—that desert desolate—
   These Ishmaels and Hagars[1] of mankind?

They lived in narrow streets and lanes obscure,
   Ghetto and Judenstrass,[2] in mirk and mire;
Taught in the school of patience to endure
   The life of anguish and the death of fire.

All their lives long, with the unleavened bread,
   And bitter herbs of exile and its fears,
The wasting famine of the heart they fed,
   And slaked its thirst with marah of their tears.

Anathema maranatha![3] was the cry
   That rang from town to town, from street to street:
At every gate the accursed Mordecai[4]
   Was mocked and jeered, and spurned by Christian
      feet.

Pride and humiliation hand in hand
   Walked with them through the world where'er they
      went;
Trampled and beaten were they as the sand,
   And yet unshaken as the continent.

For in the background figures vague and vast
   Of patriarchs and of prophets rose sublime,
And all the great traditions of the Past
   They saw reflected in the coming time.

---

[1]Gen. 16:21. Hagar, a concubine of Abraham, was driven into the desert with Ishmael, their son.
[2]Segregated Jewish quarters in European cities.
[3]A curse; see I Cor. 16:22.
[4]Cousin of Queen Esther; see Book of Esther.

And thus forever with reverted look
  The mystic volume of the world they read,
Spelling it backward, like a Hebrew book,
  Till life became a Legend of the Dead.

But ah! what once has been shall be no more!
  The groaning earth in travail and in pain
Brings forth its races, but does not restore,
  And the dead nations never rise again.

HIAWATHA'S WOOING

"As unto the bow the cord is,
So unto the man is woman,
Though she bends him, she obeys him,
Though she draws him, yet she follows,
Useless each without the other!"
  Thus the youthful Hiawatha
Said within himself and pondered,
Much perplexed by various feelings,
Listless, longing, hoping, fearing,
Dreaming still of Minnehaha,
Of the lovely Laughing Water,
In the land of the Dacotahs.
  "Wed a maiden of your people,"
Warning said the old Nokomis;
"Go not eastward, go not westward,
For a stranger, whom we know not!
Like a fire upon the hearth–stone
Is a neighbor's homely daughter,
Like the starlight or the moonlight
Is the handsomest of strangers!"
  Thus dissuading spake Nokomis,
And my Hiawatha answered
Only this: "Dear old Nokomis,
Very pleasant is the firelight,
But I like the starlight better,
Better do I like the moonlight!"
  Gravely then said old Nokomis:
"Bring not here an idle maiden,
Bring not here a useless woman,
Hands unskilful, feet unwilling;
Bring a wife with nimble fingers,
Heart and hand that move together,
Feet that run on willing errands!"
  Smiling answered Hiawatha:
"In the land of the Dacotahs

313

Lives the Arrow-maker's daughter,
Minnehaha, Laughing Water,
Handsomest of all the women.
I will bring her to your wigwam,
She shall run upon your errands,
Be your starlight, moonlight, firelight,
Be the sunlight of my people!"
　　Still dissuading said Nokomis:
"Bring not to my lodge a stranger
From the land of the Dacotahs!
Very fierce are the Dacotahs,
Often is there war between us,
There are feuds yet unforgotten,
Wounds that ache and still may open!"
　　Laughing answered Hiawatha:
"For that reason, if no other,
Would I wed the fair Dacotah,
That our tribes might be united,
That old feuds might be forgotten,
And old wounds be healed forever!"

　　Thus departed Hiawatha
To the land of the Dacotahs,
To the land of handsome women;
Striding over moor and meadow,
Through interminable forests,
Through uninterrupted silence.
　　With his moccasins of magic,
At each stride a mile he measured;
Yet the way seemed long before him,
And his heart outrun his footsteps;
And he journeyed without resting,
Till he heard the cataract's thunder,
Heard the Falls of Minnehaha
Calling to him through the silence.
"Pleasant is the sound!" he murmured,
"Pleasant is the voice that calls me!"
　　On the outskirts of the forest,
'Twixt the shadow and the sunshine,

Herds of fallow deer were feeding,
But they saw not Hiawatha;
To his bow he whispered, "Fail not!"
To his arrow whispered, "Swerve not!"
Sent it singing on its errand,
To the red heart of the roebuck;
Threw the deer across his shoulder,
And sped forward without pausing.
    At the doorway of his wigwam
Sat the ancient Arrow-maker,
In the land of the Dacotahs,
Making arrow-heads of jasper,
Arrow-heads of chalcedony.
At his side in all her beauty,
Sat the lovely Minnehaha,
Sat his daughter, Laughing Water,
Plaiting mats of flags and rushes;
Of the past the old man's thoughts were,
And the maiden's of the future.
    He was thinking, as he sat there,
Of the days when with such arrows
He had struck the deer and bison,
On the Muskoday, the meadow;
Shot the wild goose, flying southward,
On the wing, the clamorous Wawa;
Thinking of the great war-parties,
How they came to buy his arrows,
Could not fight without his arrows.
Ah, no more such noble warriors
Could be found on earth as they were!
Now the men were all like women,
Only used their tongues for weapons!
    She was thinking of a hunter,
From another tribe and country,
Young and tall and very handsome,
Who one morning, in the Spring–time,
Came to buy her father's arrows,
Sat and rested in the wigwam,

Lingered long about the doorway,
Looking back as he departed.
She had heard her father praise him,
Praise his courage and his wisdom;
Would he come again for arrows
To the Falls of Minnehaha?
On the mat her hands lay idle,
And her eyes were very dreamy.

Through their thoughts they heard a footstep,
Heard a rustling in the branches,
And with glowing cheek and forehead,
With the deer upon his shoulders,
Suddenly from out the woodlands
Hiawatha stood before them.

Straight the ancient Arrow-maker
Looked up gravely from his labor,
Laid aside the unfinished arrow,
Bade him enter at the doorway,
Saying, as he rose to meet him,
"Hiawatha, you are welcome!"

At the feet of Laughing Water
Hiawatha laid his burden,
Threw the red deer from his shoulders;
And the maiden looked up at him,
Looked up from her mat of rushes,
Said with gentle look and accent,
"You are welcome, Hiawatha!"

Very spacious was the wigwam,
Made of deer-skin dressed and whitened,
With the Gods of the Dacotahs
Drawn and painted on its curtains,
And so tall the doorway, hardly
Hiawatha stooped to enter,
Hardly touched his eagle-feathers
As he entered at the doorway.

Then uprose the Laughing Water,
From the ground fair Minnehaha,
Laid aside her mat unfinished,

Brought forth food and set before them,
Water brought them from the brooklet,
Gave them food in earthen vessels,
Gave them drink in bowls of bass–wood,
Listened while the guest was speaking,
Listened while her father answered,
But not once her lips she opened,
Not a single word she uttered.

Yes, as in a dream she listened
To the words of Hiawatha,
As he talked of old Nokomis,
Who had nursed him in his childhood,
As he told of his companions,
Chibiabos, the musician,
And the very strong man, Kwasind,
And of happiness and plenty
In the land of the Ojibways,
In the pleasant land and peaceful.

"After many years of warfare,
Many years of strife and bloodshed,
There is peace between the Ojibways
And the tribe of the Dacotahs."
Thus continued Hiawatha,
And then added, speaking slowly,
"That this peace may last forever,
And our hands be clasped more closely,
And our hearts be more united,
Give me as my wife this maiden,
Minnehaha, Laughing Water,
Loveliest of Dacotah women!"

And the ancient Arrow-maker
Paused a moment ere he answered,
Smoked a little while in silence,
Looked at Hiawatha proudly,
Fondly looked at Laughing Water,
And made answer very gravely:
"Yes, if Minnehaha wishes;
Let your heart speak, Minnehaha!"

And the lovely Laughing Water
Seemed more lovely, as she stood there,
Neither willing nor reluctant,
As she went to Hiawatha,
Softly took the seat beside him,
While she said, and blushed to say it,
"I will follow you, my husband!"
    This was Hiawatha's wooing!
Thus it was he won the daughter
Of the ancient Arrow-maker,
In the land of the Dacotahs!
    From the wigwam he departed,
Leading with him Laughing Water;
Hand in hand they went together,
Through the woodland and the meadow,
Left the old man standing lonely
At the doorway of his wigwam,
Heard the Falls of Minnehaha
Calling to them from the distance,
Crying to them from afar off,
"Fare thee well, O Minnehaha!"
    And the ancient Arrow-maker
Turned again unto his labor,
Sat down by his sunny doorway,
Murmuring to himself, and saying:
"Thus it is our daughters leave us,
Those we love, and those who love us!
Just when they have learned to help us,
When we are old and lean upon them,
Comes a youth with flaunting feathers,
With his flute of reeds, a stranger
Wanders piping through the village,
Beckons to the fairest maiden,
And she follows where he leads her,
Leaving all things for the stranger!"

    Pleasant was the journey homeward,
Through interminable forests,
Over meadow, over mountain,

Over river, hill, and hollow.
Short it seemed to Hiawatha,
Though they journeyed very slowly,
Though his pace he checked and slackened
To the steps of Laughing Water.
   Over wide and rushing rivers
In his arms he bore the maiden;
Light he thought her as a feather,
As the plume upon his head-gear;
Cleared the tangled pathway for her,
Bent aside the swaying branches,
Made at night a lodge of branches,
And a bed with boughs of hemlock,
And a fire before the doorway
With the dry cones of the pine-tree.
   All the travelling winds went with them,
O'er the meadow, through the forest;
   All the stars of night looked at them,
Watched with sleepless eyes their slumber;
From his ambush in the oak-tree
Peeped the squirrel, Adjidaumo,
Watched with eager eyes the lovers;
And the rabbit, the Wabasso,
Scampered from the path before them,
Peering, peeping from his burrow,
Sat erect upon his haunches,
Watched with curious eyes the lovers.
   Pleasant was the journey homeward!
All the birds sang loud and sweetly
Songs of happiness and heart's-ease;
Sang the bluebird, the Owaissa,
"Happy are you, Hiawatha,
Having such a wife to love you!"
Sang the Opechee, the robin,
"Happy are you, Laughing Water,
Having such a noble husband!"
   From the sky the sun benignant
Looked upon them through the branches,

Saying to them, "O my children,
Love is sunshine, hate is shadow,
Life is checkered shade and sunshine,
Rule by love, O Hiawatha!"
   From the sky the moon looked at them,
Filled the lodge with mystic splendors,
Whispered to them, "O my children,
Day is restless, night is quiet,
Man imperious, woman feeble;
Half is mine, although I follow;
Rule by patience, Laughing Water!"
   Thus it was they journeyed homeward;
Thus it was that Hiawatha
To the lodge of old Nokomis
Brought the moonlight, starlight, firelight,
Brought the sunshine of his people,
Minnehaha, Laughing Water,
Handsomest of all the women
In the land of the Dacotahs,
In the land of handsome women.

SUGGESTED ADDITIONAL READINGS

"The Theologian's Tale"
"The Indian Hunter"
Tales of a Wayside Inn

SELECTED REFERENCES

Appel, John J. "Longfellow's Presentation of the Spanish Jews."
   American Jewish Historical Society Publication, 45 (1955),
   20–34.
Griswold, M. J. "American Quaker History in the Works of
   Whittier, Hawthorne, and Longfellow." *Americana,* 34
   (1940), 220–63.
Schramm, Wilbur L. *"Hiawatha* and Its Predecessors."
   Philological Quarterly, 11 (1932), 321–43.

Thompson, Stith. "The Indian Legend of Hiawatha." *PMLA*, 37 (1922), 128–40.

PROJECTS AND PROBLEMS

Compare Longfellow's "The Slave's Dream," "The Slave in the Dismal Swamp," and "The Quadroon Girl" with similar poems by John Greenleaf Whittier and William Dean Howells.

Discuss the relationship between *Hiawatha* and the folklore of the Ojibway Indians.

Compare Longfellow's treatment of the Spanish Jew in *Tales of a Wayside Inn* with his emphasis in *Hiawatha* on the role of Jews in the mistreatment and execution of Jesus.

Does Longfellow present minority characters as people or as symbols? Does he see them as equals?

RALPH WALDO EMERSON
(1803–1882)

The following excerpt is from "Emancipation in the British West Indies," a long address delivered in Concord on August 1, 1844. Emerson spoke on the anniversary of the British Parliament's Abolition Act of 1833, which was followed by the gradual abolition of slavery in all lands under British control. "The Sage of Concord" was chief spokesman for transcendentalism and exerted a profound influence on American thought. On the issue of slavery he relinquished the ivory tower of the poet and the philosopher and used the lecture platform to advance the cause of human freedom.

THE CIVILIZATION
OF THE NEGRO

The First of August marks the entrance of a new element into modern politics, namely, the civilization of the negro. A man is added to the human family. Not the least affecting part of this history of abolition is the annihilation of the old indecent nonsense about the nature of the negro. In the case of the ship Zong, in 1781, whose master had thrown one hundred and thirty-two slaves alive into the sea, to cheat the underwriters, the first jury gave a verdict in favor of the master and owners: they had a right to do what they had done. Lord Mansfield is reported to have said on the bench, "The matter left to the jury is—Was it from necessity? For they had no doubt—though it shocks one very much—that the case of slaves was the same as if horses had been thrown overboard. It is a very shocking case." But a more enlightened and humane opinion began to prevail. Mr. Clarkson, early in his career, made a collection of African productions and manufactures, as specimens of the arts and culture of the negro; comprising cloths and loom, weapons, polished stones and woods, leather, glass, dyes, ornaments, soap, pipe-bowls and trinkets. These he showed to Mr. Pitt, who saw and handled them with extreme interest. "On sight of these," says Clarkson, "many sublime thoughts seemed to rush at once into his mind, some of which he expressed"; and hence appeared to arise a project which was always dear to him, of the civilization of Africa—a dream which forever elevates his fame. In 1791, Mr. Wilberforce announced to the House of Commons, "We have already gained one victory: we have obtained for these poor creatures the recognition of their human nature, which for a time was most shamefully denied them." It was the sarcasm of Montesquieu, "it would not do to suppose that negroes were men, lest it should turn out that whites were not"; for the white has, for ages, done what he could to keep the negro in that hoggish state. His laws have been furies. It now appears that the negro race is, more than any other, susceptible of rapid civilization. The emancipation is observed, in the islands, to have wrought for the negro a benefit as sudden as when a thermometer is brought out of the shade into the sun. It has given him eyes and ears. If, before, he was taxed with such stupidity, or such defective vision, that he could not set a table square to the walls of an apartment, he is now the principal if not the only mechanic in the West Indies; and is, besides, an architect, a physician, a lawyer, a magistrate, an editor, and a valued and increasing political power. The recent testimonies of Sturge, of Thome and Kimball, of Gurney, of Philippo, are very explicit on this point, the capacity and the success of the colored and the black population in employment of skill, of profit and of trust; and best of all is the testimony to their moderation. They receive hints and advances from the whites that they will be gladly received as subscribers to the Exchange, as members of this or that committee of trust. They hold back, and say to each other that "social position is not to be gained by pushing."

I have said that this event interests us because it came mainly from the concession of the whites; I add, that in part it is the earning of the blacks. They won the pity and respect which they have received, by their powers and native endowments. I think this is a circumstance of the highest import. Their whole future is in it. Our planet, before the age of written history, had its races of savages, like the generations of sour paste, or the animalcules that wiggle and bite in a drop of putrid water. Who cares for these or for their wars? We do not wish a world of bugs or of birds; neither afterward of Scythians, Caraibs or Feejees. The grand style of Nature, her great periods, is all we observe in them. Who cares for oppressing whites, or oppressed blacks, twenty centuries ago, more than for bad dreams? Eaters and food are in the harmony of Nature; and there too is the germ forever protected, unfolding gigantic leaf after leaf, a newer flower, a richer fruit, in every period, yet its next product is never to be guessed. It will only save what is worth saving; and it saves not by compassion, but by power. It appoints no police to guard the lion but his teeth and claws; no fort or city for the bird but his wings; no rescue for flies and mites but their spawning numbers, which no ravages can overcome. It deals with men after the same manner. If they are rude and foolish, down they must go. When at last in a race a new principle appears, an idea—*that* conserves it; ideas only save races. If the black man is feeble and not important to the existing races, not on a parity with the best race, the black man must serve, and be exterminated. But if the black man carries in his bosom an indispensable element of a new and coming civilization; for the sake of that element, no wrong nor strength nor circumstance can hurt him: he will survive and play his part. So now, the arrival in the world of such men as Toussaint, and the Haytian heroes, or of the leaders of their race in Barbadoes and Jamaica, outweighs in good omen all the English and American humanity. The anti-slavery of the whole world is dust in the balance before this—is a poor squeamishness and nervousness: the might and the right are here: here is the anti-slave: here is man: and if you have man, black or white is an insignificance. The intellect—that is miraculous! Who has it, has the talisman: his skin and bones, though they were of the color of night, are transparent, and the everlasting stars shine through, with attractive beams. But a compassion for that which is not and cannot be useful or lovely, is degrading and futile. All the songs and newspapers and money subscriptions and vituperation of such as do not think with us, will avail nothing against a fact. I say to you, you must save yourself, black or white, man or woman; other help is none. I esteem the occasion of this jubilee to be the proud discovery that the black race can contend with the white: that in the great anthem which we call history, a piece of many parts and vast compass, after playing a long time a very low and subdued accompaniment, they perceive the time arrived when they can strike in with effect and take a master's part in the music. The civility of the world has reached that pitch that their more moral genius is becoming indispensable, and the quality of this race is to be honored for itself. For this, they have been preserved in sandy deserts, in rice-swamps, in kitchens and shoe-shops, so long: now let them emerge, clothed and in their own form.

There remains the very elevated consideration which the subject opens, but which belongs to more abstract views than we are now taking, this, namely, that the civility of no race can be perfect whilst another race is degraded. It is a doctrine alike of the oldest and of the newest philosophy, that man is one, and that you cannot injure any member, without a sympathetic injury to all the members. . . .

SUGGESTED ADDITIONAL READINGS

"Ode Sung in the Town Hall"
"The Fugitive Slave Law"
"John Brown"
"The Emancipation Proclamation"

SELECTED REFERENCES

Butcher, Philip. "Emerson and the South." *Phylon*, 17 (1956), 279–85.

Deutsch, Leonard J. "Ralph Waldo Ellison and Ralph Waldo Emerson: A Shared Moral Vision." *CLA Journal*, 16 (1972), 159–78.

Marchand, Ernest. "Emerson and the Frontier." *American Literature*, 3 (1931), 149–74.

Moody, Marjory M. "The Evolution of Emerson as an Abolitionist." *American Literature*, 17 (1945), 1–21.

Nichols, William W. "Ralph Ellison's Black American Scholar." *Phylon*, 31 (1970), 70–75.

Nicoloff, Philip L. *Emerson on Race and History* (1961).

PROJECTS AND PROBLEMS

American attitudes toward the Irish are associated with attitudes toward Roman Catholicism. Were Emerson's references to the Irish in *English Traits* and elsewhere affected by religious considerations? In other words, was his view of the Irish influenced by his attitude toward Roman Catholicism?

Emerson commented in his journal in 1845 that Europeans, Africans, and Polynesians would produce in America a new race "as vigorous as the New Europe which came out of the smelting pot of the Dark Ages." But in 1851, when he was opposing the Fugitive Slave Law, he praised the immigrant of light complexion and blue eyes and scorned the "Indiscriminate masses of Europe." Discuss.

Compare Emerson's "Abraham Lincoln" with Hawthorne's "Sketch of Abraham Lincoln," or compare Emerson's writing on John Brown with that of Thoreau.

Measure Emerson against Thoreau or Whitman or Whittier in respect to his relationship with individual blacks and his opposition to slavery. Scan his journals and his correspondence for relevant material.

FREDERICK DOUGLASS
(1817–1895)

Born in slavery in Maryland, Douglass escaped to become a leader in the antislavery struggle, a figure of national importance in the years before and after the Civil War, and a symbol of achievement and determined resistance for generations of black Americans. A brilliant orator and a talented writer and editor, Douglass made an effective assault on slavery in his popular *Narrative of the Life of Frederick Douglass, An American Slave* (1845), Chapter VII of which is presented here. The second selection by Douglass is from "What I Found at the Northampton Association," one of the reminiscences in *The History of Florence, Massachusetts* (1895), ed. by Charles A. Sheffield.

THE RIGHT TO WRITE

I lived in Master Hugh's family about seven years. During this time, I succeeded in learning to read and write. In accomplishing this, I was compelled to resort to various stratagems. I had no regular teacher. My mistress, who had kindly commenced to instruct me, had, in compliance with the advice and direction of her husband, not only ceased to instruct, but had set her face against my being instructed by any one else. It is due, however, to my mistress to say of her, that she did not adopt this course of treatment immediately. She at first lacked the depravity indispensable to shutting me up in mental darkness. It was at least necessary for her to have some training in the exercise of irresponsible power, to make her equal to the task of treating me as though I were a brute.

My mistress was, as I have said, a kind and tender-hearted woman; and in the simplicity of her soul she commenced, when I first went to live with her, to treat me as she supposed one human being ought to treat another. In entering upon the duties of a slaveholder, she did not seem to perceive that I sustained to her the relation of a mere chattel, and that for her to treat me as a human being was not only wrong, but dangerously so. Slavery proved as injurious to her as it did to me. When I went there, she was a pious, warm, and tender-hearted woman. There was no sorrow or suffering for which she had not a tear. She had bread for the hungry, clothes for the naked, and comfort for every mourner that came within her reach. Slavery soon proved its ability to divest her of these heavenly qualities. Under its influence, the tender heart became stone, and the lamblike disposition gave way to one of tiger-like fierceness. The first step in her downward course was in her ceasing to instruct me. She now commenced to practise her husband's precepts. She finally became even more violent in her opposition than her husband himself. She was not satisfied with simply doing as well as he had commanded; she seemed anxious to do better. Nothing seemed to make her more angry than to see me with a newspaper. She seemed to think that here lay the danger. I have had her rush at me with a face made all up of fury, and snatch from me a newspaper, in a manner that fully revealed her apprehension. She was an apt woman; and a little experience soon demonstrated, to her satisfaction, that education and slavery were incompatible with each other.

From this time I was most narrowly watched. If I was in a separate room any considerable length of time, I was sure to be suspected of having a book, and was at once called to give an account of myself. All this, however, was too late. The first step had been taken. Mistress, in teaching me the alphabet, had given me the *inch*, and no precaution could prevent me from taking the *ell*.

The plan which I adopted, and the one by which I was most successful, was that of making friends of all the little white boys whom I met in the street. As many of these as I could, I converted into teachers. With their kindly aid, obtained at different times and in different places, I finally succeeded in learning to read. When I was sent on errands, I always took my book with me, and by doing one part of my errand quickly, I found time to get a lesson before my return. I used also to carry bread with me, enough of which was always in the house, and to which I was always welcome; for I was much better off in this regard than many of the poor white children in our neighborhood. This bread I used to bestow upon the hungry little urchins, who, in return, would give me that more valuable bread of knowledge. I am strongly tempted to give the names of two or three of those little boys, as a testimonial of the gratitude and affection I bear them; but prudence forbids; not that it would injure me, but it might embarrass them; for it is almost an unpardonable offence to teach slaves to read in this Christian country. It is enough to say of the dear little fellows, that they lived on Philpot Street, very near Durgin and Bailey's ship-yard. I used to talk this matter of slavery over with them. I would sometimes say to them, I wished I could be as free as they would be when they got to be men. "You will be free as soon as you are twenty-one, *but I am a slave for life!* Have not I as good a right to be free as you have?" These words used to trouble them; they would express for me the liveliest sympathy, and console me with the hope that something would occur by which I might be free.

I was now about twelve years old, and the thought of being *a slave for life* began to bear heavily upon my heart. Just about this time, I got hold of a book entitled "The Columbian Orator." Every opportunity I got, I used to read this book. Among much of other interesting matter, I found in it a dialogue between a master and his slave. The slave was represented as having run away from his master three times. The dialogue represented the conversation which took place between them, when the slave was retaken the third time. In this dialogue, the whole argument in behalf of slavery was brought forward by the master, all of which was disposed of by the slave. The slave was made to say some very smart as well as impressive things in reply to his master—things which had the desired though unexpected effect; for the conversation resulted in the voluntary emancipation of the slave on the part of the master.

In the same book, I met with one of Sheridan's mighty speeches on and in behalf of Catholic emancipation. These were choice documents to me. I read them over and over again with unabated interest. They gave tongue to interesting thoughts of my own soul, which had frequently flashed through my mind, and died away for want of utterance. The moral which I gained from the dialogue was the power of truth over the conscience of even a slaveholder. What I got from Sheridan was a bold denunciation of slavery, and a powerful vindication of human rights. The reading of these documents enabled me to utter my thoughts, and to meet the arguments brought forward to sustain slavery; but while they relieved me of one difficulty, they brought on another even more painful than the one of which I was relieved. The more I read, the more I was led to abhor and detest my enslavers. I could regard them in no other light than a band of successful robbers, who had left their homes, and gone to Africa, and stolen us from our homes, and in a strange land reduced us to slavery. I loathed them as being the meanest as well as the most wicked of men. As I read and contemplated the subject, behold! that very discontentment which Master Hugh had predicted would follow my learning to read had already come, to torment and sting my soul to unutterable anguish. As I writhed under it, I would at times feel that learning to read had been a curse rather than a blessing. It had given me a view of my wretched condition, without the remedy. It opened my eyes to the horrible pit, but to no ladder upon which to get out. In moments of agony, I envied my fellow-slaves for their stupidity. I have often wished myself a beast. I preferred the condition of the meanest reptile to my own. Any thing, no matter what, to get rid of thinking! It was this everlasting thinking of my condition that tormented me. There was no getting rid of it. It was pressed upon me by every object within sight or hearing, animate or inanimate. The silver trump of freedom had roused my soul to eternal wakefulness. Freedom now appeared, to disappear no more forever. It was heard in every sound, and seen in every thing. It was ever present to torment me with a sense of my wretched condition. I saw nothing without seeing it, I heard nothing without hearing it, and felt nothing without feeling it. It looked from every star, it smiled in every calm, breathed in every wind, and moved in every storm.

I often found myself regretting my own existence, and wishing myself dead; and but for the hope of being free, I have no doubt but that I should have killed myself, or done something for which I should have been killed. While in this state of mind, I was eager to hear any one speak of slavery. I was a ready listener. Every little while, I could hear something about the abolitionists. It was some time before I found what the word meant. It was always used in such connections as to make it an interesting word to me. If a slave ran away and succeeded in getting clear, or if a slave killed his master, set fire to a barn, or did any thing very wrong in the mind of a slaveholder, it was spoken of as the fruit of *abolition.* Hearing the word in this connection very often, I set about learning what it meant. The dictionary afforded me little or no help. I found it was "the act of abolishing;" but then I did not know what was to be abolished. Here I was perplexed. I did not dare to ask any one about its meaning, for I was satisfied that it was something they wanted me to know very little about. After a patient waiting, I got one of our city papers, containing an account of the number of petitions from the north, praying for the abolition of slavery in the District of Columbia, and of the slave trade between the States. From this time I understood the words *abolition* and *abolitionist,* and always drew near when that word was spoken, expecting to hear something of importance to myself and fellow-slaves. The light broke in upon me by degrees. I went one day down on the wharf of Mr. Waters; and seeing two Irishmen unloading a scow of stone, I went, unasked, and helped them. When we had finished, one of them came to me and asked me if I were a slave. I told him I was. He asked, "Are ye a slave for life?" I told him that I was. The good Irishman seemed to be deeply affected by the statement. He said to the other that it was a pity so fine a little fellow as myself should be a slave for life. He said it was a shame to hold me. They both advised me to run away to the north; that I should find friends there, and that I should be free. I pretended not to be interested in what they said, and treated them as if I did not understand them; for I feared they might be treacherous. White men have been known to encourage slaves to escape, and then, to get the reward, catch them and return them to their masters. I was afraid that these seemingly good men might use me so; but I nevertheless remembered their advice, and from that time I resolved to run away. I looked forward to a time at which it would be safe for me to escape. I was too young to think of doing so immediately; besides, I wished to learn how to write, as I might have occasion to write my own pass. I consoled myself with the hope that I should one day find a good chance. Meanwhile, I would learn to write.

The idea as to how I might learn to write was suggested to me by being in Durgin and Bailey's ship-yard, and frequently seeing the ship carpenters, after hewing, and getting a piece of timber ready for use, write on the timber the name of that part of the ship for which it was intended. When a piece of timber was intended for the larboard side, it would be marked thus—"L." When a piece was for the starboard side, it would be marked thus—"S." A piece for the larboard side forward would be marked thus—"L. F." When a piece was for starboard side forward, it would be marked thus—"S. F." For larboard aft, it would be marked thus—"L. A." For starboard aft, it would be marked thus—"S.A." I soon learned the names of these letters, and for what they were intended when placed upon a piece of timber in the ship-yard. I immediately commenced copying them, and in a short time was able to make the four letters named. After that, when I met with any boy who I knew could write, I would tell him I could write as well as he. The next word would be, "I don't believe you. Let me see you try it." I would then make the letters which I had been so fortunate as to learn, and ask him to beat that. In this way I got a good many lessons in writing, which it is quite possible I should never have gotten in any other way. During this time, my copy-book was the board fence, brick wall, and pavement; my pen and ink was a lump of chalk. With these, I learned mainly how to write. I then commenced and continued copying the Italics in Webster's Spelling Book, until I could make them all without looking on the book. By this time, my little Master Thomas had gone to school, and learned how to write, and had written over a number of copy-books. These had been brought home, and shown to some of our near neighbors, and then laid aside. My mistress used to go to class meeting at the Wilk Street meetinghouse every Monday afternoon, and leave me to take care of the house. When left thus, I used to spend the time in writing in the spaces left in Master Thomas's copy-book, copying what he had written. I continued to do this until I could write a hand very similar to that of Master Thomas. Thus, after a long, tedious effort for years, I finally succeeded in learning how to write.

DAVID RUGGLES AND
SOJOURNER TRUTH

Of the great mental wave of reform that passed over New England fifty years ago and gave rise to the Florence, Brook Farm, and Hopedale Communities, others can tell you more and better than I. The religion of good will to man; of fervent desire and courageous determination to put aside the old and to venture boldly upon the new; to change and improve conditions of human existence; to liberate mankind from the bondage of time–worn custom; to curb and fix limits to individual selfishness; to diffuse wealth among the lowly; to banish poverty; to harmonize conflicting interests, and to promote the happiness of mankind generally, had at that time such a revival as, perhaps, New England had never seen before, and has certainly never seen since. . . .

Of the various attempts to give form and substance to the broad and beneficent ideas of the times, Florence and Hopedale seemed fullest of promise. For harmony, Hopedale had a decided advantage over Florence, in that its leaders were of one religious faith, while Florence was composed both of men and women of different denominations, and of those of no religious bias or profession. It was from the first a protest against sectism and bigotry and an assertion of the paramount importance of human brotherhood.

I visited Florence almost at its beginning, when it was in the rough; when all was Spartan-like simplicity. It struck me at once that the reformers had a tremendous task before them. . . . The place and the people struck me as the most democratic I had ever met. It was a place to extinguish all aristocratic pretensions. There was no high, no low, no masters, no servants, no white, no black. . . .

My impressions of the Community are not only the impressions of a stranger, but those of a fugitive slave to whom at that time even Massachusetts opposed a harsh and repellent side. The cordial reception I met with at Florence, was, therefore, much enhanced by its contrast with many other places in that commonwealth. Here, at least, neither my color nor my condition was counted against me. I found here my old friend, David Ruggles, not only black, but blind, and measurably helpless, but a man of sterling sense and worth. He had been caught up in New York city, rescued from destitution, brought here and kindly cared for. I speak of David Ruggles as my old friend. He was such to me only as he had been to others in the same plight. Before he was old and blind he had been a co-worker with the venerable Quaker, Isaac T. Hopper, and had assisted me as well as many other fugitive slaves, on the way from slavery to freedom. It was good to see that this man who had zealously assisted others was now receiving assistance from the benevolent men and women of this Community, and if a grateful heart in a recipient of benevolence is any compensation for such benevolence, the friends of David Ruggles were well compensated. His whole theme to me was gratitude to these noble people. For his blindness he was hydropathically treated in the Community. He himself became well versed in the water cure system, and was subsequently at the head of a water cure establishment at Florence. He acquired such sensitiveness of touch that he could, by feeling the patient, easily locate the disease, and was, therefore, very successful in treating his patients.

David Ruggles was not the only colored person who found refuge in this Community. I met here for the first time that strange compound of wit and wisdom, of wild enthusiasm and flint-like common sense, who seemed to feel it her duty to trip me up in my speeches and to ridicule my efforts to speak and act like a person of cultivation and refinement. I allude to Sojourner Truth. She was a genuine specimen of the uncultured negro. She cared very little for elegance of speech or refinement of manners. She seemed to please herself and others best when she put her ideas in the oddest forms. She was much respected at Florence, for she was honest, industrious, and amiable. Her quaint speeches easily gave her an audience, and she was one of the most useful members of the Community in its day of small things.

SUGGESTED ADDITIONAL READINGS

Life and Times of Frederick Douglass
My Bondage and My Freedom
The Life and Writings of Frederick Douglass (1950-55), ed. by Philip Foner.

SELECTED REFERENCES

Quarles, Benjamin. *Frederick Douglass* (1948).

Rexroth, Kenneth. "Frederick Douglass." *Saturday Review*, Dec. 28, 1968, p. 39.

PROJECTS AND PROBLEMS

Consider the achievement of Douglass as orator and measure his service on the platform for the antislavery cause against that of William Wells Brown.

One of the causes for which Douglass labored was women's rights. "Right," he said in 1847, "is of no sex." Trace his involvement in this struggle and his relationship to the Equal Rights Party, which nominated him for Vice President of the United States.

Examine the Douglass biographies by Charles W. Chesnutt and Booker T. Washington and compare them for literary merit with one of the Douglass autobiographies.

James Russell Lowell said in 1844, "The very look and bearing of Douglass are eloquent, and are full of an irresistible logic against the oppression of his race." Assemble other quotations from writers and public figures which testify to the effect of Douglass's commanding presence and, as one observer put it, his "remarkable physiognomy."

See Harriet Beecher Stowe's "Sojourner Truth, The Libyan Sibyl," in Volume II of the Riverside Edition of her works (1896). Does her detailed portrait confirm the general picture Douglass presents?

JAMES RUSSELL LOWELL
(1819–1891)

Poet, editor, scholar, and critic, Lowell exerted great influence on literary taste and public opinion. His abolitionist sentiments were inspired largely by his first wife, whose ardent liberalism curbed the conservative tendencies of her Brahmin husband. He is best remembered for his *Fable for Critics* and *The Biglow Papers.* "The Prejudice of Color," first published in the *Pennsylvania Freeman* for February 13, 1845, is reprinted from *The Anti-Slavery Papers.*

THE PREJUDICE OF COLOR

There is nothing more sadly and pitiably ludicrous in the motley face of our social system than the prejudice of color. As if no arrangement of society could be perfect in which there was not some arbitrary distinction of rank, we Democrats, after abolishing all other artificial claims of superiority, cling with the despair of persons just drowning, in the dreadful ocean of equality, to one more absurd and more wicked than all the rest. An aristocracy of intellect may claim some leniency of judgment from the reason, and there are certain physiological arguments to bolster up an aristocracy of birth; but a patent of nobility founded on no better distinction than an accidental difference in the secreting vessels of the skin would seem ridiculous even to a German count who had earned his title by the more valid consideration of thirty-six dollars. Or is it in some assumed superiority of intellect that the white man finds his claim to enslave his colored brother? In that case the most exclusive of this chromatic *noblesse* would stand in imminent peril of the lash of the overseer at the South, or of the editor (who occupies the position and discharges the duties of that distinguished member of our democratic system) at the North. For we assume it as a primary step in our argument that, when the moral vision of a man becomes perverted enough to persuade him that he is superior to his fellow, he is in reality looking up at him from an immeasurable distance beneath.

Regarding the American people as a professedly Christian people, their anti-Christian prejudices are at first sight astonishing enough. Were this the place, the greater part of them might be traced to the timidity and unfaithfulness of the Church, which to most men supplies the place of a conscience, and whose sacredness, instead of being founded immutably upon a living inward principle, rises and falls with the popular lukewarmness or zeal. Claiming to be of divine origin and appointment, its main occupation would nevertheless seem to be to prove by its subservience to popular fallacies that it is merely a mechanical contrivance of man's ingenuity—a labor-saving national conscience. Our people go once or twice a week to hear the praises of meekness, humanity, and forbearance, so curi-

339

ously intertwined with theological dogmas that the latter seem equally sacred with the former, and then go home to practice the very reverse of these virtues without the slightest perception of their inconsistency. For example, the black men, having endured unparalleled hardships and oppressions with resignation and patience, are despised as wanting in spirit and capacity, while the red men, having returned blow for blow—having displayed, perhaps, more hideous qualities than any other savages—become the theme of novels and romances, are made the subject of rhymes almost as atrocious as one of their own war songs, and furnish even our children's books with pernicious examples of utterly barbarous and pagan virtues. This proves that we give only a theoretical assent to the doctrines of Christ, and that, like Louis the Eleventh of France, though we wear the badges of our religion most conspicuously, we contrive adroitly to hide them away whenever it suits our convenience to break any of its commandments.

Meanwhile, as a prophecy is sometimes known to bring about its own fulfillment, the national prejudice against the colored race is fast producing a plentiful crop of statistical facts on which to base an argument in its own favor. The colored people of the so-called free states are still held in slavery by something stronger than a constitution, more terrible than the cannon and the bayonet—the force of a depraved and unchristian public opinion. We shut them rigidly out from every path of emulation or ambition, and then deny to them the possession of ordinary faculties. No talent will show itself till there is a demand for its exercise, and then it leaps spontaneously and irresistibly into vigorous action. The proportion of degraded whites in this country is to the full as great as that of the colored population; it is infinitely greater if we consider the respective opportunities of the two races.

The oppressor has always endeavored to justify his sin by casting reproach upon the moral or intellectual qualities of the oppressed. The Romans held their miserable victims in contempt, until Spartacus displayed a military genius and a heroism which their ablest generals were unable to make head against until his little army was divided against itself. Yet these very slaves were among the ancestors of two nations now the most distinguished in Europe, the one for philanthropy and profound scholarship, the other for science.

The Norman barons (a race of savages, strong chiefly in their intense and selfish acquisitiveness, to whom our Southern brethren are fond of comparing themselves) looked upon their Saxon serfs as mere cattle, and indeed reduced them as nearly as might be to that degraded level by their cruelty. Yet these very serfs were part and parcel of that famous Anglo–Saxon race, concerning whom we have seen so much claptrap in the newspapers for a few years past, especially since the project of extending the area of freedom has been discussed and glorified. A still more prominent example may be found in the case of the Jews, who by a series of enormous tyrannies were reduced to the condition of the most abject degradation among nations to whom they had given a religious system, and who borrowed from them their choicest examples of eloquence and pathos and sublime genius. Here was and is a people remarkable above almost all others for the possession of the highest and clearest intellect, and yet absolutely dwarfed and contracted in mind by being sternly debarred from any but the very lowest exercise of mental capacity. But they had the advantage of a less palpable outward distinguishment from the nations among whom they underwent their latest and worst captivity, and a few of them have been enabled to raise themselves to power and distinction—but never *as Jews*.

With us the color is made the most prominent feature. The newspapers can never say simply man or woman in speaking of the African race; they must always prefix the badge of inferiority, and in the same way that they say the *Honorable* Member of Congress or the *Reverend* Doctor of Divinity to excite our favorable sympathies, they say a *colored* man or woman to indicate that there is no need of our troubling our sympathies at all. Nor is this the worst. Though it is a part of the religious faith of our Northern editors, and a part (apparently) of their constitutional compact of fealty to the South, to consider the colored race as incapable of high civilization, as incapable indeed, even of manhood, yet, so surely as a colored man commits any offense, a paragraph runs the rounds of our newspapers, religious and all, headed *"a black ruffian,"* as if his color were an aggravation of his offense, instead of being, according to their own standard, a palliation of it.

It has always seemed to us that abolitionists could in no way more usefully serve their holy cause than by seeking to elevate the condition of the colored race in the free states, and to break down every barrier of invidious distinction between them and their privileged brothers. We know that a great deal has been done, but we think that it has not been made sufficiently a primary object. A few such men as Douglass and Remond[1] are the strongest anti-slavery arguments. The very look and bearing of Douglass are eloquent, and are full of an irresistible logic against the oppression of his race.

We have never had any doubt that the African race was intended to introduce a new element of civilization, and that the Caucasian would be benefited greatly by an infusion of its gentler and less selfish qualities. The Caucasian mind, which seeks always to govern, at whatever cost, can never come to so beautiful or Christian a height of civilization, as with a mixture of those seemingly humbler, but truly more noble, qualities which teach it to obey. While our moral atmosphere is so dense and heavy with prejudice, it will be impossible for the colored man to stand erect or to breathe freely. Even if he make the attempt, he can never attain that quiet unconsciousness so necessary to a full and harmonious development, while he is continually forced to resist the terrible pressure from without. It is for us to endeavor to reduce this atmosphere to the true natural weight, and so struggle as manfully and earnestly and as constantly also against the slave system of the North as against that of the South. Had we room we might easily prove by historical examples that no race has ever so rapidly improved by being brought into contact with a higher civilization (even under the most terrible disadvantages) as the one of which we have been speaking.

[1]Frederick Douglass and Charles Lenox Remond.

A CHIPPEWA LEGEND*

The old Chief, feeling now wellnigh
    his end,
Called his two eldest children to his side,
And gave them, in few words, his parting
    charge!
"My son and daughter, me ye see no
    more;
The happy hunting–grounds await me,
    green
With change of spring and summer
    through the year:
But, for remembrance, after I am gone,
Be kind to little Sheemah for my sake:
Weakling he is and young, and knows
    not yet
To set the trap, or draw the seasoned
    bow;
Therefore of both your loves he hath
    more need,
And he, who needeth love, to love hath
    right;
It is not like our furs and stores of corn,
Whereto we claim sole title by our toil,
But the Great Spirit plants it in our
    hearts,
And waters it, and gives it sun, to be
The common stock and heritage of all:
Therefore be kind to Sheemah, that
    yourselves
May not be left deserted in your need."

Alone, beside a lake, their wigwam
    stood,

*For the leading incidents in this tale I am indebted to the very valuable "Algic
Researches" of Henry R. Schoolcraft, Esq. [Lowell's note. His prefatory quotation
from Aeschylus is omitted here.]

Far from the other dwellings of their
    tribe;
And, after many moons, the loneliness
Wearied the elder brother, and he said,
"Why should I dwell here far from men,
    shut out
From the free, natural joys that fit my
    age?
Lo, I am tall and strong, well skilled to
    hunt,
Patient of toil and hunger, and not yet
Have seen the danger which I dared not
    look
Full in the face; what hinders me to be
A mighty Brave and Chief among my
    kin?"
So, taking up his arrows and his bow,
As if to hunt, he journeyed swiftly on,
Until he gained the wigwams of his
    tribe,
Where, choosing out a bride, he soon
    forgot,
In all the fret and bustle of new life,
The little Sheemah and his father's
    charge.

Now when the sister found her brother
    gone,
And that, for many days, he came not
    back,
She wept for Sheemah more than for
    herself;
For Love bides longest in a woman's
    heart,
And flutters many times before he flies,
And then doth perch so nearly, that a
    word

May lure him back to his accustomed
    nest;
And Duty lingers even when love is
    gone,
Oft looking out in hope of his return;
And, after Duty hath been driven forth,
Then Selfishness creeps in the last of all,
Warming her lean hands at the lonely
    hearth,
And crouching o'er the embers, to shut
    out
Whatever paltry warmth and light are
    left,
With avaricious greed, from all beside.
So, for long months, the sister hunted
    wide,
And cared for little Sheemah tenderly;
But, daily more and more, the loneliness
Grew wearisome, and to herself she
    sighed,
"Am I not fair? at least the glassy pool,
That hath no cause to flatter, tells me so;
But, O, how flat and meaningless the tale,
Unless it tremble on a lover's tongue!
Beauty hath no true glass, except it be
In the sweet privacy of loving eyes."
Thus deemed she idly, and forgot the
    lore
Which she had learned of nature and the
    woods,
That beauty's chief reward is to itself,
And that Love's mirror holds no image
    long
Save of the inward fairness, blurred and
    lost
Unless kept clear and white by Duty's
    care.
So she went forth and sought the haunts

of men,
And, being wedded, in her household
        cares,
Soon, like the elder brother, quite forgot
The little Sheemah and her father's
        charge.

   But Sheemah, left alone within the
        lodge,
Waited and waited, with a shrinking
        heart,
Thinking each rustle was his sister's step,
Till hope grew less and less, and then
        went out,
And every sound was changed from hope
        to fear.
Few sounds there were:—the dropping
        of a nut,
The squirrel's chirrup, and the jay's
        harsh scream,
Autumn's sad remnants of blithe Sum-
        mer's cheer,
Heard at long intervals, seemed but to
        make
The dreadful void of silence silenter.
Soon what small store his sister left was
        gone,
And, through the Autumn, he made shift
        to live
On roots and berries, gathered in much
        fear
Of wolves, whose ghastly howl he heard
        ofttimes,
Hollow and hungry, at the dead of night.
But Winter came at last, and, when the
        snow,
Thick-heaped for gleaming leagues o'er
        hill and plain,

Spread its unbroken silence over all,
Made bold by hunger, he was fain to glean
(More sick at heart than Ruth, and all
    alone)
After the harvest of the merciless wolf,
Grim Boaz, who, sharp-ribbed and gaunt,
    yet feared
A thing more wild and starving than
    himself;
Till, by degrees, the wolf and he grew
    friends,
And shared together all the winter
    through.

    Late in the Spring, when all the ice
    was gone,
The elder brother, fishing in the lake,
Upon whose edge his father's wigwam
    stood,
Heard a low moaning noise upon the
    shore:
Half like a child it seemed, half like a
    wolf,
And straightway there was something in
    his heart
That said, "It is thy brother Sheemah's
    voice."
So, paddling swiftly to the bank, he saw,
Within a little thicket close at hand,
A child that seemed fast changing to a
    wolf,
From the neck downward, gray with
    shaggy hair,
That still crept on and upward as he
    looked.
The face was turned away, but well he
    knew
That it was Sheemah's, even his broth-

er's face.
Then with his trembling hands he hid
    his eyes,
And bowed his head, so that he might
    not see
The first look of his brother's eyes, and
    cried,
"O Sheemah! O my brother, speak to
    me!
Dost thou not know me, that I am thy
    brother?
Come to me, little Sheemah, thou shalt
    dwell
With me henceforth, and know no care
    or want!"
Sheemah was silent for a space, as if
'T were hard to summon up a human
    voice,
And, when he spake, the voice was as
    a wolf's:
"I know thee not, nor art thou what
    thou say'st;
I have none other brethren than the
    wolves,
And, till thy heart be changed from
    what it is,
Thou art not worthy to be called their
    kin."
Then groaned the other, with a choking
    tongue,
"Alas! my heart is changed right bit-
    terly;
'T is shrunk and parched within me
    even now!"
And, looking upward fearfully, he saw
Only a wolf that shrank away and ran,
Ugly and fierce, to hide among the
    woods.

SUGGESTED ADDITIONAL READINGS

"Abraham Lincoln"
"Stanzas on Freedom"
"On the Capture of Fugitive Slaves Near Washington"
The Biglow Papers

SELECTED REFERENCES

Flower, B. O. "James Russell Lowell as a Poet of Freedom and Human Rights." Arena, 41 (1909), 309–17.
Gibbs, Lincoln R. "A Brahmin's Version of Democracy." Antioch Review, 1 (1941), 50–62.

PROJECTS AND PROBLEMS

Compare Lowell's sympathy for enslaved blacks with his attitude toward the Irish, Indians, and Jews. Was he equally enlightened in dealing with all minorities?

Compare Lowell's positions on the Mexican War and the Civil War as presented in The Biglow Papers.

WILLIAM GILMORE SIMMS
(1806–1870)

Author of a prodigious number of books, Simms was a staunch supporter of his beloved South Carolina. The two main subjects of his fiction, the frontier and the Revolution, are treated in numerous romances that invite comparison with the works of James Fenimore Cooper. The first selection is from Chapter XI of "Caloya; or the Loves of the Driver," in *The Wigwam and the Cabin* (1845–46). The second is from an essay review of two books by Henry R. Schoolcraft, which Simms republished in *Views and Reviews in American Literature, History and Fiction* (1845).

PLANTATION
PHILANDERER

Meanwhile, the youthful master of the veteran Mingo, meditated in the silence of his hall, the mode by which to save that amorous personage from the threatened consequences of his impertinence. Not that he felt any desire to screen the fellow from chastisement. Had he been told that husband and wife had simply resolved to scourge him with many stripes, he would have struck hands and cried "cheer" as loudly as any more indifferent spectator. But the vengeance of the Catawba Othello, promised to be of a character far too extreme, and, the inferior moral sense and sensibility of both Indian and negro considered, too greatly disproportioned to the offence. It was therefore necessary that what he proposed to do should be done quickly; and, taking his hat, Colonel Gillison sallied forth to the negro quarter, in the centre of which stood the superior habitation of the Driver. His object was simply to declare to the unfaithful servant that his evil designs and deeds were discovered, as well by himself as by the Catawba—to promise him the due consequences of his falsehood to himself, and to warn him of what he had to fear, in the event of his again obtruding upon the privacy of the squatters. To those who insist that the working classes in the South should enjoy the good things of this world in as bountiful a measure as the wealthy proprietors of the soil, it would be very shocking to see that they lived poorly, in dwellings which, though rather better than those of the Russian boor, are yet very mean in comparison with those built by Stephen Girard, John Jacob Astor, and persons of that calibre. Nay, it would be monstrous painful to perceive that the poor negroes are constantly subjected to the danger of ophthalmic and other diseases, from the continued smokes in which they live, the fruit of those liberal fires which they keep up at all seasons, and which the more fortunate condition of the poor in the free States, does not often compel them to endure at any. It would not greatly lessen the evil of this cruel destiny, to know that each had his house to himself, exclusively; that he had his little garden plat around it, and that his cabbages, turnips, corn and potatoes, not to speak of his

351

celery, his salad, &c., are, in half the number of cases, quite as fine as those which appear on his master's table. Then, his poultry-yard, and pig-pen—are they not there also?—but then, it must be confessed that his stock is not quite so large as his owner's, and there, of course, the parallel must fail. He has one immunity, however, which is denied to the owner. The hawk, (to whose unhappy door most disasters of the poultry yard are referred,) seldom troubles his chickens —his hens lay more numerously than his master's, and the dogs always prefer to suck the eggs of a white rather than those of a black proprietor. These, it is confessed, are very curious facts, inscrutable, of course, to the uninitiated; and, in which the irreverent and sceptical alone refuse to perceive any legitimate cause of wonder. You may see in his hovel and about it, many little additaments which, among the poor of the South, are vulgarly considered comforts; with the poor of other countries, however, as they are seldom known to possess them, they are no doubt regarded as burthens, which it might be annoying to take care of and oppressive to endure. A negro slave not only has his own dwelling, but he keeps a plentiful fire within it for which he pays no taxes. That he lives upon the fat of the land you may readily believe, since he is proverbially much fatter himself than the people of any other class. He has his own grounds for cultivation, and, having a taste for field sports, he keeps his own dog for the chase—an animal always of very peculiar characteristics, some of which we shall endeavour one day to analyse and develope. He is as hardy and cheerful as he is fat, and, but for one thing, it might be concluded safely that his condition was very far before that of the North American Indian—his race is more prolific, and, by increasing rather than diminishing, multiply necessarily, and unhappily the great sinfulness of mankind. This, it is true, is sometimes urged as a proof of improving civilization, but then, every justly-minded person must agree with Miss Martineau, that it is dreadfully immoral.[1] We suspect we have been digressing.

Col. Gillison soon reached the negro quarter, and tapping at the door of the Driver's wigwam, was admitted, after a brief parley, by the legitimate spouse of that gallant. Mingo had been married to Diana, by the Reverend Jonathan Buckthorn, a preacher of the Methodist persuasion, who rode a large circuit, and had travelled,

[1]Harriet Martineau attacked slavery in *Society in America.*

with praiseworthy charity, all the way from Savannah River, in all weathers, and on a hard going nag, simply to unite this worthy couple in the holy bonds of wedlock. At that time, both the parties were devout members of the Church, but they suffered from frequent lapses; and Mingo, having been engaged in sundry *liaisons*—which, however creditable to, and frequent among the French, Italian and English nobility, are highly censurable in a slave population, and a decisive proof of the demoralizing tendency of such an institution—was, at the formal complaint of the wife, "suspended" from the enjoyment of the Communion Table, and finally, on a continuance of this foreign and fashionable practice, fully expelled from all the privileges of the brotherhood. Diana had been something of a termagant, but Mingo had succeeded in outstorming her. For the first six months after marriage, the issue was considered very doubtful; but a decisive battle took place at the close of that period, in which the vigorous woman was compelled to give in and Mingo remained undisputed master of the field. But though overthrown and conquered, she was not quiescent; and her dissatisfaction at the result, showed itself in repeated struggles, which, however, were too convulsive and transient, to render necessary any very decided exercise of the husband's energies. She growled and grumbled still, without cessation, and though she did not dare to resent his frequent infidelities, she nevertheless pursued them with an avidity, and followed the movements of her treacherous lord with a jealous watchfulness, which proved that she did not the less keenly feel them. Absolute fear alone made her restrain the fury which was yet boiling and burning in her soul. When her master declared his desire to see Mingo, what was her answer? Not, certainly, that of a very dutiful or well satisfied spouse.

"Mingo, mossa? Whay him dey? Ha! mossa, you bes' ax ebbry woman on de plantation 'fore you come to he own wife. I bin marry to Mingo by Parson Buckthorn, and de Parson bin make Mingo promis' for lub and 'bey me, but he forget all he promise tree day after we bin man and wife. He nebber bin lub 't all; and as for 'bey,—lor' ha' massy 'pon me, mossa, I speak noting but de trute when I tell you,—he 'bey ebbry woman from yer to town 'fore he 'bey he own dear wife. Der's not a woman, mossa, 'pon de tree plantation, he aint lub more dan Di. Sometime he gone to Misser Jacks place—he hab wife dere! Sometime he gone to Misser Gabeau—he hab wife dere! Nex' time, he gone to Squir' Collins,—he hab wife dere! Whay he no hab wife, mossa? Who can tell? He hab wife ebbry which whay, and now, he no *sacrify*, he gone—you aint gwine to bleeb me, mossa, I know you aint—he gone and look for wife at Indian camp, whay down by de 'Red Gulley.' De trute is, mossa, Mingo is a mos' powerful black rascal of a nigger as ebber lib on gentleman plantation."

It was fortunate for young Gillison that he knew something of the nature of a termagant wife, and could make allowances for the injustice of a jealous one. He would otherwise have been persuaded by what he heard that his driver was one of the most uncomely of all the crow family. Though yielding no very credulous faith to the complaints of Diana, he still found it impossible to refuse to hear them; and all that he could do by dint of perseverance, was to diminish the long narratives upon which she was prepared to enter to prove her liege lord to be no better than he should be. Having exhausted all his efforts and his patience in the attempt to arrive at some certain intelligence of the husband's "whereabouts," without being able to divert the stream of her volubility from the accustomed channels, he concluded by exclaiming—

"Well, d—n the fellow, let him take the consequences. He stands a chance of having his throat cut before twenty-four hours are over, and you will then be at liberty Di., to get a husband who will be more faithful. Should Mingo not see me by ten o'clock to-morrow, he's a dead man. So you had better stir your stumps, my good woman, and see after him, unless you are willing to be a widow before you have found out a better man for your husband. Find Mingo and send him to me to-night, or he's a dead man to-morrow."

"Le' 'em dead—who care? He d'zarb for dead. I sure he no care if Di bin dead twenty tousand time. Le' 'em dead!"

Gillison left the hut and proceeded to other parts of the settlement where he thought it not improbable that the driver might be found; but a general ignorance was professed by all the negroes with respect to the particular movements of that worthy; and he soon discovered that his search was fruitless. He gave it up in despair, trusting that he should be able to succeed better at an hour seasonably early in the morning, yet half disposed, from his full conviction of his roguery, to leave the fellow to his fate.

Strange to say, such was not the determination of the dissatisfied Diana. Wronged and neglected as she had been, and was, there was still a portion of the old liking left, which had first persuaded her to yield her youthful affections to the keeping of this reckless wooer; and though she had avowed her willingness to her young master, that the "powerful black rascal of a nigger" should go to the dogs, and be dog's meat in twenty-four hours, still, better feelings came back to her, after due reflection, to soften her resolves. Though not often blessed with his kind words and pleasant looks, now-a-days, still, "she could not but remember such things were, and were most precious to her."

Left to herself, she first began to repeat the numberless conjugal offences of which he had been guilty; but the memory of these offences did not return alone. She remembered that these offences brought with them an equal number of efforts at atonement on the part of the offender; and when she thought of his vigorous frame, manly, dashing and graceful carriage, his gorgeous coat, his jauntily worn cap, his white teeth, and the insinuating smile of his voluminous lips, she could not endure the idea of such a man being devoted to a fate so short and sudden as that which her young master had predicted. She had not been told, it is true, from what quarter this terrible fate was to approach. She knew not under what aspect it would come, but the sincerity of her master was evident in his looks, words, and general air of anxiety, and she was convinced that there was truth in his assurance. Perhaps, her own attachment for the faithless husband—disguised as it was by her continual grumbling and discontent—was sufficiently strong to bring about this conviction easily. Diana determined to save her husband, worthless and wicked as he was,—and possibly, some vague fancy may have filled her mind as she came to this resolution, that, gratitude alone, for so great a service, might effect a return of the false one to that allegiance which love had hitherto failed to secure. She left her dwelling to seek him within half an hour after the departure of her master. But the worst difficulty in her way was the first. She trembled with the passion of returning jealousy when she reflected that the most likely place to find him would be at the "Red Gulley" in instant communion with a hateful rival—a red Indian—a dingy squaw,

—whose colour, neither white nor black, was of that sort, which, according to Diana in her jealous mood, neither gods nor men ought to endure. Her husband's admiration she naturally ascribed to Catawba witchcraft. She doubted—she hesitated—she almost re-resolved against the endeavour. Fortunately, however, her better feelings prevailed. She resolved to go forward—to save her husband—but, raising her extended hands and parted fingers, as she came to this determination, and gnashing her teeth with vindictive resolution as she spoke, she declared her equal resolve to compensate herself for so great a charity, by sinking her ten claws into the cheeks of any copper coloured damsel whom she should discover at the Red Gulley in suspicious propinquity with that gay deceiver whom she called her lord. . . .

THE NOBLE NORTH AMERICAN INDIAN

Our imperfect knowledge of the Indian,—the terror that he inspired,—the constant warfare between his race and our own—have embittered our prejudices, and made us unwilling to see any thing redeeming either in his character or intellect. We are apt to think him no more than a surly savage, capable of showing nothing better than his teeth. The very mention of his name, recalls no more grateful images than scalping knife and tomahawk; and, shuddering at the revolting associations, we shut our eyes, and close our ears, against all the proofs which declare his better characteristics. We are unwilling to read his past as we are unable to control his future;—refuse to recognize his sensibilities, and reject with scorn the evidence of any more genial attributes, in his possession, which might persuade us to hope for him in after days—for his natural genius and his real virtues—when, shut in by the comparatively narrow empire which we have allotted him—barred from expansion by the nations which are destined to crowd upon him on every hand,—the people of Texas, of Oregon and Mississippi,—he will be forced to throw aside the license of the hunter, and place himself, by a happy necessity, within the traces of civilization.

Regarded without prejudice, and through the medium even of what we most positively know of his virtues and his talents, and the North American Indian was as noble a specimen of crude humanity as we can find, from history, any aboriginal people to have been. There is not the slightest reason to suppose that he laboured under any intellectual deficiency. On the contrary, the proofs are conclusive, that, compared with other nations—the early Romans before their amalgamation with the great Tuscan family; the Jews prior to the Egyptian captivity;—the German race to the time of Odoacer, the Saxon, to the period of the Heptarchy, and the Norman tribes in the reign of Charlemagne;—he presented as high and sufficient proofs of susceptibility for improvement and education, as any, the very noblest stocks in our catalogue. In some respects, indeed, the Indians show more impressively. The republican features in their so-

357

ciety—their leagues for common defence and necessity, and the frequency of their counsels for the adjustment of subjects in common—led to the growth of a race of politicians and orators, of whose acuteness, excellent skill in argument, and great powers of elocution, the early discoverers give us some of the most astonishing examples. The samples of their eloquence which have come down to us, are as purely Attic as the most severe critic could desire—bold, earnest, truthful—clear in style, closely thought, keenly argued, conclusive in logic, and, in the highest degree, impressive in utterance. That their action was admirable, and would have delighted Demosthenes, we know from authorities upon which we would as cheerfully rely as upon the assurances of the great Athenian orator himself. Now capacious and flowing, now terse and epigrammatic, adapting the manner to the matter, and both to the occasion,—sometimes smooth and conciliatory, anon searching and sarcastic—now persuasive and adroit, and again suddenly startling because of their vehement force and audacious imagery;—these were the acknowledged characteristics of their eloquence, which awed the most fearless spectator and would have done honour to the noblest senate. An eloquent people is capable of taking any place in letters—in mastering all forms of speech, in perfecting any species of composition—history, or poetry—the one faculty, indeed, somewhat implying all the rest, since to be a great orator, imagination must keep pace with thought,—and reason, and the capacity for historical narration, must contribute to the embodiment of the argument, to which a warm fancy must impart colour and animation, and which great energies of character must endow with force. All of these qualities and constituents were in possession of our aborigines. They had all the requisites, shown by their speeches only, even if there were no other proofs, for intellectual development in every species of literature. Tecumseh was a very great orator,—so was his brother, the prophet. The Cherokee, Attakullakullah, was one of the most persuasive and insinuating of speakers; and the renown of Logan, of the Shawanee, is already a proverb from the single speech preserved by Jefferson. Some of the sayings and orations of the Seminoles and Creeks, are equally remarkable for their significance and poetical beauty. Of the six Nations we have numerous fragments, and the Catawbas had a reputation of this sort, among the tribes of the South, though but few specimens are preserved to us. Wetherford, who roused the Southern Indians to war, while Tecumseh and his brother were fomenting the western nations, was not inferior to either of these as a statesman and an orator. His speech to Jackson, when he surrendered himself, voluntarily, a willing sacrifice, in order that his country should obtain peace, is at once one of the most touching and manly instances of eloquence on record; and, in recent times, Osceola of the Seminoles, and Mooshalatubbee of the Choctaws— the one a bold, and the other an adroit speaker,—are proofs in point, showing that the faculty was not one to die utterly out in the emasculation of their several people. We should be pleased, did our space suffice, to give examples from each of these remarkable men. Enough to say, that they betrayed the possession of a power of logical thinking, lively fancy, subdued good taste, cool judgment, and lofty imagination, such as, addressed to literature, in a community even partially civilized, would have been worthy of all fame and honour in succeeding times. And that we should doubt or be insensible to this conclusion, is only to be accounted for by reference to our blinding prejudices against the race—prejudices which seem to have been fostered as necessary to justify the reckless and unsparing hand with which we have smitten them in their habitations, and expelled them from their country. We must prove them unreasoning beings, to sustain our pretensions as human ones—show them to have been irreclaimable, to maintain our own claims to the regards and respect of civilization.

SUGGESTED ADDITIONAL READINGS

The Yemassee
Slavery in America
The Cassique of Kiawah
Carl Werner
Woodcraft
Vasconselos

SELECTED REFERENCES

Burch, Charles E. "Negro Characters in the Novels of William

Gilmore Simms." *Southern Workman,* 52 (1923), 192–95.
McDowell, Tremaine. "The Negro in the Southern Novel Prior
to 1850." *Journal of English and Germanic Philology,* 25
(1926), 455–73.
Rose, A. H. "The Image of the Negro in the Pre–Civil War
Novels of John Pendleton Kennedy and William Gilmore
Simms." *Journal of American Studies,* 4 (1971), 217–31.
Shillingsburg, Miriam J. "Politics and Art: Toward Seeing
Simms as a Whole." *Southern Literary Journal,* 7, No. 2
(1975), 133–45, 148.

PROJECTS AND PROBLEMS

Consider Mingo in the selection in this volume as an example of
the stereotype of the black stud. Discuss other stereotypes in the stories in *The Wigwam and the Cabin.*

An anonymous review in *The Literary World,* December 4, 1852,
said of *Woodcraft,* "His negroes are living and breathing specimens
of human ebony, filled with the same queer conceits, and speaking
with the very tongues of the genuine article." Is this praise de-
served?

Compare the idealized portrait of plantation life in South
Carolina that appears in the works of Simms with the pictures of
Virginia plantation life in John Pendleton Kennedy's *Swallow Barn.*
Use as one reference Francis P. Gaines, *The Southern Plantation*
(1924).

Compare Simms's portrayal of Mexicans with his treatment of
blacks and Indians.

Speculate on the reasons for Simms's comment in his *Views and
Reviews in American Literature, History and Fiction:* "Properly di-
luted there was no better blood than that of Cherokee and Natchez.
It would have been a good infusion into the paler fountain of
Quaker and Puritan. . . ."

Compare the stereotyped Jewish characters in these historical
novels: *The Bravo,* by James Fenimore Cooper, and *Pelayo,* by
Simms. Consider also Simms's "The Last Wager" (1843), a short
story.

LYDIA MARIA CHILD
(1802-1880)

A zealous abolitionist, Mrs. Child won supporters to the ranks with her pamphlets and widely circulated correspondence. She edited the *National Anti-Slavery Standard*, a New York City weekly newspaper, from 1841 to 1849. Much of her fiction also was designed to serve her humanitarian purposes. "The Black Saxons" is one of several stories in *Fact and Fiction* (1846) that treats minority characters.

THE BLACK SAXONS

Tyrants are but the spawn of ignorance,
Begotten by the slaves they trample on;
Who, could they win a glimmer of the light,
And see that tyranny is *always* weakness,
Or fear with its own bosom ill at ease,
Would laugh away in scorn the sand–wove chain,
Which their own blindness feigned for adamant.
Wrong ever builds on quicksands; but the Right
To the firm centre lays its moveless base.

J. R. LOWELL

Mr. Duncan was sitting alone in his elegantly furnished parlour, in the vicinity of Charleston, South Carolina. Before him lay an open volume, Thierry's History of the Norman Conquest. From the natural kindliness of his character, and democratic theories deeply imbibed in childhood, his thoughts dwelt more with a nation prostrated and kept in base subjection by the strong arm of violence, than with the renowned robbers, who seized their rich possesions, and haughtily trampled on their dearest rights.

"And so that bold and beautiful race became slaves!" thought he. "The brave and free-souled Harolds, strong of heart and strong of arm; the fair-haired Ediths, in their queenly beauty, noble in soul as well as ancestry; these all sank to the condition of slaves. They tamely submitted to their lot, till their free, bright beauty passed under the heavy cloud of animal dullness, and the contemptuous Norman epithet of 'base Saxon churls' was but too significantly true. Yet not without efforts did they thus sink. How often renewed, or how bravely sustained, we know not; for Troubadours rarely sing of the defeated, and conquerors write their own History. That they did not relinquish freedom without a struggle, is proved by Robin Hood and his bold followers, floating in dim and shadowy glory on the outskirts of history; brave outlaws of the free forest, and the wild mountain-passes, taking back, in the very teeth of danger, a precarious subsistence from the rich possessions that were once their own; and therefore styled thieves and traitors by the robbers who had beg-

362

gared them. Doubtless they had minstrels of their own; unknown in princely halls, untrumpeted by fame, yet singing of their exploits in spirit-stirring tones, to hearts burning with a sense of wrong. Troubled must be the sleep of those who rule a conquered nation!"

These thoughts were passing through his mind, when a dark mulatto opened the door, and making a servile reverence, said, in wheedling tones, "Would massa be so good as gib a pass to go to Methodist meeting?"

Mr. Duncan was a proverbially indulgent master; and he at once replied, "Yes, Jack, you may have a pass; but you must mind and not stay out all night."

"Oh, no, massa. Tom neber preach more than two hours."

Scarcely was the pass written, before another servant appeared with a similar request; and presently another; and yet another. When these interruptions ceased, Mr. Duncan resumed his book, and quietly read of the oppressed Saxons, until the wish for a glass of water induced him to ring the bell. No servant obeyed the summons. With an impatient jerk of the rope, he rang a second time, muttering to himself, "What a curse it is to be waited upon by slaves! If I were dying, the lazy loons would take their own time, and come dragging their heavy heels along, an hour after I was in the world of spirits. My neighbours tell me it is because I never flog them. I believe they are in the right. It is a hard case, too, to force a man to be a tyrant, whether he will or no."

A third time he rang the bell more loudly; but waited in vain for the sound of coming footsteps. Then it occurred to him that he had given every one of his slaves a pass to go to the Methodist meeting. This was instantly followed by the remembrance, that the same thing had happened a few days before.

We were then at war with Great Britain; and though Mr. Duncan often boasted the attachment of his slaves, and declared them to be the most contented and happy labourers in the world, who would not take their freedom if they could, yet, by some coincidence of thought, the frequency of Methodist meetings immediately suggested the common report that British troops were near the coast, and about to land in Charleston. Simultaneously came the remembrance of Big-boned Dick, who many months before had absconded from a neighbouring planter, and was suspected of holding a rendezvous for runaways, in the swampy depths of some dark forest. The existence of such a gang was indicated by the rapid disappearance of young corn, sweet potatoes, fat hogs, & c., from the plantations for many miles round.

"The black rascal!" exclaimed he: "If my boys *are* in league with him"—

The coming threat was arrested by a voice within, which, like a chorus from some invisible choir, all at once struck up the lively ballad of Robin Hood; and thus brought Big-boned Dick, like Banquo's Ghost, unbidden and unwelcome, into incongruous association with his spontaneous sympathy for Saxon serfs, his contempt of "base Saxon churls," who tamely submitted to their fate, and his admiration of the bold outlaws, who lived by plunder in the wild freedom of Saxon forests.

His republican sympathies, and the "system entailed upon him by his ancestors," were obviously out of joint with each other; and the skilfullest soldering of casuistry could by no means make them adhere together. Clear as the tones of a cathedral bell above the hacks and drays of a city, the voice of Reason rose above all the pretexts of selfishness, and the apologies of sophistry, and loudly proclaimed that his sympathies were right, and his practice wrong. Had there been at his elbow some honest John Woolman, or fearless Elias Hicks, that hour might perhaps have seen *him* a freeman, in giving freedom to his serfs. But he was alone; and the prejudices of education, and the habits of his whole life, conjured up a fearful array of lions in his path; and he wist not that they were phantoms. The admonitions of awakened conscience gradually gave place to considerations of personal safety, and plans for ascertaining the real extent of his danger.

The next morning he asked his slaves, with assumed nonchalance, whether they had a good meeting.

"Oh, yes, massa; bery good meeting."

"Where did you meet?"

"In the woods behind Birch Grove, massa."

The newspaper was brought, and found to contain a renewal of the report that British troops were prowling about the coast. Mr. Duncan slowly paced the room for some time, apparently studying the figures of the carpet, yet utterly unconscious whether he trod on canvas or the greensward. At length, he ordered his horse and drove to the next plantation. Seeing a gang at work in the fields, he stopped; and after some questions concerning the crop, he said to one of the most intelligent, "So you had a fine meeting last night?"

"Oh, yes, massa, bery nice meeting."

"Where was it?"

The slave pointed far *east* of Birch Grove. The white man's eye followed the direction of the bondman's finger, and a deeper cloud gathered on his brow. Without comment he rode on in another direction, and with apparent indifference made similar inquiries of another gang of labourers. They pointed *north* of Birch Grove, and replied, "In the Hugonot woods, massa."

With increasing disquietude, he slowly turned his horse toward the city. He endeavoured to conceal anxiety under a cheerful brow; for he was afraid to ask counsel, even of his most familiar friends, in a community so prone to be blinded by insane fury under the excitement of such suspicions. Having purchased a complete suit of negro clothes, and a black mask well fitted to his face, he returned home, and awaited the next request for passes to a Methodist meeting.

In a few days, the sable faces again appeared before him, one after another, asking permission to hear Tom preach. The passes were promptly given, accompanied by the cool observation, "It seems to me, boys, that you are all growing wonderfully religious of late."

To which they eagerly replied, "Ah, if massa could hear Tom preach, it make his hair stand up. Tom make ebery body tink weder he hab a soul."

When the last one had departed, the master hastily assumed his disguise, and hurried after them. Keeping them within sight, he followed over field and meadow, through woods and swamps. As he went on, the number of dark figures, all tending toward the same point, continually increased. Now and then, some one spoke to him; but he answered briefly, and with an effort to disguise his voice. At last, they arrived at one of those swamp islands, so common at the South, insulated by a broad, deep belt of water, and effectually screened from the main-land by a luxuriant growth of forest trees, matted together by a rich entanglement of vines and underwood. A large tree had been felled for a bridge; and over this dusky forms were swarming, like ants into their new-made nest.

Mr. Duncan had a large share of that animal instinct called physical courage; but his heart throbbed almost audibly, as he followed that dark multitude.

At the end of a rough and intricate passage, there opened before him a scene of picturesque and imposing grandeur. A level space, like a vast saloon, was enclosed by majestic trees, uniting their boughs over it, in fantastic resemblance to some Gothic cathedral. Spanish moss formed a thick matted roof, and floated in funereal streamers. From the points of arches hung wild vines in luxuriant profusion, some in heavy festoons, others lightly and gracefully leaping upward. The blaze of pine torches threw some into bold relief, and cast others into a shadowy background. And here, in this lone sanctuary of Nature, were assembled many hundreds of swart figures, some seated in thoughtful attitudes, others scattered in moving groups, eagerly talking together. As they glanced about, now sinking into dense shadow, and now emerging into lurid light, they seemed to the slaveholder's excited imagination like demons from the pit, come to claim guilty souls. He had, however, sufficient presence of mind to observe that each one, as he entered, prostrated himself, till his forehead touched the ground, and rising, placed his finger on his mouth. Imitating this signal, he passed in with the throng, and seated himself behind the glare of the torches. For some time, he could make out no connected meaning amid the confused buzz of voices, and half-suppressed snatches of songs. But, at last, a tall man mounted the stump of a decayed tree, nearly in the centre of the area, and requested silence.

"When we had our last meeting," said he, "I suppose most all of you know, that we all concluded it was best for to join the British, if so be we could get a good chance. But we didn't all agree about our masters. Some thought we should never be able to keep our freedom, without we killed our masters, in the first place; others didn't like the thoughts of that; so we agreed to have another meeting to talk about it. And now, boys, if the British land here in Caroliny, what shall we do with our masters?"

He sat down, and a tall, sinewy mulatto stepped into his place, exclaiming with fierce gestures, "Ravish wives and daughters before their eyes, as they have done to *us!* Hunt them with hounds, as they have hunted *us!* Shoot them down with rifles, as they have shot *us!*

Throw their carcasses to the crows, they have fattened on *our* bones; and then let the Devil take them where they never rake up fire o' nights. Who talks of *mercy* to our masters?"

"I do," said an aged black man, who rose up before the fiery youth, tottering as he leaned both hands on an oaken staff. "I do;— because the blessed Jesus always talked of mercy. I know we have been fed like hogs, and shot at like wild beasts. Myself found the body of my likeliest boy under the tree where buckra° rifles reached him. But thanks to the blessed Jesus, I feel it in my poor old heart to forgive them. I have been member of a Methodist church these thirty years; and I've heard many preachers, white and black; and they all tell me Jesus said, Do good to them that do evil to you, and pray for them that spite you. Now I say, let us love our enemies; let us pray for them; and when our masters flog us, and sell our piccaninnies, let us break out singing:

> "You may beat upon my body,
> But you cannot harm my soul;
> I shall join the forty thousand by and bye.

> "You may sell my children to Georgy,
> But you cannot harm their soul;
> They will join the forty thousand by and bye.

> "Come, slave–trader, come in too;
> The Lord's got a pardon here for you;
> You shall join the forty thousand by and bye.

> "Come, poor nigger, come in too;
> The Lord's got a pardon here for you;
> You shall join the forty thousand by and bye.

> "My skin is black, but my soul is white;
> And when we get to Heaven we'll all be alike;
> We shall join the forty thousand by and bye.

That's the way to glorify the Lord."

°Buckra is the negro term for white man. [Child's note.]

Scarcely had the cracked voice ceased the tremulous chant in which these words were uttered, when a loud altercation commenced; some crying out vehemently for the blood of the white men, others maintaining that the old man's doctrine was right. The aged black remained leaning on his staff, and mildly replied to every outburst of fury, "But Jesus said, do good for evil." Loud rose the din of excited voices; and the disguised slaveholder shrank deeper into the shadow.

In the midst of the confusion, an athletic, gracefully-proportioned young man sprang upon the stump, and throwing off his coarse cotton garments, slowly turned round and round, before the assembled multitude. Immediately all was hushed; for the light of a dozen torches, eagerly held up by fierce revengeful comrades, showed his back and shoulders deeply gashed by the whip, and still oozing with blood. In the midst of that deep silence, he stopped abruptly, and with stern brevity exclaimed, "Boys! *shall* we not murder our masters?"

"Would you murder *all?*" inquired a timid voice at his right hand. "They don't all cruellize their slaves."

"There's Mr. Campbell," pleaded another; "he never had one of his boys flogged in his life. You wouldn't murder *him*, would you?"

"Oh, no, no, no," shouted many voices; "we wouldn't murder Mr. Campbell. He's always good to coloured folks."

"And I wouldn't murder *my* master," said one of Mr. Duncan's slaves; "and I'd fight anybody that set out to murder him. I an't a going to work for him for nothing any longer, if I can help it; but he shan't be murdered; for he's a good master."

"Call him a good master, if ye like!" said the bleeding youth, with a bitter sneer in his look and tone. "I curse the word. The white men tell us God made them our masters; I say it was the Devil. When they don't cut up the backs that bear their burdens; when they throw us enough of the grain we have raised, to keep us strong for another harvest; when they forbear to shoot the limbs, that toil to make *them* rich; there *are* fools who call them good masters. Why should *they* sleep on soft beds, under silken curtains, while *we*, whose labour bought it all, lie on the floor at the threshold, or miserably coiled up in the dirt of our own cabins? Why should I clothe my master in broadcloth and fine linen, when he knows, and I know,

that he is my own brother? and I, meanwhile, have only this coarse
rag to cover my aching shoulders?" He kicked the garment scornfully, and added, "Down on your knees, if ye like, and thank them
that ye are not flogged and shot. Of *me* they'll learn another lesson!"

Mr. Duncan recognised in the speaker, the reputed son of one of
his friends, lately deceased; one of that numerous class, which southern vice is thoughtlessly raising up, to be its future scourge and terror.

The high, bold forehead, and flashing eye, indicated an intellect
too active and daring for servitude; while his fluent speech and appropriate language betrayed the fact that his highly educated parent, from some remains of instinctive feeling, had kept him near his
own person, during his lifetime, and thus formed his conversation on
another model than the rude jargon of slaves.

His poor, ignorant listeners stood spell-bound by the magic of a
superior mind; and at first it seemed as if he might carry the whole
meeting in favour of his views. But the aged man, leaning on his
oaken staff, still mildly spoke of the meek and blessed Jesus; and the
docility of African temperament responded to his gentle words.

Then rose a man of middle age, short of stature, with a quick ro-
guish eye, and a spirit of knowing drollery lurking about his mouth.
Rubbing his head in uncouth fashion, he began: "I don't know how
to speak like Bob; for I never had no chance. He says the Devil made
white men our masters. Now dat's a ting I've thought on a heap.
Many a time I've axed myself how pon arth it was, that jist as sure as
white man and black man come togeder, de white man sure to git he
foot on de black man. Sometimes I tink one ting, den I tink anoder
ting; and dey all be jumbled up in my head, jest like seed in de cotton, afore he put in de gin. At last, I find it all out. White man *always* git he foot on de black man; no mistake in *dat*. But how he do
it? I'll show you how!"

Thrusting his hand into his pocket, he took out a crumpled piece
of printed paper, and smoothing it carefully on the palm of his hand,
he struck it significantly with his finger, and exclaimed triumphantly, "Dat's de way dey do it! Dey got de *knowledge!* Now, it'll
do no more good to rise agin our masters, dan put de head in de fire
and pull him out agin; and may be you can't pull him out agin.
When I was a boy, I hear an old conjuring woman say she could con-

jure de Divil out of anybody. I ask her why she don't conjure her massa, den; and she tell me, 'Oh, nigger neber conjure buckra—can't do't.' But I say nigger *can* conjure buckra. How he do it? Get de knowledge! Dat de way. We make de sleeve wide, and fill full of de tea and de sugar, ebery time we get in missis' closet. If we take half so much pains to get de knowledge, de white man take he foot off de black man. Maybe de British land, and maybe de British no land; but tell you sons to marry de free woman, dat know how to read and write; and tell you gals to marry de free man, dat know how to read and write; and den, by'm bye, you be de British *yourselves!* You want to know how I manage to get de knowledge? I tell you. I want right bad to larn to read. My old boss is the most begrudgfullest massa, and I know he won't let me larn. So, when I see leetle massa wid he book, (he about six year old,) I say to him, What you call dat? He tell me dat is A. Oh, dat is A! So I take old newspaper, and I ax missis, may I hab dis to rub my brasses? She say yes. I put it in my pocket, and by'm by, I look to see I find A; and I look at him till I know him bery well. Den I ask my young massa, What you call dat? He say, dat is B. So I find him on my paper, and look at him, till I know him bery well. Den I ask my young massa what C A T spell? He tell me cat. Den, after great long time, I can read de newspaper. And what you tink I *find* dere? I read British going to land! Den I tell all de boys British going to land; and I say what you *do*, s'pose British land? When I stand behind massa's chair, I hear him talk, and I tell all de boys what he say. Den Bob say must hab Methodist meeting, and tell massa, Tom going to preach in de woods. But what you tink I did toder day? You know Jim, massa Gubernor's boy? Well, I want mighty bad to let Jim know British going to land. But he lib ten mile off, and old boss no let me go. Well, massa Gubernor he come dine my massa's house; and I bring he horse to de gate; and I make my bow, and say, massa Gubernor, how Jim do? He tell me Jim bery well. Den I ax him, be Jim good boy? He say yes. Den I tell him Jim and I leetle boy togeder; and I want mighty bad send Jim someting. He tell me Jim hab enough of ebery ting. Oh, yes, massa Gubernor, I know you bery good massa, and Jim hab ebery ting he want; but when leetle boy togeder, dere is always someting *here* (laying his hand on his heart). I want to send a leetle backy to Jim. I know he hab much backy he want; but Jim and I leetle boy togeder, and I want to send Jim someting. Massa Gubernor say, bery well, Jack. So I gib him de backy, done up in de bery bit o' newspaper dat tell British going to land! And massa Gubernor *himself* carry it! And massa Gubernor *himself* carry it!!"

He clapped his hands, kicked up his heels, and turned somersets like a harlequin. These demonstrations were received with loud shouts of merriment; and it was sometime before sufficient order was restored to proceed with the question under discussion.

After various scenes of fiery indignation, gentle expostulation, and boisterous mirth, it was finally decided, by a considerable majority, that in case the British landed, they would take their freedom *without* murdering their masters; not a few, however, went away in wrathful mood, muttering curses deep.

With thankfulness to Heaven, Mr. Duncan again found himself in the open field, alone with the stars. Their glorious beauty seemed to him, that night, clothed in new and awful power. Groups of shrubbery took to themselves startling forms; and the sound of the wind among the trees was like the unsheathing of swords. Again he recurred to Saxon history, and remembered how he had thought that troubled must be the sleep of those who rule a conquered people. A new significance seemed given to Wat Tyler's address to the insurgent labourers of *his* day; an emphatic, and most unwelcome application of *his* indignant question why serfs should toil unpaid, in wind and sun, that lords might sleep on down, and embroider their garments with pearl.

"And these Robin Hoods, and Wat Tylers, were my Saxon ancestors," thought he. "Who shall so balance effects and causes, as to decide what portion of my present freedom sprung from their seemingly defeated efforts? Was the place I saw to-night, in such wild and fearful beauty, like the haunts of the *Saxon* Robin Hoods? Was not the spirit that gleamed forth as brave as *theirs?* And who shall calculate what even such hopeless endeavours may do for the future freedom of this down-trodden race?"

These cogitations did not, so far as I ever heard, lead to the emancipation of his bondmen; but they did prevent his revealing a secret, which would have brought hundreds to an immediate and violent death. After a painful conflict between contending feelings and duties, he contented himself with advising the magistrates to forbid all meetings whatsoever among the coloured people until the war was ended.

He visited Boston several years after, and told the story to a gentleman, who often repeated it in the circle of his friends. In brief outline it reached my ears. I have told it truly, with some filling up by imagination, some additional garniture of language, and the adoption of fictitious names, because I have forgotten the real ones.

SUGGESTED ADDITIONAL READINGS

Hobomok
Appeal in Favor of that Class of Americans Called Africans
Letters of Lydia Maria Child

SELECTED REFERENCE

Whittier, John G. Introduction to Letters of Lydia Maria Child (1883).

PROJECTS AND PROBLEMS

Mrs. Child's humanitarianism is evident in her writing about Indians as well as in her antislavery works. Are some of her Indian characters "Noble Savages"? Was her analysis of the Seminole War, in her letter to Mrs. S. B. Shaw in 1873, basically romantic or realistic? What was her attitude toward miscegenation?

One of Mrs. Child's many services to the abolitionist cause was that of editing Incidents in the Life of a Slave Girl, by Linda Brent (Harriet Brent Jacobs). Compare the treatment of Nat Turner's Insurrection in that book with "The Black Saxons." And see her correspondence with Mrs. Mason of Virginia.

Are some of the stories in Fact and Fiction stereotypical in presenting docile black slaves and more fiery mulattos? Why did antislavery writers consider such characterizations desirable or necessary for their purposes? Do Mrs. Child's stories rely on stereotypes for her Irish and Quaker characters?

Compare Mrs. Child's "The Quadroons" in *Fact and Fiction* with Louisa May Alcott's "M. L.," a sentimental antislavery story first published in installments in the Boston *Commonwealth* in 1863 and reprinted in Lorenzo Dow Turner's *Anti-Slavery Sentiment in American Literature Prior to 1865* (1966). Do these works effectively attack slavery as an institution or merely decry the enslavement of particular individuals?

HERMAN MELVILLE
(1819-1891)

Herman Melville's works abound with representatives of the assorted races of mankind and with evidences of his conviction that all human beings are "sprung from one head, and made in one image." The first selection below is from *Redburn: His First Voyage* (1849), a novel based on Melville's voyage to Liverpool as a cabin boy. The story of poor Pip is from his masterpiece, *Moby-Dick* (1851). "Benito Cereno," from which the third selection is extracted, is the subject of numerous studies by modern critics, intrigued by its complexities. The story was collected in *The Piazza Tales* in 1856. " 'Formerly a Slave' " appeared in *Battle Pieces* (1866), his volume of Civil War poetry.

BLACK SHIPMATES AND
IRISH EMIGRANTS

The only man who seemed to be taking his ease that day, was our black cook; who according to the invariable custom at sea, always went by the name of *the doctor*.

And *doctors*, cooks certainly are, the very best medicos in the world; for what pestilent pills and potions of the Faculty are half so serviceable to man, and health-and-strength-giving, as roasted lamb and green peas, say, in spring; and roast beef and cranberry sauce in winter? Will a dose of calomel and jalap do you as much good? Will a bolus build up a fainting man? Is there any satisfaction in dining off a powder? But these doctors of the frying-pan sometimes kill men off by a surfeit; or give them the headache, at least. Well, what then? No matter. For if with their most goodly and ten times jolly medicines, they now and then fill our nights with tribulations, and abridge our days, what of the social homicides perpetrated by the Faculty? And when you die by a pill-doctor's hands, it is never with a sweet relish in your mouth, as though you died by a frying-pan-doctor; but your last breath villainously savors of ipecac and rhubarb. Then, what charges they make for the abominable lunches they serve out so stingily! One of their bills for boluses would keep you in good dinners a twelve-month.

Now, our doctor was a serious old fellow, much given to metaphysics, and used to talk about original sin. All that Sunday morning, he sat over his boiling pots, reading out of a book which was very much soiled and covered with grease spots: for he kept it stuck into a little leather strap, nailed to the keg where he kept the fat skimmed off the water in which the salt beef was cooked. I could hardly believe my eyes when I found this book was the Bible.

I loved to peep in upon him, when he was thus absorbed; for his smoky studio or study was a strange-looking place enough; not more than five feet square, and about as many high; a mere box to hold the stove, the pipe of which stuck out of the roof.

Within, it was hung round with pots and pans; and on one side was a little looking-glass, where he used to shave; and on a small

375

shelf were his shaving tools, and a comb and brush. Fronting the stove, and very close to it, was a sort of narrow shelf, where he used to sit with his legs spread out very wide, to keep them from scorching; and there, with his book in one hand, and a pewter spoon in the other, he sat all that Sunday morning, stirring up his pots, and studying away at the same time; seldom taking his eye off the page. Reading must have been very hard work for him; for he muttered to himself quite loud as he read; and big drops of sweat would stand upon his brow, and roll off, till they hissed on the hot stove before him.

But on the day I speak of, it was no wonder that he got perplexed, for he was reading a mysterious passage in the Book of Chronicles. Being aware that I knew how to read, he called me as I was passing his premises, and read the passage over, demanding an explanation. I told him it was a mystery that no one could explain; not even a parson. But this did not satisfy him, and I left him poring over it still.

He must have been a member of one of those negro churches, which are to be found in New York. For when we lay at the wharf, I remembered that a committee of three reverend looking old darkies, who, besides their natural canonicals, wore quaker-cut black coats, and broad-brimmed black hats, and white neck-cloths; these colored gentlemen called upon him, and remained conversing with him at his cook-house door for more than an hour; and before they went away they stepped inside, and the sliding doors were closed; and then we heard some one reading aloud and preaching; and after that a psalm was sung and a benediction given; when the door opened again, and the congregation came out in a great perspiration; owing, I suppose, to the chapel being so small, and there being only one seat besides the stove.

But notwithstanding his religious studies and meditations, this old fellow used to use some bad language occasionally; particularly of cold, wet stormy mornings, when he had to get up before daylight and make his fire; with the sea breaking over the bows, and now and then dashing into his stove.

So, under the circumstances, you could not blame him much, if he did rip a little, for it would have tried old Job's temper, to be set to work making a fire in the water.

Without being at all neat about his premises, this old cook was very particular about them; he had a warm love and affection for his cook-house. In fair weather, he spread the skirt of an old jacket before the door, by way of a mat; and screwed a small ring-bolt into the door for a knocker; and wrote his name, "Mr. Thompson," over it, with a bit of red chalk.

The men said he lived round the corner of *Forecastle-square*, opposite the *Liberty Pole;* because his cook-house was right behind the foremast, and very near the quarters occupied by themselves.

Sailors have a great fancy for naming things that way on shipboard. When a man is hung at sea, which is always done from one of the lower yard-arms, they say he *"takes a walk up Ladder-lane, and down Hemp-street."*

Mr. Thompson was a great crony of the steward's, who, being a handsome, dandy mulatto, that had once been a barber in West-Broadway, went by the name of Lavender. I have mentioned the gorgeous turban he wore when Mr. Jones and I visited the captain in the cabin. He never wore that turban at sea, though; but sported an uncommon head of frizzled hair, just like the large, round brush, used for washing windows, called a *Pope's Head.*

He kept it well perfumed with Cologne water, of which he had a large supply, the relics of his West-Broadway stock in trade. His clothes, being mostly cast-off suits of the captain of a London liner, whom he had sailed with upon many previous voyages, were all in the height of the exploded fashions, and of every kind of color and cut. He had claret-colored suits, and snuff-colored suits, and red velvet vests, and buff and brimstone pantaloons, and several full suits of black, which, with his dark-colored face, made him look quite clerical; like a serious young colored gentleman of Barbados, about to take orders.

He wore an uncommon large pursy ring on his forefinger, with something he called a real diamond in it; though it was very dim, and looked more like a glass eye than anything else. He was very proud of his ring, and was always calling your attention to something, and pointing at it with his ornamented finger.

He was a sentimental sort of a darky, and read the *"Three Spaniards,"* and *"Charlotte Temple,"* and carried a lock of frizzled hair in his vest pocket, which he frequently volunteered to show to people, with his handkerchief to his eyes.

Every fine evening, about sunset, these two, the cook and steward, used to sit on the little shelf in the cook-house, leaning up against each other like the Siamese twins, to keep from falling off, for the shelf was very short; and there they would stay till after dark, smoking their pipes, and gossiping about the events that had happened during the day in the cabin.

And sometimes Mr. Thompson would take down his Bible, and read a chapter for the edification of Lavender, whom he knew to be a sad profligate and gay deceiver ashore; addicted to every youthful indiscretion. He would read over to him the story of Joseph and Potiphar's wife; and hold Joseph up to him as a young man of excellent principles, whom he ought to imitate, and not be guilty of his indiscretion any more. And Lavender would look serious, and say that he knew it was all true—he was a wicked youth, he knew it—he had broken a good many hearts, and many eyes were weeping for him even then, both in New York, and Liverpool, and London, and Havre. But how could he help it? He hadn't made his handsome face, and fine head of hair, and graceful figure. It was not *he*, but the others, that were to blame; for his bewitching person turned all heads and subdued all hearts, wherever he went. And then he would look very serious and penitent, and go up to the little glass, and pass his hands through his hair, and see how his whiskers were coming on.

o   o   o   o   o

And here, I must not omit one thing, that struck me at the time. It was the absence of negroes; who in the large towns in the "free states" of America, almost always form a considerable portion of the destitute. But in these streets, not a negro was to be seen. All were whites; and with the exception of the Irish, were natives of the soil: even Englishmen; as much Englishmen, as the dukes in the House of Lords. This conveyed a strange feeling: and more than any thing else, reminded me that I was not in my own land. For *there*, such a being as a native beggar is almost unknown; and to be a born American citizen seems a guarantee against pauperism; and this, perhaps, springs from the virtue of a vote.

Speaking of negroes, recalls the looks of interest with which negro-sailors are regarded when they walk the Liverpool streets. In Liverpool indeed the negro steps with a prouder pace, and lifts his head like a man; for here, no such exaggerated feeling exists in respect to him, as in America. Three or four times, I encountered our black steward, dressed very handsomely, and walking arm in arm with a good-looking English woman. In New York, such a couple would have been mobbed in three minutes; and the steward would have been lucky to escape with whole limbs. Owing to the friendly reception extended to them, and the unwonted immunities they enjoy in Liverpool, the black cooks and stewards of American ships are very much attached to the place and like to make voyages to it.

Being so young and inexperienced then, and unconsciously swayed in some degree by those local and social prejudices, that are the marring of most men, and from which, for the mass, there seems no possible escape; at first I was surprised that a colored man should be treated as he is in this town; but a little reflection showed that, after all, it was but recognizing his claims to humanity and normal equal ity; so that, in some things, we Americans leave to other countries the carrying out of the principle that stands at the head of our Declaration of Independence.

○   ○   ○   ○   ○

We were all now very busy in getting things ready for sea. The cargo had been already stowed in the hold by the stevedores and lumpers from shore; but it became the crew's business to clear away the *between-decks*, extending from the cabin bulkhead to the forecastle, for the reception of about five hundred emigrants, some of whose boxes were already littering the decks.

To provide for their wants, a far larger supply of water was needed than upon the outward-bound passage. Accordingly, besides the usual number of casks on deck, rows of immense tierces were lashed amid-ships, all along the *between-decks*, forming a sort of aisle on each side, furnishing access to four rows of bunks,—three tiers, one above another,—against the ship's sides; two tiers being placed over the tierces of water in the middle. These bunks were rapidly knocked together with coarse planks. They looked more like dog-kennels than any thing else; especially as the place was so gloomy and dark; no light coming down except through the fore and after hatchways, both of which were covered with little houses called *"booby-hatches."* Upon the main-hatches, which were well calked and covered over with heavy tarpaulins, the *"passengers'- galley"* was solidly lashed down.

This *galley* was a large open stove, or iron range—made expressly for emigrant ships, wholly unprotected from the weather, and where alone the emigrants are permitted to cook their food while at sea.

After two days' work, everything was in readiness; most of the emigrants on board; and in the evening we worked the ship close into the outlet of Prince's Dock, with the bow against the water-gate, to go out with the tide in the morning.

In the morning, the bustle and confusion about us was indescrib-able. Added to the ordinary clamor of the docks, was the hurrying to and fro of our five hundred emigrants, the last of whom, with their baggage, were now coming on board; the appearance of the cabin passengers, following porters with their trunks; the loud orders of the dock-masters, ordering the various ships behind us to preserve their order of going out; the leave-takings, and good-by's, and God-bless-you's, between the emigrants and their friends; and the cheers of the surrounding ships.

At this time we lay in such a way, that no one could board us ex-cept by the bowsprit, which overhung the quay. Staggering along the bowsprit, now came a one-eyed *crimp* leading a drunken tar by the collar, who had been shipped to sail with us the day previous. It has been stated before, that two or three of our men had left us for good, while in port. When the crimp had got this man and another safely lodged in a bunk below, he returned on shore; and going to a miserable cab, pulled out still another apparently drunken fellow, who proved completely helpless. However, the ship now swinging her broadside more toward the quay, this stupefied sailor, with a Scotch cap pulled down over his closed eyes, only revealing a sallow Portuguese complexion, was lowered on board by a rope under his arms, and passed forward by the crew, who put him likewise into a bunk in the forecastle, the crimp himself carefully tucking him in, and bidding the bystanders not to disturb him till the ship was away from the land.

This done, the confusion increased, as we now glided out of the dock. Hats and handkerchiefs were waved; hurrahs were exchanged; and tears were shed; and the last thing I saw, as we shot into the stream, was a policeman collaring a boy, and walking him off to the guard-house.

A steam-tug, the *Goliath,* now took us by the arm, and gallanted us down the river past the fort.

The scene was most striking.

Owing to a strong breeze, which had been blowing up the river for four days past, holding wind-bound in the various docks a multitude of ships for all parts of the world; there was now under weigh, a vast fleet of merchantmen, all steering broad out to sea. The white sails glistened in the clear morning air like a great Eastern encampment of sultans; and from many a forecastle, came the deep mellow old song *Ho–o–he–yo, cheerily men!* as the crews catted their anchors.

The wind was fair; the weather mild; the sea most smooth; and the poor emigrants were in high spirits at so auspicious a beginning of their voyage. They were reclining all over the decks, talking of soon seeing America, and relating how the agent had told them, that twenty days would be an uncommonly long voyage.

Here it must be mentioned, that owing to the great number of ships sailing to the Yankee ports from Liverpool, the competition among them in obtaining emigrant passengers, who as a cargo are much more remunerative than crates and bales, is exceedingly great; so much so, that some of the agents they employ, do not scruple to deceive the poor applicants for passage, with all manner of fables concerning the short space of time, in which their ships make the run across the ocean.

This often induces the emigrants to provide a much smaller stock of provisions than they otherwise would; the effect of which sometimes proves to be in the last degree lamentable; as will be seen further on. And though benevolent societies have been long organized in Liverpool, for the purpose of keeping offices, where the emigrants can obtain reliable information and advice, concerning their best mode of embarkation, and other matters interesting to them; and though the English authorities have imposed a law, providing that every captain of an emigrant ship bound for any port of America shall see to it, that each passenger is provided with rations of food for sixty days; yet, all this has not deterred mercenary ship-masters and unprincipled agents from practicing the grossest decep-tion; nor exempted the emigrants themselves, from the very suffer-ings intended to be averted.

No sooner had we fairly gained the expanse of the Irish Sea, and, one by one, lost sight of our thousand consorts, than the weather changed into the most miserable cold, wet, and cheerless days and nights imaginable. The wind was tempestuous, and dead in our teeth; and the hearts of the emigrants fell. Nearly all of them had now hied below, to escape the uncomfortable and perilous decks: and from the two *"booby-hatches"* came the steady hum of a sub-terranean wailing and weeping. That irresistible wrestler, sea-sickness, had overthrown the stoutest of their number, and the women and children were embracing and sobbing in all the agonies of the poor emigrant's first storm at sea.

Bad enough is it at such times with ladies and gentlemen in the cabin, who have nice little state-rooms; and plenty of privacy; and stewards to run for them at a word, and put pillows under their heads, and tenderly inquire how they are getting along, and mix them a posset: and even then, in the abandonment of this soul and body subduing malady, such ladies and gentlemen will often give up life itself as unendurable, and put up the most pressing petitions for a speedy annihilation; all of which, however, only arises from their intense anxiety to preserve their valuable lives.

How, then, with the friendless emigrants, stowed away like bales of cotton, and packed like slaves in a slave-ship; confined in a place that, during storm time, must be closed against both light and air; who can do no cooking, nor warm so much as a cup of water; for the drenching seas would instantly flood their fire in their exposed gal-ley on deck? How, then, with these men, and women, and children, to whom a first voyage, under the most advantageous circum-stances, must come just as hard as to the Honorable De Lancey Fitz Clarence, lady, daughter, and seventeen servants.

Nor is this all: for in some of these ships, as in the case of the Highlander, the emigrant passengers are cut off from the most indis-pensable conveniences of a civilized dwelling. This forces them in storm time to such extremities, that no wonder fevers and plagues are the result. We had not been at sea one week, when to hold your head down the fore hatchway was like holding it down a suddenly opened cess-pool.

But still more than this. Such is the aristocracy maintained on board some of these ships, that the most arbitrary measures are enforced, to prevent the emigrants from intruding upon the most holy precincts of the quarter-deck, the only completely open space on ship-board. Consequently—even in fine weather—when they come up from below, they are crowded in the waist of the ship, and jammed among the boats, casks, and spars; abused by the seamen, and sometimes cuffed by the officers, for unavoidably standing in the way of working the vessel.

The cabin-passengers of the Highlander numbered some fifteen in all; and to protect this detachment of gentility from the barbarian incursions of the "*wild Irish*" emigrants, ropes were passed athwart-ships, by the main-mast, from side to side: which defined the boundary line between those who had paid three pounds passage-money, from those who had paid twenty guineas. And the cabin-passengers themselves were the most urgent in having this regulation maintained.

Lucky would it be for the pretensions of some parvenus, whose souls are deposited at their banker's, and whose bodies but serve to carry about purses, knit of poor men's heartstrings, if thus easily they could precisely define, ashore, the difference between them and the rest of humanity. . . .

POOR PIP!

Now, in the whale ship, it is not every one that goes in the boats. Some few hands are reserved called ship-keepers, whose province it is to work the vessel while the boats are pursuing the whale. As a general thing, these ship-keepers are as hardy fellows as the men comprising the boats' crews. But if there happen to be an unduly slender, clumsy, or timorous wight in the ship, that wight is certain to be made a ship-keeper. It was so in the Pequod with the little negro Pippin by nick-name, Pip by abbreviation. Poor Pip! ye have heard of him before; ye must remember his tambourine on that dramatic midnight, so gloomy-jolly.

In outer aspect, Pip and Dough-Boy made a match, like a black pony and a white one, of equal developments, though of dissimilar color, driven in one eccentric span. But while hapless Dough–Boy was by nature dull and torpid in his intellects, Pip, though over tender-hearted, was at bottom very bright, with that pleasant, genial, jolly brightness peculiar to his tribe; a tribe, which ever enjoy all holidays and festivities with finer, freer relish than any other race. For blacks, the year's calendar should show naught but three hundred and sixty-five Fourth of Julys and New Year's Days. Nor smile so, while I write that this little black was brilliant, for even blackness has its brilliancy; behold yon lustrous ebony, panelled in king's cabinets. But Pip loved life, and all life's peaceable securities; so that the panic-striking business in which he had somehow unaccountably become entrapped, had most sadly blurred his brightness; though, as ere long will be seen, what was thus temporarily subdued in him, in the end was destined to be luridly illumined by strange wild fires, that fictitiously showed him off to ten times the natural lustre with which in his native Tolland County in Connecticut, he had once enlivened many a fiddler's frolic on the green; and at melodious even-tide, with his gay ha-ha! had turned the round horizon into one starbelled tambourine. So, though in the clear air of day, suspended against a blue-veined neck, the pure-watered diamond drop will healthful glow; yet, when the cunning jeweller would show you the diamond in its most impressive lustre, he lays it against a gloomy ground, and then lights it up, not by the sun, but by

384

some unnatural gases. Then come out those fiery effulgences, infernally superb; then the evil-blazing diamond, once the divinest symbol of the crystal skies, looks like some crown-jewel stolen from the King of Hell. But let us to the story.

It came to pass, that in the ambergris affair Stubb's afteroarsman chanced so to sprain his hand, as for a time to become quite maimed; and, temporarily, Pip was put into his place.

The first time Stubb lowered with him, Pip evinced much nervousness; but happily, for that time, escaped close contact with the whale; and therefore came off not altogether discreditably; though Stubb observing him, took care, afterwards, to exhort him to cherish his courageousness to the utmost, for he might often find it needful.

Now upon the second lowering, the boat paddled upon the whale; and as the fish received the darted iron, it gave its customary rap, which happened, in this instance, to be right under poor Pip's seat. The involuntary consternation of the moment caused him to leap, paddle in hand, out of the boat; and in such a way, that part of the slack whale line coming against his chest, he breasted it overboard with him, so as to become entangled in it, when at last plumping into the water. That instant the stricken whale started on a fierce run, the line swiftly straightened; and presto! poor Pip came all foaming up to the chocks of the boat, remorselessly dragged there by the line, which had taken several turns around his chest and neck.

Tashtego stood in the bows. He was full of the fire of the hunt. He hated Pip for a poltroon. Snatching the boatknife from its sheath, he suspended its sharp edge over the line, and turning towards Stubb, exclaimed interrogatively, "Cut?" Meantime Pip's blue, choked face plainly looked, Do, for God's sake! All passed in a flash. In less than half a minute, this entire thing happened.

"Damn him, cut!" roared Stubb; and so the whale was lost and Pip was saved.

So soon as he recovered himself, the poor little negro was assailed by yells and execrations from the crew. Tranquilly permitting these irregular cursings to evaporate, Stubb then in a plain, business-like, but still half humorous manner, cursed Pip officially; and that done, unofficially gave him much wholesome advice. The substance was, Never jump from a boat, Pip, except—but all the rest was indefinite, as the soundest advice ever is. Now, in general, *Stick to the boat,* is your true motto in whaling; but cases will sometimes happen when *Leap from the boat*, is still better. Moreover, as if perceiving at last that if he should give undiluted conscientious advice to Pip, he would be leaving him too wide a margin to jump in for the future; Stubb suddenly dropped all advice, and concluded with a peremptory command "Stick to the boat, Pip, or by the Lord, I won't pick you up if you jump; mind that. We can't afford to lose whales by the likes of you; a whale would sell for thirty times what you would, Pip, in Alabama. Bear that in mind, and don't jump any more." Hereby perhaps Stubb indirectly hinted, that though man loved his fellow, yet man is a money-making animal, which propensity too often interferes with his benevolence.

But we are all in the hands of the Gods; and Pip jumped again. It was under very similar circumstances to the first performance; but this time he did not breast out the line; and hence, when the whale started to run, Pip was left behind on the sea, like a hurried traveller's trunk. Alas! Stubb was but too true to his word. It was a beautiful, bounteous, blue day! the spangled sea calm and cool, and flatly stretching away, all round, to the horizon, like gold-beater's skin hammered out to the extremest. Bobbing up and down in that sea, Pip's ebon head showed like a head of cloves. No boat-knife was lifted when he fell so rapidly astern. Stubb's inexorable back was turned upon him; and the whale was winged. In three minutes, a whole mile of shoreless ocean was between Pip and Stubb. Out from the centre of the sea, poor Pip turned his crisp, curling, black head to the sun, another lonely castaway, though the loftiest and the brightest.

Now, in calm weather, to swim in the open ocean is as easy to the practised swimmer as to ride in a spring-carriage ashore. But the awful lonesomeness is intolerable. The intense concentration of self in the middle of such a heartless immensity, my God! who can tell it? Mark, how when sailors in a dead calm bathe in the open sea— mark how closely they hug their ship and only coast along her sides.

But had Stubb really abandoned the poor little negro to his fate? No; he did not mean to, at least. Because there were two boats in his wake, and he supposed, no doubt, that they would of course come up to Pip very quickly, and pick him up; though, indeed, such considerations towards oarsmen jeopardized through their own timidity, is not always manifested by the hunters in all similar instances; and such instances not unfrequently occur; almost invariably in the fishery, a coward, so called, is marked with the same ruthless detestation peculiar to military navies and armies.

But it so happened, that those boats, without seeing Pip, suddenly spying whales close to them on one side, turned, and gave chase; and Stubb's boat was now so far away, and he and all his crew so intent upon his fish, that Pip's ringed horizon began to expand around him miserably. By the merest chance the ship itself at last rescued him; but from that hour the little negro went about the deck an idiot; such, at least, they said he was. The sea had jeeringly kept his finite body up, but drowned the infinite of his soul. Not drowned entirely, though. Rather carried down alive to wondrous depths, where strange shapes of the unwarped primal world glided to and fro before his passive eyes; and the miser-merman, Wisdom, revealed his hoarded heaps; and among the joyous, heartless, ever–juvenile eternities, Pip saw the multitudinous, God-omnipresent, coral insects, that out of the firmament of waters heaved the colossal orbs. He saw God's foot upon the treadle of the loom, and spoke it; and therefore his shipmates called him mad. So man's insanity is heaven's sense; and wandering from all mortal reason, man comes at last to that celestial thought, which, to reason, is absurd and frantic; and weal or woe, feels then uncompromised, indifferent as his God.

A CLOSE SHAVE

There is something in the negro which, in a peculiar way, fits him for avocations about one's person. Most negroes are natural valets and hair–dressers; taking to the comb and brush congenially as to the castanets, and flourishing them apparently with almost equal satisfaction. There is, too, a smooth tact about them in this employment, with a marvelous, noiseless, gliding briskness, not ungraceful in its way, singularly pleasing to behold, and still more so to be the manipulated subject of. And above all is the great gift of good humour. Not the mere grin or laugh is here meant. Those were unsuitable. But a certain easy cheerfulness, harmonious in every glance and gesture; as though God had set the whole negro to some pleasant tune.

When to all this is added the docility arising from the unaspiring contentment of a limited mind, and that susceptibility of blind attachment sometimes inhering in indisputable inferiors, one readily perceives why those hypochondriacs, Johnson and Byron—it may be something like the hypochondriac, Benito Cereno—took to their hearts, almost to the exclusion of the entire white race, their serving men, the negroes, Barber and Fletcher. But if there be that in the negro which exempts him from the inflicted sourness of the morbid or cynical mind, how, in his own prepossessing aspects, must he appear to a benevolent one? When at ease with respect to exterior things, Captain Delano's nature was not only benign, but familiarly and humorously so. At home, he had often taken rare satisfaction in sitting in his door, watching some free man of colour at his work or play. If on a voyage he chanced to have a black sailor, invariably he was on chatty, and half-gamesome terms with him. In fact, like most men of a good, blithe heart, Captain Delano took to negroes, not philanthropically, but genially, just as other men to Newfoundland dogs.

Hitherto the circumstances in which he found the *San Dominick* had repressed the tendency. But in the cuddy, relieved from his former uneasiness, and, for various reasons, more sociably inclined than at any previous period of the day, and seeing the coloured servant, napkin on arm, so debonair about his master, in a business so familiar as that of shaving, too, all his old weakness for negroes returned.

388

Among other things, he was amused with an odd instance of the African love of bright colours and fine shows, in the black's informally taking from the flag-locker a great piece of bunting of all hues, and lavishly tucking it under his master's chin for an apron.

The mode of shaving among the Spaniards is a little different from what it is with other nations. They have a basin, specially called a barber's basin, which on one side is scooped out, so as accurately to receive the chin, against which it is closely held in lathering; which is done, not with a brush, but with soap dipped in the water of the basin and rubbed on the face.

In the present instance salt-water was used for lack of better; and the parts lathered were only the upper lip, and low down under the throat, all the rest being cultivated beard.

These preliminaries being somewhat novel to Captain Delano he sat curiously eyeing them, so that no conversation took place, nor for the present did Don Benito appear disposed to renew any.

Setting down his basin, the negro searched among the razors, as for the sharpest, and having found it, gave it an additional edge by expertly stropping it on the firm, smooth, oily skin of his open palm; he then made a gesture as if to begin, but midway stood suspended for an instant, one hand elevating the razor, the other professionally dabbling among the bubbling suds on the Spaniard's lank neck. Not unaffected by the close sight of the gleaming steel, Don Benito nervously shuddered, his usual ghastliness was heightened by the lather, which lather, again, was intensified in its hue by the contrasting sootiness of the negro's body. Altogether the scene was somewhat peculiar, at least to Captain Delano, nor, as he saw the two thus postured, could he resist the vagary, that in the black he saw a headsman, and in the white, a man at the block. But this was one of those antic conceits, appearing and vanishing in a breath, from which, perhaps, the best regulated mind is not free.

Meantime the agitation of the Spaniard had a little loosened the bunting from around him, so that one broad fold swept curtain-like over the chair-arm to the floor, revealing, amid a profusion of armorial bars and ground-colours—black, blue and yellow—a closed castle in a blood-red field diagonal with a lion rampant in a white.

"The castle and the lion," exclaimed Captain Delano—"why, Don Benito, this is the flag of Spain you use here. It's well it's only I, and not the King, that sees this," he added with a smile, "but"—turning toward the black,—"it's all one, I suppose, so the colours be gay," which playful remark did not fail somewhat to tickle the negro.

"Now, master," he said, readjusting the flag, and pressing the head gently further back into the crotch of the chair; "now master," and the steel glanced nigh the throat.

Again Don Benito faintly shuddered.

"You must not shake so, master.—See, Don Amasa, master always shakes when I shave him. And yet master knows I never yet have drawn blood, though it's true, if master will shake so, I may some of these times. Now, master," he continued. "And now, Don Amasa, please go on with your talk about the gale, and all that, master can hear, and between times master can answer."

"Ah yes, these gales," said Captain Delano; "but the more I think of your voyage, Don Benito, the more I wonder, not at the gales, terrible as they must have been, but at the disastrous interval following them. For here, by your account, have you been these two months and more getting from Cape Horn to St. Maria, a distance which I myself, with a good wind, have sailed in a few days. True, you had calms, and long ones, but to be becalmed for two months, that is, at least, unusual. Why, Don Benito, had almost any other gentleman told me such a story, I should have been half disposed to a little incredulity."

Here an involuntary expression came over the Spaniard, similar to that just before on the deck, and whether it was the start he gave, or a sudden gawky roll of the hull in the calm, or a momentary unsteadiness of the servant's hand; however it was, just then the razor drew blood, spots of which stained the creamy lather under the throat; immediately the black barber drew back his steel, and remaining in his professional attitude, back to Captain Delano, and face to Don Benito, held up the trickling razor, saying, with a sort of half humorous sorrow, "See, master,—you shook so—here's Babo's first blood."

No sword drawn before James the First of England, no assassination in that timid King's presence, could have produced a more terrified aspect than was now presented by Don Benito.

Poor fellow, thought Captain Delano, so nervous he can't even bear the sight of barber's blood; and this unstrung, sick man, is it credible that I should have imagined he meant to spill all my blood, who can't endure the sight of one little drop of his own? Surely, Amasa Delano, you have been beside yourself this day. Tell it not when you get home, sappy Amasa. Well, well, he looks like a murderer, doesn't he? More like as if himself were to be done for. Well, well, this day's experience shall be a good lesson.

Meantime, while these things were running through the honest seaman's mind, the servant had taken the napkin from his arm, and to Don Benito had said: "But answer Don Amasa, please, master, while I wipe this ugly stuff off the razor, and strop it again."

As he said the words, his face was turned half round, so as to be alike visible to the Spaniard and the American, and seemed by its expression to hint, that he was desirous, by getting his master to go on with the conversation, considerately to withdraw his attention from the recent annoying accident. As if glad to snatch the offered relief, Don Benito resumed, rehearsing to Captain Delano, that not only were the calms of unusual duration, but the ship had fallen in with obstinate currents, and other things he added, some of which were but repetitions of former statements, to explain how it came to pass that the passage from Cape Horn to St. Maria had been so exceedingly long, now and then mingling with his words, incidental praises, less qualified than before, to the blacks, for their general good conduct.

These particulars were not given consecutively, the servant now and then using his razor, and so, between the intervals of shaving, the story and panegyric went on with more than usual huskiness.

To Captain Delano's imagination, now again not wholly at rest, there was something so hollow in the Spaniard's manner, with apparently some reciprocal hollowness in the servant's dusky comment of silence, that the idea flashed across him, that possibly master and man, for some unknown purpose, were acting out, both in word and deed, nay, to the very tremor of Don Benito's limbs, some juggling play before him. Neither did the suspicion of collusion lack apparent support, from the fact of those whispered conferences before mentioned. But then, what could be the object of enacting this play of the barber before him? At last, regarding the notion as a whimsy, insensibly suggested, perhaps, by the theatrical aspect of Don Benito in his harlequin ensign, Captain Delano speedily banished it.

The shaving over, the servant bestirred himself with a small bottle of scented waters, pouring a few drops on the head, and then diligently rubbing; the vehemence of the exercise causing the muscles of his face to twitch rather strangely.

His next operation was with comb, scissors and brush; going round and round, smoothing a curl here, clipping an unruly whisker-hair there, giving a graceful sweep to the temple-lock, with other impromptu touches evincing the hand of a master; while, like any resigned gentleman in barber's hands, Don Benito bore all, much less uneasily, at least, than he had done the razoring; indeed, he sat so pale and rigid now, that the negro seemed a Nubian sculptor finishing off a white statue-head.

All being over at last, the standard of Spain removed, tumbled up, and tossed back into the flag-locker, the negro's warm breath blowing away any stray hair which might have lodged down his master's neck; collar and cravat readjusted; a speck of lint whisked off the velvet lapel; all this being done; backing off a little space, and pausing with an expression of subdued self-complacency, the servant for a moment surveyed his master, as, in toilet at least, the creature of his own tasteful hands.

Captain Delano playfully complimented him upon his achievement; at the same time congratulating Don Benito.

But neither sweet waters, nor shampooing, nor fidelity, nor sociality, delighted the Spaniard. Seeing him relapsing into forbidding gloom, and still remaining seated, Captain Delano, thinking that his presence was undesired just then, withdrew, on pretence of seeing whether, as he had prophesied, any signs of a breeze were visible.

Walking forward to the mainmast, he stood awhile thinking over the scene, and not without some undefined misgivings, when he heard a noise near the cuddy, and turning, saw the negro, his hand to his cheek. Advancing, Captain Delano perceived that the cheek was bleeding. He was about to ask the cause, when the negro's wailing soliloquy enlightened him.

"Ah, when will master get better from his sickness; only the sour heart that sour sickness breeds made him serve Babo so; cutting Babo with the razor, because, only by accident, Babo had given master one little scratch; and for the first time in so many a day, too. Ah, ah, ah," holding his hand to his face.

Is it possible, thought Captain Delano; was it to wreak in private his Spanish spite against this poor friend of his, that Don Benito, by his sullen manner, impelled me to withdraw? Ah, this slavery breeds ugly passions in man! Poor fellow!

He was about to speak in sympathy to the negro, but with a timid reluctance he now re-entered the cuddy.

Presently master and man came forth; Don Benito leaning on his servant as if nothing had happened.

But a sort of love-quarrel, after all, thought Captain Delano. He accosted Don Benito, and they slowly walked together. They had gone but a few paces, when the steward—a tall, rajah-looking mulatto, orientally set off with a pagoda turban formed by three or four Madras handkerchiefs wound about his head, tier on tier—approaching with a salaam, announced lunch in the cabin.

On their way thither, the two captains were preceded by the mulatto, who, turning round as he advanced, with continual smiles and bows, ushered them in, a display of elegance which quite completed the insignificance of the small bare-headed Babo, who, as if not unconscious of inferiority, eyed askance the graceful steward. But in part, Captain Delano imputed his jealous watchfulness to that peculiar feeling which the full-blooded African entertains for the adulterated one. As for the steward, his manner, if not bespeaking much dignity or self-respect, yet evidenced his extreme desire to please; which is doubly meritorious, as at once Christian and Chesterfieldian.

Captain Delano observed with interest that while the complexion of the mulatto was hybrid, his physiognomy was European; classically so.

"Don Benito," whispered he, "I am glad to see this usher-of-the-golden-rod of yours; the sight refutes an ugly remark once made to me by a Barbados planter that when a mulatto has a regular European face, look out for him; he is a devil. But see, your steward here has features more regular than King George's of England; and yet there he nods, and bows, and smiles; a king, indeed—the king of kind hearts and polite fellows. What a pleasant voice he has, too."

"He has, Señor."

"But, tell me, has he not, so far as you have known him, always proved a good, worthy fellow?" said Captain Delano, pausing, while with a final genuflexion the steward disappeared into the cabin; "come, for the reason just mentioned, I am curious to know."

"Francesco is a good man," rather sluggishly responded Don Benito, like a phlegmatic appreciator, who would neither find fault nor flatter.

"Ah, I thought so. For it were strange indeed, and not very creditable to us white-skins, if a little of our blood mixed with the African's, should, far from improving the latter's quality, have the sad effect of pouring vitriolic acid into black broth; improving the hue, perhaps, but not the wholesomeness."

FORMERLY A SLAVE

An idealized portrait by E. Vedder,
in the spring exhibition
of the National Academy, 1865

The sufferance of her race is shown,
    And retrospect of life,
Which now too late deliverance dawns upon;
    Yet is she not at strife.

Her children's children they shall know
    The good withheld from her;
And so her reverie takes prophetic cheer—
    In spirit she sees the stir.

Far down the depth of thousand years,
    And marks the revel shine;
Her dusky face is lit with sober light,
    Sibylline, yet benign.

SUGGESTED ADDITIONAL READINGS

Typee
Omoo
White-Jacket
The Confidence Man
Clarel

SELECTED REFERENCES

Browne, Ray B. "Billy Budd: Gospel of Democracy." *Nineteenth Century Fiction,* 17 (1963), 321–37.
Cohen, Hennig. "Melville's Tomahawk Pipe: Artifact and Symbol." *Studies in the Novel,* 1 (1969), 397–401.
Cook, Fred J. "The Slave Ship Rebellion." *American Heritage,* 8, No. 2 (1957), 61–64, 104–106.

D'Azevedo, Warren. "Revolt on the San Dominick." *Phylon,* 17 (1956), 129–40.

Grejda, Edward S. *The Common Continent of Men: Racial Equality in the Writings of Herman Melville* (1974).

Guttmann, Allen. "The Enduring Innocence of Captain Amasa Delano." *Boston University Studies in English,* 5 (1961), 35–45.

Harap, Louis. *The Image of the Jew in American Literature* (1974).

Jackson, Kenny. "Israel Potter: Melville's 'Fourth of July Story.'" *CLA Journal,* 6 (1963), 498–534.

Jackson, Margaret Y. "Melville's Use of a Real Slave Mutiny in 'Benito Cereno.'" *CLA Journal,* 4 (1960), 79–93.

Kaplan, Sidney. "Herman Melville and the American National Sin: The Meaning of 'Benito Cereno.'" *Journal of Negro History,* 41 (1956), 311–38, and 42 (1957), 11–37.

Keeler, Clinton. "Melville's Delano: Our Cheerful Axiologist." *CLA Journal,* 10 (1966), 49–55.

Margolies, Edward. "Melville and Blacks." *CLA Journal,* 18 (1975), 364–73.

Rosenberry, Edward H. "Queequeg's Coffin-Canoe: Made in *Typee." American Literature,* 30 (1959), 529–30.

Simboli, David. " 'Benito Cereno' as Pedagogy." *CLA Journal,* 9 (1965), 159–64.

Simpson, Eleanor E. "Melville and the Negro: From *Typee* to 'Benito Cereno.'" *American Literature,* 41 (1969), 19–38.

Welsh, Howard. "The Politics of Race in 'Benito Cereno.'" *American Literature,* 46 (1975), 556–66.

Yellin, Jean Fagan. "Black Masks: Melville's 'Benito Cereno.'" *American Quarterly,* 22 (1970), 678–89.

PROJECTS AND PROBLEMS

Discuss the contrasting attitudes toward Polynesian society in *Typee* and *Omoo.* The second book shows some changes in Melville's views.

Compare Melville's poem about John Brown, "Shenandoah," with what Emerson and Thoreau wrote about Brown.

What is the reader to make of the cripple, Black Guinea, in *The Confidence Man?* What does Melville really say about "Indian depravity" in that book?

Locate incidental references to Jews and Italians in Melville's works (*Redburn* and *The Confidence Man*, for example). Is he generous or otherwise in his comments?

Study Melville's treatment of the hundreds of Irish immigrants in *Redburn*, "packed like slaves in a slave-ship." Is the picture stereotyped? Is it essentially favorable or unfavorable?

Compare Pip, the black cabin boy in *Moby-Dick*, with Harry Bolton, the somewhat effeminate English youth in *Redburn*. Do they seem at all like such other Melville characters as Billy Budd and Bartleby?

In 1839, Melville wrote a letter to his brother in Negro dialect and signed it "your friend/Tawney." Does this youthful prank foreshadow his treatment of black characters in fiction?

Study the minority characters in *Moby-Dick* and compare them with those in other Melville narratives or in other nautical fiction of the time.

Discuss the changes Melville made in his sources when he wrote "Benito Cereno" and his use of the records of the Amistad Mutiny. Decide whether his changes strengthen or weaken the story.

Is the position Melville expresses in "Benito Cereno" comparable to the defense John Quincy Adams provided for Cinque, who was acquitted in 1840 for his role in a mutiny? See Morris Bishop's "Cinque, The Noble Mutineer" in *The New Yorker*, December 20, 1941, or David Holland's "The Slaves Who Wouldn't Be Sold" in *True, The Man's Magazine*, March, 1957.

Compare Melville's "Benito Cereno" with the drama of the same name by Robert Lowell, published in 1964. Account for differences in theme and symbols.

FRANCIS PARKMAN
(1823–1893)

Parkman is important for his many volumes of history, but his first work, *The Oregon Trail* (1849), was an account of a journey to the West motivated by his interest in studying Indian life and his hope of improving his frail health. Member of a prominent Boston family, Parkman lived with a band of Sioux and mingled with trappers and other frontiersmen. This selection from the book he dictated to a companion is from Chapter XI.

AT A DAHCOTAH VILLAGE

As this Indian village and its inhabitants will hold a prominent place in the rest of the story, perhaps it may not be amiss to glance for an instant at the savage people of which they form a part. The Dahcotah or Sioux range over a vast territory, from the river St. Peter to the Rocky Mountains. They are divided into several independent bands, united under no central government, and acknowledging no common head. The same language, usages, and superstitions form the sole bond between them. They do not unite even in their wars. The bands of the east fight the Ojibwas on the Upper Lakes; those of the west make incessant war upon the Snake Indians in the Rocky Mountains. As the whole people is divided into bands, so each band is divided into villages. Each village has a chief, who is honored and obeyed only so far as his personal qualities may command respect and fear. Sometimes he is a mere nominal chief; sometimes his authority is little short of absolute, and his fame and influence reach beyond his own village, so that the whole band to which he belongs is ready to acknowledge him as their head. This was, a few years since, the case with the Ogillallah. Courage, address, and enterprise may raise any warrior to the highest honor, especially if he be the son of a former chief, or a member of a numerous family, to support him and avenge his quarrels; but when he has reached the dignity of chief, and the old men and warriors, by peculiar ceremony, have formally installed him, let it not be imagined that he assumes any of the outward signs of rank and honor. He knows too well on how frail a tenure he holds his station. He must conciliate his uncertain subjects. Many a man in the village lives better, owns more squaws and more horses, and goes better clad than he. Like the Teutonic chiefs of old, he ingratiates himself with his young men by making them presents, thereby often impoverishing himself. If he fails to gain their favor, they will set his authority at naught, and may desert him at any moment; for the usages of his people have provided no means of enforcing his authority. Very seldom does it happen, at least among these western bands, that a chief attains to much power, unless he is the head of a numerous family. Frequently the village is principally made up of his relatives and descendants,

399

and the wandering community assumes much of the patriarchal character.

The western Dahcotah have no fixed habitations. Hunting and fighting, they wander incessantly, through summer and winter. Some follow the herds of buffalo over the waste of prairie; others traverse the Black Hills, thronging, on horseback and on foot, through the dark gulfs and sombre gorges, and emerging at last upon the "Parks," those beautiful but most perilous hunting-grounds. The buffalo supplies them with the necessaries of life; with habitations, food, clothing, beds, and fuel; strings for their bows, glue, thread, cordage, trail-ropes for their horses, coverings for their saddles, vessels to hold water, boats to cross streams, and the means of purchasing all that they want from the traders. When the buffalo are extinct, they too must dwindle away.

War is the breath of their nostrils. Against most of the neighboring tribes they cherish a rancorous hatred, transmitted from father to son, and inflamed by constant aggression and retaliation. Many times a year, in every village, the Great Spirit is called upon, fasts are made, the war-parade is celebrated, and the warriors go out by handfuls at a time against the enemy. This fierce spirit awakens their most eager aspirations, and calls forth their greatest energies. It is chiefly this that saves them from lethargy and utter abasement. Without its powerful stimulus they would be like the unwarlike tribes beyond the mountains, scattered among the caves and rocks like beasts, and living on roots and reptiles. These latter have little of humanity except the form; but the proud and ambitious Dahcotah warrior can sometimes boast heroic virtues. It is seldom that distinction and influence are attained among them by any other course than that of arms. Their superstition, however, sometimes gives great power to those among them who pretend to the character of magicians; and their orators, such as they are, have their share of honor.

But to return. Look into our tent, or enter, if you can bear the stifling smoke and the close air. There, wedged close together, you will see a circle of stout warriors, passing the pipe around, joking, telling stories, and making themselves merry after their fashion. We were also infested by little copper-colored naked boys and snake-eyed girls. They would come up to us, muttering certain words, which

being interpreted conveyed the concise invitation, "Come and eat."
Then we would rise, cursing the pertinacity of Dahcotah hospitality,
which allowed scarcely an hour of rest between sun and sun, and to
which we were bound to do honor, unless we would offend our en-
tertainers. This necessity was particularly burdensome to me, as I
was scarcely able to walk, from the effects of illness, and was poorly
qualified to dispose of twenty meals a day. So bounteous an entertainment looks like an outgushing of goodwill; but, doubtless, half
at least of our kind hosts, had they met us alone and unarmed on the
prairie, would have robbed us of our horses, and perhaps have bestowed an arrow upon us besides.

One morning we were summoned to the lodge of an old man, the
Nestor of his tribe. We found him half sitting, half reclining, on a
pile of buffalo-robes; his long hair, jetblack, though he had seen
some eighty winters, hung on either side of his thin features. His
gaunt but symmetrical frame did not more clearly exhibit the wreck
of bygone strength, than did his dark, wasted features, still prominent and commanding, bear the stamp of mental energies. Opposite
the patriarch was his nephew, the young aspirant Mahto-Tatonka;
and besides these, there were one or two women in the lodge.

The old man's story is peculiar, and illustrative of a superstition
that prevails in full force among many of the Indian tribes. He was
one of a powerful family, renowned for warlike exploits. When a
very young man, he submitted to the singular rite to which most of
the tribe subject themselves before entering upon life. He painted
his face black; then seeking out a cavern in a sequestered part of the
Black Hills, he lay for several days, fasting, and praying to the spirits. In the dreams and visions produced by his weakened and excited
state, he fancied, like all Indians, that he saw supernatural revela-
tions. Again and again the form of an antelope appeared before him.
The antelope is the graceful peace spirit of the Ogillallah; but seldom is it that such a gentle visitor presents itself during the initia-
tory fasts of their young men. The terrible grizzly bear, the divinity
of war, usually appears to fire them with martial ardor and thirst for
renown. At length the antelope spoke. It told the young dreamer
that he was not to follow the path of war; that a life of peace and
tranquillity was marked out for him; that thenceforward he was to
guide the people by his counsels, and protect them from the evils of

their own feuds and dissensions. Others were to gain renown by fighting the enemy; but greatness of a different kind was in store for him.

The visions beheld during the period of this fast usually determine the whole course of the dreamer's life. From that time, Le Borgne, which was the only name by which we knew him, abandoned all thoughts of war, and devoted himself to the labors of peace. He told his vision to the people. They honored his commission and respected him in his novel capacity.

A far different man was his brother, Mahto-Tatonka, who had left his name, his features, and many of his qualities, to his son. He was the father of Henry Chatillon's squaw, a circumstance which proved of some advantage to us, as it secured the friendship of a family perhaps the most noted and influential in the whole Ogillallah band; Mahto-Tatonka, in his way, was a hero. No chief could vie with him in warlike renown, or in power over his people. He had a fearless spirit, and an impetuous and inflexible resolution. His will was law. He was politic and sagacious, and with true Indian craft, always befriended the whites, knowing that he might thus reap great advantages for himself and his adherents. When he had resolved on any course of conduct, he would pay to the warriors the compliment of calling them together to deliberate upon it, and when their debates were over, quietly state his own opinion, which no one ever disputed. It fared hard with those who incurred his displeasure. He would strike them or stab them on the spot; and this act, which, if attempted by any other chief would have cost him his life, the awe inspired by his name enabled him to repeat again and again with impunity. In a community where, from immemorial time, no man has acknowledged any law but his own will, Mahto-Tatonka raised himself to power little short of despotic. His career came at last to an end. He had a host of enemies patiently biding their time; and our old friend Smoke in particular, together with all his kinsmen, hated him cordially. Smoke sat one day in his lodge, in the midst of his own village, when Mahto-Tatonka entered it alone, and approaching the dwelling of his enemy, challenged him in a loud voice to come out, and fight. Smoke would not move. At this, Mahto-Tatonka proclaimed him a coward and an old woman, and, striding to the entrance of the lodge, stabbed the chief's best horse, which

was picketed there. Smoke was daunted, and even this insult failed
to bring him out. Mahto-Tatonka moved haughtily away; all made
way for him; but his hour of reckoning was near.

One hot day, five or six years ago, numerous lodges of Smoke's
kinsmen were gathered about some of the Fur Company's men, who
were trading in various articles with them, whiskey among the rest.
Mahto-Tatonka was also there with a few of his people. As he lay in
his own lodge, a fray arose between his adherents and the kinsmen of
his enemy. The war-whoop was raised, bullets and arrows began to
fly, and the camp was in confusion. The chief sprang up, and rushing
in a fury from the lodge, shouted to the combatants on both sides to
cease. Instantly—for the attack was preconcerted—came the reports
of two or three guns, and the twanging of a dozen bows, and the
savage hero, mortally wounded, pitched forward headlong to the
ground. Rouleau was present, and told me the particulars. The tu-
mult became general, and was not quelled until several had fallen on
both sides. When we were in the country the feud bel..een the two
families was still rankling.

Thus died Mahto-Tatonka; but he left behind him a goodly army
of descendants, to perpetuate his renown and avenge his fate. Besides daughters, he had thirty sons, a number which need not stagger
the credulity of those acquainted with Indian usages and practices.
We saw many of them, all marked by the same dark complexion,
and the same peculiar cast of features. Of these, our visitor, young
Mahto-Tatonka, was the eldest, and some reported him as likely to
succeed to his father's honors. Though he appeared not more than
twenty-one years old, he had oftener struck the enemy, and stolen
more horses and more squaws, than any young man in the village.
Horse-stealing is well known as an avenue to distinction on the
prairies, and the other kind of depredation is esteemed equally meritorious. Not that the act can confer fame from its own intrinsic merits. Any one can steal a squaw, and if he chooses afterwards to make
an adequate present to her rightful proprietor, the easy husband for
the most part rests content, his vengeance falls asleep, and all danger from that quarter is averted. Yet this is regarded as a pitiful and
mean-spirited transaction. The danger is averted, but the glory of
the achievement also is lost. Mahto-Tatonka proceeded after a more
dashing fashion. Out of several dozen squaws whom he had stolen,

he could boast that he had never paid for one, but snapping his fingers in the face of the injured husband, had defied the extremity of his indignation, and no one yet had dared to lay the finger of violence upon him. He was following close in the footsteps of his father. The young men and the young squaws, each in their way, admired him. The former would always follow him to war, and he was esteemed to have an unrivalled charm in the eyes of the latter. Perhaps his impunity may excite some wonder. An arrow-shot from a ravine, or a stab given in the dark, require no great valor, and are especially suited to the Indian genius; but Mahto-Tatonka had a strong protection. It was not alone his courage and audacious will that enabled him to career so dashingly among his compeers. His enemies did not forget that he was one of thirty warlike brethren, all growing up to manhood. Should they wreak their anger upon him, many keen eyes would be ever upon them, and many fierce hearts thirst for their blood. The avenger would dog their footsteps everywhere. To kill Mahto-Tatonka would be an act of suicide.

Though he found such favor in the eyes of the fair, he was no dandy. He was indifferent to the gaudy trappings and ornaments of his companions, and was content to rest his chances of success upon his own warlike merits. He never arrayed himself in gaudy blanket and glittering necklaces, but left his statue-like form, limbed like an Apollo of bronze, to win its way to favor. His voice was singularly deep and strong, and sounded from his chest like the deep notes of an organ. Yet, after all, he was but an Indian. See him as he lies there in the sun before our tent, kicking his heels in the air and cracking jokes with his brother. Does he look like a hero? See him now in the hour of his glory, when at sunset the whole village empties itself to behold him, for to-morrow their favorite young partisan goes out against the enemy. His head-dress is adorned with a crest of the war-eagle's feathers, rising in a waving ridge above his brow, and sweeping far behind him. His round white shield hangs at his breast, with feathers radiating from the centre like a star. His quiver is at his back; his tall lance in his hand, the iron point flashing against the declining sun, while the long scalp–locks of his enemies flutter from the shaft. Thus, gorgeous as a champion in panoply, he rides round and round within the great circle of lodges, balancing with a graceful buoyancy to the free movements of his war–horse, while with a sedate brow he sings his song to the Great Spirit. Young rival warriors look askance at him; vermilion–cheeked girls gaze in admiration; boys whoop and scream in a thrill of delight, and old women yell forth his name and proclaim his praises from lodge to lodge.

Mahto–Tatonka was the best of all our Indian friends. Hour after hour, and day after day, when swarms of savages of every age, sex, and degree beset our camp, he would lie in our tent, his lynx–eye ever open to guard our property from pillage.

The Whirlwind invited us one day to his lodge. The feast was finished, and the pipe began to circulate. It was a remarkably large and fine one, and I expressed admiration of it.

"If the Meneaska likes the pipe," asked The Whirlwind, "why does he not keep it?"

Such a pipe among the Ogillallah is valued at the price of a horse. The gift seemed worthy of a chieftain and a warrior; but The Whirlwind's generosity rose to no such pitch. He gave me the pipe, confidently expecting that I in return would make him a present of equal or superior value. This is the implied condition of every gift among the Indians, and should it not be complied with, the present is usually reclaimed. So I arranged upon a gaudy calico handkerchief, an assortment of vermilion, tobacco, knives, and gunpowder, and summoning the chief to camp, assured him of my friendship, and begged his acceptance of a slight token of it. Ejaculating, "How! how!" he folded up the offerings and withdrew to his lodge.

Late one afternoon a party of Indians on horseback came suddenly in sight from behind some clumps of bushes that lined the bank of the stream, leading with them a mule, on whose back was a wretched negro, sustained in his seat by the high pommel and cantle of the Indian saddle. His cheeks were shrunken in the hollow of his jaws; his eyes were unnaturally dilated, and his lips shrivelled and drawn back from his teeth like those of a corpse. When they brought him before our tent, and lifted him from the saddle, he could not walk or stand, but crawled a short distance, and with a look of utter misery sat down on the grass. All the children and women came pouring out of the lodges, and with screams and cries made a circle about him, while he sat supporting himself with his hands, and looking from side to side with a vacant stare. The wretch was starving to death. For thirty-three days he had wandered alone

on the prairie, without weapon of any kind; without shoes, moccasins, or any other clothing than an old jacket and trousers; without
intelligence to guide his course, or any knowledge of the productions of the prairie. All this time he had subsisted on crickets and
lizards, wild onions, and three eggs which he found in the nest of a
prairie-dove. He had not seen a human being. Bewildered in the
boundless, hopeless desert that stretched around him, he had walked
on in despair, till he could walk no longer, and then crawled on his
knees, till the bone was laid bare. He chose the night for travelling,
lying down by day to sleep in the glaring sun, always dreaming, as he
said, of the broth and corn-cake he used to eat under his old master's
shed in Missouri. Every man in the camp, both white and red, was
astonished at his escape not only from starvation, but from the grizzly bears, which abound in that neighborhood, and the wolves which
howled around him every night.

Reynal recognized him the moment the Indians brought him in.
He had run away from his master about a year before and joined the
party of Richard, who was then leaving the frontier for the mountains. He had lived with Richard until, at the end of May, he with
Reynal and several other men went out in search of some stray
horses, when he was separated from the rest in a storm, and had
never been heard of to this time. Knowing his inexperience and
helplessness, no one dreamed that he could still be living. The Indians had found him lying exhausted on the ground.

As he sat there, with the Indians gazing silently on him, his hag-
gard face and glazed eye were disgusting to look upon. Deslauriers
made him a bowl of gruel, but he suffered it to remain untasted before him. At length he languidly raised the spoon to his lips; again
he did so, and again; and then his appetite seemed suddenly inflamed into madness, for he seized the bowl, swallowed all its contents in a few seconds, and eagerly demanded meat. This was refused, telling him to wait until morning; but he begged so eagerly
that we gave him a small piece, which he devoured, tearing it like a
dog. He said he must have more. We told him that his life was in
danger if he ate so immoderately at first. He assented, and said he
knew he was a fool to do so, but he must have meat. This was absolutely refused, to the great indignation of the senseless squaws, who,
when we were not watching him, would slyly bring dried meat and

pommes blanches, and place them on the ground by his side. Still this was not enough for him. When it grew dark he contrived to creep away between the legs of the horses and crawl over to the Indian camp. Here he fed to his heart's content, and was brought back again in the morning, when Gingras, the trapper, put him on horseback and carried him to the fort. He managed to survive the effects of his greediness. Though slightly deranged when we left this part of the country, he was otherwise in tolerable health, and expressed his firm conviction that nothing could ever kill him.

SUGGESTED ADDITIONAL READING

The Conspiracy of Pontiac

SELECTED REFERENCES

Pease, Otis. *Parkman's History: The Historian as Literary Artist* (1953).

Russell, J. "Francis Parkman and the Real Indians." *Journal of American History,* 22 (1928), 121–29.

PROJECTS AND PROBLEMS

Compare the literary works and public careers of Parkman and Richard Henry Dana, both New Englanders and graduates of Harvard Law School.

Find the passage in Chapter XXI of *The Oregon Trail* that spurred Herman Melville to write, in an anonymous review in *The Literary World* for March 31, 1849, "We are all of us—Anglo-Saxons, Dyaks, and Indians—sprung from one head, and made in one image." Is the point Melville makes in the review—reprinted in *The Indian and the White Man* (1964), ed. by Wilcomb E. Washburn—important to Parkman's stature as historian?

Compare Parkman's description of the Sioux in *The Oregon Trail* with Melville's representation of the Marquesan Islanders in *Typee.* Or compare Parkman's first-hand account of the Sioux with Poe's second-hand account in "The Journal of Julius Rodman."

MAYNE REID
(1818–1883)

Born in Ireland, Reid first came to the United States in 1840 and pursued varied occupations during his years here. Overseer, actor, frontiersman, and soldier, he wrote many adventure tales that endeared him to boys. Henry James called him, in *The American Scene,* "idol of my childhood." One of Reid's popular novels, *The Quadroon* (1856), was dramatized by the author and served as the basis for Dion Boucicault's play, *The Octoroon.* This selection is from *Osceola, the Seminole,* a romance about a notable Indian leader and guerrilla fighter. To the publisher of the English edition, *The Half-Blood* seemed a better title for this tale about a warrior who was supposedly the child of a Seminole mother and a white father. The narrator and other characters are also of mixed ancestry.

BLACK, WHITE, AND RED IN SEMINOLE LAND

CHAPTER II

THE INDIGO PLANTATION

My father was an indigo planter; his name was Randolph. I bear his name in full—George Randolph.

There is Indian blood in my veins. My father was of the Randolphs of Roanoke—hence descended from the Princess Pocahontas. He was proud of his Indian ancestry—almost vain of it.

It may sound paradoxical, especially to European ears; but it is true, that white men in America, who have Indian blood in them, are proud of the taint. Even to be a "half-breed" is no badge of shame—particularly where the *sang mêlé* has been gifted with fortune. Not all the volumes that have been written bear such strong testimony to the grandeur of the Indian character as this one fact— we are not ashamed to acknowledge them as ancestry!

Hundreds of white families lay claim to descent from the Virginian princess. If their claims be just, then must the fair Pocahontas have been a blessing to her lord.

I think my father *was* of the true lineage; at all events, he belonged to a proud family in the "Old Dominion;" and during his early life had been surrounded by sable slaves in hundreds. But his rich patrimonial lands became at length worn out—profuse hospitality well-nigh ruined him; and not brooking an inferior station, he gathered up the fragments of his fortune, and "moved" southward— there to begin the world anew.

I was born before this removal, and am therefore a native of Virginia: but my earliest impressions of a home were formed upon the banks of the beautiful Suwanee in Florida. That was the scene of my boyhood's life—the spot consecrated to me by the joys of youth and the charms of early love.

I would paint the picture of my boyhood's home. Well do I remember it; so fair a scene is not easily effaced from the memory.

409

A handsome "frame"-house, coloured white, with green Venetians over the windows, and a wide verandah extending all round. Carved wooden porticoes support the roof of this verandah, and a low balustrade with light railing separates it from the adjoining grounds—from the flower parterre in front, the orangery on the right flank and a large garden on the left. From the outer edge of the parterre, a smooth lawn slopes gently to the bank of the river—here expanding to the dimensions of a noble lake, with distant wooded shores, islets that seem suspended in the air, wild-fowl upon the wind, and wild-fowl in the water.

Upon the lawn, behold tall tapering palms, with pinnatifid leaves —a species of *oreodoxia*—others with broad fan–shaped fronds—the *palmettoes* of the south; behold magnolias, clumps of fragrant illicium, and radiating crowns of the *yucca gloriosa*—all indigenous to the soil. Another native presents itself to the eye—a huge live-oak extending its long horizontal boughs, covered thickly with evergreen coriaceous leaves, and broadly shadowing the grass beneath. Under its shade behold a beautiful girl, in light summer robes—her hair loosely coifed with a white kerchief, from the folds of which have escaped long tresses glittering with the hues of gold. That is my sister Virginia, my only sister, still younger than myself. Her golden hair bespeaks not her Indian descent, but in that she takes after our mother. . . .

The rear of the dwelling presents a different aspect—perhaps not so bright, though not less cheerful. Here is exhibited a scene of active life—a picture of the industry of an indigo plantation. . . .

In the inclosure, and over the indigo-fields, a hundred human forms are moving; with one or two exceptions, they are all of the African race—all slaves. They are not all of black skin—scarcely the majority of them are negroes. There are mulattoes, samboes, and quadroons. Even some who are of pure African blood are not black, only bronze-coloured; but with the exception of the "overseer" and the owner of the plantation, all are slaves. Some are hideously ugly, with thick lips, low retreating foreheads, flat noses, and ill–formed bodies! others are well proportioned; and among them are some that might be accounted good-looking. There are women nearly white— quadroons. Of the latter are several that are more than good looking —some even beautiful.

CHAPTER III
THE TWO JAKES

Every plantation has its "bad fellow"—often more than one but always one who holds preëminence in evil. "Yellow Jake" was the fiend of ours.

He was a young mulatto, in person not ill-looking, but of sullen habit and morose disposition. On occasions he had shewn himself capable of fierce resentment and cruelty.

Instances of such character are more common among mulattoes than negroes. Pride of color on the part of the yellow man—confidence in a higher organism, both intellectual and physical, and consequently a keener sense of the injustice of his degraded position, explain this psychological difference.

As for the pure negro, he rarely enacts the unfeeling savage. In the drama of human life, he is the victim, not the villain. No matter where lies the scene—in his own land, or elsewhere—he has been used to play the *rôle* of the sufferer; yet his soul is still free from resentment or ferocity. In all the world, there is no kinder heart than that which beats within the bosom of the African black.

Yellow Jake was wicked without provocation. Cruelty was innate in his disposition—no doubt inherited. He was a Spanish mulatto; that is, paternally of Spanish blood—maternally, negro. His father had sold him to mine!

A slave-mother, a slave-son. The father's freedom affects not the offspring. Among the black and red races of America, the child follows the fortunes of the mother. Only she of Caucasian race can be the mother of white men.

There was another "Jacob" upon the plantation—hence the distinctive sobriquet of "Yellow Jake." This other was "Black Jake;" and only in age and size was there any similarity between the two. In disposition they differed even more than in complexion. If Yellow Jake had the brighter skin, Black Jake had the lighter heart. Their countenances exhibited a complete contrast—the contrast between a sullen frown and a cheerful smile. The white teeth of the latter were ever set in smiles: the former smiled only when under the influence of some malicious prompting.

Black Jake was a Virginian. He was one of those belonging to the old plantation—had "moved" along with his master; and felt those ties of attachment which in many cases exist strongly between master and slave. He regarded himself as one of our family, and gloried in bearing our name. Like all negroes born in the "Old Dominion," he was proud of his nativity. In caste, a "Vaginny nigger" takes precedence of all others.

Apart from his complexion, Black Jake was not ill-looking. His features were as good as those of the mulatto. He had neither the thick lips, flat nose, nor retreating forehead of his race—for these characteristics are not universal. I have known negroes of pure African blood with features perfectly regular, and such a one was Black Jake. In form, he might have passed for the Ethiopian Apollo.

There was one who thought him handsome—handsomer than his yellow namesake. This was the quadroon Viola, the belle of the plantation. . . .

●　　●　　●　　●　　●

CHAPTER LIII

MY SISTER'S SPIRIT

. . . My sister, then, was an heiress—quite independent of either mother or brother—bound by no authority to either, except that which exists in the ties of the heart—in filial and sororal affection.

I have been minute with these circumstances, in order to explain the delicate duty I had to perform, in calling my sister to an account.

Strange that I reflected not on my own anomalous position. At that hour, it never entered my thoughts. Here was I affianced to the sister of this very man, with the sincere intention of making her my wife.

I could perceive nothing unnatural, nothing disgraceful in the alliance—neither would society. Such in earlier times had done honour to Rolfe, who had mated with a maiden of darker skin, less beauty, and far slighter accomplishments than Maümee. In later days, hundreds of others had followed his example, without the loss either of *caste* or character; and why should not I? In truth, the question had never occurred to me for it never entered my thoughts that my purpose in regard to my Indian *fiancée* was otherwise than perfectly *en règle*.

It would have been different had there been a taint of *African blood* in the veins of my intended. Then, indeed, might I have dreaded the frowns of society—for in America it is not the colour of the skin that condemns, but the blood—the blood. The white gentleman may marry an Indian wife; she may enter society without protest—if beautiful, become a belle.

All this I knew, while, at the same time, I was slave to a belief in the monstrous anomaly that where the blood is mingled from the other side—where the woman is white and the man red—the union becomes a *mésalliance*, a disgrace. By the friends of the former, such a union is regarded as a misfortune—a fall; and when the woman chances to be a *lady*—ah! then, indeed.

Little regard as I had for many of my country's prejudices, regarding race and colour, I was not free from the influence of this social maxim. To believe my sister in love with an Indian, would be to regard her as lost—fallen! No matter how high in rank among his own people—no matter how brave—how accomplished he might be —no matter if it were Osceola himself!

SUGGESTED ADDITIONAL READINGS

The Quadroon
The Scalp Hunters
Cris Rock

SELECTED REFERENCES

Gaines, Francis P. "The Racial Bar Sinister in American Romance," *South Atlantic Quarterly*, 25 (1926), 396–402.

Meyer, Roy W. "The Western Fiction of Mayne Reid." *Western American Literature*, 3 (1968), 115–32.

Zanger, Jules. "The 'Tragic Octoroon' in Pre–Civil War Fiction." *American Quarterly*, 18 (1966), 63–70.

PROJECTS AND PROBLEMS

Did Reid's experience as slave overseer, Indian fighter, and officer in the Mexican War give authority to his romances and juvenile novels? Do his works show the objectivity of a foreign perspective or the conventional biases of his adopted society?

Compare Reid's treatment of the quadroon with that of Nathaniel Parker Willis in *Health Trip to the Tropics* (1853). Do the two writers, from different backgrounds, agree in their assessment of race relations in New Orleans in the 1850s?

Does Reid's picture of slavery support his disclaimer that he wrote, "neither to aid the abolitionist, nor glorify the planter"?

Discuss the refinements of Reid's treatment in *Cris Rock* of Mexicans of pure Spanish descent and those of Indian ancestry.

In his preface to *The Quadroon* Reid described his book as "a romance, nothing more." Consider that Hawthorne's preface to *The House of Seven Gables* a few years earlier called that work a romance and said that its author had not "professed to be writing a novel." In what ways do the two writers use the latitude granted by the more popular and less serious literary form?

Compare Reid's treatment of Indians with James Fenimore Cooper's, noting particularly the attitude toward miscegenation.

Does Walt Whitman's "Osceola" agree with Reid's interpretation of the Indian leader's character?

For modern fiction on Osceola and the Seminole War to compare with Reid's work, see Henry Carlisle, *The Land Where the Sun Died* (1975).

Compare Reid's interpretation of Seminole character with that of the black poet Albery A. Whitman, whose *Twasinta's Seminoles; or The Rape of Florida* appeared in 1885.

GEORGE L. AIKEN
(1830-1876)

An actor and playwright, Aiken was called upon to dramatize Harriet Beecher Stowe's *Uncle Tom's Cabin* when the phenomenal success of that novel encouraged producers to exploit its appeal on the stage. His version of the story opened in New York on September 27, 1853, and ran for over two hundred performances. Later touring companies presented it in many cities and hamlets. This and other dramatic representations of Mrs. Stowe's work over the years had a greater impact on the American imagination than did the novel itself. It was the Tom shows that made Uncle Tom, Topsy, Simon Legree, and Little Eva familiar to every American. The shows, which transformed romance into melodrama and pathos into bathos, were a major influence in converting Mrs. Stowe's protagonist from an honorable Christian martyr to an infamous stereotype.

UNCLE TOM'S CABIN (BASED ON THE NOVEL BY HARRIET BEECHER STOWE)

Act I -SCENE THREE

Snowy landscape. UNCLE TOM's *cabin.—Snow on roof. Practicable door and window. Dark stage. Music.*

ELIZA *(enters hastily, with* HARRY *in her arms)*. My poor boy! they have sold you, but your mother will have you yet! *(Goes to cabin and taps on window.)*

CHLOE *(appears at window with a large white nightcap on)*. Good Lord! what's that? My sakes alive if it ain't Lizy! Get on your clothes, old man, quick! I'm gwine to open the door.

(The door opens and CHLOE *enters followed by* UNCLE TOM *in his shirt sleeves holding a tallow candle.)*

TOM *(holding the light towards* ELIZA*)*. Lord bless you! I'm skeered to look at ye, Lizy! Are ye tuck sick, or what's come over ye?

ELIZA. I'm running away, Uncle Tom and Aunt Chloe, carrying off my child! Master sold him!

TOM *and* CHLOE. Sold him!

ELIZA. Yes, sold him! I crept into the closet by mistress' door to-night and heard master tell mistress that he had sold my Harry and you, Uncle Tom, both, to a trader, and that the man was to take possession tomorrow.

CHLOE. The good lord have pity on us! Oh! it don't seem as if it was true. What has he done that master should sell *him?*

ELIZA. He hasn't done anything—it isn't for that. Master don't want to sell, and mistress—she's always good. I heard her plead and beg for us, but he told her 'twas no use—that he was in this man's debt, and he had got the power over him, and that if he did not pay him off clear, it would end in his having to sell the place and all the people and move off.

416

CHLOE. Well, old man, why don't you run away, too? Will you wait to be toted down the river, where they kill niggers with hard work and starving? I'd a heap rather die than go there, any day! There's time for ye, be off with Lizy—you've got a pass to come and go any time. Come, bustle up, and I'll get your things together.

TOM. No, no—I ain't going. Let Eliza go—it's her right. I wouldn't be the one to say no—t'aint in nature for her to stay; but you heard what she said? If I must be sold, or all the people on the place, and everything go to rack, why, let me be sold. I s'pose I can bear it as well as any one. Mas'r always found me on the spot—he always will. I never have broken trust, nor used my pass no ways contrary to my word, and I never will. It's better for me to go alone, than to break up the place and sell all. Mas'r ain't to blame, and he'll take care of you and the poor little 'uns! (*Overcome.*)

CHLOE. Now, old man, what is you gwine to cry for? Does you want to break this old woman's heart? (*Crying.*)

ELIZA. I saw my husband only this afternoon, and I little knew then what was to come. He told me he was going to run away. Do try, if you can, to get word to him. Tell him how I went and why I went, and tell him I'm going to try and find Canada. You must give my love to him, and tell him if I never see him again on earth, I trust we shall meet in heaven!

TOM. Dat is right, Lizy, trust in the Lord—he is our best friend— our only comforter.

ELIZA. You won't go with me, Uncle Tom?

TOM. No; time was when I would, but the Lord's given me a work among these yer poor souls, and I'll stay with 'em and bear my cross with 'em till the end. It's different with you—it's more'n you could stand, and you'd better go if you can.

ELIZA. Uncle Tom, I'll try it!

TOM. Amen! The Lord help ye!

(*Exit* ELIZA *and* HARRY.)

CHLOE. What is you gwine to do, old man! What's to become of you?

TOM. (*solemnly*). Him that saved Daniel in the den of lions—that saved the children in the fiery furnace—Him that walked on the sea and bade the winds be still—He's alive yet! and I've faith to believe he can deliver me.

CHLOE. You is right, old man.

TOM. The Lord is good unto all that trust him, Chloe.

(They go into the cabin.)

o   o   o   o   o

SCENE FIVE

Snow landscape. Music.

ELIZA. *(enters with* HARRY, *hurriedly).* They press upon my footsteps—the river is my only hope. Heaven grant me strength to reach it, ere they overtake me! Courage, my child!—we will be free—or perish! *(Rushes off, as music continues.)*

(Enter LOKER, HALEY, *and* MARKS.)

HALEY. We'll catch her yet; the river will stop her!

MARKS. No, it won't, for look! she has jumped upon the ice! She's a brave gal, anyhow!

LOKER. She'll be drowned!

HALEY. Curse that young 'un! I shall lose him, after all.

LOKER. Come on, Marks, to the ferry!

HALEY. Aye, to the ferry!—a hundred dollars for a boat!

(Music. They rush off.)

SCENE SIX

The entire depth of stage, representing the Ohio River, is filled with floating ice.

*(*ELIZA *appears, with* HARRY, *on a cake of ice, and floats slowly across.* HALEY, LOKER, *and* MARKS *on bank, observing,* PHINEAS *on opposite bank.)*

SELECTED REFERENCES

Birdoff, Harry. *The World's Greatest : Uncle Tom's Cabin* (1947).

Hewitt, Bernard. *Theatre, U.S.A.* (1959).

Moody, Richard. "Uncle Tom, The Theater and Mrs. Stowe." *American Heritage*, 6, No. 6 (1955), 29–33, 102–103.

PROJECTS AND PROBLEMS

Discuss the relationship between the Tom show and other plays dealing with slavery. See Monroe Lippman's "Uncle Tom and His Poor Relations: American Slavery Plays," *Southern Speech Journal*, Spring, 1963. Comment on the connection between the Tom show and the minstrel show.

Select characters and incidents for a comparison of Mrs. Stowe's novel and Aiken's dramatization. Use as one reference Bernard Hewitt's "Uncle Tom and Uncle Sam: New Light from an Old Play," in the February, 1951, *Quarterly Journal of Speech*.

Compare Eliza in *Uncle Tom's Cabin* with Zoe, the heroine of Dion Boucicault's *The Octoroon*. Both dramas are in *Best Plays of the Early American Theatre* (1967), ed. by John Gassner.

WILLIAM WELLS BROWN
(1816–1884)

William Wells Brown escaped from slavery and spent his life speaking and writing in support of abolition, temperance, women's suffrage, and prison reform. A prolific author, he was the first black American to write a novel, a play, and a book of travels, and he was among the first to write history. He shared with many of his fellows the honor of publishing a slave narrative, in 1847. His novel, *Clotel: or The President's Daughter*, was published in London in 1853. It was later reprinted in different versions under variant titles.

The first section of the following selection is from the opening chapter, entitled "The Negro Sale." In Chapter XIV Althesa Morton, who is Clotel's sister and Salome's mistress, is living in comfort in New Orleans with her white husband. The text is that of the first version of the novel.

LIGHT SLAVE AND WHITE SLAVE: CLOTEL AND SALOME

... The appearance of Clotel on the auction block created a deep sensation amongst the crowd. There she stood, with a complexion as white as most of those who were waiting with a wish to become her purchasers; her features as finely defined as any of her sex of pure Anglo-Saxon; her long black wavy hair done up in the neatest manner; her form tall and graceful, and her whole appearance indicating one superior to her position. The auctioneer commenced by saying, that "Miss Clotel had been reserved for the last, because she was the most valuable. How much, gentlemen? Real Albino, fit for a fancy girl for any one. She enjoys good health, and has a sweet temper. How much do you say?"

"Five hundred dollars."

"Only five hundred for such a girl as this? Gentlemen, she is worth a deal more than that sum; you certainly don't know the value of the article you are bidding upon. Here, gentlemen, I hold in my hand a paper certifying that she has a good moral character."

"Seven hundred."

"Ah; gentlemen, that is something like. This paper also states that she is very intelligent."

"Eight hundred."

"She is a devoted Christian, and perfectly trustworthy."

"Nine hundred."

"Nine fifty."

"Ten."

"Eleven."

"Twelve hundred." Here the sale came to a dead stand. The auctioneer stopped, looked around, and began in a rough manner to relate some anecdotes relative to the sale of slaves, which, he said, had come under his own observation. At this juncture the scene was indeed strange. Laughing, joking, swearing, smoking, spitting, and talking kept up a continual hum and noise amongst the crowd; while the slave-girl stood with tears in her eyes, at one time looking towards her mother and sister, and at another towards the young man whom she hoped would become her purchaser.

"The chastity of this girl is pure; she has never been from under her mother's care; she is a virtuous creature."

"Thirteen."

"Fourteen."

"Fifteen."

"Fifteen hundred dollars," cried the auctioneer, and the maiden was struck for that sum. This was a Southern auction, at which the bones, muscles, sinews, blood, and nerves of a young lady of sixteen were sold for five hundred dollars; her moral character for two hundred; her improved intellect for one hundred; her Christianity for three hundred; and her chastity and virtue for four hundred dollars more. And this, too, in a city thronged with churches, whose tall spires look like so many signals pointing to heaven, and whose ministers preach that slavery is a God-ordained institution!

What words can tell the inhumanity, the atrocity, and the immorality of that doctrine which, from exalted office, commends such a crime to the favour of enlightened and Christian people? What indignation from all the world is not due to the government and people who put forth all their strength and power to keep in existence such an institution? Nature abhors it; the age repels it; and Christianity needs all her meekness to forgive it.

Clotel was sold for fifteen hundred dollars, but her purchaser was Horatio Green. Thus closed a Negro sale, at which two daughters of Thomas Jefferson, the writer of the Declaration of American Independence, and one of the presidents of the great republic, were disposed of to the highest bidder!

> "O God! my every heart-string cries,
>   Dost thou these scenes behold
> In this our boasted Christian land,
>   And must the truth be told?

> "Blush, Christian, blush! for e'en the dark,
>   Untutored heathen see
> Thy inconsistency; and, lo!
>   They scorn thy God, and thee!"

o   o   o   o   o

Althesa found in Henry Morton a kind and affectionate husband;
and his efforts to purchase her mother, although unsuccessful, had
doubly endeared him to her. Having from the commencement resolved not to hold slaves, or rather not to own any, they were compelled to hire servants for their own use. Five years had passed
away, and their happiness was increased by two lovely daughters.
Mrs. Morton was seated, one bright afternoon, busily engaged with
her needle, and near her sat Salome, a servant that she had just taken
into her employ. The woman was perfectly white; so much so, that
Mrs. Morton had expressed her apprehensions to her husband, when
the woman first came, that she was not born a slave. The mistress
watched the servant, as the latter sat sewing upon some coarse
work, and saw the large silent tear in her eye. This caused an uneasiness to the mistress, and she said, "Salome, don't you like your situation here?"

"Oh yes, madam," answered the woman in a quick tone, and then
tried to force a smile.

"Why is it that you often look sad, and with tears in your eyes?"
The mistress saw that she had touched a tender chord, and continued, "I am your friend; tell me your sorrow, and, if I can, I will
help you." As the last sentence was escaping the lips of the mistress,
the slave woman put her check apron to her face and wept. Mrs.
Morton saw plainly that there was cause for this expression of grief,
and pressed the woman more closely. "Hear me, then," said the
woman calming herself: "I will tell you why I sometimes weep. I
was born in Germany, on the banks of the Rhine. Ten years ago my
father came to this country, bringing with him my mother and
myself. He was poor, and I, wishing to assist all I could, obtained a
situation as nurse to a lady in this city. My father got employment as
a labourer on the wharf, among the steamboats; but he was soon
taken ill with the yellow fever, and died. My mother then got a situation for herself, while I remained with my first employer. When
the hot season came on, my master, with his wife, left New Orleans
until the hot season was over, and took me with them. They stopped
at a town on the banks of the Mississippi river, and said they should

remain there some weeks. One day they went out for a ride, and they had not been gone more than half an hour, when two men came into the room and told me that they had bought me, and that I was their slave. I was bound and taken to prison, and that night put on a steamboat and taken up the Yazoo river, and set to work on a farm. I was forced to take up with a Negro, and by him had three children. A year since my master's daughter was married, and I was given to her. She came with her husband to this city, and I have ever since been hired out."

"Unhappy woman," whispered Althesa, "why did you not tell me this before?"

"I was afraid," replied Salome, "for I was once severely flogged for telling a stranger that I was not born a slave."

On Mr. Morton's return home, his wife communicated to him the story which the slave woman had told her an hour before, and begged that something might be done to rescue her from the situation she was then in. In Louisiana as well as many others of the slave states, great obstacles are thrown in the way of persons who have been wrongfully reduced to slavery regaining their freedom. A person claiming to be free must prove his right to his liberty. This, it will be seen, throws the burden of proof upon the slave, who, in all probability, finds it out of his power to procure such evidence. And if any free person shall attempt to aid a freeman in regaining his freedom, he is compelled to enter into security in the sum of one thousand dollars, and if the person claiming to be free shall fail to establish such fact, the thousand dollars are forfeited to the state. This cruel and oppressive law has kept many a freeman from espousing the cause of persons unjustly held as slaves. Mr. Morton inquired and found that the woman's story was true, as regarded the time she had lived with her present owner; but the latter not only denied that she was free, but immediately removed her from Morton's. Three months after Salome had been removed from Morton's and let out to another family, she was one morning cleaning the door steps, when a lady passing by, looked at the slave and thought she recognised some one that she had seen before. The lady stopped and asked the woman if she was a slave.

"I am," said she.

"Were you born a slave?"

"No, I was born in Germany."

"What's the name of the ship in which you came to this country?" inquired the lady.

"I don't know," was the answer.

"Was it the *Amazon?*"

At the sound of this name, the slave woman was silent for a moment, and then the tears began to flow freely down her careworn cheeks.

"Would you know Mrs. Marshall, who was a passenger in the *Amazon*, if you should see her?" inquired the lady.

At this the woman gazed at the lady with a degree of intensity that can be imagined better than described, and then fell at the lady's feet. The lady was Mrs. Marshall. She had crossed the Atlantic in the same ship with this poor woman. Salome, like many of her countrymen, was a beautiful singer, and had often entertained Mrs. Marshall and the other lady passengers on board the *Amazon*. The poor woman was raised from the ground by Mrs. Marshall, and placed upon the door step that she had a moment before been cleaning. "I will do my utmost to rescue you from the horrid life of a slave," exclaimed the lady, as she took from her pocket her pencil, and wrote down the number of the house, and the street in which the German woman was working as a slave.

After a long and tedious trial of many days, it was decided that Salome Miller was by birth a free woman, and she was set at liberty. The good and generous Althesa had contributed some of the money toward bringing about the trial, and had done much to cheer on Mrs. Marshall in her benevolent object. Salome Miller is free, but where are her three children? They are still slaves, and in all human probability will die as such.

This, reader, is no fiction; if you think so, look over the files of the New Orleans newspapers of the years 1845–6, and you will there see reports of the trial.

SUGGESTED ADDITIONAL READINGS

> *Narrative of William Wells Brown, a Fugitive Slave*
> *Three Years in Europe; or, Places I Have Seen and People I Have Met*

The Escape; or, A Leap for Freedom
The Black Man: His Antecedents, His Genius, and His Achievements
The Negro in the American Rebellion, His Heroism and His Fidelity
The Rising Son; or The Antecedents and the Advancement of the Colored Race
My Southern Home, or The South and Its People

SELECTED REFERENCES

Bell, Bernard W. "Literary Sources of the Early Afro–American Novel." *CLA Journal*, 18 (1974), 29–43.

Farrison, W. Edward. *William Wells Brown: Author and Reformer* (1969).

Yellin, Jean Fagan. *The Intricate Knot: Black Figures in American Literature, 1776–1863* (1972).

PROJECTS AND PROBLEMS

Discuss the range of Brown's literary work. Appraise his importance as artist and as propagandist.

Study Brown's use of Lydia Maria Child's "The Quadroons" as a source for portions of *Clotel*. Did he improve this material in adapting it to his purpose?

Evaluate the relative literary merits of the autobiographies of Brown and Frederick Douglass and compare their careers.

Compare *Clotel*, the first novel by a black American, and Nathan Mayer's *Differences* (1867), the first significant American Jewish novel.

Compare the report of the tragic history of Salome Miller provided by Brown with George W. Cable's version in his *Strange True Stories of Louisiana* (1888).

HENRY DAVID THOREAU (1817–1862)

The passages here are selected from Thoreau's most famous book, *Walden* (1854). This classic of American romanticism documents his talent as writer and naturalist, his commitment to transcendental philosophy, and his disparate reactions to the nation's minorities. If he was insensitive to the plight of some of America's underpriviliged people, he was notable for giving ardent service to the antislavery cause and attaining a rare appreciation of Indian culture. His "Civil Disobedience" (1849) has won a legion of converts to movements for independence and equality around the world.

IRISHMEN AND OTHERS IN WALDEN WOODS

But how do the poor *minority* fare? Perhaps it will be found, that just in proportion as some have been placed in outward circumstances above the savage, others have been degraded below him. The luxury of one class is counterbalanced by the indigence of another. On the one side is the palace, on the other are the almshouse and "silent poor." The myriads who built the pyramids to be the tombs of the Pharaohs were fed on garlic, and it may be were not decently buried themselves. The mason who finishes the cornice of the palace returns at night perchance to a hut not so good as a wigwam. It is a mistake to suppose that, in a country where the usual evidences of civilization exist, the condition of a very large body of the inhabitants may not be as degraded as that of savages. I refer to the degraded poor, not now to the degraded rich. To know this I should not need to look farther than to the shanties which everywhere border our railroads, that last improvement in civilization; where I see in my daily walks human beings living in sties, and all winter with an open door, for the sake of light, without any visible, often imaginable, wood pile, and the forms of both old and young are permanently contracted by the long habit of shrinking from cold and misery, and the development of all their limbs and faculties is checked. It certainly is fair to look at that class by whose labor the works which distinguish this generation are accomplished. Such too, to a greater or less extent, is the condition of the operatives of every denomination in England, which is the great workhouse of the world. Or I could refer you to Ireland, which is marked as one of the white or enlightened spots on the map. Contrast the physical condition of the Irish with that of the North American Indian, or the South Sea Islander, or any other savage race before it was degraded by contact with the civilized man. Yet I have no doubt that that people's rulers are as wise as the average of civilized rulers. Their condition only proves what squalidness may consist with civilization. I hardly need refer now to the laborers in our Southern States who produce the staple exports of this country, and are themselves a staple production of the South. . . .

Near the end of March, 1845, I borrowed an axe and went down to the woods by Walden Pond, nearest to where I intended to build my house, and began to cut down some tall arrowy white pines, still in their youth, for timber. It is difficult to begin without borrowing, but perhaps it is the most generous course thus to permit your fellow-men to have an interest in your enterprise. The owner of the axe, as he released his hold on it, said that it was the apple of his eye; but I returned it sharper than I received it. It was a pleasant hillside where I worked, covered with pine woods, through which I looked out on the pond, and a small open field in the woods where pines and hickories were springing up. The ice in the pond was not yet dissolved, though there were some open spaces, and it was all dark-colored and saturated with water. There were some slight flurries of snow during the days that I worked there; but for the most part when I came out on to the railroad, on my way home, its yellow sand heap stretched away gleaming in the hazy atmosphere, and the rails shone in the spring sun . . . .

By the middle of April, for I made no haste in my work, but rather made the most of it, my house was framed and ready for the raising. I had already bought the shanty of James Collins, an Irishman who worked on the Fitchburg Railroad, for boards. James Collins' shanty was considered an uncommonly fine one. When I called to see it he was not at home. I walked about the outside, at first unobserved from within, the window was so deep and high. It was of small dimensions, with a peaked cottage roof, and not much else to be seen, the dirt being raised five feet all around as if it were a compost heap. The roof was the soundest part, though a good deal warped and made brittle by the sun. Doorsill there was none, but a perennial passage for the hens under the door board. Mrs. C. came to the door and asked me to view it from the inside. The hens were driven in by my approach. It was dark, and had a dirt floor for the most part, dank, clammy, and aguish, only here a board and there a board which would not bear removal. She lighted a lamp to show me the inside of the roof and the walls, and also that the board floor extended under the bed, warning me not to step into the cellar, a sort of dust-hole two feet deep. In her own words, they were "good boards overhead, good boards all around, and a good window,"—of two whole squares originally, only the cat had passed out that way lately. There was a stove, a bed, and a place to sit, an infant in the house where it was born, a silk parasol, gilt-framed looking-glass, and a patent new coffee-mill nailed to an oak sapling, all told. The bargain was soon concluded, for James had in the meanwhile returned. I to pay four dollars and twenty-five cents to-night, he to vacate at five to-morrow morning, selling to nobody else meanwhile: I to take possession at six. It were well, he said, to be there early, and anticipate certain indistinct but wholly unjust claims on the score of ground-rent and fuel. This he assured me was the only encumbrance. At six I passed him and his family on the road. One large bundle held their all,—bed, coffee-mill, looking-glass, hens,—all but the cat, she took to the woods and became a wild cat, and, as I learned afterward, trod in a trap set for woodchucks, and so became a dead cat at last.

I took down this dwelling the same morning, drawing the nails, and removed it to the pond-side by small cartloads, spreading the boards on the grass there to bleach and warp back again in the sun. One early thrush gave me a note or two as I drove along the woodland path. I was informed treacherously by a young Patrick[1] that neighbor Seeley, an Irishman, in the intervals of the carting, transferred the still tolerable, straight, and drivable nails, staples, and spikes to his pocket, and then stood when I came back to pass the time of day, and look freshly up, unconcerned, with spring thoughts at the devastation; there being a dearth of work, as he said. He was there to represent spectatordom, and help make this seemingly insignificant event one with the removal of the gods of Troy. . . .

Such is the universal law, which no man can ever outwit, and with regard to the railroad even we may say it is as broad as it is long. To make a railroad round the world available to all mankind is equivalent to grading the whole surface of the planet. Men have an indistinct notion that if they keep up this activity of joint stocks and spades long enough all will at length ride somewhere, in next to no time, and for nothing; but though a crowd rushes to the depot, and the conductor shouts "All aboard!" when the smoke is blown away and the vapor condensed, it will be perceived that a few are riding, but the rest are run over,—and it will be called, and will be, "A melancholy accident." No doubt they can ride at last who shall have

[1]Common name for any Irishman.

earned their fare, that is, if they survive so long, but they will probably have lost their elasticity and desire to travel by that time. This spending of the best part of one's life earning money in order to enjoy a questionable liberty during the least valuable part of it, reminds me of the Englishman who went to India to make a fortune first, in order that he might return to England and live the life of a poet. He should have gone up garret at once. "What!" exclaim a million Irishmen starting up from all the shanties in the land, "is not this railroad which we have built a good thing?" Yes, I answer, *comparatively* good, that is, you might have done worse; but I wish, as you are brothers of mine, that you could have spent your time better than digging in this dirt.

. . .I was wont to pity the clumsy Irish laborers who cut ice on the pond, in such mean and ragged clothes, while I shivered in my more tidy and somewhat more fashionable garments, till, one bitter cold day, one who had slipped into the water came to my house to warm him, and I saw him strip off three pairs of pants and two pairs of stockings ere he got down to the skin, though they were dirty and ragged enough, it is true, and that he could afford to refuse the *extra* garments which I offered him, he had so many *intra* ones. This ducking was the very thing he needed. Then I began to pity myself, and I saw that it would be a greater charity to bestow on me a flannel shirt than a whole slop-shop on him. There are a thousand hacking at the branches of evil to one who is striking at the root, and it may be that he who bestows the largest amount of time and money on the needy is doing the most by his mode of life to produce that misery which he strives in vain to relieve. It is the pious slave-breeder devoting the proceeds of every tenth slave to buy a Sunday's liberty for the rest. Some show their kindness to the poor by employing them in their kitchens. Would they not be kinder if they employed themselves there? You boast of spending a tenth part of your income in charity; may be you should spend the nine-tenths so, and done with it. . . .

o   o   o   o   o

. . .By the way there came up a shower, which compelled me to stand half an hour under a pine, piling boughs over my head, and wearing my handkerchief for a shed; and when at length I had made one cast over the pickerel-weed, standing up to my middle in water, I found myself suddenly in the shadow of a cloud, and the thunder began to rumble with such emphasis that I could do no more than listen to it. The gods must be proud, thought I, with such forked flashes to rout a poor unarmed fisherman. So I made haste for shelter to the nearest hut, which stood half a mile from any road, but so much the nearer to the pond, and had long been uninhabited:—

> "And here a poet builded,
>   In the completed years,
> For behold a trivial cabin
>   That to destruction steers."

So the Muse fables. But therein, as I found, dwelt now John Field, an Irishman, and his wife, and several children, from the broad-faced boy who assisted his father at his work, and now came running by his side from the bog to escape the rain, to the wrinkled, sibyl-like, cone-headed infant that sat upon its father's knee as in the palaces of nobles, and looked out from its home in the midst of wet and hunger inquisitively upon the stranger, with the priviledge of infancy, not knowing but it was the last of a noble line, and the hope and cynosure of the world, instead of John Field's poor starveling brat. There we sat together under that part of the roof which leaked the least, while it showered and thundered without. I had sat there many times of old before the ship was built that floated this family to America. An honest, hard-working, but shiftless man plainly was John Field; and his wife, she too was brave to cook so many successive dinners in the recesses of that lofty stove; with round greasy face and bare breast, still thinking to improve her condition one day; with the never-absent mop in one hand, and yet no effects of it visible anywhere. The chickens, which had also taken shelter here from the rain, stalked about the room like members of the family, too humanized methought to roast well. They stood and looked in my eye or pecked at my shoe significantly. Meanwhile my host told me his story, how hard he worked "bogging" for a neighboring farmer, turning up a meadow with a spade or bog hoe at the rate of ten dollars an acre and the use of the land with manure for one year, and his little broad-faced son worked cheerfully at his father's side the while, not knowing how poor a bargain the latter had made. I tried to help him with my experience, telling him that he was one of my nearest neighbors, and that I too, who came a-fishing here, and looked like a loafer, was getting my living like himself; that I lived in a tight, light, and clean house, which hardly cost more than the annual rent of such a ruin as his commonly amounts to; and how, if he chose, he might in a month or two build himself a palace of his own; that I did not use tea, nor coffee, nor butter, nor milk, nor fresh meat, and so did not have to work to get them; again, as I did not work hard, I did not have to eat hard, and it cost me but a trifle for my food; but as he began with tea, and coffee, and butter, and milk, and beef, he had to work hard to pay for them, and when he had worked hard he had to eat hard again to repair the waste of his system,—and so it was as broad as it was long, indeed it was broader than it was long, for he was discontented and wasted his life into the bargain; and yet he had rated it as a gain in coming to America, that here you could get tea, and coffee, and meat every day. But the only true America is that country where you are at liberty to pursue such a mode of life as may enable you to do without these, and where the state does not endeavor to compel you to sustain the slavery and war and other superfluous expenses which directly or indirectly result from the use of such things. For I purposely talked to him as if he were a philosopher, or desired to be one. I should be glad if all the meadows on the earth were left in a wild state, if that were the consequence of men's beginning to redeem themselves. A man will not need to study history to find out what is best for his own culture. But alas! the culture of an Irishman is an enterprise to be undertaken with a sort of moral bog hoe. I told him, that as he worked so hard at bogging, he required thick boots and stout clothing, which yet were soon soiled and worn out, but I wore light shoes and thin clothing, which cost not half so much, though he might think that I was dressed like a gentleman, (which, however, was not the case,) and in an hour or two, without labor, but as a recreation, I could, if I wished, catch as many fish as I should want for two days, or earn enough money to support me a week. If he and his family would live simply, they might all go a-huckleberrying in the summer for their amusement. John heaved a sigh at this, and his wife stared with arms a-kimbo, and both appeared to be wondering if they had capital enough to begin such a course with, or arithmetic enough to carry it through. It was sailing by dead reckoning to them, and they saw not clearly how to make their port so; therefore I suppose they still take life bravely, after their fashion, face to face, giving it tooth and nail, not having skill to split its massive columns with any fine entering wedge, and rout it in detail;—thinking to deal with it roughly, as one should handle a thistle. But they fight at an overwhelming disadvantage,—living, John Field, alas! without arithmetic, and failing so.

"Do you ever fish?" I asked. "O yes, I catch a mess now and then when I am lying by; good perch I catch." "What's your bait?" "I catch shiners with fish-worms, and bait the perch with them." "You'd better go now, John," said his wife with glistening and hopeful face; but John demurred.

The shower was now over, and a rainbow above the eastern woods promised a fair evening; so I took my departure. When I had got without I asked for a dish, hoping to get a sight of the well bottom, to complete my survey of the premises; but there, alas! are shallows and quicksands, and rope broken withal, and bucket irrecoverable. Meanwhile the right culinary vessel was selected, water was seemingly distilled, and after consultation and long delay passed out to the thirsty one,—not yet suffered to cool, not yet to settle. Such gruel sustains life here, I thought; so, shutting my eyes, and excluding the motes by a skilfully directed undercurrent, I drank to genuine hospitality the heartiest draught I could. I am not squeamish in such cases when manners are concerned.

As I was leaving the Irishman's roof after the rain, bending my steps again to the pond, my haste to catch pickerel, wading in retired meadows, in sloughs and bog-holes, in forlorn and savage places, appeared for an instant trivial to me who had been sent to school and college; but as I ran down the hill toward the reddening west, with the rainbow over my shoulder, and some faint tinkling sounds borne to my ear through the cleansed air, from I know not what quarter, my Good Genius seemed to say,—Go fish and hunt far and wide day by day,—farther and wider,—and rest thee by many brooks and hearth-sides without misgiving. Remember thy Creator in the days of thy youth. Rise free from care before the dawn, and seek adventures. Let the noon find thee by other lakes, and the night overtake thee everywhere at home. There are no larger fields than these, no worthier games than may here be played. Grow wild according to thy nature, like these sedges and brakes, which will never become English hay. Let the thunder rumble; what if it threaten ruin to farmers' crops? that is not its errand to thee. Take shelter under the cloud, while they flee to carts and sheds. Let not to get a living be thy trade, but thy sport. Enjoy the land, but own it not. Through want of enterprise and faith men are where they are, buying and selling, and spending their lives like serfs. . . .

Before I had reached the pond some fresh impulse had brought out John Field, with altered mind, letting go "bogging" ere this sunset. But he, poor man, disturbed only a couple of fins while I was catching a fair string, and he said it was his luck; but when we changed seats in the boat luck changed seats too. Poor John Field!— I trust he does not read this, unless he will improve by it,— thinking to live by some derivative old country mode in this primitive new country,—to catch perch with shiners. It is good bait sometimes, I allow. With his horizon all his own, yet he a poor man, born to be poor, with his inherited Irish poverty or poor life, his Adam's grandmother and boggy ways, not to rise in this world, he nor his posterity, till their wading webbed bog-trotting feet get *talaria* to their heels.

°   °   °   °   °

East of my bean-field, across the road, lived Cato Ingraham, slave of Duncan Ingraham, Esquire, gentleman of Concord Village; who built his slave a house, and gave him permission to live in Walden Woods;—Cato, not Uticensis, but Concordiensis.[1] Some say that he was a Guinea Negro. There are a few who remember his little patch among the walnuts, which he let grow up till he should be old and need them; but a younger and whiter speculator got them at last. He too, however, occupies an equally narrow house at present. Cato's half-obliterated cellar hole still remains, though known to few, being concealed from the traveller by a fringe of pines. It is now filled with the smooth sumach, *(Rhus glabra,)* and one of the earliest

[1]Cato of Concord, not the Roman statesman who died in Utica.

species of goldenrod *(Solidago stricta)* grows there luxuriantly.

Here, by the very corner of my field, still nearer to town, Zilpha, a colored woman, had her little house, where she spun linen for the townsfolk, making the Walden Woods ring with her shrill singing, for she had a loud and notable voice. At length, in the war of 1812, her dwelling was set on fire by English soldiers, prisoners on parole, when she was away, and her cat and dog and hens were all burned up together. She led a hard life, and somewhat inhumane. One old frequenter of these woods remembers, that as he passed her house one noon he heard her muttering to herself over her gurgling pot,— "Ye are all bones, bones!" I have seen bricks amid the oak copse there.

Down the road, on the right hand, on Brister's Hill, lived Brister Freeman, "a handy Negro," slave of Squire Cummings once,—there where grow still the apple trees which Brister planted and tended; large old trees now, but their fruit still wild and ciderish to my taste. Not long since I read his epitaph in the old Lincoln burying-ground, a little on one side, near the unmarked graves of some British grenadiers who fell in the retreat from Concord,—where he is styled "Sippio Brister,"—Scipio Africanus he had some title to be called,— "a man of color," as if he were discolored. It also told me, with staring emphasis, when he died; which was but an indirect way of informing me that he ever lived. With him dwelt Fenda, his hospitable wife, who told fortunes, yet pleasantly,—large, round, and black, blacker than any of the children of night, such a dusky orb as never rose on Concord before or since.

SUGGESTED ADDITIONAL READINGS

    A Week on the Concord and Merrimack Rivers
    The Maine Woods
    "Civil Disobedience"
    "Slavery in Massachusetts"
    "A Plea for Captain John Brown"
    "The Last Days of John Brown"

SELECTED REFERENCES

Adams, Raymond. "An Irishman on Thoreau: A Stillborn View of *Walden.*" *New England Quarterly*, 13 (1940), 697–99.

Buckley, Frank. "Thoreau and the Irish." *New England Quarterly*, 13 (1940), 389–400.

Ford, Nick Aaron. "Henry David Thoreau, Abolitionist." *New England Quarterly*, 19 (1946), 359–71.

Harding, Walter. "Thoreau and the Negro." *Negro History Bulletin.* 10 (1946), 29–35.

Hendrick, George. "The Influence of Thoreau's 'Civil Disobedience' on Ghandi's *Satyagraha.*" *New England Quarterly*, 29 (1956), 462–71.

Keiser, Albert. "Thoreau's Manuscripts on the Indians." *Journal of English and German Philology*, 27 (1928), 183–99.

King, Martin Luther, Jr. "A Legacy of Creative Protest." *Massachusetts Review*, 4 (1962), 43.

Nelson, William Stewart. "Thoreau and American Non-Violent Resistance." *Massachusetts Review*, 4 (1962), 56-60.

Nichols, William W. "Individualism and Autobiographical Art: Frederick Douglass and Henry Thoreau." *CLA Journal*, 16 (1972), 145–58.

Russell, James Almust. "Thoreau: The Interpreter of the Real Indian." *Queens Quarterly*, 35 (1927), 37–48.

PROJECTS AND PROBLEMS

Examine Thoreau's journals and correspondence for illuminating references to minorities. Compare these with his published works.

Explain the appeal of "Civil Disobedience" to both philosophical equalitarians and practical political leaders of exploited or oppressed minorities. Discuss instances of its influence on particular people. Is Thoreau's doctrine, which rejects majority rule, undemocratic?

The Irish immigrants during the time of Thoreau and Emerson were generally of agrarian background. Did their closeness to nature influence Thoreau and Emerson to adopt generous attitudes toward them?

In "Thoreau," Emerson said that his friend occasionally observed Penobscot Indians who visited Concord, "though he well knew that asking questions of Indians is like catechizing beavers and rabbits." Would Thoreau have approved of this comment?

Did Thoreau show any sensitivity to the plight of the Indian woman, who, as Margaret Fuller remarked in *Summer on the Lakes* (1844), "occupies a position inferior to that of man"? Did he share her view that the Indians suffered less harm from French Catholics that from the "stern Presbyterian"?

SELECTED BIBLIOGRAPHY

I. Reference Books

Brown, Sterling A. *The Negro in American Fiction.* Washington, D. C.: Associates in Negro Folk Education, 1937.

———. *Negro Poetry and Drama.* Washington, D. C.: Associates in Negro Folk Education, 1937.

Butcher, Margaret Just. *The Negro in American Culture.* New York: Knopf, 1956.

Friedman, Lawrence J. *The White Savage: Racial Fantasies in the Post-Bellum South.* Englewood Cliffs, N. J.: Prentice-Hall, 1970.

Gloster, Hugh Morris. *Negro Voices in American Fiction.* Chapel Hill: Univ. of North Carolina Press, 1948.

Gross, Seymour L., and John Edward Hardy, eds. *Images of the Negro in American Literature.* Chicago: Univ. of Chicago Press, 1966.

Harap, Louis. *The Image of the Jew in American Literature: From Early Republic to Mass Immigration.* Philadelphia: The Jewish Publication Society of America, 1974.

Keiser, Albert. *The Indian in American Literature.* New York: Oxford Univ. Press, 1933.

Liptzin, Sol. *The Jew in American Literature.* New York: Bloch Publishing Co., 1966.

Robinson, Cecil. *With the Ears of Strangers: The Mexican in American Literature.* Tucson: Univ. of Arizona Press, 1963.

Skaggs, Merrill Maguire. *The Folk of Southern Fiction.* Athens: Univ. of Georgia Press, 1972.

Starke, Catherine Juanita. *Black Portraiture in American Fiction.* New York: Basic Books, 1971.

Turner, Darwin T., comp. *Afro-American Writers.* A Bibliography. New York: Appleton-Century-Crofts, 1970.

Turner, Lorenzo Dow. *Anti-Slavery Sentiment in American Literature Prior to 1865.* Port Washington, N. Y.: Kennikat Press, 1966.

Yellin, Jean Fagan. *The Intricate Knot: Black Figures in American Literature, 1776-1863.* New York: New York Univ. Press, 1972.

II. Anthologies

Anderson, David D., and Robert L. Wright, eds. *The Dark and Tangled Path: Race in America.* Boston: Houghton Mifflin, 1971.

Armstrong, Virginia Irving, comp. *I Have Spoken: American History Through the Voices of the Indians.* Chicago: The Swallow Press, 1971.

Barksdale, Richard, and Keneth Kinnamon, eds. *Black Writers in America.* New York: The Macmillan Company, 1972.

Black, Nancy B. and Bette S. Weidman, eds. *White on Red: Images of the American Indian.* Port Washington, N.Y.: Kennikat Press, 1976.

Brown, Sterling A., Arthur P. Davis, and Ulysses Lee, eds. *Negro Caravan.* New York: Dryden Press, 1941.

Chapman, Abraham, ed. *Literature of the American Indians: Views and Interpretations.* New York: New American Library, 1975.

Curti, Merle, Willard Thorp, and Carlos Baker, eds. *American Issues: The Social Record.* Fourth ed. Philadelphia: J. B. Lippincott Co., 1960.

Davis, Arthur P., and Saunders Redding, eds. *Cavalcade: Negro American Writing from 1760 to the Present.* Boston: Houghton Mifflin, 1971.

Freimarck, Vincent, and Bernard Rosenthal, eds. *Race and the American Romantics.* New York: Schocken Books, 1971.

Kearns, Francis E., ed. *The Black Experience: An Anthology of American Literature for the 1970s.* New York: Viking Press, 1970.

Lerner, Gerda, ed. *Black Women in White America: A Documentary History.* New York: Vantage Books, 1973.

Moquin, Wayne, ed. *Great Documents in American Indian History.* New York: Praeger Publishers, 1973.

VanDerBeets, Richard, ed. *Held Captive by Indians: Selected Narratives, 1642-1836.* Knoxville: Univ. of Tennessee Press, 1973.

Washburn, Wilcomb E., ed. *The Indian and the White Man.* Garden City, N. Y.: Doubleday, 1964.

III. Background

Allport, Gordon W. *The Nature of Prejudice*. Garden City, N. Y. : Doubleday, 1958.

Barron, Milton L., ed. *American Minorities: A Textbook of Readings in Intergroup Relations*. New York: Alfred A. Knopf, 1962.

Bissell, Benjamin. *The American Indian in English Literature of the Eighteenth Century*. New Haven: Yale Univ. Press, 1925.

Brandon, William. *The American Heritage Book of Indians*. New York: American Heritage Publishing Co., 1961.

Brown, Dee. *Bury My Heart at Wounded Knee: An Indian History of the American West*. New York: Holt, Rinehart & Winston, 1970.

Brown, Francis J., and Joseph S. Roucek, eds. *One America: The History, Contributions and Present Problems of Our Racial and National Minorities*. Third ed. Englewood Cliffs, N. J.: Prentice-Hall, 1952.

Burrows, Edwin G. *Hawaiian Americans: An Account of the Mingling of Japanese, Chinese, Polynesian, and American Cultures*. New Haven: Yale Univ. Press, 1947.

Coffin, Tristram P., and Hennig Cohen, eds. *Folklore in America*. Garden City, N. Y.: Doubleday, 1970.

Dorson, Richard M. *American Folklore*. Chicago: Univ. of Chicago Press, 1959.

Dykes, Eva Beatrice. *The Negro in English Romantic Thought*. Washington, D. C.: Associated Publishers, 1942.

Fiedler, Leslie A. *The Return of the Vanishing American*. New York: Stein & Day, 1968.

Franklin, John Hope. *From Slavery to Freedom*. Rev. ed. New York: Knopf, 1968.

Gossett, Thomas F. *Race: The History of an Idea in America*. Dallas: Southern Methodist Univ. Press, 1963.

Halliburton, Warren J., and William Loren Katz. *American Majorities and Minorities: A Syllabus of United States History for Secondary Schools*. New York: Arno, 1970.

Handlin, Oscar. *Adventure in Freedom: Three Hundred Years of Jewish Life in America*. New York: McGraw-Hill, 1954.

Hosokawa, Bill. *Nisei: The Quiet Americans*. New York: William Morrow, 1969.

Howe, Irving. *World of Our Fathers: The Journey of the East European Jews to America and the Life They Found and Made*. New York: Harcourt Brace Jovanovich, 1976.

Huthmacher, J. Joseph. *A Nation of Newcomers: Ethnic Minority Groups in American History.* New York: Dell, 1967.

Johnston, James Hugo. *Race Relations in Virginia and Miscegenation in the South, 1776–1860.* Amherst: University of Massachusetts Press, 1970.

Jordan, Winthrop D. *Historical Origins of Racism in the United States.* New York: Oxford Univ. Press, 1974.

————. *White Over Black: American Attitudes Toward the Negro. 1550–1812.* Baltimore: Penguin Books, 1969.

Kennedy, John F. *A Nation of Immigrants.* New York: Harper & Row, 1964.

Lader, Lawrence. *The Bold Brahmins: New England's War Against Slavery: 1831–1863.* New York: E. P. Dutton, 1961.

Litwack, Leon F. *North of Slavery: The Negro in the Free States, 1790–1860.* Chicago: Phoenix Books, 1965.

Logan, Rayford W., and Irving S. Cohen. *The American Negro: Old World Background and New World Experience.* Boston: Houghton Mifflin, 1970.

McIlwaine, Shields. *The Southern Poor-White from Lubberland to Tobacco Road.* Norman: Univ. of Oklahoma Press, 1939.

McPherson, James M., *et al. Blacks in America: Bibliographical Essays.* Garden City, N. Y.: Doubleday, 1971.

Marden, Charles F., and Gladys Meyer. *Minorities in American Society.* Fourth ed. New York: D. Van Nostrand Co., 1973.

Marr, Warren, II, and Maybelle Ward, eds. *Minorities and the American Dream: A Bicentennial Perspective.* New York: Arno Press, Inc., 1976.

Marriott, Alice, and Carol K. Rachlin. *American Epic: The Story of the American Indian.* New York: New American Library, 1969.

Marzio, Peter C., ed. *A Nation of Nations: The People Who Came to America as Seen Through Objects, Prints, and Photographs at the Smithsonian Institution.* New York: Harper & Row, 1976.

Melendy, H. Brett. *The Oriental Americans.* New York: Twayne Publishers, 1972.

Mellon, Matthew T. *Early American Views on Negro Slavery.* New York: New American Library, 1969.

Miller, John C. *The First Frontier: Life in Colonial America.* New York: Dell, 1966.

Nash, Gary B. *Red, White, and Black: The Peoples of Early America.* Englewood Cliffs, N. J.: Prentice-Hall, 1974.

Nye, Russel. *The Unembarassed Muse: The Popular Arts in America.* New York: Dial Press, 1970.

Quarles, Benjamin. *The Negro in the Making of America.* New York: Collier Books, 1964.

Ruchames, Louis, ed. *Racial Thought in America: From the Puritans to Abraham Lincoln.* New York: Grosset & Dunlap, 1970.

Williamson, Juanita V., and Virginia M. Burke, eds. *A Various Language: Perspectives on American Dialects.* New York: Holt, Rinehart and Winston, 1971.

Wittke, Carl. *We Who Built America: the Saga of the Immigrant.* Cleveland: Western Reserve Univ. Press, 1964.

Wright, Louis B. *The Cultural Life of the American Colonies.* New York: Harper & Row, 1962.

IV. Articles in Periodicals

Appel, John J. "American Negro and Immigrant Experience: Similarities and Differences." *American Quarterly,* 18 (1966), 95–103.

Brown, Sterling A. "The American Race Problem as Reflected in American Literature." *Journal of Negro Education,* 7 (1939), 275–90.

――――. "A Century of Negro Portraiture in American Literature." *Massachusetts Review,* 7 (1966), 73–96.

――――. "Negro Character as Seen by White Authors." *Journal of Negro Education,* 2 (1933), 179–203.

Cantor, Milton, "The Image of the Negro in Colonial Literature." *New England Quarterly,* 36 (1963), 452–77.

Fine, David M. "Immigrant Ghetto Fiction, 1885–1918: An Annotated Bibliography." *American Literary Realism, 1870–1910,* 6 (1973), 169–95.

Gross, Theodore L. "The Negro in the Literature of Reconstruction." *Phylon,* 22 (1961), 5–14.

Jordan, Winthrop D. "American Chiaroscuro: The Status and Definition of Mulattoes in the British Colonies." *William and Mary Quarterly,* 19 (1962), 183–200.

Kaiser, Ernest. "American Indians and Mexican Americans: A Selected Bibliography." *Freedomways,* 9 (1969), 298–327.

Kent, George E. "Ethnic Impact in American Literature: Reflections on a Course." *CLA Journal,* 11 (1967), 1–17.

Lamplugh, G. R. "The Image of the Negro in Popular Magazine Fiction, 1875–1900." *Journal of Negro History,* 57 (1972), 177–89.

Levy, David W. "Racial Stereotypes in Anti-Slavery Fiction." *Phylon,* 31 (1970), 265–79.

MacDonald, J. Frederick. " 'The Foreigner' in Juvenile Series Fiction, 1900–1945." *Journal of Popular Culture,* 8 (1974), 534–48.

Mead, Margaret. "Racial Differences and Cultural Attitudes." *Columbia University Forum,* 10 (1967), 35–36.

Mintz, Sidney W. "Creating Culture in the Americas." *Columbia Forum,* 13 (1970), 4–11.

Moore, Jack B. "Images of the Negro in Early American Short Fiction." *Mississippi Quarterly,* 22 (1969), 47–57.

Musgrave, Marian E. "Patterns of Violence and Non-Violence in Pro-Slavery and Anti-Slavery Fiction." *CLA Journal,* 16 (1973), 426–37.

Nichols, Charles H., Jr. "Slave Narratives and the Plantation Legend." *Phylon,* 10 (1949), 201–10.

Patterson, Orlando. "Ethnicity and the Pluralist Fallacy." *Change,* March, 1975, pp. 10–11.

Rassekh, Nosratollah. "Melting Pot or Boiling Cauldron: The Ethnic Experience in America." *World Order,* 10, No. 3 (1976), 13–25.

Read, Allen Walker. "The Speech of Negroes in Colonial America." *Journal of Negro History,* 24 (1939), 247–58.

Rollins, H. E. "The Negro in the Southern Short Story." *Sewanee Review,* 24 (1916), 42–60.

Simms, H. H. "A Critical Analysis of Abolition Literature, 1830–1840." *Journal of Southern History,* 6 (1940), 368–82.

Soderbergh, Peter A. "Bibliographical Essay: The Negro in Juvenile Series Books, 1899–1930." *Journal of Negro History,* 58 (1973), 179–86.

Tandy, Jeanette. "Pro-Slavery Propaganda in American Fiction of the Fifties." *South Atlantic Quarterly,* 21 (1922), 41–50, 170–78.

Thompson, Lawrence S. "The Negro in Kentucky Fiction." *Midwest Journal,* 5 (1953), 75–81.

Towner, Lawrence W. " 'A Fondness for Freedom': Servant Protest in Puritan Society." *William and Mary Quarterly,* 19 (1962), 201–19.

Turner, Darwin T. "The Teaching of Afro-American Literature." *College English,* 31 (1970), 666–70.

Twombly, Robert C., and Richard H. Moore. "Black Puritan: The Negro in Seventeenth Century Massachusetts." *William and Mary Quarterly,* 24 (1967), 224–42.

VanDerBeets, Richard. "The Indian Captivity Narrative as Ritual." *American Literature,* 43 (1972), 548–62.

Wilson, Charles R. "Racial Reservations: Indians and Blacks in American Magazines, 1865–1900." *Journal of Popular Culture,* 10 (1976), 70–79.

Zanger, Jules. "The 'Tragic Octoroon' in Pre-Civil War Fiction." *American Quarterly,* 18 (1966), 63–70.

INDEX